501

delicious
diabetic
recipes

for you and your family

Oxmoor
House®

Library of Congress Catalog Number: 00-134141
ISBN: 0-8487-2387-2
Printed in the United States of America
Third Printing 2002

Be sure to check with your health-care provider before making any changes in your diet.

Editor-in-Chief: Nancy Fitzpatrick Wyatt
Senior Foods Editor: Katherine M. Eakin
Senior Editor, Editorial Services: Olivia Kindig Wells
Art Director: James Boone

501 Delicious Diabetic Recipes for You and Your Family

Editor: Anne Chappell Cain, M.S., M.P.H., R.D.
Associate Art Director: Cynthia R. Cooper
Designer: Melissa Clark
Senior Copy Editor: Keri Bradford Anderson
Copy Editor: Donna Baldone
Editorial Assistant: Heather Averett
Director, Test Kitchens: Elizabeth Tyler Luckett
Assistant Director, Test Kitchens: Julie Christopher
Recipe Editor: Gayle Hays Sadler
Test Kitchens Staff: Rebecca Mohr Boggan; Gretchen Feldtman, R.D.; David Gallent; Ana Kelly; Jan A. Smith
Senior Photographer: Jim Bathie
Photographer: Brit Huckabay
Senior Photo Stylist: Kay E. Clarke
Photo Stylist: Virginia Cravens
Director, Production and Distribution: Phillip Lee
Books Production Manager: Theresa L. Beste
Production Assistant: Faye Porter Bonner

Cover: Strawberry-Banana Tart, page 132

We're Here for You!

We at Oxmoor House are dedicated to serving you with reliable information that expands your imagination and enriches your life. We welcome your comments and suggestions. Please write us at:

Oxmoor House, Inc.
Editor, *501 Delicious Diabetic Recipes for You and Your Family*
2100 Lakeshore Drive
Birmingham, AL 35209

To order additional publications, call 1-205-877-6560. Or, if you have any diabetic recipes to share, please send them to the address above. Be sure to include your name and daytime telephone number.

Contents

Recipes

Dear Friends,

Our mission for *501 Delicious Diabetic Recipes for You and Your Family* is to help you enjoy wonderful food as you live with diabetes. There is no doubt that keeping your blood glucose under control will help prevent diabetes complications. Since food plays a big part in this control, why not make the food you eat the best it can be?

Our staff of registered dietitians and cooking experts have put together over 500 recipes that will help you control your diabetes while you enjoy delicious food. Each recipe has nutrient information and diabetic exchanges so you can work it into your meal plan whether you're counting carbohydrates or using exchange lists.

> ❧ If it tastes fabulous, if every bite delights, if we really pay attention, we will end up eating less, not to deprive ourselves, but because we are satisfied.
>
> Barbara Kafka,
> American author and columnist

We realize that you don't have all day to spend in the kitchen, so we've identified the "Super-Quick" recipes (15 minutes or less). We've also kept the ingredient lists simple by using items that you can find easily in your local grocery store.

Use these recipes to provide all your family with healthy, great-tasting meals. Eating delicious food with people you care about is something no one should miss. Welcome, and please join us in the joy of good food.

The Editors

Introduction

How To Use This Book

Meal planning is an essential part of diabetes management—whether you control your diabetes with insulin, pills, diet or a combination of these methods. And no longer do we have just one "diabetic diet." The diabetes experts now recommend that you have an individualized meal plan that matches your food preferences and lifestyle as much as possible. The recipes in this book can fit into most meal plans. You'll find a variety of recipes, all reduced in sugar, fat, and salt. Use the nutrient values and/or exchange values with each recipe and see how easily the recipes can fit into your plan. If you need help with meal planning, talk to a registered dietitian (RD) or other members of your health-care team.

For help with shopping we've included a quick guide to reading food labels. (See page 8.) And since people with diabetes often have questions about using sugar substitutes, we've provided some information and tips on a variety of substitutes. (See page 9.)

Nutrient Analysis

Each recipe comes with a nutrient analysis and exchange values. Refer to the example below as a guide for using the recipes in this book in your meal plan.

YIELD: 6 servings

All values are for one serving of the recipe.

EXCHANGES PER SERVING:
3 Very Lean Meat
1 Starch
2 Vegetable

Use this information if you use diabetic exchanges for meal planning.

PER SERVING:
Calories 257
Carbohydrate 25.4g
Protein 27.9g
Fat 4.6g
Cholesterol 76mg
Fiber 3.4g
Sodium 296mg

Use this value if you count carbohydrates for meal planning

Limit sodium to 2400mg a day

Grams are abbreviated "g."
Milligrams are abbreviated "mg."

Diabetic Exchanges

Exchange values for all recipes are provided for people who use them for meal planning. The exchange values are based on the *Exchange Lists for Meal Planning* developed by the American Diabetes Association and The American Dietetic Association.

Carbohydrates

If you count carbohydrates, look for the value in the nutrient analysis. The current American Diabetes Association guidelines loosen the restriction on sugar and encourage you to look at the total grams of carbohydrate in a serving. Sugar does not appear to raise blood glucose any more than other types of carbohydrate; it's the total amount of carbohydrate that's important.

We have used small amounts of sugar in some recipes. We've also used a variety of sugar substitutes when the use of a substitute yields a quality product.

Fiber

There is some evidence that increasing your fiber intake will help control blood glucose levels. Try to eat 25 to 30 grams of fiber each day.

Sodium

Current dietary recommendations advise a daily sodium intake of 2400mg or less. (One teaspoon of salt has 2,325 milligrams of sodium.) We've limited the use of sodium in these recipes by using reduced-sodium products whenever possible.

Salt does not have a direct effect on your blood glucose, but if you have high blood pressure or heart disease, your doctor might have told you to limit sodium. If you must restrict sodium in your diet, please note the sodium value per serving and see if you should modify the recipe further.

READ THE LABEL

The Nutrition Facts panel printed on most packaged foods gives you information to make healthy food choices. Use this sample label to understand what the numbers mean.

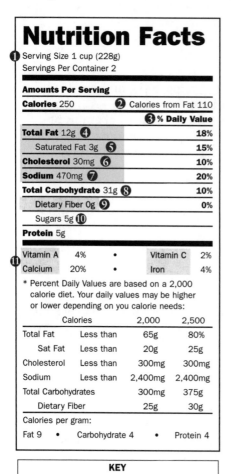

2 Calories from Fat: Choose foods with a big difference between total calories and calories from fat.

3 % Daily Value (DV): This percentage indicates which part of your daily requirement you get from one serving of the food. For fat, saturated fat, and sodium, choose foods with a low % DV. For fiber, vitamins, and minerals, the goal should be 100 percent each day. The carbohydrate % DV is not a useful value for people with diabetes because individual carbohydrate requirements and recommendations vary.

4 Total Fat: Try to keep calories from fat at 30 percent or less of total calories.

5 Saturated Fat: The value for saturated fat is included in Total Fat. A high intake of saturated fat is associated with the risk of heart disease.

6 Cholesterol: A high intake of cholesterol is associated with the risk of heart disease. Try to keep cholesterol intake to less than 300 milligrams a day.

7 Sodium: Try to keep your sodium intake to no more than 2400 milligrams a day.

1 Serving Size: Values are for one serving of the food. The serving size on the label doesn't always correspond with the serving size in diabetic exchange lists.

8 Total Carbohydrate: Use this value if you count carbohydrates for meal planning.

9 Dietary Fiber: This value is included in Total Carbohydrate. Try to eat at least 25 to 30 grams of fiber every day.

10 Sugars: This value is included in Total Carbohydrate. You can't tell from this value which type of sugar the product contains.

11 Vitamins and Minerals: The goal is 100 percent each day for each nutrient.

SUGAR SUBSTITUTE TIPS

Many sugar substitutes are available for people with diabetes and for those trying to lose weight. Sugar substitutes don't have the same properties as sucrose (table sugar) but do give food a sweet taste. Although some substitutes do contain calories, most are used in such small quantities that they don't significantly contribute to caloric intake.

When using sugar substitutes, remember that they don't have the same cooking properties as table sugar, so you don't get the same brownness, lightness, or tenderness. Some sugar substitutes undergo chemical changes when heated, causing a bitter taste in the finished product. Other sugar substitutes are not recommended for baking because they lose their sweetness when subjected to high temperatures for a long time.

Although we don't endorse any one brand of sugar substitute, see the chart below for the ones we use most often in recipe testing and how we call for them in the ingredient lists.

SEND IN A SUBSTITUTE

When a recipe calls for . . .	We tested with . . .
granulated sugar substitute	Sugar Twin
granulated brown sugar substitute	Sugar Twin Brown
granulated sugar substitute with aspartame	Equal Spoonful
1 packet sugar substitute	Sweet 'N Low
liquid sugar substitute	Liquid Sweet 'N Low

Types Of Sugar Substitutes

You may want to try several types and brands of sugar substitutes to see which type you prefer.

Granulated Sugar Substitutes: Substitutes such as *Sugar Twin* and *Sprinkle Sweet* have saccharin and work better in baked goods like cookies and cakes. They can be measured like regular granulated sugar, so if a recipe calls for ½ cup of sugar, you could substitute ½ cup of Sugar Twin. (You won't get the exact same product as you would with sugar, but you will get a similar amount of sweetness.)

Brown Sugar Substitute: One example of a granulated brown sugar substitute is *Sugar Twin Brown*. It works in recipes that call for brown sugar for sweetness, but not for tenderness.

Liquid Sweeteners: Liquid sweeteners blend easily with other ingredients and are especially good for salad dressing and marinade recipes. For most brands, about 10 drops is equal in sweetness to 1 teaspoon of granulated sugar.

Aspartame Sweeteners: Sugar substitutes with aspartame (Nutrasweet) lose some sweetness in high heat, so they work better in recipes that have short cooking times. You don't get the aftertaste that you get with some saccharin products.
• *Nutrasweet* or other aspartame sweeteners now come in a variety of forms, from fine powder to granules. It can be a challenge to figure out which form to use.
• *Equal* packets and *Equal Measure* (also called Equal for Recipes) are the same fine powder product. Equal Measure is packaged in bulk form so you don't have to open a lot of little packets when you use it in recipes.
• *Equal Spoonful* has a fluffy appearance and looks more like granulated sugar. Use it in similar amounts to regular sugar.

These are only a few examples of the sugar substitutes on the market. Others include:

• **Acesulfame-K (Sunette)**   • **Fructose**   • **Sucralose (Splenda)**
• **Stevia extract (herbal product)**

When you're using any type of sugar substitute, read the manufacturer's package information to find out how best to use the product in recipes.

SUGAR SUBSTITUTIONS

Use this chart to determine how much sugar substitute to use when you're replacing sugar in recipes. It's usually best to follow recipes that have already been tested with sugar substitutes, and to use the amount in the ingredient list.

Brand Name of Sugar Substitute	Amount of Sugar Substitute	Equivalent Amount of Sugar
Equal	1 packet	2 teaspoons sugar
	6 packets	¼ cup sugar
	12 packets	½ cup sugar
	18 packets	¾ cup sugar
Equal for Recipes	½ teaspoon	1 tablespoon sugar
	1¾ teaspoons	¼ cup sugar
	3½ teaspoons	½ cup sugar
	5½ teaspoons	¾ cup sugar
Equal Spoonful	1 teaspoon	1 teaspoon sugar
	1 tablespoon	1 tablespoon sugar
	¼ cup	¼ cup sugar
	½ cup	½ cup sugar
	¾ cup	¾ cup sugar
Sugar Twin	1 teaspoon	1 teaspoon sugar
	1 tablespoon	1 tablespoon sugar
	¼ cup	¼ cup sugar
	½ cup	½ cup sugar
	¾ cup	¾ cup sugar
Sugar Twin Brown	1 teaspoon	1 teaspoon brown sugar
	1 tablespoon	1 tablespoon sugar
	¼ cup	¼ cup sugar
	½ cup	½ cup sugar
	¾ cup	¾ cup sugar
Sweet 'N Low	¹⁄₁₀ teaspoon	1 teaspoon sugar
	1 packet	2 teaspoons sugar
	⅓ teaspoon	1 tablespoon sugar
	1½ teaspoons	¼ cup sugar
	1 tablespoon	½ cup sugar
	2 tablespoons	1 cup sugar

Brand Name of Sugar Substitute	Amount of Sugar Substitute	Equivalent Amount of Sugar
Sweet One	1 packet	2 teaspoons sugar
	3 packets	¼ cup sugar
	4 packets	⅓ cup sugar
	6 packets	½ cup sugar
	12 packets	1 cup sugar
Sucaryl (liquid)	⅛ teaspoon	1 teaspoon sugar
	⅓ teaspoon	1 tablespoon sugar
	½ teaspoon	4 teaspoons sugar
	1½ teaspoons	¼ cup sugar
	1 tablespoon	½ cup sugar
Superose (liquid)	4 drops	1 teaspoon sugar
	⅛ teaspoon	2 teaspoons sugar
	¼ teaspoon	1 tablespoon sugar
	1½ teaspoons	½ cup sugar
	1 tablespoon	1 cup sugar
Sweet-10 (liquid)	10 drops	1 teaspoon sugar
	½ teaspoon	4 teaspoons sugar
	1½ teaspoons	¼ cup sugar
	1 tablespoon	½ cup sugar
	2 tablespoons	1 cup sugar
Zero-Cal (liquid)	10 drops	1 teaspoon sugar
	30 drops	1 tablespoon sugar
	¾ teaspoon	2 tablespoons sugar
	1 tablespoon	½ cup sugar
	2 tablespoons	1 cup sugar

Note: Sugar equivalents for various brand names of sugar substitutes are listed for your convenience and are not an endorsement of any product.

Appetizers & Beverages

super·quick

SESAME WONTON CHIPS

EXCHANGES PER
SERVING:
1 Starch

PER SERVING:
Calories 90
Carbohydrate 14.8g
Protein 3.7g
Fat 1.6g
Cholesterol 2mg
Fiber 0.1g
Sodium 248mg

2 egg whites, lightly beaten
2 tablespoons low-sodium soy sauce
1 teaspoon garlic powder
¼ teaspoon ground ginger
24 fresh or frozen wonton skins, thawed
    Vegetable cooking spray
2 tablespoons sesame seeds, toasted

1 Combine first 4 ingredients in a small bowl; set aside.

2 Cut each wonton skin in half diagonally. Place in a 15- x 10- x 1-inch jellyroll pan coated with cooking spray. Brush egg white mixture over skins, and sprinkle evenly with sesame seeds.

3 Bake at 375° for 6 to 7 minutes or until crisp and lightly browned. Remove from pan; let cool completely on wire racks.
Yield: 8 servings (serving size: 6 chips).

Poppy Seed Pretzels

For a variation, omit the poppy seeds and sprinkle pretzels evenly with ⅓ cup freshly grated Parmesan cheese.

1 cup water
2 tablespoons margarine
1 (16-ounce) package hot roll mix
1 egg white, lightly beaten
1 teaspoon all-purpose flour
  Vegetable cooking spray
1 egg white
1 tablespoon water
1 tablespoon poppy seeds

1 Combine 1 cup water and margarine in a small saucepan; heat until margarine melts, stirring occasionally. Cool to 120° to 130°. Combine roll mix and yeast from packet in a large mixing bowl. Gradually add margarine mixture and beaten egg white, beating at medium speed of an electric mixer 4 minutes or until blended.

2 Sprinkle 1 teaspoon flour evenly over work surface. Turn dough out onto a floured surface, and knead until smooth and elastic (about 10 minutes). Cover and let rest 10 minutes.

3 Divide dough into 16 equal portions. Roll each portion into a 22-inch rope. Twist each rope into a pretzel shape. Place on baking sheets coated with cooking spray. Cover and let rest 15 minutes.

4 Combine egg white and 1 tablespoon water; stir well. Brush pretzels with egg white mixture; sprinkle with poppy seeds. Bake at 375° for 10 minutes or until lightly browned. Let cool on wire racks. Yield: 16 pretzels.

YIELD: 16 pretzels

EXCHANGES PER PRETZEL:
1 Starch

PER PRETZEL:
Calories 119
Carbohydrate 19.9g
Protein 3.3g
Fat 2.4g
Cholesterol 0mg
Fiber 0.5g
Sodium 650mg

SNACK MIX

EXCHANGES PER SERVING:
1 Starch
1 Fat

PER SERVING:
Calories 106
Carbohydrate 12.4g
Protein 2.4g
Fat 6.0g
Cholesterol 0mg
Fiber 1.9g
Sodium 47mg

Expecting company and need a snack mix to serve? This recipe can easily be doubled.

> 2 cups bite-size shredded whole wheat cereal biscuits
> ⅓ cup lightly salted dry roasted mixed nuts
> ¼ cup reduced-calorie margarine, melted
> 2 teaspoons celery seeds
> ½ teaspoon ground thyme
> ½ teaspoon garlic powder
> ½ teaspoon onion powder
> 3 cups popped corn (cooked without salt or fat)

1 Combine cereal and nuts in a 2-quart baking dish. Combine margarine and next 4 ingredients; pour over cereal mixture, tossing to coat.

2 Bake at 350° for 15 minutes, stirring every 5 minutes. Remove from oven; add popcorn immediately, tossing gently to combine.

3 Let mixture cool completely; store in an airtight container. Yield: 10 (½-cup) servings.

Fresh Tomato Salsa

YIELD: 2 cups

2 cups finely chopped tomato (about
   3 medium)
¼ cup chopped green onions
1 tablespoon finely chopped fresh cilantro
1 tablespoon fresh lime juice
1 teaspoon minced fresh jalapeño pepper
¼ teaspoon salt
   Fresh cilantro sprigs (optional)
   Fresh jalapeño pepper (optional)

**EXCHANGES PER
TABLESPOON:**
Free

PER TABLESPOON:
Calories 3
Carbohydrate 0.7g
Protein 0.1g
Fat 0.0g
Cholesterol 0mg
Fiber 0.2g
Sodium 20mg

1 Combine first 6 ingredients in a medium bowl; stir well. Cover and chill at least 2 hours. Serve with no-oil baked tortilla chips (chips not included in analysis). If desired, garnish with cilantro sprigs and a jalapeño pepper. Yield: 2 cups.

super·quick

Santa Fe Salsa

YIELD: 1¾ cups

1 cup finely chopped tomato (about
   1 large)
½ cup finely chopped purple onion
⅛ teaspoon salt
1 (4½-ounce) can chopped green chiles,
   undrained
1 large clove garlic, minced

**EXCHANGES PER
TABLESPOON:**
Free

PER TABLESPOON:
Calories 4
Carbohydrate 1.0g
Protein 0.2g
Fat 0.0g
Cholesterol 0mg
Fiber 0.2g
Sodium 11mg

1 Combine all ingredients in a medium bowl; stir well. Cover and chill at least 2 hours. Serve with no-oil baked tortilla chips (chips not included in analysis). Yield: 1¾ cups.

super·quick

HUMMUS DIP

YIELD: 1½ cups

EXCHANGES PER TABLESPOON:
Free

PER TABLESPOON:
Calories 18
Carbohydrate 2.8g
Protein 0.7g
Fat 0.5g
Cholesterol 0mg
Fiber 0.7g
Sodium 33mg

1 (15-ounce) can garbanzo beans, rinsed and drained
1 green onion, cut into ½-inch pieces
2 tablespoons plain nonfat yogurt
2 tablespoons sesame seeds
1 tablespoon lemon juice
1 small clove garlic

1 Position knife blade in food processor bowl; add all ingredients, and process until bean mixture is smooth.

2 Transfer mixture to a small serving bowl. Cover and chill thoroughly. Serve with assorted fresh vegetables like carrots, celery, snow peas, broccoli flowerets, and radishes (vegetables not included in analysis).
Yield: 1½ cups.

SHRIMP DIPPERS

YIELD: 28 appetizers

EXCHANGES PER APPETIZER:
Free

PER APPETIZER:
Calories 7
Carbohydrate 0.1g
Protein 1.4g
Fat 0.1g
Cholesterol 12mg
Fiber 0.0g
Sodium 14mg

14 fresh snow pea pods, trimmed
28 large cooked, peeled, and deveined shrimp

1 Arrange pea pods in a vegetable steamer over boiling water. Cover and steam 1 minute or until crisp-tender. Remove pea pods, and chill.

2 Separate pea pods lengthwise into 2 pieces. Wrap a pea pod half around each shrimp, and secure with a plastic pick. Yield: 28 appetizers.

super·quick

DILLED GARDEN DIP

YIELD: 1¾ cups

1 (16-ounce) carton 1% low-fat cottage
   cheese
2 tablespoons tarragon vinegar
1 tablespoon finely chopped green onions
1 tablespoon dried parsley flakes
½ teaspoon dried dillweed
1 tablespoon skim milk
   Dash of coarsely ground pepper
   Fresh parsley sprigs (optional)

**EXCHANGES PER
TABLESPOON:**
Free

PER TABLESPOON:
Calories 13
Carbohydrate 0.5g
Protein 2.1g
Fat 0.2g
Cholesterol 1mg
Fiber 0.0g
Sodium 70mg

1 Place cottage cheese and vinegar in container of an electric blender or food processor; cover and process until smooth.

2 Combine cottage cheese mixture, green onions, and next 4 ingredients in a medium bowl; stir well. Transfer cheese mixture to a small serving bowl; cover and chill. If desired, garnish with parsley sprigs, and serve with Shrimp Dippers on previous page. Yield: 1¾ cups.

PIMIENTO CHEESE DIP

YIELD: 1¼ cups

EXCHANGES PER
TABLESPOON:
Free (up to 3
tablespoons)

PER TABLESPOON:
Calories 19
Carbohydrate 0.8g
Protein 1.7g
Fat 1.0g
Cholesterol 2mg
Fiber 0.0g
Sodium 66mg

¾ cup 1% low-fat cottage cheese
3 tablespoons reduced-fat mayonnaise
½ teaspoon vinegar
⅛ teaspoon pepper
   Dash of hot sauce
¼ cup (1 ounce) shredded reduced-fat
   sharp Cheddar cheese
1 (2-ounce) jar diced pimiento, drained

1 Combine first 5 ingredients in container of an electric blender or food processor; cover and process until smooth. Cover and chill.

2 Stir in cheese and pimiento. Serve with vegetable crudités (not included in analysis). Yield: 1¼ cups.

HERB-CHEESE DIP

YIELD: 1⅔ cups

EXCHANGES PER
TABLESPOON:
½ Fat

PER TABLESPOON:
Calories 27
Carbohydrate 0.5g
Protein 1.6g
Fat 2.1g
Cholesterol 7mg
Fiber 0.0g
Sodium 60mg

1 (8-ounce) package Neufchâtel cheese,
   softened
⅔ cup 1% low-fat cottage cheese
1 tablespoon chopped fresh parsley
1 clove garlic, minced
1½ teaspoons skim milk
1 teaspoon red wine vinegar
½ teaspoon Worcestershire sauce
⅛ teaspoon dried marjoram
⅛ teaspoon dried thyme
⅛ teaspoon dried basil
⅛ teaspoon ground savory

1 Combine all ingredients in a small bowl; beat at medium speed of an electric mixer until smooth. Cover and chill thoroughly. Serve with Melba toast rounds (not included in analysis). Yield: 1⅔ cups.

super·quick

CREAMY CRAB DIP

For a colorful presentation, serve this appetizer in a hollowed-out head of radicchio (radicchio not included in analysis).

½ cup plain nonfat yogurt
⅓ cup reduced-fat mayonnaise
1 tablespoon grated onion
2 teaspoons minced fresh parsley
2 teaspoons lemon juice
½ teaspoon Dijon mustard
¼ teaspoon dried dillweed
6 ounces fresh lump crabmeat, drained

1 Combine first 7 ingredients in a small bowl; stir well. Stir in crabmeat. Cover and chill.

2 To serve, transfer mixture to a serving bowl. Serve with Melba toast or fresh raw vegetables (Melba toast and vegetables not included in analysis). Yield: 1½ cups.

YIELD: 1½ cups

EXCHANGES PER TABLESPOON:
Free

PER TABLESPOON:
Calories 19
Carbohydrate 0.7g
Protein 1.7g
Fat 1.0g
Cholesterol 5mg
Fiber 0.0g
Sodium 107mg

YIELD: 2 cups

super·quick

SNAPPY SPINACH DIP

EXCHANGES PER
TABLESPOON:
Free

PER TABLESPOON:
Calories 13
Carbohydrate 0.9g
Protein 1.2g
Fat 0.6g
Cholesterol 1mg
Fiber 0.3g
Sodium 43mg

1 (10-ounce) package frozen chopped
   spinach, thawed and drained
1 cup 1% low-fat cottage cheese
¼ cup low-fat sour cream
2 tablespoons reduced-fat mayonnaise
2 tablespoons minced fresh parsley
2 teaspoons extra spicy salt-free herb and
   spice blend
2 teaspoons lemon juice
¼ teaspoon garlic powder
   Celery leaves (optional)

1 Press spinach between layers of paper towels to remove excess moisture.

2 Position knife blade in food processor bowl; add cottage cheese and sour cream. Process until smooth, stopping once to scrape down sides. Add spinach, mayonnaise, and next 4 ingredients; process until smooth.

3 Transfer dip to a bowl. Serve with assorted fresh vegetables (vegetables not included in analysis). Garnish with celery leaves, if desired. Yield: 2 cups.

HOT SPINACH DIP

YIELD: 12 servings

1 (1-pound) round loaf sourdough bread
1 (10-ounce) package frozen chopped
   spinach, thawed
2 tablespoons reduced-calorie margarine
1½ tablespoons all-purpose flour
1 tablespoon chopped onion
¼ cup evaporated skimmed milk
3 ounces light process cream cheese
¼ cup (1 ounce) shredded Monterey Jack
   cheese with jalapeño peppers
2 teaspoons low-sodium Worcestershire
   sauce
¼ teaspoon garlic powder
¼ teaspoon pepper
⅛ teaspoon dried crushed red pepper
1 (2-ounce) jar diced pimiento, drained

EXCHANGES PER SERVING:
½ Starch
1 Vegetable
1 Fat

PER SERVING:
Calories 91
Carbohydrate 11.3g
Protein 4.1g
Fat 3.6g
Cholesterol 6mg
Fiber 1.1g
Sodium 190mg

🌿 You can also serve this dip with assorted fresh vegetables and fat-free crackers.

1 Cut off top one-fourth of loaf; set top aside. Hollow out center of loaf to form a shell about ½ inch thick. Cut bread from center and top of loaf into 48 (1-inch) cubes. Place bread cubes on a baking sheet, and bake at 350° for 15 to 20 minutes or until lightly browned. Set aside.

2 Cook spinach according to package directions, omitting salt; drain well, reserving ¼ cup liquid. Set spinach and liquid aside.

3 Melt margarine in a medium saucepan over medium heat. Add flour and onion; cook 1 minute, stirring constantly. Gradually add reserved spinach liquid and milk; cook, stirring constantly, until slightly thickened. Add cream cheese and next 5 ingredients, stirring until cheeses melt. Stir in spinach and pimiento. Cook 1 minute or until thoroughly heated.

4 Spoon mixture into bread round; serve with bread cubes. Yield: 12 appetizer servings (serving size: 4 bread cubes and 2½ tablespoons dip).

Spicy Black-Eyed Pea Dip

YIELD: 2 cups

EXCHANGES PER
TABLESPOON:
Free

PER TABLESPOON:
Calories 17
Carbohydrate 1.8g
Protein 1.4g
Fat 0.4g
Cholesterol 1mg
Fiber 0.2g
Sodium 33mg

Unsalted corn tortilla chips are naturals
for scooping up this hot, spicy dip.

1 (15-ounce) can black-eyed peas,
   drained
½ cup plain nonfat yogurt
1 teaspoon chili powder
½ teaspoon garlic powder
¼ to ½ teaspoon ground red pepper
   Vegetable cooking spray
½ cup (2 ounces) shredded reduced-fat
   Cheddar cheese
1 tablespoon sliced green onions

1 Position knife blade in food processor bowl;
add first 5 ingredients. Process 30 seconds,
stopping once to scrape down sides of bowl;
process 30 additional seconds or until smooth.
Transfer to a 1-quart casserole coated with
cooking spray.

2 Bake at 400° for 15 to 20 minutes or until
thoroughly heated. Remove from oven;
sprinkle with cheese, and bake 2 additional minutes or until cheese melts.

3 Top with green onions. Serve dip with
unsalted corn tortilla chips (not included in
analysis). Yield: 2 cups.

LAYERED PIZZA DIP

YIELD: 12 appetizer
servings

Be sure to include the carbohydrate
from the chips in your meal plan. Ten chips
have about 16 grams of carbohydrate.

EXCHANGES PER
SERVING:
½ Lean Meat
1 Vegetable

1 (8-ounce) carton nonfat cream cheese,
 softened
½ cup nonfat sour cream
⅛ teaspoon garlic powder
⅛ teaspoon ground red pepper
 Vegetable cooking spray
½ cup no-salt-added tomato sauce
¼ teaspoon dried oregano
⅛ teaspoon garlic powder
⅛ teaspoon onion powder
½ cup chopped frozen artichoke hearts,
 thawed
¼ cup sliced green onions
¼ cup chopped sweet red pepper
¼ cup sliced ripe olives
½ cup (2 ounces) shredded part-skim
 mozzarella cheese
½ teaspoon dried Italian seasoning

PER SERVING:
Calories 48
Carbohydrate 3.5g
Protein 4.9g
Fat 1.4g
Cholesterol 6mg
Fiber 0.5g
Sodium 189mg

1 Combine first 4 ingredients in a small bowl;
beat at low speed of an electric mixer until
smooth. Spread cream cheese mixture in a
9-inch pieplate coated with cooking spray.

2 Combine tomato sauce and next 3 ingredients in a small bowl, stirring well. Pour
tomato sauce mixture over cream cheese
mixture in pieplate. Layer artichokes and next
4 ingredients over tomato sauce. Sprinkle with
Italian seasoning. Bake, uncovered, at 350° for
15 to 20 minutes or until thoroughly heated.
Serve with no-oil baked tortilla chips (chips
not included in analysis). Yield: 12 appetizer
servings.

EGGPLANT CAPONATA

YIELD: 3½ cups

EXCHANGES PER
TABLESPOON:
Free

PER TABLESPOON:
Calories 7
Carbohydrate 1.1g
Protein 0.2g
Fat 0.3g
Cholesterol 0mg
Fiber 0.2g
Sodium 17mg

Serve this flavorful appetizer with toasted
cocktail pumpernickel bread or Melba toast
(bread and toast not included in analysis).

1 medium eggplant (about 1½ pounds)
   Vegetable cooking spray
1 tablespoon olive oil
1 cup chopped onion
1 cup chopped green pepper
2 cloves garlic, minced
⅔ cup no-salt-added tomato sauce
3 tablespoons no-salt-added tomato paste
3 tablespoons sliced ripe olives
2 tablespoons chopped salad olives
2 tablespoons red wine vinegar
2 teaspoons granulated sugar substitute
¼ teaspoon salt
¼ teaspoon dried oregano
¼ teaspoon pepper
   Fresh oregano sprigs (optional)

1 Cut eggplant in half lengthwise. Scoop out
pulp, reserving shells; finely chop pulp.

2 Coat a nonaluminum Dutch oven with cooking spray; add oil. Place over medium-high
heat until hot. Add chopped eggplant, onion,
green pepper, and garlic; sauté 5 minutes. Add
tomato sauce and next 8 ingredients; stir well.
Cook over low heat 20 minutes, stirring often.
Remove from heat, and let cool slightly.

3 Spoon vegetable mixture evenly into reserved
eggplant shells. Cover and chill. Garnish
with oregano sprigs, if desired. Yield: 3½ cups.

LAYERED SOUTHWESTERN SPREAD

YIELD: 10 servings

EXCHANGES PER SERVING:
1 Medium-Fat Meat
1 Vegetable

PER SERVING:
Calories 98
Carbohydrate 4.9g
Protein 7.6g
Fat 5.6g
Cholesterol 13mg
Fiber 0.9g
Sodium 214mg

2 cups (8 ounces) shredded part-skim mozzarella cheese
⅓ cup 1% low-fat cottage cheese
1 (4½-ounce) can chopped green chiles, drained
2 tablespoons reduced-calorie mayonnaise
¼ teaspoon garlic powder
1 cup seeded, chopped tomato
1 cup shredded lettuce
½ cup red kidney beans, rinsed and drained
1½ tablespoons sliced green onions
8 ripe olives, sliced
Pita chips (optional)

1 Combine first 5 ingredients in a medium bowl; stir well.

2 Spread cheese mixture in a 9-inch quiche dish. Bake at 350° for 20 minutes or until bubbly. Let cool 3 minutes.

3 Arrange chopped tomato around edge of dish, leaving a 1-inch border. Arrange lettuce next to tomato, forming a ring. Arrange beans in center. Sprinkle evenly with green onions and olives. Serve warm with pita chips, if desired. Yield: 10 appetizer servings.

Microwave Instructions: Prepare cheese mixture as directed. Cover with heavy-duty plastic wrap, and microwave at HIGH 4 to 6 minutes or until thoroughly heated, stirring after 2 minutes. Proceed with recipe as directed.

YIELD: 16 appetizer
servings

EXCHANGES PER
SERVING:
1 Lean Meat
1 Starch

PER SERVING:
Calories 134
Carbohydrate 14.1g
Protein 7.7g
Fat 3.6g
Cholesterol 25mg
Fiber 1.2g
Sodium 256mg

CRAB MOUSSE

Vegetable cooking spray
1 envelope unflavored gelatin
3 tablespoons skim milk
1 (8-ounce) package Neufchâtel cheese,
    softened
1 (8-ounce) carton plain nonfat yogurt
½ pound fresh lump crabmeat, drained
1 cup minced celery
⅓ cup sliced green onions
1 tablespoon lemon juice
1 teaspoon pepper
½ teaspoon prepared horseradish
    Fresh radishes (optional)
64 slices Melba toast

1 Coat a 4-cup mold with cooking spray; set aside.

2 Sprinkle gelatin over skim milk in a small saucepan; let stand 1 minute. Add Neufchâtel cheese, and cook over low heat, stirring until gelatin dissolves and mixture is smooth. Add yogurt, stirring until well blended. Remove from heat. Add crabmeat and next 5 ingredients, stirring well.

3 Pour mixture into prepared mold. Cover and chill until firm. To serve, unmold onto a serving plate; garnish with fresh radishes, if desired. Serve with Melba toast. Yield: 16 appetizer servings (serving size: ¼ cup mousse and 4 slices Melba toast).

✿ To soften Neufchâtel cheese quickly, stir it vigorously. Or unwrap the cheese and place it in a microwave-safe bowl. Microwave, uncovered, at HIGH 15 to 20 seconds.

COCKTAIL CHEESE BALL

You can prepare this crowd-pleasing appetizer up to a week ahead, but wait until party time to add the parsley.

1 (8-ounce) package Neufchâtel cheese, softened
¼ cup plain nonfat yogurt
1 cup (4 ounces) shredded 40% less-fat Cheddar cheese
1 cup (4 ounces) shredded reduced-fat Swiss cheese
2 teaspoons grated onion
2 teaspoons prepared horseradish
1 teaspoon country-style Dijon mustard
¼ cup chopped fresh parsley

1 Combine Neufchâtel cheese and yogurt in a large mixing bowl; beat at medium speed of an electric mixer until smooth. Add Cheddar cheese and next 4 ingredients; stir well. Cover and chill at least 1 hour.

2 Shape cheese mixture into a ball, and sprinkle with parsley. Press parsley gently into cheese ball. Wrap in heavy-duty plastic wrap, and chill. Serve with fat-free crackers. Yield: 2 cups.

Ham and Cheese Ball: Substitute ¾ cup finely chopped lean cooked ham for Swiss cheese. Substitute 2 tablespoons finely chopped green onions for grated onion. Proceed with recipe as directed. Yield: 2 cups.

Caraway-Swiss Cheese Ball: Omit Cheddar cheese. Increase Swiss cheese to 2 cups. Omit horseradish. Stir 1 tablespoon caraway seeds into cheese mixture. Proceed with recipe as directed. Yield: 2 cups.

YIELD: 2 cups

EXCHANGES PER TABLESPOON:
½ Medium-Fat Meat

PER TABLESPOON:
Calories 41
Carbohydrate 0.6g
Protein 3.1g
Fat 3.0g
Cholesterol 10mg
Fiber 0g
Sodium 67mg

✍ The two variations have about the same amount of carbohydrate as the Cocktail Cheese Ball and are both counted as ½ Medium-Fat Meat Exchange.

BAKED CHEESE WITH TOMATO CHUTNEY

YIELD: 12 appetizer servings

EXCHANGES PER SERVING:
1 Medium-Fat Meat

PER SERVING:
Calories 78
Carbohydrate 1.1g
Protein 4.0g
Fat 5.5g
Cholesterol 32mg
Fiber 0.4g
Sodium 146mg

✘ Try serving this appetizer with small French bread slices. Two slices will add about 20 calories.

1 large egg, lightly beaten
½ teaspoon ground red pepper
1 (8-ounce) round farmer cheese
¼ cup toasted wheat germ
 Vegetable cooking spray
 Tomato Chutney

1 Combine egg and red pepper. Dip cheese in egg mixture; dredge in wheat germ. Place on a baking sheet coated with cooking spray. Cut a piece of aluminum foil long enough to fit around cheese, allowing a 1-inch overlap; fold foil lengthwise into thirds. Lightly coat one side of foil with cooking spray; wrap around outside of cheese, coated side in, allowing foil to extend ¼ inch above cheese. Secure with string.

2 Bake at 375° for 10 minutes or just until cheese melts. Let stand 5 minutes. Remove foil; transfer cheese to a serving plate. Serve warm with Tomato Chutney and toasted French bread rounds, if desired. Yield: 12 appetizer servings.

TOMATO CHUTNEY

1 (8-ounce) can no-salt-added whole tomatoes, undrained and chopped
¼ cup water
2 tablespoons red wine vinegar
¼ teaspoon ground ginger
¼ teaspoon ground cloves
⅛ teaspoon ground cinnamon
2 cloves garlic, minced
1 tablespoon granulated sugar substitute
1 tablespoon currants

1 Combine first 7 ingredients in a saucepan; bring to a boil. Reduce heat; cook 15 minutes or until slightly thickened, stirring often. Remove from heat; stir in sugar substitute and currants. Yield: ¾ cup.

Tofu-Stuffed Eggs

YIELD: 6 servings

To hard-cook eggs, place them in a saucepan and cover with water. Cover and bring to a boil. Remove pan from heat, and let eggs stand, covered, in hot water about 15 minutes.

6 hard-cooked eggs, peeled
¾ cup firm tofu
2 tablespoons nonfat mayonnaise
1 teaspoon prepared mustard
¼ teaspoon curry powder
⅛ teaspoon paprika
   Fresh parsley sprigs (optional)

EXCHANGES PER SERVING:
1 Lean Meat

PER SERVING:
Calories 44
Carbohydrate 2.0g
Protein 5.8g
Fat 1.5g
Cholesterol 0mg
Fiber 0.4g
Sodium 129mg

1 Slice eggs in half lengthwise; carefully remove and discard yolks.

2 Position knife blade in food processor bowl; add tofu and next 4 ingredients. Process mixture 30 seconds or until smooth, scraping down sides of bowl twice.

3 Spoon tofu mixture evenly into egg whites. (If desired, spoon tofu mixture into a decorating bag fitted with a No. 1B star tip, and pipe tofu mixture evenly into egg whites.) Garnish with parsley sprigs, if desired. Yield: 6 servings.

✒ Look for tofu, a curd made from soybeans, in the produce department of your supermarket.

TORTELLINI-VEGETABLE KABOBS

EXCHANGES PER
APPETIZER:
1 Vegetable

PER APPETIZER:
Calories 26
Carbohydrate 4.5g
Protein 1.4g
Fat 0.4g
Cholesterol 0mg
Fiber 0.1g
Sodium 43mg

If you use dried tortellini, the cooking time will be about 15 minutes instead of 5 for the fresh.

24 small fresh spinach tortellini with
    cheese, uncooked
12 small fresh cheese tortellini, uncooked
1 teaspoon cornstarch
1 teaspoon dried basil
1 teaspoon dried oregano
½ teaspoon dry mustard
¼ teaspoon onion powder
¼ teaspoon garlic powder
¼ teaspoon salt
⅔ cup water
½ cup cider vinegar
1 (14-ounce) can artichoke hearts, drained
12 small cherry tomatoes, halved

1 Cook tortellini according to package directions, omitting salt and fat. Drain and set aside.

2 Combine cornstarch and next 6 ingredients in a small saucepan; gradually stir in water and vinegar. Bring to a boil; cook 30 seconds, stirring with a wire whisk. Remove from heat, and let cool.

3 Cut 6 artichoke hearts into quarters; reserve remaining artichoke hearts for another use. Alternate tortellini, tomato halves, and artichoke quarters on 6-inch wooden skewers; place in a 13- x 9- x 2-inch dish. Pour vinegar mixture over kabobs, turning to coat. Cover and marinate in refrigerator at least 4 hours, turning occasionally.

4 Drain well, discarding marinade. Transfer kabobs to a serving platter. Yield: 24 appetizers.

ARTICHOKE SQUARES

YIELD: 16 appetizers

Use a hot tray, griddle, or bun warmer to keep these appetizers warm at the serving table.

Vegetable cooking spray
3 tablespoons chopped green onions
1 (14-ounce) can artichoke hearts, drained and chopped
1/4 cup chopped fresh parsley
2 eggs
2 egg whites
3/4 cup (3 ounces) shredded reduced-fat Swiss cheese
1/2 cup plain nonfat yogurt
1/2 cup fine, dry breadcrumbs
1/4 teaspoon salt
Fresh parsley sprigs (optional)

EXCHANGES PER SERVING:
1 Vegetable
1/2 Fat

PER SERVING:
Calories 54
Carbohydrate 4.9g
Protein 4.4g
Fat 2.0g
Cholesterol 31mg
Fiber 0.2g
Sodium 108mg

1 Coat a small nonstick skillet with cooking spray; place over medium-high heat until hot. Add green onions; sauté 3 minutes or until tender. Remove from heat. Add artichoke hearts and chopped parsley; stir gently.

2 Beat eggs and egg whites in a large bowl with a wire whisk. Add cheese, yogurt, breadcrumbs, and salt; stir well. Stir in artichoke mixture.

3 Spread mixture in a 9-inch square pan coated with cooking spray. Bake at 350° for 20 minutes or until set. Cut into squares. Transfer to a serving tray, and garnish with parsley, if desired. Serve warm. Yield: 16 appetizers.

Microwave Instructions: Prepare steps 1 and 2 as directed. Spread mixture in a 9-inch square baking dish coated with cooking spray. Place in microwave oven on an inverted saucer. Microwave, uncovered, at MEDIUM-HIGH (70% power) 11 to 12 minutes or until set, rotating a half-turn every 3 minutes. Let stand 5 minutes before serving.

YIELD: 24 appetizers

EXCHANGES PER
APPETIZER:
1 Vegetable

PER SERVING:
Calories 26
Carbohydrate 4.8g
Protein 0.8g
Fat 0.5g
Cholesterol 0mg
Fiber 0.6g
Sodium 54mg

MARINATED EGGPLANT APPETIZERS

1 medium eggplant (about 1¼ pounds)
½ teaspoon salt
 Olive oil-flavored vegetable cooking
  spray
⅓ cup balsamic vinegar
2 tablespoons minced fresh basil
3 cloves garlic, crushed
1 teaspoon olive oil
1½ tablespoons minced fresh thyme
2 teaspoons minced fresh oregano
½ teaspoon freshly ground pepper
24 (¼-inch-thick) slices French bread
1½ cups peeled, seeded, and chopped
  tomato
 Fresh basil sprigs (optional)

1 Slice eggplant into 24 slices. Place eggplant in a colander, and sprinkle with salt; let stand 30 minutes. Rinse well, and pat dry.

2 Coat both sides of each eggplant slice with cooking spray; place on rack of a broiler pan. Broil 5½ inches from heat (with electric oven door partially opened) 3 to 4 minutes on each side or until lightly browned and tender.

3 Combine vinegar and next 6 ingredients in a small bowl. Brush on both sides of eggplant, and let stand 1 hour.

4 Coat bread with cooking spray; place on rack of broiler pan. Broil 5½ inches from heat until golden. Top each with an eggplant slice and 1 tablespoon tomato. Garnish with basil sprigs, if desired. Yield: 2 dozen appetizers.

ITALIAN-STUFFED MUSHROOMS

For variety, use reduced-fat Cheddar in place of part-skim mozzarella; the fat and calorie content will be about the same.

30 medium-size fresh mushrooms
½ cup (2 ounces) shredded part-skim mozzarella cheese
¼ cup minced fresh parsley
¼ cup commercial fat-free Italian dressing

YIELD: 30 mushrooms

EXCHANGES PER MUSHROOM:
Free

PER MUSHROOM:
Calories 8
Carbohydrate 0.8g
Protein 0.7g
Fat 0.3g
Cholesterol 1mg
Fiber 0.1g
Sodium 31mg

1 Clean mushrooms with damp paper towels. Remove mushroom stems, and finely chop; set caps aside.

2 Combine chopped mushroom stems, cheese, parsley, and dressing in a bowl, stirring well. Spoon evenly into mushroom caps, and place in a shallow baking dish. Bake at 350° for 15 to 20 minutes or until cheese melts. Yield: 30 mushrooms.

Microwave Instructions: Prepare mushroom mixture as directed above. Spoon chopped mushroom mixture evenly into mushroom caps. Arrange mushroom caps in a shallow baking dish. Microwave, uncovered, at HIGH 3 to 4 minutes or until cheese melts, rotating a quarter-turn every minute.

SPINACH CUPS

PER SERVING:
Calories 19
Carbohydrate 2.3g
Protein 0.9g
Fat 0.8g
Cholesterol 2mg
Fiber 0.4g
Sodium 51mg

These vegetable-filled bread cups
can be refrigerated up to 2 hours before
baking without getting soggy.

9 (½-ounce) slices very thinly sliced
 whole wheat bread
 Vegetable cooking spray
1 (10-ounce) package frozen chopped
 spinach, thawed
2 teaspoons reduced-calorie margarine
½ cup finely chopped onion
½ cup light process cream cheese,
 softened
1 (2-ounce) jar diced pimiento, drained
1 small clove garlic, minced
1 teaspoon hot sauce
⅛ teaspoon salt
⅛ teaspoon pepper

1 Trim crusts from bread; reserve bread crusts
 for another use. Flatten bread slices, using
a rolling pin. Cut slices into quarters. Press into
miniature (1¾-inch) muffin pans coated with
cooking spray. Bake at 350° for 5 to 7 minutes
or until lightly browned.

2 Drain spinach; press between paper towels
 to remove excess moisture.

3 Coat a large nonstick skillet with cooking
 spray; add margarine. Place over medium
heat until margarine melts. Add onion, and
sauté 4 to 5 minutes or until tender. Stir in
spinach; cook 2 to 3 minutes or until thoroughly heated.

4 Combine cream cheese and next 5 ingredients in a bowl; add spinach mixture, stirring
well. Spoon into bread cups (about 2 teaspoons
per cup). Bake at 350° for 5 minutes or until
thoroughly heated. Yield: 3 dozen.

PEPPY PIZZA WEDGES

YIELD: 16 appetizers

4 (6-inch) pita bread rounds
½ cup fat-free spaghetti sauce
4 plum tomatoes, thinly sliced
½ teaspoon dried basil
¼ teaspoon dried thyme
1 sweet yellow pepper, seeded and cut into thin strips
4 thin slices purple onion, separated into rings
1 cup (4 ounces) shredded part-skim mozzarella cheese
2 tablespoons grated Romano cheese
Fresh thyme sprigs (optional)

EXCHANGES PER SERVING:
1 Starch

PER SERVING:
Calories 72
Carbohydrate 10.4g
Protein 3.1g
Fat 1.7g
Cholesterol 5mg
Fiber 2.0g
Sodium 102mg

1 Arrange pita bread rounds on an ungreased baking sheet. Broil 5½ inches from heat (with electric oven door partially opened) 2 minutes on each side.

2 Spread 2 tablespoons spaghetti sauce over 1 side of each pita round, leaving a ½-inch border; top rounds evenly with tomato. Sprinkle basil and thyme over tomato. Arrange yellow pepper and onion over tomato. Sprinkle cheeses evenly over pita rounds.

3 Broil 5½ inches from heat (with electric oven door partially opened) 3 to 4 minutes or until cheese melts and pita rounds are thoroughly heated. Cut each round into 4 wedges. Garnish with thyme sprigs, if desired. Yield: 16 appetizers.

PIZZA SQUARES

EXCHANGES PER
SERVING:
1 Medium-Fat Meat
1 Starch
1 Vegetable

PER SERVING:
Calories 173
Carbohydrate 19.4g
Protein 11.6g
Fat 5.2g
Cholesterol 21mg
Fiber 1.0g
Sodium 299mg

Vegetable cooking spray
½ pound ground round
⅔ cup chopped green pepper
½ cup chopped onion
1 clove garlic, minced
¾ cup (3 ounces) shredded reduced-fat
   sharp Cheddar cheese
¾ cup (3 ounces) shredded part-skim
   mozzarella cheese
⅓ cup no-salt-added tomato sauce
¾ teaspoon dried Italian seasoning
¼ teaspoon freshly ground pepper
1 (11-ounce) package refrigerated crusty
   French loaf dough
1 tablespoon grated Parmesan cheese

1 Coat a large nonstick skillet with cooking spray; add ground round and next 3 ingredients. Cook over medium heat until meat is browned, stirring until it crumbles. Drain and pat dry with paper towels. Wipe drippings from skillet with a paper towel.

2 Combine meat mixture, Cheddar cheese, and next 4 ingredients; stir well.

3 Unroll dough into a large rectangle; cut into 36 (2-inch) squares. Place squares on a large baking sheet coated with cooking spray. Spoon about 1½ teaspoons meat mixture onto each dough square. Sprinkle Parmesan cheese evenly over squares.

4 Bake at 425° for 10 to 12 minutes or until bread is crisp and lightly browned. Serve warm. Yield: 12 appetizer servings (serving size: 3 squares).

Stuffed Miniature Popovers

YIELD: 32 appetizers

EXCHANGES PER
SERVING:
1 Vegetable

PER APPETIZER:
Calories 44
Carbohydrate 3.8g
Protein 3.0g
Fat 1.8g
Cholesterol 20mg
Fiber 0.0g
Sodium 61mg

1½ cups diced cooked chicken breast
    (skinned before cooking and cooked
    without salt)
¼ cup plus 2 tablespoons minced fresh
    mushrooms
¼ cup plus 2 tablespoons reduced-calorie
    mayonnaise
2 tablespoons chopped fresh parsley
2 tablespoons diced pimiento
1 tablespoon lemon juice
¼ teaspoon salt
½ teaspoon dried tarragon
4 drops of hot sauce
1 cup bread flour
1 cup skim milk
2 eggs, lightly beaten
2 tablespoons grated Parmesan cheese
1 tablespoon reduced-calorie margarine
    Vegetable cooking spray

1 Combine first 9 ingredients in a small bowl;
stir well. Cover and chill thoroughly.

2 Combine flour and next 4 ingredients in
container of an electric blender; cover and
process just until smooth.

3 Place miniature (1¾-inch) muffin pans coated
with cooking spray in a 450° oven for 3 minutes or until a drop of water sizzles when
dropped in muffin cup. Remove pans from oven;
fill each muffin cup half full with batter. Bake at
450° for 10 minutes; reduce heat to 350°, and
bake 5 minutes. Remove popovers from pan, and
let cool on a wire rack.

4 Slice each popover in half to, but not through,
other side; fill each with 2 teaspoons chicken
mixture. Place on a baking sheet; bake at 400°
for 5 minutes or until thoroughly heated.
Yield: 32 appetizers.

MINIATURE CHICKEN TOSTADAS

EXCHANGES PER
SERVING:
1 Very Lean Meat
½ Starch

PER SERVING:
Calories 72
Carbohydrate 8.8g
Protein 5.6g
Fat 1.6g
Cholesterol 12mg
Fiber 0.9g
Sodium 129mg

1 cup finely chopped cooked chicken
    breast (skinned before cooking and
    cooked without salt)
½ cup chopped jicama
½ cup (2 ounces) shredded reduced-fat
    Cheddar cheese
¼ cup nonfat mayonnaise
1 tablespoon diced pimiento, drained
1 (4½-ounce) can chopped green chiles,
    drained
6 (6-inch) corn tortillas

✄ For a different
look, use scissors to
cut each tortilla
into 6 wedges.

1 Combine first 6 ingredients in a small bowl; stir well. Set aside.

2 Cut each tortilla into 6 rounds, using a 2-inch biscuit cutter. Place tortilla rounds on an ungreased baking sheet. Bake at 350° for 6 minutes. Turn rounds, and bake 2 to 3 additional minutes or until golden and crisp.

3 Spread chicken mixture evenly over chips (about 1 tablespoon per chip). Broil 5½ inches from heat (with electric oven door partially opened) 3 minutes or until hot and bubbly. Serve warm. Yield: 12 appetizer servings (serving size: 3 tostadas).

Hawaiian Quesadillas

8 (8-inch) fat-free flour tortillas
1 (8-ounce) can pineapple tidbits in juice, drained
1 (5-ounce) can chunk chicken in water, drained and flaked
1 cup (4 ounces) shredded part-skim farmer cheese
⅓ cup sliced green onions
¼ teaspoon pepper
1 cup commercial no-salt-added chunky salsa
Fresh cilantro sprigs (optional)

EXCHANGES PER APPETIZER:
½ Medium-Fat Meat
1 Starch

PER APPETIZER:
Calories 100
Carbohydrate 14.1g
Protein 5.6g
Fat 2.3g
Cholesterol 5mg
Fiber 0.1g
Sodium 272mg

1 Place 2 tortillas on each of two ungreased baking sheets. Combine pineapple and chicken; spoon over tortillas. Top each tortilla evenly with cheese, green onions, and pepper; top with remaining 4 tortillas.

2 Bake at 350° for 8 to 10 minutes or until cheese softens. Cut each tortilla into 4 wedges. Spoon 1 tablespoon salsa over each wedge, and garnish with cilantro sprigs, if desired. Serve immediately. Yield: 16 appetizers.

✒ Fresh cilantro sprigs are the leaves of the coriander plant. This herb, also known as Chinese parsley, has a strong flavor that lends itself to highly seasoned foods. Store fresh cilantro, stems down, in a glass of water with a plastic bag over the leaves. You can store cilantro in the refrigerator in this manner up to a week.

EXCHANGES PER
SERVING:
1 Very Lean Meat
1 Vegetable

PER SERVING:
Calories 70
Carbohydrate 3.8g
Protein 11.2g
Fat 0.9g
Cholesterol 81mg
Fiber 0.6g
Sodium 162mg

SOUTHWESTERN
SHRIMP COCKTAIL

1¼ pounds unpeeled medium-size fresh
   shrimp
4 cups water
1 (8-ounce) can no-salt-added tomato
   sauce
¼ cup chopped fresh cilantro
1 tablespoon finely chopped onion
1½ tablespoons lime juice
1 tablespoon prepared horseradish
1 jalapeño pepper, seeded and chopped
½ teaspoon garlic powder
½ teaspoon onion powder
½ teaspoon salt
⅛ teaspoon hot sauce
   Fresh jalapeño pepper (optional)

1 Peel and devein shrimp leaving tails intact,
if desired. Bring water to a boil in a large
saucepan. Add shrimp; cook 3 to 5 minutes
or until shrimp turn pink. Drain well. Cover
and chill.

2 Combine tomato sauce and next 9 ingredients in a bowl; stir well. Cover and chill
3 hours. Transfer to a serving bowl; garnish
with jalapeño pepper, if desired. Serve with
shrimp. Yield: 8 appetizer servings.

HOT AND SPICY OYSTERS

These broiled oysters are similar to
Oysters Bienville, a popular Creole appetizer.
The red-hot flavor is characteristic of
many Creole dishes.

12 oysters on the half shell
   Vegetable cooking spray
⅓ cup chopped green onions
½ cup soft breadcrumbs
 3 tablespoons grated Parmesan cheese
½ teaspoon black pepper
¼ teaspoon ground red pepper

YIELD: 12 appetizers

EXCHANGES PER
APPETIZER:
Free

PER SERVING:
Calories 20
Carbohydrate 2.0g
Protein 1.5g
Fat 0.7g
Cholesterol 6mg
Fiber 0.1g
Sodium 48mg

1 Place oysters on a baking sheet, and set aside.

2 Coat a small nonstick skillet with cooking spray; place over medium-high heat until hot. Add green onions; sauté until tender. Add breadcrumbs and remaining 3 ingredients, stirring well.

3 Spoon breadcrumb mixture evenly over oysters. Broil 5½ inches from heat (with electric oven door partially opened) 2 minutes or until golden. Serve immediately.
Yield: 12 appetizers.

Fajita Potato Skins

YIELD: 4 appetizer
servings

EXCHANGES PER
SERVING:
1 Lean Meat
½ Starch

PER SERVING:
Calories 83
Carbohydrate 9.6g
Protein 6.6g
Fat 2.2g
Cholesterol 13mg
Fiber 1.0g
Sodium 153mg

1 tablespoon chopped onion
1 tablespoon chopped fresh cilantro
1 tablespoon lime juice
¼ teaspoon garlic powder
⅛ teaspoon salt
⅛ teaspoon ground cumin
⅛ teaspoon ground red pepper
2 ounces lean boneless round steak
2 small baking potatoes (about 3½ ounces each)
   Vegetable cooking spray
¼ cup (1 ounce) shredded reduced-fat Cheddar cheese
2 tablespoons mild salsa

1 Combine first 7 ingredients in a small bowl, stirring well. Trim fat from steak; slice steak diagonally across grain into ¼-inch-wide strips. Add steak to onion mixture. Cover and marinate in refrigerator 2 hours.

2 Scrub potatoes. Bake at 400° for 35 minutes or until tender. Let cool to touch. Cut potatoes in half lengthwise. Carefully scoop out pulp, leaving ¼-inch-thick shells; set shells aside. Mash pulp.

3 Coat a small nonstick skillet with cooking spray; place over medium heat until hot. Add meat mixture; cook 2 minutes or until meat is browned. Add mashed potato to skillet, and cook 1 minute.

4 Place potato shells in a small baking dish. Spoon steak mixture evenly into shells, and top with cheese. Bake at 350° for 10 to 12 minutes or until thoroughly heated. Top evenly with salsa. Yield: 4 appetizer servings.

APPETIZER MEATBALLS

YIELD: 14 servings

EXCHANGES PER
SERVING:
1 Medium-Fat Meat

PER SERVING:
Calories 83
Carbohydrate 2.3g
Protein 6.6g
Fat 4.6g
Cholesterol 19mg
Fiber 0.1g
Sodium 150mg

You can freeze these meatballs, uncooked, and then use them as needed. Broil frozen meatballs for about 15 minutes.

1 pound ground chuck
½ cup soft breadcrumbs
2 tablespoons chopped green pepper
2 tablespoons skim milk
1 teaspoon low-sodium Worcestershire sauce
2 egg whites, lightly beaten
   Vegetable cooking spray
1 tablespoon plus 1 teaspoon cornstarch
¼ cup water
¼ cup granulated brown sugar substitute
¼ cup red wine vinegar
¼ cup low-sodium soy sauce
1 teaspoon peeled, minced gingerroot
⅛ teaspoon garlic powder

1 Combine first 6 ingredients in a large bowl; stir well. Shape mixture into 42 (1-inch) meatballs. Arrange meatballs on rack of a broiler pan coated with cooking spray. Broil 5½ inches from heat (with electric oven door partially opened) 10 minutes or until browned, turning often.

2 Combine cornstarch and water in a large saucepan; stir well. Add brown sugar substitute and remaining 4 ingredients; stir well. Place over medium heat; bring to a boil, stirring constantly. Reduce heat, and simmer 3 to 5 minutes or until thickened, stirring constantly. Add meatballs, stirring lightly to coat. Transfer to a chafing dish, and serve warm. Yield: 14 appetizer servings (serving size: 3 meatballs).

ROSEMARY LEMONADE

EXCHANGES PER
SERVING:
½ Fruit

PER SERVING:
Calories 24
Carbohydrate 7.0g
Protein 0.2g
Fat 0.0g
Cholesterol 0mg
Fiber 0.0g
Sodium 1mg

5 cups water
1½ cups fresh lemon juice (about 10
　　large lemons)
1 tablespoon minced fresh rosemary
½ cup granulated sugar substitute with
　　aspartame (such as Equal Spoonful)
Fresh rosemary sprigs (optional)

1 Combine water and lemon juice in a large
nonaluminum saucepan; bring to a boil.

2 Remove from heat. Add rosemary; let stand
10 minutes. Strain mixture discarding rosemary. Stir in sugar substitute. Cover and chill.
Serve over ice. Garnish with fresh rosemary
sprigs, if desired. Yield: 6 (1-cup) servings.

🌿 The two variations have the
same nutrient and
exchange values
as the Rosemary
Lemonade.

Mint Lemonade: Substitute 2 tablespoons
minced fresh mint for the rosemary. Garnish
with fresh mint sprigs, if desired.

Lavender Lemonade: Substitute 1 tablespoon
minced fresh lavender for the rosemary. Garnish
with fresh lavender sprigs, if desired.

Gingered Watermelon Spritzer

3 tablespoons peeled, grated gingerroot
2 cups seeded, cubed watermelon
3 tablespoons frozen orange juice
    concentrate, undiluted
1 tablespoon lemon juice
1¾ cups lemon-lime-flavored sparkling
    mineral water, chilled

1 Place gingerroot on an 8-inch square of cheese-cloth. Bring edges together at top, and hold securely. Squeeze cheesecloth over a small bowl, reserving 2 teaspoons juice; discard gingerroot.

2 Combine ginger juice, watermelon, orange juice concentrate, and lemon juice in a container of an electric blender; cover and process until smooth. Stir in mineral water. Serve over ice. Yield: 4 (1-cup) servings.

YIELD: 4 servings

EXCHANGES PER
SERVING:
1 Fruit

PER SERVING:
Calories 50
Carbohydrate 11.5g
Protein 0.9g
Fat 0.4g
Cholesterol 0mg
Fiber 0.6g
Sodium 23mg

TANGY CRANBERRY COOLERS

YIELD: 4 servings

EXCHANGES PER
SERVING:
1½ Fruit

PER SERVING:
Calories 91
Carbohydrate 22.3g
Protein 0.9g
Fat 0.2g
Cholesterol 0mg
Fiber 0.1g
Sodium 13mg

¾ cup reduced-calorie cranberry juice
    cocktail, chilled
½ cup unsweetened apple juice, chilled
2 tablespoons fresh lime juice, chilled
1 tablespoon granulated sugar substitute
1 (6-ounce) can unsweetened pink
    grapefruit juice, chilled
Fresh lime slices (optional)

1 Combine first 5 ingredients in a small pitcher, stirring well. Serve juice mixture over crushed ice. Garnish with lime slices, if desired. Yield: 4 (½-cup) servings.

CRANBERRY FIZZ

YIELD: 5 servings

EXCHANGES PER
SERVING:
1 Fruit

PER SERVING:
Calories 56
Carbohydrate 13.9g
Protein 0.5g
Fat 0.0g
Cholesterol 0mg
Fiber 0.1g
Sodium 29mg

2¼ cups reduced-calorie cranberry juice
    cocktail
1½ cups unsweetened orange juice
1¼ cups club soda, chilled

1 Combine cranberry juice and orange juice in a large pitcher, stirring well. Cover and chill.

2 Stir in club soda just before serving. Serve over ice. Yield: 5 (1-cup) servings.

super·quick

SPARKLING PEACH COOLERS

YIELD: 4 servings

For nonalcoholic versions of both coolers, use 1 cup sugar-free lemon-lime soft drink instead of the champagne.

EXCHANGES PER SERVING:
1 Fruit

2 cups frozen sliced peaches, thawed
1 cup apricot nectar
1 cup champagne, chilled
½ cup club soda, chilled

PER SERVING:
Calories 111
Carbohydrate 17.8g
Protein 0.9g
Fat 0.1g
Cholesterol 0mg
Fiber 1.5g
Sodium 10mg

1 Combine peaches and apricot nectar in container of an electric blender; cover and process until smooth, stopping once to scrape down sides. Pour into a pitcher.

2 Stir champagne and club soda into peach mixture just before serving. Yield: 4 (1-cup) servings.

super·quick

STRAWBERRY COOLERS

YIELD: 4 servings

2½ cups fresh or frozen strawberries, thawed
1 cup unsweetened orange juice
1 cup champagne, chilled
½ cup club soda, chilled

EXCHANGES PER SERVING:
1 Fruit

1 Combine strawberries and orange juice in container of an electric blender; top with cover, and process until smooth, stopping once to scrape down sides. Pour into a pitcher.

PER SERVING:
Calories 110
Carbohydrate 16.1g
Protein 1.4g
Fat 0.5g
Cholesterol 0mg
Fiber 3.3g
Sodium 10mg

2 Stir champagne and club soda into peach mixture just before serving. Yield: 4 (1-cup) servings.

super·quick

PEACHES AND CREAM SIPPER

EXCHANGES PER
SERVING:
1 Fruit
½ Skim Milk

PER SERVING:
Calories 91
Carbohydrate 19.7g
Protein 3.4g
Fat 0.2g
Cholesterol 1mg
Fiber 0.9g
Sodium 50mg

✖ The two variations have about the same amount of carbohydrate as the Peaches and Cream Sipper and are both counted as 1 Fruit Exchange and ½ Skim Milk Exchange.

Use your electric blender to transform frozen fruit into creative beverages. You can use fresh fruit, but the drink will have a thinner consistency.

1 (16-ounce) package frozen unsweetened peaches, slightly thawed
1 (6-ounce) can frozen apple juice concentrate
1 (8-ounce) carton vanilla nonfat yogurt sweetened with aspartame
⅓ cup instant nonfat dry milk powder
¼ cup water
⅛ teaspoon vanilla extract
Ice cubes
Fresh strawberries (optional)

1 Combine first 6 ingredients in container of an electric blender; cover and process until smooth.

2 Gradually add enough ice to measure 4 cups in blender; cover and process until smooth.

3 Pour mixture into glasses. Garnish each serving with a fresh strawberry, if desired. Yield: 4 (1-cup) servings.

Banana-Strawberry Sipper: Substitute 2 large frozen bananas, peeled and sliced, for peaches. Substitute 1 (8-ounce) carton strawberry low-fat yogurt sweetened with aspartame for vanilla yogurt. Proceed with recipe as directed. Yield: 4 (1-cup) servings.

Raspberry Sipper: Substitute 1 (16-ounce) package frozen unsweetened raspberries, thawed and strained, for peaches. Substitute 1 (8-ounce) carton raspberry low-fat yogurt sweetened with aspartame for vanilla yogurt. Proceed with recipe as directed. Yield: 4 (1-cup) servings.

super·quick

CHILLED TOMATO COCKTAIL

YIELD: 6 servings

4 cups no-salt-added tomato juice
1 teaspoon low-sodium Worcestershire
   sauce
½ teaspoon coarsely ground pepper
½ teaspoon prepared horseradish
2 cups club soda, chilled
   Lemon slices (optional)
   Green onions (optional)

**EXCHANGES PER
SERVING:**
1 Vegetable

PER SERVING:
Calories 34
Carbohydrate 8.4g
Protein 1.6g
Fat 0.0g
Cholesterol 0mg
Fiber 0.0g
Sodium 37mg

1 Combine first 4 ingredients in a large pitcher;
stir well. Cover and chill.

2 Gently stir club soda into juice mixture just
before serving. Serve over ice. If desired,
garnish with lemon slices and green onions.
Yield: 6 (1-cup) servings.

CHOOSE-A-COCOA

YIELD: 12 servings

**EXCHANGES PER
SERVING:**
1 Skim Milk

PER SERVING:
Calories 97
Carbohydrate 13.3g
Protein 9.1g
Fat 0.5g
Cholesterol 5mg
Fiber 0.0g
Sodium 126mg

❧ Both of the variations have about the same amount of carbohydrate as the basic cocoa recipe, and both count as 1 Skim Milk Exchange.

2⅓ cups instant nonfat dry milk powder
⅓ cup unsweetened cocoa
⅓ cup granulated sugar substitute with
aspartame (such as Equal Spoonful)

1 Combine all ingredients in a large bowl; stir well. Store in an airtight container.

2 To serve, spoon ¼ cup cocoa mixture into each mug. Add 1 cup boiling water, and stir well. Yield: 12 (1-cup) servings.

Velvet Hot Cocoa: Prepare cocoa as directed above. Stir 1 teaspoon amaretto and ⅛ teaspoon rum extract into each serving. Yield: 12 (1-cup) servings.

Mocha Cocoa: Prepare cocoa as directed above. Stir 1½ teaspoons instant coffee granules and ⅛ teaspoon vanilla extract into each serving. Yield: 12 (1-cup) servings.

Orange Cappuccino

In a hurry? You can speed up the time it takes to chill the milk by setting the bowl in another larger bowl filled with ice.

¼ cup evaporated skimmed milk
3 cups hot strongly brewed coffee
2 tablespoons unsweetened orange juice
½ teaspoon orange extract
½ teaspoon grated semisweet chocolate

1 Place milk in a small, narrow glass or stainless steel bowl; freeze 30 minutes or until small ice crystals form around the top.

2 Beat milk at high speed of an electric mixer 5 minutes or until stiff peaks form.

3 Combine coffee, juice, and orange extract. Pour ¾ cup coffee mixture into each of 4 coffee cups. Top with whipped milk. Sprinkle each with ⅛ teaspoon grated chocolate. Serve immediately. Yield: 4 servings.

YIELD: 4 servings

EXCHANGES PER SERVING:
½ Skim Milk

PER SERVING:
Calories 55
Carbohydrate 7.7g
Protein 2.9g
Fat 1.4g
Cholesterol 1mg
Fiber 0.1g
Sodium 41mg

HOLIDAY GLÖGG

This lightened version of a traditional Swedish holiday punch helps take the chill off a cold winter night. Serve it warm with almonds and raisins in the cup.

EXCHANGES PER
SERVING:
2 Fruit
½ Fat

PER SERVING:
Calories 131
Carbohydrate 27.7g
Protein 1.2g
Fat 2.4g
Cholesterol 0mg
Fiber 1.0g
Sodium 22mg

3½ cups water
1 tablespoon whole cloves
¼ teaspoon ground cardamom
2 (3-inch) sticks cinnamon
2 (750-milliliter) bottles nonalcoholic
   dry red wine
1 cup raisins
½ cup granulated sugar substitute (such as
   Sugar Twin)
½ cup blanched whole almonds

✿ Nonalcoholic wines differ from sparkling ciders. Nonalcoholic varieties are fully fermented wines with almost all of the alcohol removed. The fermented flavor of the wine remains, but without the alcohol. These wines are 99.5 percent alcohol-free and have about 55 percent less calories than regular wines.

1 Combine first 4 ingredients in a large saucepan; bring to a boil. Reduce heat, and simmer, uncovered, 20 minutes.

2 Pour liquid through a wire-mesh strainer, discarding cloves and cinnamon sticks. Return liquid to saucepan. Stir in nonalcoholic wine and remaining ingredients. Cook over medium heat just until sugar substitute is dissolved and mixture is thoroughly heated, stirring often. To serve, pour into individual cups. Serve warm. Yield: 16 (½-cup) servings.

Breads

SESAME-HORSERADISH TOAST

YIELD: 4 servings

EXCHANGES PER SERVING:
1 Starch

PER SERVING:
Calories 105
Carbohydrate 18.1g
Protein 3.7g
Fat 2.1g
Cholesterol 1mg
Fiber 0.6g
Sodium 231mg

1½ tablespoons prepared horseradish
  1 tablespoon plain nonfat yogurt
  1 tablespoon reduced-fat mayonnaise
    Dash of hot sauce
  4 (1¼-ounce) slices Italian sourdough bread
  1 teaspoon sesame seeds, toasted

1 Combine first 4 ingredients in a small bowl, stirring well. Spread 1 side of each bread slice with 2 teaspoons horseradish mixture; sprinkle each slice with ¼ teaspoon toasted sesame seeds.

2 Place bread slices on a baking sheet. Broil 5½ inches from heat (with electric oven door partially opened) until lightly browned. Serve immediately. Yield: 4 servings.

super·quick

HERB-SEASONED FRENCH BREAD

YIELD: 6 servings

EXCHANGES PER SERVING:
1 Starch
½ Fat

PER SERVING:
Calories 98
Carbohydrate 15.9g
Protein 2.6g
Fat 2.4g
Cholesterol 1mg
Fiber 0.7g
Sodium 194mg

1½ tablespoons reduced-calorie margarine, melted
  1 teaspoon dried parsley flakes
  ½ teaspoon low-sodium Worcestershire sauce
  ¼ teaspoon dried basil
  ⅛ teaspoon garlic powder
  6 (1-inch-thick) slices French bread

1 Combine first 5 ingredients in a small bowl; stir well. Lightly brush 1 side of each bread slice with margarine mixture.

2 Wrap bread in heavy-duty aluminum foil. Place grill rack on grill over medium coals (300° to 350°). Place bread packet on rack; grill, covered, 6 minutes or until thoroughly heated. Yield: 6 servings.

super·quick
TWO-ALARM PEPPER BREAD

4 (1-inch-thick) slices French bread
1 tablespoon reduced-calorie margarine,
  melted
1 teaspoon dried parsley flakes
⅛ teaspoon dried crushed red pepper
  Dash of coarsely ground pepper

1 Place bread slices on an ungreased baking
  sheet.

2 Combine margarine and remaining ingredients in a small bowl. Brush one side of each
bread slice with margarine mixture. Bake at 350°
for 10 minutes or until thoroughly heated. Serve
warm. Yield: 4 servings.

YIELD: 4 servings

**EXCHANGES PER
SERVING:**
1½ Starch
½ Fat

PER SERVING:
Calories 139
Carbohydrate 23.7g
Protein 3.9g
Fat 2.7g
Cholesterol 1mg
Fiber 1.0g
Sodium 275mg

super·quick
GRILLED PEPPERED BREAD

2 teaspoons water
1½ teaspoons olive oil
¼ teaspoon ground white pepper
¼ teaspoon dried thyme
1 clove garlic, crushed
6 (1-inch-thick) slices Italian bread

1 Combine first 5 ingredients in a small bowl;
  stir well. Brush one side of each bread slice
with oil mixture.

2 Wrap bread in heavy-duty aluminum foil.
  Place grill rack on grill over medium
coals (300° to 350°). Place bread on rack, and
grill 6 minutes or until thoroughly heated.
Yield: 6 servings.

YIELD: 6 servings

**EXCHANGES PER
SERVING:**
1½ Starch

PER SERVING:
Calories 129
Carbohydrate 24.3g
Protein 3.9g
Fat 1.5g
Cholesterol 0mg
Fiber 1.2g
Sodium 249mg

BAKED PITA WEDGES

YIELD: 4 servings

EXCHANGES PER
SERVING:
1 Starch

PER SERVING:
Calories 77
Carbohydrate 14.1g
Protein 1.4g
Fat 0.9g
Cholesterol 0mg
Fiber 2.6g
Sodium 349mg

2 pita bread rounds
1 teaspoon Greek seasoning
Olive oil-flavored vegetable cooking spray

1 Split pita bread rounds in half horizontally. Cut each half into 8 wedges. Arrange wedges, cut sides up, on a baking sheet. Sprinkle evenly with Greek seasoning, and generously coat with cooking spray.

2 Bake at 400° for 6 to 7 minutes or until crisp. Yield: 4 servings (serving size: 8 wedges).

TORTILLA WEDGES

YIELD: 4 servings

EXCHANGES PER
SERVING:
1½ Starch
½ Fat

PER SERVING:
Calories 140
Carbohydrate 23.6g
Protein 3.7g
Fat 3.2g
Cholesterol 0mg
Fiber 1.3g
Sodium 203mg

4 (8-inch) flour tortillas
Butter -flavored vegetable cooking spray

1 Cut tortillas into wedges, and coat with butter-flavored cooking spray. Bake at 400° for 4 to 5 minutes or until lightly browned and crisp. Yield: 4 servings (serving size: 4 wedges).

ITALIAN FLATBREAD

Serve these flavorful bread rounds with your favorite Italian dish and a tossed green salad.

½ (32-ounce) package frozen bread dough, thawed
    Vegetable cooking spray
1 tablespoon water
2 teaspoons dried basil
¾ teaspoon garlic powder
2 tablespoons Italian-seasoned breadcrumbs
2 tablespoons freshly grated Parmesan cheese

1 Divide dough into 3 equal portions. Roll each portion into a 6½-inch circle. Place on a baking sheet coated with cooking spray. Brush dough with water. Combine basil and garlic powder; sprinkle evenly over dough.

2 Combine breadcrumbs and cheese in a small bowl; sprinkle evenly over dough. Bake at 375° for 10 to 12 minutes or until golden. Let cool slightly on baking sheet. Cut each round into 4 wedges. Yield: 12 wedges.

YIELD: 12 wedges

EXCHANGES PER WEDGE:
1 Starch

PER WEDGE:
Calories 97
Carbohydrate 17.1g
Protein 3.6g
Fat 1.5g
Cholesterol 1mg
Fiber 1.4g
Sodium 224mg

❧ You can thaw frozen bread dough overnight in the refrigerator. Or place frozen loaf in a loaf-pan coated with cooking spray. Cover dough lightly with wax paper or plastic wrap. The dough will thaw in approximately 1½ to 2 hours at room temperature.

CHEESE CRACKERS

YIELD: 56 crackers

SERVING SIZE:
8 crackers

EXCHANGES PER
SERVING:
1 Starch
1½ Fat

PER SERVING:
Calories 151
Carbohydrate 14.9g
Protein 6.9g
Fat 7.5g
Cholesterol 11mg
Fiber 0.9g
Sodium 264mg

1 cup (4 ounces) shredded reduced-fat
    sharp Cheddar cheese
¾ cup all-purpose flour
¼ cup whole wheat flour
¼ cup cold reduced-calorie margarine
¼ teaspoon salt
¼ teaspoon dry mustard
¼ teaspoon ground red pepper
3 tablespoons cold water

1 Position knife blade in food processor bowl. Add first 7 ingredients, and process until mixture is crumbly. Add water, 1 tablespoon at a time, and process until mixture forms a ball.

2 Divide dough in half. Roll each portion to ⅛-inch thickness on a lightly floured surface. Cut 1 portion into stars, using a 2-inch star-shaped cutter. Using a small knife, cut remaining portion into 3- x ½-inch strips.

3 Place stars and stripes on an ungreased baking sheet. Bake at 350° for 15 minutes. Remove crackers to wire racks to cool. Store in an airtight container. Yield: 56 crackers.

Sesame Wafers

Try these toasted wafers as snacks, or serve them with salads and soups.

½ cup whole wheat flour
½ cup all-purpose flour
¼ teaspoon baking soda
⅛ teaspoon salt
1 tablespoon sugar
2 tablespoons margarine
¼ cup plus 2 tablespoons plain nonfat
    yogurt
  Vegetable cooking spray
1 egg white
1 tablespoon water
2 tablespoons sesame seeds, toasted

1 Combine first 5 ingredients in a medium bowl; stir well. Cut in margarine with pastry blender until mixture is crumbly. Add yogurt, stirring just until dry ingredients are moistened.

2 Turn dough out onto a lightly floured surface, and knead 20 times. Roll dough to ¼-inch thickness; cut into rounds with a 2-inch biscuit cutter. Place on a baking sheet coated with cooking spray.

3 Combine egg white and water; stir well with a wire whisk. Brush over dough rounds, and sprinkle with sesame seeds. Bake at 400° for 8 to 10 minutes or until golden. Remove from baking sheet; cool completely on wire racks. Store in an airtight container. Yield: 48 wafers.

YIELD: 48 wafers

SERVING SIZE:
6 wafers

EXCHANGES PER
SERVING:
1 Starch
1 Fat

PER SERVING:
Calories 112
Carbohydrate 13.7g
Protein 3.8g
Fat 5.1g
Cholesterol 0mg
Fiber 1.2g
Sodium 114mg

✄ Store whole wheat flour in a tightly covered container in a cool, dry place. For longer storage store flour in the refrigerator or freezer.

FRENCH TOAST

EXCHANGES PER
SERVING:
½ Medium-Fat Meat
1 Starch

PER SERVING:
Calories 134
Carbohydrate 18.1g
Protein 6.9g
Fat 3.3g
Cholesterol 57mg
Fiber 0.7g
Sodium 241mg

If you serve this toast with fresh
berries, be sure to count the carbohydrate
from the fruit into your meal plan.

½ cup skim milk
¼ cup granulated sugar substitute with
    aspartame (such as Equal Spoonful),
    divided
2 teaspoons reduced-calorie margarine,
    melted
1 egg
2 egg whites
¼ teaspoon ground cinnamon
4 (1-ounce) slices French bread (1 inch
    thick)
    Butter-flavored vegetable cooking spray
    Sugar-free syrup (optional)
    Assorted fresh berries (optional)

1 Combine milk, 2 tablespoons sugar substitute, margarine, and next 3 ingredients in an
8-inch square baking dish; stir well. Arrange
bread slices over egg mixture, and let soak 5
minutes on each side.

2 Coat a nonstick griddle with cooking spray,
and preheat to 350°. Cook bread slices 6
minutes on each side or until golden. Sprinkle
evenly with remaining 2 tablespoons sugar
alternative. If desired, serve with sugar-free
syrup and fresh berries (syrup and berries not
included in analysis). Yield: 4 servings.

super·quick

SHREDDED WHEAT PANCAKES

YIELD: 8 pancakes

¾ cup all-purpose flour
½ cup crushed shredded whole wheat
    cereal biscuits
1 tablespoon baking powder
2 teaspoons granulated sugar substitute
    (such as Sugar Twin)
¼ teaspoon salt
1 egg, beaten
1 cup skim milk
1 tablespoon vegetable oil
    Vegetable cooking spray

EXCHANGES PER
PANCAKE:
1 Starch
½ Fat

PER SERVING:
Calories 90
Carbohydrate 13.2g
Protein 3.4g
Fat 2.6g
Cholesterol 28mg
Fiber 0.6g
Sodium 98mg

1 Combine first 5 ingredients in a medium bowl; make a well in center of mixture.

2 Combine egg, milk, and oil; add to dry ingredients, stirring just until moistened.

3 For each pancake, pour ¼ cup batter onto a hot griddle or skillet coated with cooking spray. Turn pancakes when tops are covered with bubbles and edges look cooked. Serve with Fresh Strawberry Sauce, if desired. Yield: 8 (4-inch) pancakes.

super·quick

FRESH STRAWBERRY SAUCE

YIELD: 1 cup

½ cup water
1 teaspoon cornstarch
1 cup fresh strawberries, sliced
2 teaspoons granulated sugar substitute
    (such as Sugar Twin)
⅛ teaspoon almond extract

EXCHANGES PER
TABLESPOON:
Free

PER SERVING:
Calories 3
Carbohydrate 0.7g
Protein 0.0g
Fat 0.0g
Cholesterol 0mg
Fiber 0.2g
Sodium 0mg

1 Combine water and cornstarch in a small saucepan. Add strawberries and sugar substitute; cook over medium heat, stirring constantly, until thickened and bubbly. Stir in almond extract. Yield: 1 cup.

EXCHANGES PER
SERVING:
1 Starch

PER SERVING:
Calories 79
Carbohydrate 12.2g
Protein 3.5g
Fat 1.9g
Cholesterol 0mg
Fiber 1.0g
Sodium 134mg

super·quick

BANANA-OAT BRAN PANCAKES

⅔ cup unprocessed oat bran
⅔ cup all-purpose flour
1 teaspoon baking powder
1 teaspoon baking soda
2 teaspoons granulated sugar substitute
    (such as Sugar Twin)
1 (8-ounce) carton plain nonfat yogurt
⅓ cup mashed ripe banana
1 tablespoon vegetable oil
2 teaspoons vanilla extract
3 egg whites
    Vegetable cooking spray

1 Combine first 5 ingredients in a medium bowl; make a well in center of mixture. Combine yogurt and next 3 ingredients; add to dry ingredients, stirring until moistened.

2 Beat egg whites in a medium bowl at high speed of an electric mixer until stiff peaks form; gently fold into batter.

3 For each pancake, pour ¼ cup batter onto a hot griddle or skillet coated with cooking spray. Turn pancakes when tops are covered with bubbles and edges look cooked.
Yield: 12 (4-inch) pancakes.

super·quick

WHOLE WHEAT-APPLE PANCAKES

YIELD: 10 pancakes

EXCHANGES PER PANCAKE:
1 Starch

PER PANCAKE:
Calories 97
Carbohydrate 17.6g
Protein 3.1g
Fat 1.8g
Cholesterol 23mg
Fiber 1.3g
Sodium 200mg

½ cup all-purpose flour
½ cup whole wheat flour
1 tablespoon granulated sugar substitute
  (such as Sugar Twin)
1 teaspoon baking soda
⅛ teaspoon salt
1 cup nonfat buttermilk
2 teaspoons vegetable oil
1 egg, lightly beaten
½ cup peeled, finely chopped apple
  Vegetable cooking spray
½ cup unsweetened applesauce
½ cup reduced-calorie apple jelly
½ teaspoon apple pie spice

1 Combine first 5 ingredients in a medium bowl; make a well in center of mixture. Combine buttermilk, oil, and egg; add to dry ingredients, stirring just until dry ingredients are moistened. Stir in apple.

2 For each pancake, pour ¼ cup batter onto a hot griddle or skillet coated with cooking spray, spreading batter to a 4-inch circle. Turn pancakes when tops are covered with bubbles and edges look cooked.

3 Combine applesauce, jelly, and apple pie spice in a small saucepan. Cook over low heat until jelly melts, stirring occasionally. Top pancakes evenly with applesauce mixture. Yield: 10 (4-inch) pancakes.

YIELD: 8 waffles

EXCHANGES PER
WAFFLE:
1 Starch
1 Fat

PER WAFFLE:
Calories 121
Carbohydrate 16.4g
Protein 3.9g
Fat 4.2g
Cholesterol 56mg
Fiber 0.5g
Sodium 106mg

BUTTERMILK-LEMON WAFFLES

1¼ cups all-purpose flour
1½ teaspoons sugar
1 teaspoon baking powder
¼ teaspoon baking soda
⅛ teaspoon salt
½ cup lemon-flavored sparkling water
¼ cup nonfat buttermilk
1½ tablespoons vegetable oil
¾ teaspoon grated lemon rind
2 eggs, separated
Vegetable cooking spray
Sugar-free maple syrup (optional)

1 Combine first 5 ingredients in a medium bowl; stir well, and set aside.

2 Combine sparkling water, buttermilk, oil, lemon rind, and egg yolks in a bowl; stir with a wire whisk until well blended. Add to flour mixture, stirring just until dry ingredients are moistened.

3 Beat egg whites at high speed of an electric mixer until stiff; gently fold into batter.

4 For each waffle, pour ⅓ cup batter onto a hot waffle iron coated with cooking spray, spreading batter to edges. Cook 4 to 5 minutes or until steaming stops. Repeat procedure with remaining batter. Serve with sugar-free syrup, if desired (syrup not included in analysis). Yield: 8 (4-inch) waffles.

BELGIAN WAFFLES

YIELD: 12 waffles

2 cups all-purpose flour
1 tablespoon plus 1 teaspoon baking
   powder
2 teaspoons granulated sugar substitute
   (such as Sugar Twin)
¼ teaspoon salt
1½ cups skim milk
½ cup frozen egg substitute, thawed
¼ cup reduced-calorie margarine, melted
½ teaspoon vanilla extract
   Vegetable cooking spray
   Fresh blueberries (optional)
   Fresh mint sprigs (optional)

**EXCHANGES PER
WAFFLE:**
1 Starch
1 Fat

PER SERVING:
Calories 119
Carbohydrate 17.4g
Protein 4.1g
Fat 3.7g
Cholesterol 34mg
Fiber 0.5g
Sodium 261mg

1 Combine first 4 ingredients in a medium bowl. Combine milk, egg substitute, margarine, and vanilla; add to dry ingredients, beating well at medium speed of an electric mixer.

2 Coat a Belgian waffle iron with cooking spray; allow waffle iron to preheat. For each waffle, spoon ¼ cup batter onto hot waffle iron, spreading batter to edges. Bake 4 to 5 minutes or until steaming stops. Repeat procedure with remaining batter. If desired, serve with fresh blueberries, and garnish with mint sprigs. Yield: 12 (4-inch) waffles.

LIGHT BISCUITS

YIELD: 6 biscuits

EXCHANGES PER BISCUIT:
1 Starch
½ Fat

PER BISCUIT:
Calories 104
Carbohydrate 16.6g
Protein 3.0g
Fat 2.9g
Cholesterol 1mg
Fiber 0.5g
Sodium 165mg

1 cup all-purpose flour
1½ teaspoons baking powder
⅛ teaspoon baking soda
¼ teaspoon salt
2 tablespoons reduced-calorie stick
    margarine
½ cup plain low-fat yogurt
½ teaspoon honey
    No-sugar-added fruit spread (optional)

1 Combine first 4 ingredients in a medium bowl; cut in margarine with pastry blender until mixture is crumbly. Add yogurt and honey, stirring just until dry ingredients are moistened.

2 Turn biscuit dough out onto lightly floured surface, and knead lightly 4 or 5 times.

3 Roll dough to ½-inch thickness; cut into rounds with a 2½-inch biscuit cutter. Transfer dough rounds to an ungreased baking sheet. Bake at 425° for 10 to 12 minutes or until golden. Serve with fruit spread, if desired, (fruit spread not included in analysis). Yield: 6 biscuits.

Peppery Cheese Biscuits

1¾ cups all-purpose flour
2 tablespoons grated Romano cheese
2 teaspoons baking powder
¼ teaspoon ground red pepper
¼ teaspoon salt
⅔ cup nonfat buttermilk
2 tablespoons vegetable oil
   Butter-flavored vegetable cooking spray

1 Combine first 5 ingredients in a large bowl; stir well.

2 Combine buttermilk and oil; add milk mixture to dry ingredients. Stir with a fork just until dry ingredients are moistened.

3 Turn dough out onto a lightly floured surface, and knead lightly 3 or 4 times. Roll dough to ½-inch thickness; cut into rounds with a 1½-inch biscuit cutter.

4 Place biscuits on an ungreased baking sheet; lightly coat tops of biscuits with cooking spray. Bake at 400° for 15 minutes. Yield: 2 dozen.

YIELD: 2 dozen
biscuits

EXCHANGES PER
BISCUIT:
½ Starch

PER SERVING:
Calories 49
Carbohydrate 7.5g
Protein 1.4g
Fat 1.5g
Cholesterol 1mg
Fiber 0.3g
Sodium 40mg

CORNMEAL DAISY BISCUITS

YIELD: 1½ dozen
biscuits

EXCHANGES PER
BISCUIT:
1 Starch

PER BISCUIT:
Calories 78
Carbohydrate 12.7g
Protein 1.9g
Fat 2.1g
Cholesterol 0mg
Fiber 0.5g
Sodium 86mg

1½ cups all-purpose flour
½ cup cornmeal
2 teaspoons baking powder
¼ teaspoon baking soda
¼ teaspoon salt
1 tablespoon granulated sugar substitute
   (such as Sugar Twin)
3 tablespoons margarine
¾ cup nonfat buttermilk
1 tablespoon all-purpose flour
1½ tablespoons no-sugar-added strawberry
   spread

1 Combine first 6 ingredients in a medium bowl; cut in margarine with pastry blender until mixture resembles coarse meal. Add buttermilk, stirring just until dry ingredients are moistened.

2 Sprinkle 1 tablespoon flour over work surface. Turn dough out onto surface, and knead 3 or 4 times. Roll dough to ½-inch thickness; cut into rounds, using a 2-inch biscuit cutter.

3 Place rounds on ungreased baking sheets. With a knife, cut 6 (½-inch) slashes evenly around edge of each biscuit to form petals. Press thumb in center of each biscuit, leaving an indentation. Place ¼ teaspoon strawberry spread in each indentation. Bake at 425° for 10 minutes or until lightly browned. Yield: 1½ dozen.

ANGEL BISCUITS

YIELD: 1 dozen
biscuits

1 package active dry yeast
2 tablespoons warm water (105° to 115°)
1 cup nonfat buttermilk
2½ cups all-purpose flour
1½ teaspoons sugar
1 teaspoon baking powder
½ teaspoon salt
¼ teaspoon baking soda
3 tablespoons margarine
   Vegetable cooking spray

EXCHANGES PER BISCUIT:
1½ Starch
½ Fat

PER BISCUIT:
Calories 132
Carbohydrate 21.8g
Protein 3.7g
Fat 3.2g
Cholesterol 1mg
Fiber 0.9g
Sodium 179mg

1 Combine yeast and warm water in a small bowl; let stand 5 minutes. Add buttermilk, stirring well.

2 Combine flour and next 4 ingredients in a large bowl; cut in margarine with pastry blender until mixture is crumbly. Add buttermilk mixture, stirring with a fork until dry ingredients are moistened. Turn dough out onto a lightly floured surface, and knead lightly 3 or 4 times.

3 Roll dough to ½-inch thickness; cut into rounds with a 2½-inch biscuit cutter. Place on a baking sheet coated with cooking spray. Cover and let rise in a warm place (85°), free from drafts, 10 to 15 minutes. Bake at 400° for 10 to 12 minutes or until biscuits are golden. Yield: 1 dozen.

CURRANT SCONES

YIELD: 8 scones

EXCHANGES PER
SCONE:
1 Starch
1 Fruit
½ Fat

PER SERVING:
Calories 155
Carbohydrate 26.9g
Protein 4.2g
Fat 3.3g
Cholesterol 0.6mg
Fiber 0.5g
Sodium 186mg

¼ cup currants
¼ cup boiling water
1 cup all-purpose flour
1 cup sifted cake flour
2 tablespoons granulated brown sugar
  substitute
2 teaspoons baking powder
½ teaspoon baking soda
¼ teaspoon salt
2 tablespoons margarine
1 (8-ounce) carton vanilla nonfat yogurt
  sweetened with aspartame
1 tablespoon all-purpose flour
  Vegetable cooking spray
1 egg white, lightly beaten
  No-sugar-added fruit spread (optional)

1 Combine currants and water; let stand 10 minutes. Drain well, and set aside.

2 Combine all-purpose flour and next 5 ingredients; cut in margarine with pastry blender until mixture is crumbly. Add currants; toss well. Add yogurt to dry ingredients, stirring just until moistened.

3 Sprinkle 1 tablespoon flour evenly over work surface. Turn dough out onto floured surface, and knead 3 or 4 times. Pat dough into an 8-inch round on a baking sheet coated with cooking spray. Cut round into 8 wedges, cutting to, but not through, bottom of dough. Brush wedges with egg white. Bake at 425° for 15 minutes or until lightly browned. Serve with no-sugar-added fruit spread, if desired (spread not included in analysis). Yield: 8 scones.

BLUEBERRY MUFFINS

YIELD: 1 dozen
muffins

1⅓ cups all-purpose flour
1 cup quick-cooking oats, uncooked
¼ cup granulated brown sugar substitute
2 teaspoons baking powder
½ teaspoon ground cinnamon
¼ teaspoon salt
1 cup skim milk
¼ cup frozen egg substitute, thawed
3 tablespoons vegetable oil
1 cup fresh or frozen blueberries, thawed
Vegetable cooking spray

EXCHANGES PER MUFFIN:
1 Starch
1 Fat

PER MUFFIN:
Calories 130
Carbohydrate 19.0g
Protein 3.8g
Fat 4.3g
Cholesterol 0mg
Fiber 1.5g
Sodium 73mg

1 Combine first 6 ingredients in a medium bowl; make a well in center of mixture. Combine milk, egg substitute, and oil; add to dry ingredients, stirring just until moistened. Fold in blueberries.

2 Spoon batter into muffin pans coated with cooking spray, filling three-fourths full. Bake at 425° for 25 minutes or until golden. Yield: 1 dozen.

SAVORY ROSEMARY MUFFINS

EXCHANGES PER
MUFFIN:
1½ Starch
1 Fat

PER MUFFIN:
Calories 133
Carbohydrate 20.9g
Protein 4.4g
Fat 3.8g
Cholesterol 37mg
Fiber 1.3g
Sodium 74mg

¾ cup all-purpose flour
¼ cup whole wheat flour
1 teaspoon baking powder
⅛ teaspoon salt
1 tablespoon granulated sugar substitute
    (such as Sugar Twin)
1½ teaspoons minced fresh rosemary
½ cup skim milk
1 tablespoon olive oil
1 large egg, lightly beaten
    Vegetable cooking spray
1 tablespoon toasted wheat germ
    Fresh rosemary sprig

1 Combine first 6 ingredients in a medium bowl; stir well. Make a well in center of flour mixture. Combine milk, oil, and egg in a small bowl, stirring well. Add to flour mixture, stirring just until dry ingredients are moistened.

2 Spoon batter into muffin pans coated with cooking spray, filling two-thirds full. Sprinkle wheat germ evenly over muffins.

3 Bake at 400° for 18 to 20 minutes or until lightly browned. Garnish with fresh rosemary sprig, if desired. Yield: 6 muffins.

Harvest Corn Muffins

YIELD: 18 muffins

1 cup all-purpose flour
1 cup cornmeal
1 tablespoon plus 1 teaspoon baking
   powder
¼ teaspoon salt
2 tablespoons granulated brown sugar
   substitute
½ teaspoon dried oregano
¼ teaspoon ground white pepper
1 cup cooked mashed pumpkin
1 cup skim milk
3 tablespoons diced pimiento, drained
2 tablespoons vegetable oil
1 egg, lightly beaten
2 egg whites, lightly beaten
1 jalapeño pepper, seeded and minced
   Vegetable cooking spray
½ cup (2 ounces) finely shredded reduced-
   fat Cheddar cheese

EXCHANGES PER
MUFFIN:
1 Starch

PER MUFFIN:
Calories 96
Carbohydrate 13.8g
Protein 3.7g
Fat 2.9g
Cholesterol 15mg
Fiber 1.2g
Sodium 74mg

1 Combine first 4 ingredients in a large bowl; add brown sugar substitute, oregano, and white pepper. Make a well in center of mixture.

2 Combine pumpkin and next 6 ingredients; add to dry ingredients, stirring just until dry ingredients are moistened.

3 Spoon batter into muffin pans coated with cooking spray, filling two-thirds full. Sprinkle cheese over batter. Bake at 400° for 20 minutes or until lightly browned. Remove from pans immediately. Yield: 18 muffins.

SAUSAGE-CHEESE MUFFINS

YIELD: 1 dozen
muffins

EXCHANGES PER SERVING:
1 Starch
1 Fat

PER SERVING:
Calories 112
Carbohydrate 11.4g
Protein 5.1g
Fat 5.0g
Cholesterol 28mg
Fiber 0.7g
Sodium 304mg

Vegetable cooking spray
⅓ pound freshly ground raw turkey breakfast sausage
¼ cup chopped green pepper
¼ cup chopped green onions
1 cup all-purpose flour
¼ cup cornmeal
1 teaspoon baking soda
¼ teaspoon salt
⅛ teaspoon ground red pepper
1 cup nonfat buttermilk
2 teaspoons margarine, melted
1 egg, lightly beaten
⅓ cup (1.3 ounces) shredded reduced-fat sharp Cheddar cheese

1 Coat a nonstick skillet with cooking spray. Place over medium heat until hot. Add sausage, green pepper, and onions. Cook until sausage browns, stirring until it crumbles; drain.

2 Combine flour and next 4 ingredients in a bowl; make a well in center of mixture. Combine buttermilk, margarine, and egg; add to dry ingredients, stirring just until dry ingredients are moistened. Gently fold in sausage mixture and cheese.

3 Spoon batter into muffin pans coated with cooking spray, filling two-thirds full. Bake at 400° for 20 minutes or until golden. Remove muffins from pans immediately. Yield: 1 dozen.

ONION PINWHEELS

YIELD: 10 pinwheels

Vegetable cooking spray
½ cup chopped green onions
2 tablespoons chopped fresh parsley
¼ teaspoon garlic powder
¼ teaspoon onion powder
⅛ teaspoon ground red pepper
1¼ cups all-purpose flour
1 teaspoon baking powder
¼ teaspoon salt
3 tablespoons margarine
3 tablespoons skim milk
1 egg, lightly beaten

EXCHANGES PER PINWHEEL:
1 Starch
1 Fat

PER PINWHEEL:
Calories 101
Carbohydrate 12.7g
Protein 2.5g
Fat 4.3g
Cholesterol 22mg
Fiber 0.5g
Sodium 109mg

1 Coat a nonstick skillet with cooking spray; place over medium-high heat until hot. Add green onions and parsley; sauté 3 minutes. Stir in garlic powder, onion powder, and red pepper. Set aside.

2 Combine flour, baking powder, and salt in a large bowl; cut in margarine with a pastry blender until mixture resembles coarse meal. Make a well in center of mixture. Combine milk and egg; add to dry ingredients, stirring just until moistened.

3 Turn dough out onto a lightly floured surface, and knead lightly 5 or 6 times. Shape dough into a ball; wrap in heavy-duty plastic wrap, and freeze 10 minutes.

4 Remove plastic wrap. Roll dough into a 10- x 8-inch rectangle on a lightly floured surface. Spread onion mixture over dough. Carefully roll up dough, jellyroll fashion, starting at long end. Pinch seam and ends to seal. Wrap in plastic wrap, and freeze 10 minutes.

5 Remove plastic wrap. Cut roll into 1-inch slices. Place slices, cut side down, in muffin pan cups coated with cooking spray. Bake at 400° for 15 to 20 minutes or until golden. Remove from pans, and serve warm. Yield: 10 pinwheels.

HERB POPOVERS

YIELD: 6 popovers

EXCHANGES PER
POPOVER
1½ Starch
½ Fat

PER POPOVER:
Calories 131
Carbohydrate 18.8g
Protein 6.4g
Fat 3.1g
Cholesterol 38mg
Fiber 0.7g
Sodium 148mg

Break open this crusty muffin-size bread,
and you'll find a hollow center. Very thin batter
and a high baking temperature produce steam
that causes the bread to rise rapidly and
"pop over" into one-of-a-kind puffed shapes.

1 cup bread flour
1 cup skim milk
1 egg
2 egg whites
2 teaspoons vegetable oil
1 teaspoon dried dillweed
¼ teaspoon salt
  Vegetable cooking spray

✒ This variation
has about the same
amount of carbohy-
drate as the Herb
Popovers and is
counted as 1½ Starch
and ½ Fat Exchange.

1 Combine first 7 ingredients in a medium bowl; beat at low speed of an electric mixer just until blended and smooth.

2 Fill six 6-ounce custard cups coated with cooking spray three-fourths full. Bake at 425° for 25 to 30 minutes or until crusty and dark brown. Serve immediately.
Yield: 6 popovers.

Parmesan Popovers: Substitute 1 teaspoon dried basil for dillweed. Stir 2 tablespoons grated Parmesan cheese into batter just before filling custard cups. Proceed with recipe as directed. Yield: 6 popovers.

SOUTHERN CORN STICKS

½ cup yellow cornmeal
½ cup all-purpose flour
2 teaspoons granulated sugar substitute
 (such as Sugar Twin)
2 teaspoons baking powder
¼ teaspoon salt
1 egg, beaten
½ cup evaporated skimmed milk
2 tablespoons vegetable oil
 Vegetable cooking spray

1 Combine first 5 ingredients in a medium bowl; stir well.

2 Combine egg, milk, and oil; add to dry ingredients, stirring just until smooth.

3 Coat a cast-iron corn stick pan with cooking spray. Heat pan in a 425° oven 3 to 5 minutes or until hot. Remove pan from oven; spoon batter into pan, filling two-thirds full. Bake at 425° for 10 to 12 minutes or until lightly browned. Yield: 1 dozen.

YIELD: 1 dozen corn sticks

EXCHANGES PER SERVING:
1 Starch
½ Fat

PER SERVING:
Calories 76
Carbohydrate 10.0g
Protein 2.4g
Fat 2.9g
Cholesterol 19mg
Fiber 0.4g
Sodium 67mg

MEXICAN CORN STICKS

YIELD: 16 corn sticks

EXCHANGES PER
CORN STICK:
1 Starch

PER CORN STICK:
Calories 91
Carbohydrate 16.7g
Protein 3.8g
Fat 1.2g
Cholesterol 3mg
Fiber 0.9g
Sodium 194mg

1¼ cups all-purpose flour
¾ cup cornmeal
2 teaspoons baking powder
1 teaspoon baking soda
¼ teaspoon salt
   Dash of ground red pepper
¾ cup nonfat buttermilk
1 (8¾-ounce) can no-salt-added
   cream-style corn
1 (4½-ounce) can chopped green chiles,
   undrained
2 egg whites, lightly beaten
½ cup (2 ounces) shredded reduced-fat
   sharp Cheddar cheese
   Vegetable cooking spray

1 Combine first 6 ingredients in a medium bowl; make a well in center of mixture.

2 Combine buttermilk and next 3 ingredients; add to dry ingredients, stirring just until moistened. Fold in cheese.

3 Spoon batter into cast-iron cornstick pans coated with cooking spray, filling two-thirds full. Bake at 425° for 18 to 20 minutes or until golden. Remove from pans immediately. Yield: 16 corn sticks.

Oven-Baked Hush Puppies

YIELD: 2 dozen
hush puppies

2/3 cup yellow cornmeal
2/3 cup all-purpose flour
 2 teaspoons baking powder
1/2 teaspoon salt
1/2 teaspoon granulated sugar substitute
    (such as Sugar Twin)
1/4 teaspoon onion powder
1/4 teaspoon garlic powder
1/8 teaspoon ground red pepper
1/2 cup evaporated skimmed milk
 2 tablespoons vegetable oil
 3 egg whites, lightly beaten
   Vegetable cooking spray

**EXCHANGES PER
2 HUSH PUPPIES:**
1 Starch

PER SERVING:
Calories 91
Carbohydrate 12.9g
Protein 3.0g
Fat 2.9g
Cholesterol 0mg
Fiber 0.6g
Sodium 124mg

1 Combine first 8 ingredients in a medium bowl; make a well in center of mixture. Combine milk, oil, and egg whites in a small bowl; stir well. Add milk mixture to cornmeal mixture, stirring just until dry ingredients are moistened.

2 Spoon batter evenly into miniature (1¾-inch) muffin pans coated with cooking spray, filling three-fourths full. Bake at 425° for 13 to 15 minutes or until lightly browned. Remove from pans immediately. Yield: 2 dozen (serving size: 2 hush puppies).

CALICO CORNBREAD

YIELD: 10 wedges

EXCHANGES PER
WEDGE:
1½ Starch
½ Fat

PER SERVING:
Calories 136
Carbohydrate 22.3g
Protein 3.9g
Fat 3.4g
Cholesterol 22mg
Fiber 1.2g
Sodium 114mg

Vegetable cooking spray
1 cup all-purpose flour
⅔ cup yellow cornmeal
2 teaspoons granulated sugar substitute
   (such as Sugar Twin)
2 teaspoons baking powder
¼ teaspoon salt
¼ teaspoon pepper
⅔ cup skim milk
1 (8¾-ounce) can no-salt-added whole
   kernel corn, drained
1 (4½-ounce) can chopped green chiles,
   drained
1 (4-ounce) jar diced pimiento, drained
½ cup chopped onion
2 tablespoons margarine, melted
1 egg, lightly beaten

1 Coat a 10-inch cast-iron skillet with cooking spray. Place in a 450° oven 5 minutes or until skillet is hot.

2 Combine flour and next 5 ingredients in a bowl; make a well in center of mixture. Combine milk and remaining ingredients; add to dry ingredients, stirring just until dry ingredients are moistened.

3 Pour batter into hot skillet. Bake at 450° for 25 to 27 minutes or until golden. Cut into wedges. Yield: 10 wedges.

PEPPERED SPOONBREAD

YIELD: 6 servings

EXCHANGES PER
SERVING:
1 Starch

PER SERVING:
Calories 107
Carbohydrate 16.8g
Protein 5.9g
Fat 1.8g
Cholesterol 2mg
Fiber 0.9g
Sodium 216mg

1½ cups nonfat buttermilk
¾ cup water
¾ cup yellow cornmeal
 1 tablespoon reduced-calorie margarine
¾ teaspoon cracked pepper
¼ teaspoon salt
 2 egg whites
¼ cup frozen egg substitute, thawed
 Vegetable cooking spray

1 Combine first 6 ingredients in a medium saucepan; cook over medium heat 5 minutes or until thickened, stirring constantly. Remove from heat.

2 Beat egg whites at medium speed of an electric mixer until stiff peaks form. With mixer running, slowly add egg substitute. Gradually stir about one-third of hot cornmeal mixture into egg mixture; add to remaining hot cornmeal mixture, stirring constantly. Pour into a 1½-quart soufflé dish coated with cooking spray.

3 Bake at 350° for 25 to 30 minutes or until lightly browned. Serve immediately.
Yield: 6 servings.

MINI-BLUEBERRY LOAF

YIELD: 4 slices or
4 muffins

EXCHANGES PER
SLICE or MUFFIN:
1 Starch
½ Fruit

PER SERVING:
Calories 127
Carbohydrate 20.7g
Protein 4.1g
Fat 2.8g
Cholesterol 0mg
Fiber 1.1g
Sodium 167mg

⅓ cup fresh or frozen blueberries, thawed
⅔ cup all-purpose flour, divided
½ teaspoon baking powder
¼ teaspoon baking soda
⅛ teaspoon salt
3 tablespoons granulated sugar substitute
    (such as Sugar Twin)
¼ cup plus 2 tablespoons plain nonfat
    yogurt
2 teaspoons vegetable oil
½ teaspoon vanilla extract
1 egg white, lightly beaten
    Vegetable cooking spray

1 Toss blueberries with 2 teaspoons flour, and set aside. Combine remaining flour, baking powder, and next 3 ingredients in a medium bowl; make a well in center of mixture. Combine yogurt and next 3 ingredients; add to dry ingredients, stirring just until dry ingredients are moistened. Fold blueberries into batter.

2 Spoon batter into a 6- x 3- x 2-inch loafpan coated with cooking spray. Bake at 350° for 35 to 40 minutes or until a wooden pick inserted in center comes out clean. Remove from pan immediately, and let cool on a wire rack. Yield: 4 slices.

Blueberry Muffins: Prepare batter as directed above. Spoon batter evenly into 4 muffin cups coated with cooking spray. Bake at 375° for 18 minutes. Remove from pan immediately, and let cool on a wire rack. Yield: 4 muffins.

Lemon-Apricot Soda Bread.

2¾ cups all-purpose flour
  1 teaspoon baking powder
  1 teaspoon baking soda
  ¼ teaspoon salt
  ¼ cup granulated sugar substitute
      (such as Sugar Twin)
  ¼ teaspoon ground nutmeg
1⅓ cups nonfat buttermilk
  ½ cup chopped dried apricot halves
  ¼ cup margarine, melted
  1 teaspoon grated lemon rind
  1 egg, lightly beaten
    Vegetable cooking spray

1 Combine first 6 ingredients in a medium bowl; make a well in center of mixture. Combine buttermilk, chopped apricot, margarine, lemon rind, and egg. Add to dry ingredients, stirring just until dry ingredients are moistened.

2 Spoon batter into an 8½- x 4½- x 3-inch loafpan coated with cooking spray. Bake at 350° for 45 minutes or until a wooden pick inserted in center comes out clean. Let cool in pan 10 minutes; remove from pan. Yield: 16 (½-inch) slices.

YIELD: 16 slices

EXCHANGES PER SLICE:
1 Starch
1 Fat

PER SERVING:
Calories 125
Carbohydrate 20.0g
Protein 3.4g
Fat 3.5g
Cholesterol 14mg
Fiber 0.7g
Sodium 155mg

FIVE-GRAIN LOAF

YIELD: 16 slices

EXCHANGES PER
SLICE:
1 Starch
½ Fat

PER SERVING:
Calories 109
Carbohydrate 17.4g
Protein 3.5g
Fat 2.8g
Cholesterol 1.9mg
Fiber 0.8g
Sodium 138mg

1 cup no-salt-added, low-fat Swiss-style
   cereal
1½ cups nonfat buttermilk
¼ cup frozen egg substitute, thawed
2 tablespoons granulated brown sugar
   substitute
2 tablespoons plus 1 teaspoon
   vegetable oil
2 cups all-purpose flour
1 teaspoon baking powder
1 teaspoon baking soda
1 teaspoon ground cinnamon
¼ teaspoon salt
   Vegetable cooking spray

1 Combine cereal and buttermilk in a small bowl; let stand 5 minutes. Add egg substitute, sugar substitute, and oil; stir well.

2 Combine flour and next 4 ingredients in a bowl, stirring well. Make a well in center of mixture. Add cereal mixture to dry ingredients; stir just until dry ingredients are moistened.

3 Spoon batter into an 8½- x 4½- x 3-inch loafpan coated with cooking spray. Bake at 350° for 45 to 50 minutes or until a wooden pick inserted in center comes out clean. Cool in pan 10 minutes; remove from pan, and let cool on a wire rack. Yield: 16 (½-inch) slices.

DILLED BROWN BREAD

YIELD: 16 servings

½ cup bulgur, uncooked
½ cup boiling water
1¾ cups all-purpose flour
1 cup whole wheat flour
¼ cup toasted wheat germ
½ teaspoon baking powder
1 teaspoon baking soda
¼ teaspoon salt
2 tablespoons minced fresh dillweed
1⅔ cups nonfat buttermilk
2 tablespoons vegetable oil
2 tablespoons honey
1 egg, lightly beaten
Vegetable cooking spray

EXCHANGES PER SERVING:
1½ Starch

PER SERVING:
Calories 139
Carbohydrate 24.2g
Protein 4.9g
Fat 2.7g
Cholesterol 15mg
Fiber 1.8g
Sodium 149mg

1 Combine bulgur and boiling water, stirring well. Let stand 5 to 10 minutes or until water is absorbed and bulgur is tender.

2 Combine all-purpose flour and next 6 ingredients in a medium bowl; make a well in center of mixture. Combine buttermilk and next 3 ingredients, stirring well. Add buttermilk mixture and bulgur to dry ingredients, stirring just until dry ingredients are moistened.

3 Spoon batter into a 9-inch pieplate coated with cooking spray. Bake at 375° for 45 to 50 minutes or until bread is golden. Let bread cool in pieplate 10 minutes. Remove bread from pieplate, and let cool on a wire rack. Cut into wedges. Yield: 16 servings.

EXCHANGES PER
SLICE:
1 Starch

PER SERVING:
Calories 108
Carbohydrate 21.8g
Protein 3.6g
Fat 0.4g
Cholesterol 0mg
Fiber 1.9g
Sodium 84mg

GOLDEN RAISIN WHOLE WHEAT BREAD

2 cups all-purpose flour
1½ cups whole wheat flour
1 tablespoon baking powder
3 tablespoons granulated brown sugar
   substitute
2 teaspoons caraway seeds
½ teaspoon salt
3 tablespoons golden raisins, chopped
1 (12-ounce) can light beer, at room
   temperature
¼ cup egg substitute
   Vegetable cooking spray

1 Combine first 7 ingredients; make a well in center of mixture. Add beer and egg substitute, stirring just until dry ingredients are moistened.

2 Spoon batter into an 8½- x 4½- x 3-inch loafpan coated with cooking spray. Bake at 375° for 45 to 50 minutes or until a wooden pick inserted in center comes out clean. Let cool in pan 10 minutes. Remove from pan; let cool completely on a wire rack. Yield: 16 slices.

SAFFRON-PISTACHIO BREAD

YIELD: 12 servings

Brush this loaf with an egg white before
baking for a shiny, golden crust.

1½ cups all-purpose flour
 ½ cup whole wheat flour
 1 teaspoon baking powder
 ½ teaspoon baking soda
 ½ teaspoon salt
 ¼ cup chopped pistachios
 1 tablespoon granulated brown
     sugar substitute
 ¼ teaspoon dried rosemary
 ⅛ teaspoon ground saffron
 ¾ cup low-fat buttermilk
 2 tablespoons olive oil
 1 egg
     Vegetable cooking spray
 1 egg white, beaten

**EXCHANGES PER
SERVING:**
1 Starch
1 Fat

PER SERVING:
Calories 126
Carbohydrate 16.6g
Protein 4.3g
Fat 4.9g
Cholesterol 18mg
Fiber 1.4g
Sodium 152mg

1 Combine first 9 ingredients in a large bowl;
make a well in center of flour mixture.
Combine buttermilk, oil, and egg; stir well. Add
to dry ingredients, stirring just until dry ingredients are moistened.

2 Turn dough out onto a floured surface, and
knead lightly 4 or 5 times. Shape dough into
a ball, gently smoothing surface. Place dough on
a baking sheet coated with cooking spray. Gently cut 2 (½-inch-deep) slits crosswise in top of
loaf, using a sharp knife. Brush loaf with egg
white.

3 Bake at 375° for 25 to 30 minutes or until
golden and loaf sounds hollow when tapped.
Remove bread from baking sheet, and let cool
5 minutes on a wire rack. Yield: 12 servings.

✒ Saffron is made
from the dried
stigmas of a type
of crocus. It's
expensive, but you
can keep it in the
freezer for 1 year.
Look for both
ground saffron
and saffron threads
in the spice section
of your grocery
store.

FENNEL CASSEROLE LOAF

YIELD: 18 wedges

EXCHANGES PER
SERVING:
1 Starch

PER WEDGE:
Calories 93
Carbohydrate 16.0g
Protein 4.3g
Fat 1.3g
Cholesterol 13mg
Fiber 1.1g
Sodium 115mg

2 cups all-purpose flour, divided
⅔ cup whole wheat flour
2 tablespoons sugar
2 tablespoons finely chopped green onion
½ teaspoon fennel seeds, crushed
¼ teaspoon salt
1 package active dry yeast
1 cup 1% low-fat cottage cheese
¼ cup skim milk
1 tablespoon margarine
1 egg, lightly beaten
Vegetable cooking spray

1 Combine ½ cup all-purpose flour and next 6 ingredients in a large bowl; stir well.

2 Combine cottage cheese, milk, and margarine in a small saucepan; cook over medium heat until margarine melts, stirring occasionally. Cool to 120° to 130°.

3 Gradually add cottage cheese mixture to flour mixture, beating at low speed of an electric mixer until blended. Beat 2 additional minutes at medium speed. Add egg; beat 2 additional minutes. Gradually stir in enough remaining 1½ cups all-purpose flour to make a soft dough. (Dough will be sticky.)

4 Place dough in a large bowl coated with cooking spray, turning to coat top. Cover and let rise in a warm place (85°), free from drafts, 1 hour or until doubled in bulk.

5 Punch dough down; shape into a ball, gently smoothing surface of dough. Place in a 2-quart casserole coated with cooking spray. Cover and let rise in a warm place, free from drafts, 30 to 40 minutes or until doubled in bulk. Bake at 350° for 25 minutes or until loaf sounds hollow when tapped. Remove from casserole immediately, and let cool on a wire rack. Cut into wedges. Yield: 18 wedges.

WHEAT AND CHEESE PRETZELS

YIELD: 16 pretzels

EXCHANGES PER
PRETZEL:
1 Starch

PER PRETZEL:
Calories 67
Carbohydrate 11.3g
Protein 2.6g
Fat 1.3g
Cholesterol 2mg
Fiber 0.8g
Sodium 94mg

1½ teaspoons sugar
　1 teaspoon active dry yeast
½ teaspoon salt
⅔ cup warm water (105° to 115°)
1⅓ cups all-purpose flour
½ cup whole wheat flour
⅓ cup (1.3 ounces) shredded reduced-fat
　　Cheddar cheese
1½ teaspoons vegetable oil
　　Vegetable cooking spray
　1 egg white, lightly beaten
　2 tablespoons water
1½ teaspoons poppy seeds

1 Combine first 4 ingredients in a 1-cup liquid measuring cup; let stand 5 minutes.

2 Combine flours and cheese in a mixing bowl; stir well. Add yeast mixture and oil; beat at low speed of an electric mixer until well blended. Turn dough out onto a lightly floured surface; knead until smooth (about 5 minutes).

3 Using kitchen shears dipped in flour, cut dough into 16 pieces; roll each into a ball. With floured hands, roll each ball to form a 12-inch rope. Twist each rope into a pretzel shape. Place 1½ inches apart on baking sheets coated with cooking spray.

4 Combine egg white and 2 tablespoons water. Brush over pretzels; sprinkle with poppy seeds. Bake at 425° for 12 minutes or until lightly browned. Remove from baking sheets immediately; cool on wire racks. Store in an airtight container. Yield: 16 pretzels.

EXCHANGES PER
BREADSTICK:
1 Starch

PER SERVING:
Calories 63
Carbohydrate 10.6g
Protein 2.0g
Fat 1.3g
Cholesterol 0mg
Fiber 0.1g
Sodium 104mg

ONION AND POPPY SEED BREADSTICKS

1 (16-ounce) package hot roll mix
2 tablespoons instant minced onion, toasted
2 tablespoons grated Parmesan cheese
1 cup warm water (120° to 130°)
¼ cup frozen egg substitute, thawed
2 tablespoons all-purpose flour
    Vegetable cooking spray
1 egg white, lightly beaten
1 tablespoon water
2 teaspoons poppy seeds

1 Combine hot roll mix, yeast from foil packet, onion, and cheese. Add warm water and egg substitute; stir until dry ingredients are moistened. Shape dough into a ball.

2 Sprinkle 2 tablespoons flour over work surface. Turn dough out onto floured surface; knead until smooth and elastic (about 5 minutes). Cover and let rest 5 minutes.

3 Divide dough into 32 equal portions; roll each portion into a 10-inch strip, and twist into a rope. (Keep unrolled dough covered.) Place ropes 1 inch apart on baking sheets coated with cooking spray. Cover and let rise in a warm place (85°), free from drafts, 15 minutes.

4 Combine egg white and 1 tablespoon water in a small bowl, stirring well. Brush breadsticks with egg white mixture, and sprinkle with poppy seeds. Bake at 375° for 14 minutes or until golden. Remove from baking sheets; let cool on wire racks. Yield: 32 breadsticks.

HERBED DINNER ROLLS

YIELD: 2½ dozen rolls

2 packages active dry yeast
½ cup warm water (105° to 115°)
1 cup skim milk
2 tablespoons margarine
1 tablespoon sugar
1 teaspoon dried Italian seasoning
½ teaspoon salt
¼ teaspoon garlic powder
¼ cup frozen egg substitute, thawed
2 cups whole wheat flour
¼ cup grated Parmesan cheese
2½ cups plus 2 tablespoons all-purpose flour
Vegetable cooking spray

EXCHANGES PER ROLL:
1 Starch

PER ROLL:
Calories 81
Carbohydrate 14.6g
Protein 3.1g
Fat 1.3g
Cholesterol 1mg
Fiber 1.4g
Sodium 108mg

1 Sprinkle yeast over water; let stand 5 minutes. Combine milk and next 5 ingredients in a saucepan. Cook over medium heat until margarine melts, stirring often. Cool to 105° to 115°.

2 Combine yeast, milk, egg substitute, and whole wheat flour. Beat at low speed of an electric mixer just until blended; beat at high speed 3 minutes. Stir in cheese and enough of the 2½ cups flour to make a stiff dough. Sprinkle 1 tablespoon all-purpose flour over work surface. Turn dough out; knead until smooth and elastic (about 6 minutes). Place in a bowl coated with cooking spray, turning to coat top. Cover and let rise in a warm place (85°), free from drafts, 45 minutes or until doubled in bulk.

3 Sprinkle remaining 1 tablespoon flour over work surface. Punch dough down; turn out. Cover; let rest 10 minutes.

4 Shape dough into 30 balls. Place in two 9-inch round cakepans coated with cooking spray. Cover and let rise in a warm place 35 minutes or until doubled in bulk. Bake at 375° for 25 minutes. Yield: 2½ dozen.

Basic White Bread

YIELD: 17 slices

EXCHANGES PER
SLICE:
1 Starch

PER SLICE:
Calories 84
Carbohydrate 15.0g
Protein 2.9g
Fat 1.2g
Cholesterol 0mg
Fiber 2.1g
Sodium 145mg

1 package active dry yeast
1 cup warm water (105° to 115°)
3 tablespoons instant nonfat dry milk
   powder
1 tablespoon vegetable oil
1 teaspoon sugar
1 teaspoon salt
2¼ cups bread flour
2 tablespoons bread flour, divided
   Vegetable cooking spray

1 Combine yeast and warm water in a 2-cup liquid measuring cup; let stand 5 minutes.

2 Combine yeast mixture, milk powder, and next 3 ingredients in a large mixing bowl; beat at medium speed of an electric mixer until well blended. Gradually stir in enough of the 2¼ cups flour to make a soft dough.

3 Sprinkle 1 tablespoon flour over work surface. Turn dough out onto floured surface, and knead until smooth and elastic (about 8 minutes). Place in a bowl coated with cooking spray, turning to coat top. Cover and let rise in a warm place (85°), free from drafts, 1 hour or until doubled in bulk.

4 Punch dough down. Sprinkle remaining 1 tablespoon bread flour evenly over work surface. Turn dough out onto floured surface, and roll into a 10- x 6-inch rectangle.

5 Roll up dough, starting at short side, pressing firmly to eliminate air pockets; pinch ends to seal. Place dough, seam side down, in an 8½- x 4½- x 3-inch loafpan coated with cooking spray.

6 Cover and let rise in a warm place 1 hour or until doubled in bulk. Bake at 375° for 25 minutes or until loaf sounds hollow when tapped. Remove from pan immediately; let cool on a wire rack. Yield: 17 (½-inch) slices.

WHOLE WHEAT CASSEROLE BREAD

YIELD: 10 wedges

EXCHANGES PER WEDGE:
1 Starch

PER SERVING:
Calories 101
Carbohydrate 19.1g
Protein 3.4g
Fat 1.5g
Cholesterol 0mg
Fiber 2.0g
Sodium 139mg

1 package active dry yeast
¾ cup warm water (105° to 115°)
1 cup all-purpose flour, divided
1 cup whole wheat flour
1 tablespoon sugar
2 tablespoons egg substitute
1½ tablespoons reduced-calorie margarine, melted
½ teaspoon salt
  Vegetable cooking spray

1 Combine yeast and water in a 1-cup liquid measuring cup; let stand 5 minutes. Combine yeast mixture, ½ cup all-purpose flour, whole wheat flour, and next 4 ingredients in a medium bowl, stirring well. Gradually stir in enough remaining ½ cup all-purpose flour to make a soft dough. (Dough will be sticky.) Let dough stand 15 minutes; shape into a ball.

2 Place dough in a round 1-quart casserole dish heavily coated with cooking spray. Cover and let rise in a warm place (85°), free from drafts, 30 minutes or until dough is doubled in bulk.

3 Bake at 375° for 25 minutes or until loaf sounds hollow when tapped. (Cover with aluminum foil the last 10 minutes of baking to prevent excessive browning, if necessary.) Remove from dish immediately, and let cool on a wire rack. Yield: 10 wedges.

COUNTRY HERB BREAD

YIELD: 22 wedges

EXCHANGES PER
WEDGE:
1 Starch

PER SERVING:
Calories 92
Carbohydrate 18.3g
Protein 3.4g
Fat 0.8g
Cholesterol 0mg
Fiber 2.0g
Sodium 54mg

2 packages active dry yeast
2 cups warm water (105° to 115°)
1 tablespoon dried rosemary, crushed
1 tablespoon dried thyme, crushed
1 teaspoon olive oil
½ teaspoon salt
2 cloves garlic, crushed
2 cups whole wheat flour
2 cups bread flour
2 tablespoons bread flour
    Vegetable cooking spray
2 teaspoons bread flour

1 Sprinkle yeast over water in a large bowl; let stand 5 minutes. Add rosemary and next 4 ingredients; beat at medium speed of an electric mixer until well blended. Add whole wheat flour and enough of 2 cups bread flour to make a soft dough.

2 Sprinkle 2 tablespoons bread flour over work surface. Turn dough out onto surface; knead until smooth and elastic (about 8 to 10 minutes). Place in a bowl coated with cooking spray, turning to coat top. Cover and let rise in a warm place (85°), free from drafts, 1½ hours or until doubled in bulk.

3 Coat a 9-inch round, closely woven wicker basket (about 3 inches deep) with cooking spray. Dust with 2 teaspoons bread flour.

4 Punch dough down, and shape into a ball. Place in basket. Cover and let rise in a warm place, free from drafts, 30 minutes or until doubled in bulk. Place unglazed tiles on middle rack of oven to cover about 16 inches square.

5 Heat tiles at 400° until hot. Place a pan of boiling water on lower rack. Invert dough onto hot tiles, and remove basket. Bake at 400° for 35 minutes or until loaf sounds hollow when tapped. Remove from oven; let cool on a wire rack. Cut into wedges. Yield: 22 wedges.

Desserts

CREAMY FRUIT AMBROSIA

EXCHANGES PER
SERVING:
2 Fruit

PER SERVING:
Calories 130
Carbohydrate 27.2g
Protein 2.4g
Fat 2.4g
Cholesterol 0.8mg
Fiber 2.6g
Sodium 32mg

4 cups cubed fresh pineapple
2 cups peeled, coarsely chopped fresh
   peaches
1 (8-ounce) carton vanilla nonfat yogurt
   sweetened with aspartame
¼ cup no-sugar-added peach spread
2 tablespoons shredded unsweetened
   coconut, toasted
1 tablespoon finely chopped pecans,
   toasted

1 Combine pineapple and peaches in a large bowl; cover and chill.

2 Combine yogurt and peach spread in a small bowl; stir well.

3 Spoon fruit mixture evenly into 6 dessert dishes. Top with yogurt mixture; sprinkle with coconut and pecans. Yield: 6 servings.

LAYERED FRUIT DESSERT

YIELD: 6 servings

1 fresh pineapple, peeled and cored
1 medium cantaloupe, peeled, seeded, and
   thinly sliced
4 kiwifruit, peeled and thinly sliced
   Fresh mint sprigs (optional)

**EXCHANGES PER
SERVING:**
2 Fruit

PER SERVING:
Calories 120
Carbohydrate 28.7g
Protein 1.6g
Fat 1.1g
Cholesterol 0mg
Fiber 4.5g
Sodium 6mg

1 Slice pineapple into ⅛-inch-thick slices. Arrange half of pineapple in bottom of an 8-inch springform pan, covering bottom of pan. Press gently with fingertips.

2 Arrange half of cantaloupe slices over pineapple, covering pineapple. Press gently with fingertips.

3 Arrange half of kiwifruit over cantaloupe, covering cantaloupe. Press gently with fingertips.

4 Repeat layers with remaining pineapple, cantaloupe, and kiwifruit slices. Place springform pan on a plate. Cover and chill at least 45 minutes.

5 Remove sides of pan; transfer to a serving plate. Garnish with mint sprigs, if desired. Yield: 6 servings.

CHERRIES JUBILEE

To flambé, heat the brandy just until warm or until vapors rise. If the brandy gets too hot, there will be no alcohol left to ignite.

EXCHANGES PER
SERVING:
1 Starch
1 Fruit

PER SERVING:
Calories 137
Carbohydrate 32.3g
Protein 4.7g
Fat 0.3g
Cholesterol 0mg
Fiber 1.3g
Sodium 76mg

2 tablespoons granulated sugar substitute with aspartame (such as Equal Spoonful)
1 tablespoon plus 1 teaspoon cornstarch
¼ cup unsweetened apple juice
¼ cup water
1 (16-ounce) package frozen unsweetened dark cherries, partially thawed
¼ cup brandy
3 cups sugar-free, fat-free vanilla ice cream

✦ Alcohol evaporates at 172°F, so when liqueurs, wines, and spirits are used in cooking, most of the alcohol evaporates, leaving only the flavor behind. The amount of alcohol that evaporates depends on the type of heat applied, the source of the alcohol, and the cooking time.

1 Combine sugar substitute and cornstarch in a large saucepan; stir well. Stir in apple juice and water. Place over medium heat; bring to a boil, stirring constantly. Add cherries; bring to a boil. Reduce heat, and simmer 10 minutes, stirring lightly. Remove from heat.

2 Place brandy in a small long-handled saucepan, and heat just until warm (do not boil). Ignite brandy with a long match, and pour over cherry mixture. Stir mixture lightly until flame dies down. Serve immediately over ½-cup portions of vanilla ice cream. Yield: 6 servings.

Minty Melon Compote

3 cups cantaloupe balls
3 cups watermelon balls
1 cup unsweetened apple juice
2 tablespoons finely chopped fresh mint
½ teaspoon grated orange rind
4 kiwifruit, peeled and sliced
    Fresh mint sprigs (optional)

1 Combine cantaloupe and watermelon balls in a large bowl.

2 Combine apple juice, chopped mint, and orange rind; stir well. Pour over melon balls; toss gently. Cover and chill 30 minutes. Add kiwifruit, and toss gently. Garnish with mint sprigs, if desired. Yield: 6 (1-cup) servings.

YIELD: 6 servings

EXCHANGES PER SERVING:
1 Fruit

PER SERVING:
Calories 77
Carbohydrate 17.5g
Protein 1.4g
Fat 0.7g
Cholesterol 0mg
Fiber 2.4g
Sodium 8mg

Midori Melon Balls

Midori is a honeydew-flavored liqueur.
For a nonalcoholic version, replace the Midori with 2 tablespoons orange juice.

¼ cup unsweetened orange juice
2 tablespoons Midori
1 tablespoon lemon juice
1 teaspoon grated gingerroot
1 cup watermelon balls
1 cup honeydew melon balls
1 cup cantaloupe balls
2 tablespoons chopped fresh mint

1 Combine first 4 ingredients in a large bowl, stirring well.

2 Add melon balls and mint, and toss gently. Cover and chill at least 2 hours. Yield: 3 (1-cup) servings.

YIELD: 3 servings

EXCHANGES PER SERVING:
1 Fruit

PER SERVING:
Calories 82
Carbohydrate 17.6g
Protein 1.4g
Fat 0.4g
Cholesterol 0mg
Fiber 1.6g
Sodium 14mg

QUICK PEACH CRISP

EXCHANGES PER
SERVING:
½ Starch
1 Fruit

PER SERVING:
Calories 100
Carbohydrate 22.9g
Protein 1.7g
Fat 0.9g
Cholesterol 0mg
Fiber 1.3g
Sodium 50mg

1 (16-ounce) can sliced peaches in juice,
   drained
2 tablespoons granulated sugar substitute
   (such as Sugar Twin)
1 teaspoon cornstarch
   Vegetable cooking spray
¼ cup low-fat granola without raisins

1 Combine first 3 ingredients in a bowl. Spoon peach mixture evenly into 2 (10-ounce) custard cups coated with cooking spray.

2 Place cups on a baking sheet; top each with 2 tablespoons granola. Bake, uncovered, at 375° for 18 to 20 minutes or until peach mixture is thoroughly heated and topping is crisp. Yield: 2 servings.

Pear Crisp: Substitute canned pear slices in juice for the peaches. Proceed with recipe as directed.

Pineapple Crisp: Substitute canned pineapple chunks in juice for the peaches. Proceed with recipe as directed.

BLUSHING PEARS

YIELD: 4 servings

1¼ cups reduced-calorie cranberry juice
    cocktail
  3 (6- x ¼-inch) strips orange rind
  3 whole cloves
  1 (3-inch) stick cinnamon
  2 medium-size firm pears, peeled, cored,
    and halved lengthwise
1½ teaspoons cornstarch
  1 packet sugar substitute with aspartame
    (such as Equal)
  ½ teaspoon lemon juice
    Fresh mint sprigs (optional)
    Orange rind curls (optional)

**EXCHANGES PER
SERVING:**
1 Fruit

PER SERVING:
Calories 58
Carbohydrate 14.9g
Protein 0.2g
Fat 0.3g
Cholesterol 0mg
Fiber 1.7g
Sodium 12mg

1 Combine first 4 ingredients in a large saucepan; bring to a boil. Add pears; cover, reduce heat, and simmer 15 minutes or until pears are tender.

2 Reserve ½ cup juice mixture. Transfer pears and remaining juice mixture to a shallow dish; cover and chill, turning once.

3 Combine reserved ½ cup juice mixture, cornstarch, and sugar substitute in a small saucepan. Bring to a boil, stirring constantly. Remove from heat, and stir in lemon juice. Cover and chill thoroughly.

4 Drain pears, discarding juice mixture. Cut lengthwise slits in pears to within ½ inch of core end, forming a fan. Spoon sauce evenly onto 4 dessert plates. Arrange pear halves over sauce. If desired, garnish with mint sprigs and orange rind curls. Yield: 4 servings.

RUBY PEACH MELBA

EXCHANGES PER
SERVING:
1 Starch
½ Fruit

PER SERVING:
Calories 95
Carbohydrate 21.7g
Protein 2.9g
Fat 0.2g
Cholesterol 0mg
Fiber 3.2g
Sodium 43mg

1½ cups fresh raspberries
 2 tablespoons granulated sugar substitute
   with aspartame (such as Equal
   Spoonful)
 2 teaspoons lemon juice
 1 (16-ounce) can peach halves in juice,
   drained
1½ cups sugar-free vanilla nonfat ice cream

1 Combine first 3 ingredients in a small bowl,
  tossing lightly to coat. Let stand 5 minutes.

2 Spoon raspberry mixture evenly into individual dessert dishes. Place 1 peach half,
cut side up, in each dish, and spoon ¼ cup ice
cream over each serving. Serve immediately.
Yield: 6 servings.

Mint Chocolate Chip Ice Milk

⅔ cup granulated sugar substitute with
    aspartame (such as Equal Spoonful)
2 cups evaporated skimmed milk
1 cup skim milk
½ cup frozen egg substitute, thawed
½ teaspoon imitation peppermint extract
6 drops of green liquid food coloring (optional)
4 ounces bittersweet chocolate, coarsely
    chopped

1 Combine first 6 ingredients in a large bowl; beat at medium speed of an electric mixer until well blended. Stir in chocolate.

2 Pour mixture into freezer can of a 2-quart hand-turned electric freezer. Freeze according to manufacturer's instructions. Scoop ice milk into individual dessert bowls. Serve immediately. Yield: 12 (½-cup) servings.

YIELD: 12 servings

EXCHANGES PER SERVING:
1 Milk

PER SERVING:
Calories 97
Carbohydrate 12.7g
Protein 5.3g
Fat 2.9g
Cholesterol 2mg
Fiber 0.0g
Sodium 76mg

BANANA-YOGURT ICE MILK

YIELD: 9 servings

EXCHANGES PER
SERVING:
1 Fruit

PER SERVING:
Calories 90
Carbohydrate 17.5g
Protein 4.6g
Fat 0.7g
Cholesterol 3mg
Fiber 1.6g
Sodium 52mg

1 envelope unflavored gelatin
3 tablespoons cold water
1 cup mashed ripe banana
1 cup evaporated skimmed milk
1 (8-ounce) carton plain low-fat yogurt
2 tablespoons honey
1 kiwifruit, peeled and thinly sliced
¼ cup fresh blueberries
¼ cup fresh raspberries

1 Sprinkle gelatin over cold water in a saucepan; let stand 1 minute. Cook over medium heat, stirring until gelatin dissolves; remove from heat.

2 Combine banana, milk, yogurt, and honey. Stir into gelatin mixture. Spoon mixture into an 8-inch square pan; cover and freeze until firm.

3 Remove from freezer, and let stand at room temperature 15 minutes to soften. Break into chunks. Position knife blade in food processor bowl; add mixture, and process until smooth. Return mixture to pan; cover and freeze until firm.

4 To serve, scoop into individual dessert glasses. Top each serving with kiwifruit, blueberries, and raspberries.
Yield: 9 (½-cup) servings.

SPUMONI PARFAITS

YIELD: 4 servings

1 cup lime sherbet, softened
2 tablespoons chopped pistachios, divided
¼ cup crushed pineapple in juice, drained
¾ cup sugar-free, fat-free vanilla ice cream,
  softened
1 cup raspberry sherbet, softened

1 Combine lime sherbet and 1 tablespoon chopped pistachios; stir well. Spoon ¼ cup lime sherbet mixture into each of 4 (6-ounce) chilled parfait glasses. Freeze 15 minutes or until firm.

2 Press drained pineapple between paper towels to remove excess moisture. Combine pineapple and ice cream; stir well. Spoon ¼ cup ice cream mixture over lime sherbet in each glass. Freeze 15 minutes or until firm.

3 Spoon ¼ cup raspberry sherbet over ice cream mixture in each glass. Top evenly with remaining 1 tablespoon pistachios. Freeze until firm. Yield: 4 servings.

EXCHANGES PER SERVING:
1 Starch
1 Fruit
½ Fat

PER SERVING:
Calories 170
Carbohydrate 35.1g
Protein 3.3g
Fat 2.8g
Cholesterol 0mg
Fiber 0.5g
Sodium 95mg

CHOCOLATE-PECAN PARFAITS

YIELD: 4 servings

EXCHANGES PER
SERVING:
3 Starch
1 Fat

PER SERVING:
Calories 208
Carbohydrate 44.4g
Protein 3.7g
Fat 4.8g
Cholesterol 0mg
Fiber 0.5g
Sodium 141mg

2 cups sugar-free, fat-free vanilla ice
    cream
½ cup reduced-calorie chocolate syrup
¼ cup chopped Spiced Pecans
    Fresh mint sprigs (optional)

1 Spoon ¼ cup ice cream into each of 4 parfait glasses; top each with 1 tablespoon chocolate syrup. Repeat procedure with remaining ice cream and chocolate syrup. Sprinkle 1 tablespoon Spiced Pecans over each serving. Garnish with mint sprigs, if desired. Serve immediately. Yield: 4 servings.

SPICED PECANS

YIELD: 20 servings

EXCHANGES PER
SERVING:
2 Fat

PER SERVING:
Calories 97
Carbohydrate 2.8g
Protein 1.3g
Fat 9.7g
Cholesterol 0mg
Fiber 1.0g
Sodium 32mg

½ cup granulated sugar substitute (such as
    Sugar Twin)
1½ teaspoons ground cinnamon
1 teaspoon ground nutmeg
¼ teaspoon salt
1 egg white
1 tablespoon plus 1½ teaspoons water
2½ cups pecan halves
    Vegetable cooking spray

1 Combine first 4 ingredients in a medium-size bowl, stirring well.

2 Beat egg white and water at medium speed of an electric mixer until foamy. Gradually add sugar substitute mixture, 1 tablespoon at a time, beating until stiff peaks form; fold in pecan halves.

3 Pour pecan mixture onto a jellyroll pan coated with cooking spray. Bake at 300° for 25 minutes, stirring every 10 minutes. Let cool completely in pan. Store pecans in an airtight container. Yield: 2½ cups (serving size: 2 tablespoons).

GRAPEFRUIT SORBET

YIELD: 8 servings

1½ cups water
 ½ cup granulated sugar substitute (such as
     Sugar Twin)
     Orange rind strips from 2 oranges
1½ cups fresh pink or red grapefruit juice
     (about 3 medium grapefruit)
 1 tablespoon lemon juice

1 Combine water and sugar substitute in a
  saucepan; bring to a boil. Add orange rind;
reduce heat, and simmer 5 minutes. Strain mixture, discarding rind. Cool completely.

2 Add grapefruit juice and lemon juice to sugar
  substitute mixture; stir well. Pour into a 9-
inch square pan; cover and freeze until firm.

3 Break frozen mixture into pieces. Position
  knife blade in food processor. Add frozen
mixture, in batches, and process until smooth
but not thawed. Serve immediately.
Yield: 8 (½-cup) servings.

**EXCHANGES PER
SERVING:**
½ Fruit

PER SERVING:
Calories 29
Carbohydrate 6.9g
Protein 0.2g
Fat 0.0g
Cholesterol 0mg
Fiber 0.0g
Sodium 17mg

Blush Slush

YIELD: 6 servings

EXCHANGES PER
SERVING:
3½ Fruit

PER SERVING:
Calories 219
Carbohydrate 54.4g
Protein 1.3g
Fat 0.0g
Cholesterol 0mg
Fiber 0.0g
Sodium 10mg

1 (12-ounce) can frozen unsweetened
    white grape juice concentrate,
    thawed and undiluted
3 tablespoons chopped fresh mint
1½ cups nonalcoholic blush wine
    Lemon rind curls (optional)

1 Combine grape juice and chopped mint in
a saucepan. Bring to a boil; reduce heat, and
simmer 5 minutes. Strain grape juice mixture,
discarding chopped mint. Cool completely.

2 Add nonalcoholic wine to grape juice mixture; stir well. Pour into a 9-inch square pan;
freeze at least 2 hours or until slushy, stirring
once. Serve immediately. Garnish with lemon
rind curls, if desired. Yield: 6 (½-cup) servings.

BERRY SORBET

YIELD: 6 servings

1 (16-ounce) package frozen unsweetened
   strawberries, thawed
1 (14-ounce) package frozen unsweetened
   raspberries, thawed
½ cup unsweetened white grape juice
3 tablespoons granulated sugar substitute
   with aspartame (such as Equal Spoonful)

EXCHANGES PER SERVING:
1 Fruit

PER SERVING:
Calories 63
Carbohydrate 15.5g
Protein 0.8g
Fat 0.4g
Cholesterol 0mg
Fiber 4.7g
Sodium 2mg

1 Position knife blade in food processor bowl; add strawberries and raspberries. Process 30 seconds or until smooth, stopping once to scrape down sides.

2 Place fruit mixture in a wire-mesh strainer; press with back of a spoon against the sides of the strainer to squeeze out juice. Discard pulp and seeds remaining in strainer.

3 Combine fruit juice, grape juice, and sugar substitute; stir well. Pour mixture into an 8-inch square pan. Cover and freeze until mixture is almost firm.

4 Position knife blade in food processor. Break frozen mixture into large pieces, and place in processor bowl; process until fluffy but not thawed. Serve immediately, or cover and freeze. Yield: 6 (½-cup) servings.

Strawberry Sorbet

YIELD: 6 servings

EXCHANGES PER
SERVING:
1 Fruit

PER SERVING:
Calories 61
Carbohydrate 14.7g
Protein 0.9g
Fat 0.4g
Cholesterol 0mg
Fiber 2.9g
Sodium 2mg

½ teaspoon unflavored gelatin
3 tablespoons cold water
4 cups sliced fresh strawberries
¼ cup granulated sugar substitute with aspartame (such as Equal Spoonful)
1 cup unsweetened sparkling white grape juice, chilled
Fresh mint sprigs (optional)

1 Sprinkle gelatin over cold water in a small saucepan; let stand 1 minute. Cook over low heat, stirring until gelatin dissolves. Set aside.

2 Position knife blade in food processor bowl; add strawberries and sugar alternative. Process 30 seconds or until smooth, scraping sides of processor bowl once. Transfer to a medium bowl. Add gelatin mixture and grape juice; stir well.

3 Pour into freezer can of a 2-quart hand-turned or electric freezer. Freeze according to manufacturer's instructions. Let stand 1 hour, if desired. Scoop mixture into stemmed dessert glasses. Garnish with mint, if desired. Serve immediately. Yield: 6 (1-cup) servings.

ICE CREAM SANDWICHES

YIELD: 9 servings

For variety, use another flavor of sugar-free, fat-free ice cream besides strawberry. The carbohydrate, fat, and calories will be about the same.

2½ cups sugar-free, fat-free vanilla or strawberry ice cream, softened
½ teaspoon ground cinnamon
18 (2¼- x 2¼-inch) graham crackers

1 Line an 8-inch square pan with heavy-duty plastic wrap. Set aside.

2 Combine ice cream and cinnamon; stir until blended. Spread evenly in prepared pan; cover and freeze until firm.

3 Cut ice cream into 9 squares; place each square between 2 graham crackers. Wrap in heavy-duty plastic wrap; store in freezer. To serve, unwrap desired number of sandwiches. Yield: 9 servings.

EXCHANGES PER SERVING:
1½ Starch

PER SERVING:
Calories 104
Carbohydrate 22.8g
Protein 3.4g
Fat 1.3g
Cholesterol 0mg
Fiber 1.1g
Sodium 136mg

EXCHANGES PER
SERVING:
2 Starch
1 Fat

PER SERVING:
Calories 205
Carbohydrate 31.4g
Protein 8.0g
Fat 7.1g
Cholesterol 0mg
Fiber 1.9g
Sodium 138mg

super·quick

CHOCOLATE-PEANUT BUTTER SUNDAES

You can vary the flavor of the sugar-free cookies or the sugar-free ice cream (see variations below) and the exchange values will remain the same.

2 cups sugar-free, fat-free vanilla ice cream, softened
2 tablespoons creamy peanut butter
5 sugar-free chocolate sandwich cookies, divided

1 Combine ice cream and peanut butter; stir well. Coarsely crumble 3 cookies; stir into ice cream mixture.

2 Spoon ice cream mixture evenly into 4 individual bowls. Coarsely crumble remaining 2 cookies; sprinkle over ice cream. Cover and store in freezer until ready to serve.
Yield: 4 (½-cup) servings.

Peanut Butter Sundaes: Use sugar-free peanut butter sandwich cookies instead of chocolate.

Double Chocolate Sundaes: Use sugar-free, fat-free chocolate ice cream instead of vanilla.

Applesauce-Currant Cookies

½ cup vegetable oil
¼ cup granulated sugar substitute (such as Sugar Twin)
1 egg
½ cup unsweetened applesauce
1 teaspoon vanilla extract
½ cup whole wheat flour
½ cup all-purpose flour
2 teaspoons baking powder
½ teaspoon baking soda
½ cup quick-cooking oats, uncooked
½ cup currants
1 teaspoon ground allspice
Vegetable cooking spray

YIELD: 26 cookies

EXCHANGES PER COOKIE:
½ Starch
1 Fat

PER COOKIE:
Calories 75
Carbohydrate 7.6g
Protein 1.2g
Fat 4.7g
Cholesterol 8mg
Fiber 0.6g
Sodium 31mg

1 Combine oil and sugar substitute in a medium bowl. Add egg, and beat at medium speed of an electric mixer until fluffy. Add applesauce and vanilla, stirring well.

2 Combine whole wheat flour and next 6 ingredients; add to oil mixture, stirring well. Cover and chill at least 15 minutes.

3 Drop dough by heaping teaspoonfuls onto baking sheets coated with cooking spray. Bake at 375° for 10 minutes. Remove from baking sheets, and let cool on wire racks. Yield: 26 cookies.

CRISPY CEREAL TREATS

YIELD: 18 bars

EXCHANGES PER
BAR:
1 Starch

PER BAR:
Calories 72
Carbohydrate 13.0g
Protein 0.8g
Fat 2.0g
Cholesterol 0mg
Fiber 0.3g
Sodium 114mg

3 tablespoons margarine
⅓ cup granulated brown sugar substitute
2 cups miniature marshmallows
4 cups oven-toasted rice cereal
2 cups whole wheat flake cereal
  Vegetable cooking spray

1 Melt margarine in a large saucepan over medium heat. Add sugar substitute; stir well. Add marshmallows; cook, stirring constantly, until marshmallows melt. Remove from heat, stir in cereals.

2 Press cereal mixture evenly into the bottom of a 13- x 9- x 2-inch baking pan coated with cooking spray. Let cool 1 hour. Cut into 3- x 2-inch bars. Yield: 18 bars.

DATE BARS

1 (8-ounce) package pitted dates, chopped
1 cup water
1 tablespoon plus 2¼ teaspoons
   granulated sugar substitute with
   aspartame (such as Equal Spoonful)
½ cup plus 2 tablespoons margarine
1 egg, lightly beaten
2 egg whites
1 teaspoon vanilla extract
1¾ cups all-purpose flour
½ teaspoon baking powder
¼ teaspoon salt
¼ cup all-purpose flour, divided
   Vegetable cooking spray
1 egg white, lightly beaten

EXCHANGES PER BAR:
1 Starch
1 Fat

PER BAR:
Calories 112
Carbohydrate 15.1g
Protein 2.0g
Fat 5.1g
Cholesterol 9mg
Fiber 1.1g
Sodium 90mg

1 Place dates and water in a saucepan; bring to a boil. Reduce heat; simmer 10 minutes. Add 1 tablespoon sugar substitute. Process in container of an electric blender until smooth.

2 Beat margarine and 2¼ teaspoons sugar substitute at medium-high speed of an electric mixer until creamy. Add egg, 2 egg whites, and vanilla; beat well. Combine 1¾ cups flour, baking powder, and salt. Add to margarine mixture, stirring just until blended.

3 Divide dough into 4 equal portions; wrap each in plastic wrap. Freeze 15 minutes or until firm. Shape each portion, still covered, into a 4- x 2- x ½-inch log. Freeze 15 additional minutes.

4 Sprinkle 1 tablespoon flour over work surface; roll 1 portion of dough into a 12- x 4-inch rectangle. Spread ¼ cup filling down center in a 1-inch-wide strip to within ½ inch from ends. Fold sides over filling, pressing edges to seal. Cut in half crosswise; place, seam side down, on a baking sheet coated with cooking spray. Repeat procedure. Brush with egg white. Bake at 400° for 12 minutes. Remove from baking sheet; let cool on a wire rack. Slice into 2-inch bars. Yield: 2 dozen.

FIG BARS

YIELD: 2 dozen bars

**EXCHANGES PER
BAR:**
1 Starch
1 Fat

PER BAR:
Calories 95
Carbohydrate 13.5g
Protein 1.5g
Fat 4.6g
Cholesterol 0mg
Fiber 2.9g
Sodium 43mg

1½ cups chopped dried figs
 1 tablespoon all-purpose flour
 ½ cup water
 ¾ cup unsweetened flaked coconut
 ½ cup reduced-calorie margarine
 ⅓ cup granulated sugar substitute
      (such as Sugar Twin)
1¾ cups quick-cooking oats, toasted
 ½ teaspoon vanilla extract
      Vegetable cooking spray

1 Combine figs and flour in a medium bowl; toss lightly to coat.

2 Bring water to a boil in a medium saucepan. Add fig mixture, coconut, margarine, and sugar substitute to saucepan, stirring well. Cook, uncovered, over medium heat 5 to 7 minutes or until mixture is thickened, stirring often. Add oats and vanilla, stirring until oats are moistened.

3 Press mixture in bottom of a 9-inch square pan coated with cooking spray. Cover and chill thoroughly. Cut into bars. Yield: 2 dozen.

Microwave Instructions: Place ½ cup water in a 1-cup liquid measure. Microwave at HIGH 2 to 3 minutes or until water boils; pour water over fig mixture. Add coconut, margarine, and sugar substitute to fig mixture, stirring well. Microwave, uncovered, at HIGH 2 to 3 minutes or until mixture is thickened, stirring after every minute. Add oats and vanilla, stirring until oats are moistened. Proceed with recipe as directed.

Frozen Strawberry Angel Cake

YIELD: 10 servings

1 (10½-ounce) loaf angel food cake
1½ cups sugar-free, fat-free vanilla ice cream, softened
1 cup unsweetened frozen strawberries, thawed and chopped
1 envelope whipped topping mix (such as Dream Whip)
½ cup water
½ teaspoon vanilla extract
¼ cup water
2 tablespoons granulated sugar substitute (such as Sugar Twin)
1 (16-ounce) package frozen unsweetened strawberries
1 tablespoon lemon juice
Fresh strawberries (optional)

EXCHANGES PER SERVING:
1 Starch
1 Fruit
1 Fat

PER SERVING:
Calories 174
Carbohydrate 28.1g
Protein 3.4g
Fat 6.7g
Cholesterol 0.1mg
Fiber 1.4g
Sodium 201mg

1 Slice cake horizontally into 3 layers, and set aside.

2 Combine 1½ cups ice cream and 1 cup chopped strawberries; stir well. Place bottom layer of cake on a serving plate; spread half of ice cream mixture over cake, and top with middle layer. Freeze cake and remaining ice cream mixture 30 minutes. Let ice cream mixture soften slightly; spread over middle layer. Top with remaining layer. Freeze 30 minutes.

3 Combine whipped topping, ½ cup water, and vanilla in a medium bowl. Beat at high speed of an electric mixer until stiff peaks form. Spread over cake. Freeze until firm.

4 Combine ¼ cup water and sugar substitute, stirring until sugar substitute dissolves. Place 16 ounces strawberries and sugar substitute mixture in container of an electric blender. Cover and process until smooth. Press through a sieve to remove seeds. Add lemon juice; stir well.

5 Slice cake into 1-inch-thick slices, and place on dessert plates. Spoon about 3 tablespoons puree around each slice. Garnish with strawberries. Yield: 10 servings.

FRUIT SHORTCAKES

YIELD: 6 servings

EXCHANGES PER
SERVING:
1 Starch
1 Fruit

PER SERVING:
Calories 133
Carbohydrate 26.7g
Protein 2.2g
Fat 1.9g
Cholesterol 74mg
Fiber 1.6g
Sodium 48mg

If your grocery store doesn't carry
sugar-free chocolate sauce, you can make
your own, using the recipe below.

6 (³/₄-ounce) commercial shortcakes
1½ cups cubed nectarine (about 1 large)
½ cup fresh raspberries
1 tablespoon lemon juice
¾ cup commercial sugar-free chocolate
sauce

1 Place shortcakes on individual dessert
plates.

2 Combine nectarine, raspberries, and lemon
juice in a small bowl; toss well.

3 Spoon 1 tablespoon chocolate sauce over
each shortcake. Top each with ⅓ cup fruit
mixture; drizzle each with 1 additional tablespoon chocolate sauce. Yield: 6 servings.

MILK CHOCOLATE SAUCE

YIELD: ¾ cup plus
2 tablespoons

EXCHANGES PER
TABLESPOON:
Free

PER TABLESPOON:
Calories 14
Carbohydrate 2.0g
Protein 0.8g
Fat 0.1g
Cholesterol 0mg
Fiber 0g
Sodium 23mg

2½ tablespoons granulated brown sugar
substitute
2 tablespoons unsweetened cocoa
2 teaspoons cornstarch
1 cup skim milk
¼ teaspoon vanilla extract
Dash of salt

1 Combine first 3 ingredients in a small
saucepan. Gradually stir in milk. Cook
over medium heat, stirring constantly, until mixture begins to boil. Cook 1 minute, stirring
constantly. Remove from heat; stir in vanilla
and salt. Serve warm.
Yield: ¾ cup plus 2 tablespoons.

Strawberry Shortcakes

YIELD: 6 servings

2 cups fresh strawberries, sliced
2 tablespoons granulated sugar substitute
  (such as Sugar Twin)
2 tablespoons low-sugar strawberry spread
1¾ cups plus 2 teaspoons all-purpose flour
2 teaspoons baking powder
¼ teaspoon baking soda
¼ teaspoon salt
2 teaspoons granulated sugar substitute
3 tablespoons reduced-calorie margarine
¾ cup plain nonfat yogurt
  Sugar-free, fat-free vanilla ice cream,
    softened (optional)
  Fresh mint sprigs (optional)

EXCHANGES PER SERVING:
1½ Starch
1 Fruit
1 Fat

PER SERVING:
Calories 206
Carbohydrate 36.7g
Protein 5.7g
Fat 4.6g
Cholesterol 2mg
Fiber 2.4g
Sodium 234mg

1 Combine first 3 ingredients; stir lightly. Set aside.

2 Combine 1¾ cups flour, baking powder, and next 3 ingredients in a medium bowl; cut in margarine with pastry blender until mixture is crumbly. Add yogurt, stirring just until dry ingredients are moistened.

3 Sprinkle remaining 2 teaspoons flour evenly over work surface. Turn dough out onto floured surface, and knead 4 or 5 times. Roll dough to ½-inch thickness; cut into 6 rounds with a 3-inch biscuit cutter. Place on an ungreased baking sheet. Bake at 425° for 10 minutes or until golden. Remove from baking sheet; let cool on a wire rack.

4 Cut each biscuit in half horizontally; place each bottom half on an individual dessert plate. Spoon strawberry mixture evenly over bottom halves of biscuits. Place tops of biscuits on strawberries, cut side down. If desired, top each with about 2 tablespoons ice cream, and serve immediately (ice cream not included in analysis). Garnish with mint sprigs, if desired. Yield: 6 servings.

APPLESAUCE SPICE CAKE

YIELD: 20 servings

EXCHANGES PER
SERVING:
1 Starch
1 Fruit
2 Fat

PER SERVING:
Calories 206
Carbohydrate 36.7g
Protein 5.7g
Fat 4.6g
Cholesterol 2mg
Fiber 2.4g
Sodium 234mg

1 cup water
1½ cups golden raisins
3 tablespoons self-rising flour
2 cups unsweetened applesauce
2 eggs, lightly beaten
¾ cup granulated sugar substitute
  (such as Sugar Twin)
¾ cup vegetable oil
2 tablespoons vanilla extract
3 cups self-rising flour
¼ teaspoon baking soda
2 teaspoons ground cinnamon
½ teaspoon ground allspice
  Vegetable cooking spray

1 Combine 1 cup water and raisins in a medium saucepan; bring to a boil. Boil until water is completely absorbed; remove from heat. Add 3 tablespoons flour; toss well.

2 Combine applesauce and next 4 ingredients; stir well. Combine 3 cups flour and next 3 ingredients. Gradually add to applesauce mixture, stirring just until dry ingredients are moistened. Fold in raisins.

3 Pour batter into a 10-inch Bundt pan coated with cooking spray. Bake at 350° for 45 minutes or until a wooden pick inserted in center comes out clean. Cool in pan 10 minutes; remove from pan, and cool completely on a wire rack. Yield: 20 servings.

CARROT CAKE

YIELD: 18 servings

2 cups sifted cake flour
⅓ cup whole wheat flour
2 teaspoons baking soda
⅛ teaspoon salt
1½ teaspoons ground cinnamon
½ teaspoon pumpkin pie spice
1 (8-ounce) can crushed pineapple in
  juice, undrained
½ cup firmly packed brown sugar
3 tablespoons vegetable oil
4 egg whites
3 cups shredded carrot
⅔ cup nonfat buttermilk
2 teaspoons vanilla extract
  Vegetable cooking spray
  Cream Cheese Frosting

EXCHANGES PER
SERVING:
1½ Starch
1½ Fat

PER SERVING:
Calories 174
Carbohydrate 23.7g
Protein 4.6g
Fat 7.0g
Cholesterol 15mg
Fiber 1.7g
Sodium 266mg

1 Combine first 6 ingredients; set aside. Drain pineapple, reserving 2 tablespoons juice for Cream Cheese Frosting.

2 Combine sugar and oil in a medium bowl. Add egg whites; beat at medium speed of an electric mixer 1 minute. Stir in pineapple, carrot, buttermilk, and vanilla. Add flour mixture; stir well. Pour batter into a 13- x 9- x 2-inch pan coated with cooking spray. Bake at 350° for 23 to 25 minutes or until a wooden pick inserted in center comes out clean. Let cool. Spread frosting over cake. Cut into squares. Yield: 18 servings.

CREAM CHEESE FROSTING

1½ (8-ounce) packages Neufchâtel cheese
½ cup granulated sugar substitute with
  aspartame (such as Equal Spoonful)
2 tablespoons pineapple juice
½ teaspoon grated orange rind
½ teaspoon vanilla extract

1 Beat cheese at medium speed of an electric mixer just until creamy. Add sugar substitute, juice, orange rind, and vanilla; beat until creamy. Yield: 1¾ cups plus 2 tablespoons.

ORANGE CHIFFON CAKE

YIELD: 16 servings

EXCHANGES PER
SERVING:
1 Starch
1 Fat

PER SERVING:
Calories 174
Carbohydrate 23.7g
Protein 4.6g
Fat 7.0g
Cholesterol 15mg
Fiber 1.7g
Sodium 266mg

2½ cups all-purpose flour
1 tablespoon plus 1 teaspoon baking
   powder
¾ teaspoon salt
1 cup unsweetened orange juice
¼ cup vegetable oil
3 tablespoons liquid sugar substitute
1 teaspoon orange extract
4 egg yolks
10 egg whites
½ teaspoon cream of tartar
1 teaspoon vanilla extract
   Edible flowers (optional)

1 Combine first 3 ingredients in a large mixing bowl; make a well in center of mixture.

2 Add orange juice and next 4 ingredients; beat at medium speed of an electric mixer until smooth.

3 Beat egg whites at high speed of an electric mixer until foamy; add cream of tartar, beating until stiff peaks form.

4 Gently fold flour mixture into beaten egg whites. Fold in vanilla. Pour into an ungreased 10-inch tube pan. Bake at 325° for 45 to 50 minutes or until cake springs back when lightly touched. Invert pan; cool completely. Loosen cake from sides of pan, using a metal spatula; remove cake from pan. Garnish with edible flowers, if desired. Yield: 16 servings.

LIGHT FRUITCAKE

YIELD: 16 servings

1 cup fresh cranberries, chopped
¼ cup brandy
1 (6-ounce) can frozen orange juice
    concentrate, thawed and undiluted
1 cup chopped pecans
1 tablespoon grated orange rind
1 teaspoon vanilla extract
2 eggs, lightly beaten
1 (8-ounce) package unsweetened pineapple
    tidbits, drained
1 (8-ounce) package unsweetened pitted
    dates, chopped
2 cups all-purpose flour
1¼ teaspoons baking soda
¼ teaspoon salt
½ teaspoon ground cinnamon
¼ teaspoon ground nutmeg
¼ teaspoon ground allspice
    Vegetable cooking spray
½ cup brandy

**EXCHANGES PER
SERVING:**
1 Starch
1 Fruit
1 Fat

PER SERVING:
Calories 182
Carbohydrate 30.2g
Protein 3.6g
Fat 6.0g
Cholesterol 28mg
Fiber 2.5g
Sodium 145mg

1 Combine first 3 ingredients in a large bowl; cover and let stand 1 hour.

2 Combine pecans and next 5 ingredients. Add to cranberry mixture; stir well.

3 Combine flour and next 5 ingredients. Add to fruit mixture; stir well.

4 Spoon batter into a 6-cup Bundt pan coated with cooking spray. Bake at 325° for 45 minutes or until a wooden pick inserted in cake comes out clean. Cool cake in pan 20 minutes; remove from pan, and let cool completely on a wire rack.

5 Bring ½ cup brandy to a boil; let cool. Moisten several layers of cheesecloth in brandy, and wrap cake in cheesecloth. Cover with plastic wrap, and then aluminum foil. Store in cool place at least 1 week before serving. Yield: 16 servings.

STRAWBERRY CHEESECAKE

EXCHANGES PER
SERVING:
1½ Starch
3 Fat

PER SERVING:
Calories 253
Carbohydrate 20.2g
Protein 7.1g
Fat 16.2g
Cholesterol 36mg
Fiber 1.0g
Sodium 354mg

2 cups graham cracker crumbs
⅓ cup reduced-calorie margarine, melted
    Vegetable cooking spray
1 envelope unflavored gelatin
1 cup skim milk
2½ (8-ounce) packages Neufchâtel cheese
1 tablespoon lemon juice
2 teaspoons vanilla extract
¾ cup Equal Spoonful
3 cups medium-size fresh strawberries,
    halved
2 tablespoons Equal Spoonful
¼ cup low-sugar strawberry spread
    Fresh mint sprigs (optional)

❧ This creamy
dessert, while low
in sugar, has about
16 grams of fat
(3 Fat Exchanges).
If you're watching
your fat intake,
enjoy this dessert
only on special
occasions.

1 Combine graham cracker crumbs and margarine in a medium bowl, stirring well. Press mixture into bottom and 1 inch up sides of a 9-inch springform pan coated with cooking spray. Bake at 350° for 8 minutes. Remove from oven, and let cool on a wire rack.

2 Sprinkle gelatin over milk in a small saucepan; let stand 1 minute. Cook over low heat, stirring until gelatin dissolves, about 2 minutes. Let cool slightly.

3 Beat cheese at medium speed of an electric mixer until creamy. Gradually add lemon juice and vanilla, beating well. Gradually add gelatin mixture, beating until smooth and scraping down sides, if necessary. Add ¾ cup sugar substitute, and beat just until blended. Pour mixture into prepared crust. Cover and chill at least 3 hours or until set.

4 Combine strawberries, 2 tablespoons sugar substitute, and strawberry spread in a medium saucepan. Cook over medium-low heat, stirring constantly, until spread melts and strawberries are coated. Spoon strawberry mixture over chilled cheesecake. Garnish with mint sprigs, if desired. Yield: 12 servings.

BLUEBERRY-PEAR COBBLER

YIELD: 6 servings

1 (16-ounce) can pear halves in juice,
    undrained
2½ tablespoons granulated sugar
    substitute (such as Sugar Twin)
1 tablespoon cornstarch
2 cups fresh or frozen blueberries, thawed
    Vegetable cooking spray
¾ cup all-purpose flour
2 teaspoons granulated sugar substitute
1 teaspoon baking powder
1 tablespoon margarine
⅓ cup skim milk

**EXCHANGES PER
SERVING:**
1 Starch
½ Fruit
½ Fat

PER SERVING:
Calories 136
Carbohydrate 27.0g
Protein 2.6g
Fat 2.5g
Cholesterol 0mg
Fiber 3.6g
Sodium 32mg

1 Drain pears, reserving ¾ cup liquid. Chop pears, and set aside.

2 Combine 2½ tablespoons sugar substitute and cornstarch in a saucepan; stir well. Stir in reserved liquid; bring to a boil over medium heat. Cook 1 minute, stirring constantly. remove from heat, and gently stir in pears and blueberries. Spoon into an 8-inch square baking dish coated with cooking spray.

3 Combine flour, 2 teaspoons sugar substitute, and baking powder in a bowl; cut in margarine with pastry blender until crumbly. Add milk, stirring just until dry ingredients are moistened. Drop by tablespoonfuls over fruit mixture. Bake at 400° for 20 to 25 minutes or until golden. Yield: 6 servings.

HOMESTYLE APPLE PIE

EXCHANGES PER
SERVING:
1 Starch
2 Fruit
1½ Fat

PER SERVING:
Calories 258
Carbohydrate 46.1g
Protein 3.7g
Fat 7.0g
Cholesterol 0mg
Fiber 3.6g
Sodium 168mg

Serve pie with sugar-free ice cream, if desired.
(Ice cream is not included in analysis.)

  2 cups all-purpose flour
  ½ teaspoon salt
  ¼ teaspoon ground cinnamon
  ¼ cup vegetable shortening
  ½ cup plus 2 tablespoons ice water
     Vegetable cooking spray
  6 medium cooking apples, peeled, cored,
     and sliced
  ¼ cup plus 2 tablespoons frozen apple
     juice concentrate, undiluted
  2 tablespoons all-purpose flour
  1 tablespoon granulated sugar substitute
  1 tablespoon reduced-calorie margarine,
     melted
  1 teaspoon ground cinnamon
  1 teaspoon vanilla extract

1 Combine first 3 ingredients in a medium
  bowl; cut in shortening with a pastry blender
until mixture resembles coarse meal. Sprinkle
ice water, 1 tablespoon at a time, over surface;
toss with a fork until dry ingredients are moistened and mixture is crumbly.

2 Divide dough into 2 equal portions. Press
  1 portion into a 4-inch circle on heavy-duty
plastic wrap; cover with additional plastic wrap.
Roll to ⅛-inch thickness. Place in freezer 5 minutes. Remove one sheet of plastic; invert dough
into a 9-inch pieplate coated with cooking
spray. Remove remaining plastic.

3 Combine apple and next 6 ingredients in a
  large bowl. Spoon mixture into pastry shell.

4 Roll remaining pastry to ⅛-inch thickness;
  transfer to top of pie. Fold edges under; crimp.
Cut slits in top. Cover edges with aluminum foil.
Bake at 450° for 15 minutes. Reduce temperature
to 350°; bake 35 minutes, removing foil after 25
minutes. Cool on a wire rack. Yield: 8 servings.

Peaches 'n' Cream Pie

1¼ cups graham cracker crumbs
¼ cup reduced-calorie margarine, melted
3 packets sugar substitute with aspartame (such as Equal)
1 (8-ounce) package Neufchâtel cheese, softened
2 tablespoons skim milk
4 packets sugar substitute with aspartame
3½ cups frozen, reduced-calorie whipped topping, thawed and divided
4 medium-size ripe peaches, peeled and pitted
1 (1-ounce) package sugar-free vanilla pudding mix sweetened with aspartame
1 cup skim milk
¼ teaspoon vanilla extract
1 tablespoon lemon juice

EXCHANGES PER SERVING:
1 Starch
1 Fruit
3 Fat

PER SERVING:
Calories 258
Carbohydrate 46.1g
Protein 3.7g
Fat 7.0g
Cholesterol 0mg
Fiber 3.6g
Sodium 168mg

1 Combine first 3 ingredients, stirring well. Press into bottom and up sides of a 9-inch pieplate. Bake at 350° for 6 minutes. Set aside.

2 Beat Neufchâtel cheese at medium speed of an electric mixer until creamy; gradually add 2 tablespoons milk and sugar substitute, beating mixture well. Fold in 1½ cups whipped topping; spread into prepared crust. Dice 2 peaches; press lightly into topping mixture. Cover and chill thoroughly.

3 Prepare pudding according to package directions, using 1 cup milk. Stir in vanilla, and let stand 5 minutes. Fold in remaining 2 cups whipped topping; spread over diced peaches.

4 Slice 2 peaches; toss with lemon juice. Arrange decoratively on top of pie. Cover and chill 3 hours. Yield: 8 servings.

PIÑA COLADA PIE

YIELD: 8 servings

EXCHANGES PER SERVING:
1 Starch
1½ Fat
½ Milk

PER SERVING:
Calories 177
Carbohydrate 22.2g
Protein 5.1g
Fat 7.6g
Cholesterol 7mg
Fiber 0.7g
Sodium 142mg

✒ To chill a gelatin mixture to the consistency of unbeaten egg white, refrigerate the mixture only until it's slightly thick. Chilling takes between 20 to 40 minutes, depending on the amount of mixture. If a gelatin mixture becomes too firm to add remaining ingredients, set the container of gelatin in a bowl of warm water, and stir until gelatin softens slightly.

¾ cup graham cracker crumbs
3 tablespoons reduced-calorie margarine, melted
1 tablespoon granulated sugar substitute with aspartame (such as Equal Spoonful)
1 envelope unflavored gelatin
2 tablespoons cold water
¼ cup unsweetened pineapple juice
¾ cup part-skim ricotta cheese
¼ cup evaporated skimmed milk
1 tablespoon rum or 1 teaspoon rum extract
1 teaspoon coconut extract
1 (20-ounce) can crushed pineapple in juice, undrained
¼ cup shredded unsweetened coconut
2 tablespoons shredded unsweetened coconut, toasted

1 Combine first 3 ingredients; press mixture evenly into bottom and up sides of a 9-inch pieplate. Bake at 350° for 8 to 10 minutes or until lightly browned. Cool and set aside.

2 Sprinkle gelatin over cold water in a saucepan; let stand 1 minute. Add juice. Cook over low heat, stirring until gelatin dissolves.

3 Combine gelatin mixture, ricotta cheese, and next 3 ingredients in container of an electric blender or food processor; cover and process until smooth.

4 Combine ricotta cheese mixture, pineapple, and ¼ cup coconut in a medium bowl. Chill mixture 30 to 40 minutes or until the consistency of unbeaten egg white, stirring occasionally. Pour into cooled crust. Cover and chill 1 hour or until set. Before serving, sprinkle toasted coconut over top of pie. Yield: 8 servings.

MAPLE PUMPKIN PIE

YIELD: 10 servings

1 (15-ounce) can pumpkin
½ cup egg substitute
⅓ cup granulated brown sugar substitute
3 tablespoons sugar-free maple syrup
1¼ teaspoons pumpkin pie spice
¼ teaspoon salt
1 (12-ounce) can evaporated skimmed
   milk
½ (15-ounce) package refrigerated
   piecrusts (1 piecrust)
½ cup plus 2 tablespoons frozen reduced-
   calorie whipped topping, thawed
   Granulated brown sugar substitute
   (optional)
   Pastry Pumpkins (optional)

1 Combine first 6 ingredients in a large bowl, stirring well. Gradually stir in evaporated milk. Pour mixture into piecrust.

2 Bake at 425° for 15 minutes; reduce heat to 350°, and bake 35 to 40 minutes or until set. Cover pastry with aluminum foil to prevent excessive browning, if necessary. Let cool completely on a wire rack.

3 Top each serving with 1 tablespoon whipped topping, and sprinkle with additional brown sugar substitute, if desired. Garnish with Pastry Pumpkins, if desired. Yield: 10 servings.

EXCHANGES PER
SERVING:
1½ Starch
1½ Fat

PER SERVING:
Calories 174
Carbohydrate 21.9g
Protein 5.6g
Fat 7.1g
Cholesterol 4mg
Fiber 1.8g
Sodium 356mg

✎ Use a small pumpkin cookie cutter to make pastry pumpkins from part of the remaining piecrust. Sprinkle with additional brown sugar substitute, and bake at 375° for 8 minutes.

STRAWBERRY-BANANA TART

**EXCHANGES PER
SERVING:**
½ Starch
½ Fruit
2 Fat

PER SERVING:
Calories 180
Carbohydrate 17.4g
Protein 4.3g
Fat 10.6g
Cholesterol 21mg
Fiber 1.4g
Sodium 158mg

1 cup sifted cake flour
1 teaspoon granulated sugar substitute
   (such as Sugar Twin)
¼ cup margarine
2 tablespoons ice water
   Vegetable cooking spray
1 (8-ounce) package Neufchâtel cheese,
   softened
⅔ cup lemon-flavored nonfat yogurt
   sweetened with aspartame
1 tablespoon granulated sugar substitute
1 medium banana, peeled and sliced
1 tablespoon lemon juice
2 cups sliced fresh strawberries
2 tablespoons sugar-free apple jelly, melted
   Fresh mint sprig (optional)

1 Combine flour and 1 teaspoon sugar substitute in a large bowl; cut in margarine with pastry blender until mixture resembles coarse meal and is pale yellow (about 3½ minutes). Sprinkle ice water, 1 tablespoon at a time, over surface; toss with a fork just until dry ingredients are moistened and mixture is crumbly.

2 Roll dough into a 10-inch circle between 2 sheets of plastic wrap; refrigerate dough 15 minutes. Coat bottom of a 9-inch round removable-bottom tart pan with cooking spray. Press dough in bottom and up sides of pan; flute edges. Bake at 400° for 10 minutes. Cool completely.

3 Beat cheese, yogurt, and 1 tablespoon sugar substitute with a wire whisk until smooth. Spread cheese mixture in tart shell.

4 Combine banana slices and lemon juice in a small bowl; toss. Arrange banana and strawberries over cheese mixture. Brush fruit evenly with melted jelly. Garnish with a mint sprig, if desired. Yield: 8 servings.

Rum-Raisin Pear Turnovers

YIELD: 6 turnovers

EXCHANGES PER
TURNOVER:
1 Starch
1 Fruit

PER TURNOVER:
Calories 162
Carbohydrate 16.9g
Protein 3.2g
Fat 9.2g
Cholesterol 11mg
Fiber 0.9g
Sodium 128mg

3 medium-size ripe pears, peeled, cored,
　　and thinly sliced
2 tablespoons lemon juice
1/4 cup diced dried apricot halves
3 tablespoons raisins
1 tablespoon granulated brown sugar
　　substitute
1 tablespoon dark rum
1/2 teaspoon ground cinnamon
1/4 teaspoon ground nutmeg
6 sheets frozen phyllo pastry, thawed
　　Butter-flavored vegetable cooking spray

1 Combine pears and lemon juice in a large
bowl; toss gently. Add apricot and next
5 ingredients, stirring gently; set aside.

2 Place one sheet of phyllo on a damp towel
(keep remaining phyllo covered with a damp
towel). Lightly coat phyllo with cooking spray.
Fold in half lengthwise; spray again.

3 Place one-sixth of pear mixture at base
of phyllo sheet; fold right bottom corner over
filling, making a triangle. Continue folding back
and forth into a triangle to end of sheet. Place
triangle, seam side down, on a baking sheet
coated with cooking spray. (Keep triangles covered before baking.) Repeat process with remaining phyllo and pear mixture.

4 Bake at 400° for 15 minutes or until golden.
Cool 5 minutes on wire racks; serve warm.
Yield: 6 turnovers.

BANANA PUDDING

EXCHANGES PER SERVING:
1 Starch
1 Fruit
1 Fat

PER SERVING:
Calories 195
Carbohydrate 30.8g
Protein 5.5g
Fat 5.6g
Cholesterol 56mg
Fiber 1.1g
Sodium 134mg

1 tablespoon sugar
2 teaspoons cornstarch
2 tablespoons skim milk
1 egg, separated
¾ cup skim milk
¼ teaspoon vanilla extract
16 vanilla wafers
1 cup peeled, sliced ripe banana
1 egg white
Dash of cream of tartar
1 tablespoon sugar

1 Combine 1 tablespoon sugar and cornstarch in top of a double boiler. Add 2 tablespoons milk and egg yolk; stir well, and set aside.

2 Place ¾ cup milk in saucepan. Cook over medium heat until thoroughly heated. Add hot milk to cornstarch mixture; stir constantly. Place over boiling water; cook 10 minutes or until smooth and thickened, stirring constantly. Remove from heat; stir in vanilla, and let cool.

3 Place 1 vanilla wafer in bottom of each of four 6-ounce custard cups. Arrange 3 wafers around sides of each cup. Combine pudding mixture and sliced banana; stir gently. Spoon into cups over vanilla wafers.

4 Beat 2 egg whites and cream of tartar at high speed of an electric mixer until foamy. Gradually add 1 tablespoon sugar, beating until stiff peaks form (2 to 4 minutes). Spread meringue over individual puddings, sealing to edge of cups. Bake at 350° for 20 minutes or until golden. Yield: 4 servings.

CHOCOLATE-PEPPERMINT PUDDING

1 (1.4-ounce) package sugar-free
    chocolate instant pudding mix
2 cups skim milk
½ teaspoon peppermint extract
4 sugar-free peppermint candy pieces,
    coarsely crushed

1 Combine pudding mix and milk in a medium bowl, stirring with a wire whisk until smooth. Stir in extract. Cover and chill.

2 Spoon pudding into individual dessert dishes. Just before serving, sprinkle evenly with crushed candy. Yield: 4 (½-cup) servings.

White Chocolate-Peppermint Pudding: Substitute 1 (1.4-ounce) package sugar-free white chocolate instant pudding mix for the chocolate.

Butterscotch Pudding: Substitute 1 (1.4-ounce) package sugar-free butterscotch instant pudding mix for the chocolate. Add ½ teaspoon vanilla extract instead of peppermint extract. Substitute 4 sugar-free butterscotch candy pieces for peppermint candy.

YIELD: 4 servings

EXCHANGES PER SERVING:
1 Starch
½ Skim Milk

PER SERVING:
Calories 96
Carbohydrate 18.9g
Protein 5.2g
Fat 0.2g
Cholesterol 2mg
Fiber 1.0g
Sodium 394mg

❧ Both variations of the pudding count as 1 Starch and ½ Skim Milk per serving.

FRESH STRAWBERRY MOUSSE

YIELD: 7 servings

EXCHANGES PER
SERVING:
½ Fruit

PER SERVING:
Calories 50
Carbohydrate 7.2g
Protein 2.7g
Fat 1.3g
Cholesterol 0mg
Fiber 2.1g
Sodium 23mg

1 envelope unflavored gelatin
½ cup skim milk
¼ cup spoonable sugar alternative
4 cups fresh strawberries, divided
⅓ cup nonfat sour cream
¼ cup plus 3 tablespoons prepared
    reduced-calorie whipped topping mix

1 Sprinkle gelatin over cold milk in a small saucepan; let stand 1 minute. Cook over low heat, stirring until gelatin dissolves, about 2 minutes. Remove from heat; add sugar alternative, stirring until it dissolves.

2 Reserve 7 strawberries for garnish; set aside. Place remaining strawberries in container of an electric blender; cover and process until smooth, stopping once to scrape down sides. Add gelatin mixture and sour cream; cover and process until blended.

3 Spoon evenly into seven 4-ounce parfait glasses. Cover and chill until firm. Top with whipped topping, and garnish with reserved strawberries, if desired. Yield: 7 servings.

MIXED FRUIT TRIFLE

YIELD: 8 servings

1 (1-ounce) package sugar-free vanilla
   pudding mix sweetened with aspartame
2 cups skim milk
12 ladyfingers
3 tablespoons no-sugar-added strawberry
   spread, melted
1 cup halved fresh strawberries
1 cup diced fresh pineapple
½ cup halved seedless green grapes
½ cup halved seedless red grapes
1 fresh strawberry, sliced (optional)
   Fresh mint sprig (optional)

**EXCHANGES PER
SERVING:**
1 Starch
1 Fruit

PER SERVING:
Calories 132
Carbohydrate 28.3g
Protein 4.3g
Fat 1.2g
Cholesterol 27mg
Fiber 1.4g
Sodium 366mg

1 Prepare vanilla pudding according to package directions, using 2 cups skim milk. Cover and chill thoroughly.

2 Tear ladyfingers into bite-size pieces. Place half the torn ladyfingers in a 1½-quart trifle bowl; brush with melted strawberry spread.

3 Combine strawberries, pineapple, and grapes in a medium bowl. Place half the fruit mixture over ladyfingers. Top with half of pudding. Repeat procedure with remaining ladyfingers, fruit mixture, and pudding. Cover and chill. If desired, garnish with strawberry slices and a mint sprig. Yield: 8 servings.

PEACH TRIFLE

EXCHANGES PER
SERVING:
1 Starch
1 Fruit
½ Skim Milk

PER SERVING:
Calories 162
Carbohydrate 34.3g
Protein 5.6g
Fat 0.2g
Cholesterol 1mg
Fiber 0.8g
Sodium 210mg

1 (8-ounce) carton vanilla nonfat yogurt
   sweetened with aspartame
1 (3.4-ounce) package sugar-free vanilla
   instant pudding mix
2 cups skim milk
⅓ cup low-sugar strawberry spread
1 tablespoon dry sherry
8 ounces angel food cake, cut into ¾-
   inch cubes and divided
2 cups canned sliced peaches in juice,
   drained and divided
   Fresh strawberry slices (optional)
   Fresh mint sprigs (optional)

1 Spoon yogurt onto several layers of heavy-duty paper towels; spread to ½-inch thickness. Cover with additional paper towels; let stand 5 minutes. Scrape yogurt into a bowl, using a rubber spatula.

2 Combine pudding mix and milk, stirring with a wire whisk until blended. Stir drained yogurt into pudding mixture; set aside.

3 Combine strawberry spread and sherry, stirring with a wire whisk until blended; set aside.

4 Arrange half of cake cubes in a 2-quart trifle bowl or straight-sided glass bowl. Spread half of pudding mixture over cake cubes. Drizzle strawberry mixture evenly over pudding. Arrange 1 cup sliced peaches over strawberry mixture. Repeat layering procedure with remaining cake, pudding and peaches. If desired, garnish with strawberry slices and mint sprigs. Yield: 8 servings.

Fish &
Shellfish

BAKED FISH AND CHIPS

YIELD: 4 servings

EXCHANGES PER
SERVING:
3 Lean Meat
2 Starch

PER SERVING:
Calories 312
Carbohydrate 32.9g
Protein 25.5g
Fat 8.8g
Cholesterol 59mg
Fiber 3.4g
Sodium 418mg

✿ It takes 2 slices of whole wheat bread to make 1 cup of soft breadcrumbs.

½ pound baking potatoes, very thinly sliced
½ pound sweet potatoes, very thinly sliced
   Vegetable cooking spray
 1 tablespoon olive oil
 1 teaspoon dried rosemary, crushed
¼ teaspoon dried thyme
¼ teaspoon salt
⅛ teaspoon coarsely ground pepper
 3 tablespoons reduced-fat mayonnaise
¾ teaspoon grated lemon rind
 1 tablespoon fresh lemon juice
 1 tablespoon water
 4 (4-ounce) flounder fillets
 1 cup soft whole wheat breadcrumbs, toasted
 1 teaspoon coarsely ground pepper
¾ teaspoon garlic powder
   Fresh rosemary sprigs (optional)
   Lemon wedges (optional)

1 Place sliced potatoes in a single layer on a large baking sheet coated with cooking spray. Brush evenly with oil. Sprinkle rosemary and next 3 ingredients over potato slices. Bake at 425° for 30 to 35 minutes or until potato slices are lightly browned, turning once.

2 Combine mayonnaise and next 3 ingredients. Brush both sides of fish fillets with mixture. Combine breadcrumbs, 1 teaspoon pepper, and garlic powder; dredge fish in breadcrumb mixture. Place on a baking sheet coated with cooking spray. Bake at 425° for 25 minutes. Serve fish with potato slices. If desired, garnish with rosemary sprigs and lemon wedges. Yield: 4 servings.

FLOUNDER EN PAPILLOTE

YIELD: 2 servings

Vegetable cooking spray
¼ cup chopped green onions
2 teaspoons minced garlic
2 tablespoons dry white wine
2 (4-ounce) flounder fillets
¾ cup sliced mushrooms
½ cup chopped plum tomato
2 teaspoons chopped fresh oregano
2 teaspoons chopped fresh basil
¼ teaspoon salt
¼ teaspoon pepper
¼ teaspoon chopped serrano chili pepper
2 bay leaves

EXCHANGES PER SERVING:
3 Very Lean Meat
1 Vegetable

PER SERVING:
Calories 136
Carbohydrate 6.2g
Protein 23.0g
Fat 2.1g
Cholesterol 54mg
Fiber 1.4g
Sodium 394mg

1 Coat a medium nonstick skillet with cooking spray; place over medium-high heat until hot. Add green onions and garlic; sauté until tender. Remove skillet from heat; stir in wine. Set aside.

2 Cut 2 (12-inch) squares of parchment paper; fold each square in half, and trim each into a heart shape. Place parchment hearts on a baking sheet, and open out flat. Coat open side of parchment paper with cooking spray.

3 Place 1 fillet on half of each parchment heart near the crease. Spoon mushrooms evenly over fillets; top evenly with tomato. Combine oregano and next 4 ingredients; sprinkle evenly over fillets. Top each fillet with a bay leaf. Spoon onion mixture evenly over fillets.

4 Fold paper edges over to seal securely. Starting with rounded edges of hearts, pleat and crimp edges of parchment to make an airtight seal. Bake at 425° for 15 minutes or until packets are puffed and lightly browned.

5 Place packets on individual plates; cut an opening in the top of each packet; fold paper back. Serve immediately. Yield: 2 servings.

CATFISH BARBECUE

EXCHANGES PER
SERVING:
3 Lean Meat

PER SERVING:
Calories 155
Carbohydrate 1.8g
Protein 20.7g
Fat 6.5g
Cholesterol 66mg
Fiber 0.0g
Sodium 79mg

⅓ cup reduced-calorie ketchup
1 tablespoon lemon juice
1 teaspoon granulated brown sugar
  substitute
2 teaspoons vegetable oil
1 teaspoon low-sodium Worcestershire
  sauce
½ teaspoon dried marjoram
¼ teaspoon garlic powder
¼ teaspoon ground red pepper
6 (4-ounce) catfish fillets
  Vegetable cooking spray
  Lemon rind curls (optional)
  Fresh parsley sprigs (optional)

1 Combine first 8 ingredients in a small bowl. Arrange fillets in a 13- x 9- x 2-inch baking dish coated with cooking spray. Pour ketchup mixture over fillets; cover and marinate in refrigerator 30 minutes, turning once.

2 Remove fillets from marinade, reserving marinade. Place marinade in a small saucepan; bring to a boil. Remove from heat; set aside.

3 Place fillets on rack of a broiler pan coated with cooking spray. Broil 5½ inches from heat (with electric oven door partially opened) 14 to 15 minutes or until fish flakes easily when tested with a fork, basting occasionally with marinade. Transfer to a serving platter. If desired, garnish with lemon rind curls and parsley sprigs. Yield: 6 servings.

OVEN-FRIED CATFISH

YIELD: 4 servings

1 tablespoon reduced-calorie mayonnaise
1 tablespoon low-fat sour cream
1 teaspoon lemon juice
4 (4-ounce) farm-raised catfish fillets
½ cup crushed corn flakes cereal
2 tablespoons dried parsley flakes
½ teaspoon paprika
¼ teaspoon pepper
⅛ to ¼ teaspoon garlic powder
  Vegetable cooking spray
  Lemon wedges

EXCHANGES PER SERVING:
3 Lean Meat
½ Starch

PER SERVING:
Calories 186
Carbohydrate 8.8g
Protein 21.7g
Fat 6.6g
Cholesterol 68mg
Fiber 0.3g
Sodium 191mg

1 Combine first 3 ingredients; stir well. Coat fillets with mayonnaise mixture.

2 Combine cereal and next 4 ingredients; dredge one side of each fillet in cereal mixture.

3 Place fillets, coated side up, on a baking sheet coated with cooking spray. Sprinkle any remaining cereal mixture over fillets. Bake at 450° for 12 to 15 minutes or until fish flakes easily when tested with a fork. Serve with lemon wedges, if desired. Yield: 4 servings.

BAKED CATFISH FILLETS

EXCHANGES PER
SERVING:
2 Lean Meat
1 Vegetable

PER SERVING:
Calories 144
Carbohydrate 4.9g
Protein 16.5g
Fat 6.5g
Cholesterol 51mg
Fiber 0.5g
Sodium 95mg

6 (4-ounce) farm-raised catfish fillets
  Vegetable cooking spray
2 tablespoons reduced-calorie margarine,
  melted
1 tablespoon lemon juice
¼ teaspoon ground ginger
¼ teaspoon curry powder
¼ teaspoon dried crushed red pepper
  Tricolored Pepper Relish

1 Place catfish fillets on rack of a broiler pan coated with cooking spray.

2 Combine margarine and next 4 ingredients; stir well. Brush fillets with margarine mixture.

3 Bake at 400° for 25 to 30 minutes or until fish flakes easily when tested with a fork. Transfer fillets to a serving platter. Top each serving with ¼ cup Tricolored Pepper Relish. Yield: 6 servings.

TRICOLORED PEPPER RELISH

½ cup pineapple tidbits in juice, drained
½ cup chopped sweet red pepper
⅓ cup chopped green pepper
⅓ cup chopped sweet yellow or orange
  pepper
1 tablespoon cider vinegar
1 tablespoon unsweetened pineapple juice
1 packet sugar substitute with aspartame
1 teaspoon peeled, minced gingerroot
⅛ to ¼ teaspoon dried crushed red pepper

1 Combine all ingredients in a small bowl; stir well. Cover and chill at least 30 minutes. Yield: 1½ cups.

GARLIC FLOUNDER

YIELD: 6 servings

6 (4-ounce) flounder fillets
¼ cup low-sodium soy sauce
2 tablespoons minced garlic
1½ tablespoons lemon juice
2 teaspoons granulated sugar substitute
1 tablespoon mixed peppercorns, crushed
  Vegetable cooking spray
  Fresh parsley sprigs (optional)

EXCHANGES PER SERVING:
3 Very Lean Meat

PER SERVING:
Calories 113
Carbohydrate 1.6g
Protein 21.5g
Fat 1.5g
Cholesterol 60mg
Fiber 0.3g
Sodium 225mg

1 Place fish fillets in a shallow baking dish. Combine soy sauce and next 3 ingredients; pour over fish. Cover and marinate in refrigerator 30 minutes.

2 Remove fish from marinade; discard marinade. Sprinkle fish evenly with crushed peppercorns, gently pressing pepper into fish.

3 Place fish on rack of a broiler pan coated with cooking spray. Broil 5½ inches from heat (with electric oven door partially opened) 8 to 10 minutes or until fish flakes easily when tested with a fork. Transfer to a serving platter, and garnish with parsley sprigs, if desired. Yield: 6 servings.

ASIAN-STYLE GROUPER

EXCHANGES PER
SERVING:
3 Very Lean Meat
2 Vegetable
1 Fat

PER SERVING:
Calories 193
Carbohydrate 8.1g
Protein 26.6g
Fat 5.5g
Cholesterol 53mg
Fiber 2.6g
Sodium 133mg

2 (8-ounce) grouper or other white fish
   steaks (1 inch thick)
2 teaspoons low-sodium soy sauce
½ teaspoon peeled, finely grated
   gingerroot
2 teaspoons dark sesame oil
2 cups fresh snow pea pods, trimmed
   (about ½ pound)
1½ cups thinly sliced fresh mushrooms
4 green onions, sliced into ½-inch pieces
1 teaspoon sesame seeds, toasted

1 Cut each steak into 2 equal portions, and arrange in an 8-inch square baking dish. Top with soy sauce and gingerroot. Cover and bake at 425° for 25 minutes or until fish flakes easily when tested with a fork.

2 Heat oil in a nonstick skillet over medium-high heat. Add snow peas, mushrooms, and green onions; sauté 5 minutes or until crisp tender. Sprinkle with sesame seeds. Serve snow pea mixture with fish. Yield: 4 servings.

GRILLED GROUPER TANGERINE

3 (8-ounce) grouper fillets
¼ cup frozen tangerine juice concentrate, thawed and undiluted
2 tablespoons dry vermouth
2 teaspoons vegetable oil
½ teaspoon dried rosemary
¼ teaspoon dried thyme
¼ teaspoon pepper
   Vegetable cooking spray
2 tablespoons thinly sliced green onions
2 tablespoons finely chopped sweet red pepper
   Fresh rosemary and thyme sprigs (optional)

1 Place grouper fillets in a 13- x 9- x 2-inch baking dish.

2 Combine tangerine concentrate and next 5 ingredients in a small bowl; stir well. Pour tangerine mixture over fillets; cover and marinate in refrigerator 2 hours, turning once.

3 Remove fillets from marinade, reserving marinade. Bring marinade to a boil in a small saucepan; remove from heat, and set aside.

4 Coat grill rack with cooking spray; place rack on grill over medium-hot coals (350° to 400°). Place fillets on rack; grill, uncovered, 5 minutes on each side or until fish flakes easily when tested with a fork, basting frequently with marinade.

5 Transfer fillets to a serving platter. Combine green onions and red pepper; spoon mixture evenly over fillets. If desired, garnish with rosemary and thyme sprigs. Yield: 6 servings.

YIELD: 6 servings

EXCHANGES PER SERVING:
3 Very Lean Meat
1 Vegetable

PER SERVING:
Calories 143
Carbohydrate 4.7g
Protein 22.3g
Fat 2.8g
Cholesterol 42mg
Fiber 0.2g
Sodium 62mg

🐟 If you prefer, substitute 2 tablespoons of water for vermouth.

HALIBUT WITH VEGETABLES

All you need to steam the fish in this recipe is a sheet of aluminum foil. Make the foil packets slightly larger than the food so that the steam can circulate.

EXCHANGES PER
SERVING:
3 Very Lean Meat
1 Vegetable

PER SERVING:
Calories 140
Carbohydrate 3.2g
Protein 24.6g
Fat 2.7g
Cholesterol 53mg
Fiber 1.2g
Sodium 73mg

4 (4-ounce) halibut steaks
1 cup small frozen broccoli flowerets, thawed
½ cup shredded carrot
2 tablespoons chopped green onions
2 tablespoons dry white wine
¾ teaspoon garlic powder
½ teaspoon dried dillweed

1 Cut 4 (18- x 12-inch) pieces of heavy-duty aluminum foil. Center 1 halibut steak on lower half of each piece of foil; top each with ¼ cup broccoli, 2 tablespoons carrot, and 1½ teaspoons green onions. Combine wine, garlic powder, and dillweed; stir well. Spoon wine mixture evenly over vegetables.

2 Fold upper halves of foil over steaks, meeting bottom edges of foil. Seal edges together, making a tight ½-inch fold. Fold again. Allow space for heat circulation and expansion. Fold side edges of foil to seal.

3 Place packets on a baking sheet. Bake at 450° for 10 minutes. Cut an "X" in tops of packets; fold foil back. Transfer vegetable-topped steaks to warm plates, spooning juices over each. Yield: 4 servings.

CRISPY ORANGE ROUGHY

Sprinkle fillets with flour, dip in an egg white wash, and then coat with seasoned cornmeal for a surprisingly crisp crust.

2 egg whites, lightly beaten
2 tablespoons water
¼ cup cornmeal
¼ cup grated Parmesan cheese
½ teaspoon dried oregano
½ teaspoon dried parsley flakes
¼ teaspoon salt
¼ teaspoon pepper
6 (4-ounce) orange roughy fillets
3 tablespoons all-purpose flour
    Vegetable cooking spray
1 tablespoon vegetable oil
    Lemon wedges (optional)
    Fresh parsley sprigs (optional)

1 Combine egg whites and water in a shallow dish. Combine cornmeal and next 5 ingredients in a medium bowl; stir well.

2 Sprinkle each side of fillets with flour. Dip fillets into egg white mixture, and dredge in cornmeal mixture.

3 Coat a large nonstick skillet with cooking spray; add oil. Place skillet over medium-high heat until hot. Add fillets, and cook 4 to 5 minutes on each side or until golden and fish flakes easily when tested with a fork. If desired, garnish with lemon wedges and parsley. Yield: 6 servings.

YIELD: 6 servings

EXCHANGES PER SERVING:
2½ Lean Meat
1 Vegetable

PER SERVING:
Calories 148
Carbohydrate 7.2g
Protein 19.6g
Fat 4.0g
Cholesterol 25mg
Fiber 0.7g
Sodium 233mg

❧ Orange roughy, a firm-flesh fish, is readily available in specialty fish markets and most supermarkets. This versatile fish can be poached, baked, broiled, or grilled.

Orange Roughy Olé

YIELD: 4 servings

EXCHANGES PER
SERVING:
2 Very Lean Meat
2 Vegetable

PER SERVING:
Calories 150
Carbohydrate 12.0g
Protein 18.5g
Fat 3.2g
Cholesterol 23mg
Fiber 1.1g
Sodium 335mg

2 teaspoons olive oil
1 cup sliced onion
2 cloves garlic, minced
1 sweet yellow pepper, cut into rings
1 (14½-ounce) can Mexican-style stewed
    tomatoes with jalapeño peppers and
    spices, undrained
4 (4-ounce) orange roughy fillets
    Dash of garlic powder
    Dash of ground red pepper

1 Heat oil in a large nonstick skillet over medium heat. Add onion and garlic; sauté 7 minutes or until tender. Add yellow pepper and tomato; cook over medium-high heat 3 minutes. Add fish; sprinkle with garlic powder and red pepper. Cover, reduce heat, and simmer 5 minutes.

2 Turn fish; cover and simmer 5 additional minutes or until fish flakes easily when tested with a fork. Transfer fish to individual serving plates, and keep warm. Reserve tomato mixture in skillet.

3 Cook tomato mixture over medium-high heat 3 minutes or until thickened, stirring often. Spoon tomato mixture evenly over fish. Yield: 4 servings.

ASIAN-GRILLED SALMON

YIELD: 2 servings

1½ tablespoons granulated brown
    sugar substitute
3 tablespoons water
1 tablespoon low-sodium soy sauce
2 teaspoons peeled, minced gingerroot
2 teaspoons minced green onions
2 teaspoons lemon juice
½ teaspoon minced garlic
    Dash of dried crushed red pepper
2 (4-ounce) salmon steaks (½ inch thick)
    Vegetable cooking spray
2 tablespoons nonfat mayonnaise
1 tablespoon finely chopped cilantro
½ teaspoon peeled, grated gingerroot
¼ teaspoon crushed garlic
    Fresh cilantro sprigs (optional)

EXCHANGES PER SERVING:
3 Lean Meat
½ Starch

PER SERVING:
Calories 226
Carbohydrate 7.2g
Protein 24.5g
Fat 10.0g
Cholesterol 77mg
Fiber 0.3g
Sodium 458mg

1 Combine first 8 ingredients in a large heavy-duty, zip-top plastic bag; add salmon. Seal bag, and marinate salmon in refrigerator 2 hours, turning bag occasionally. Remove salmon from marinade, reserving marinade. Place marinade in a small saucepan; bring to a boil. Remove from heat, and set aside.

2 Coat grill rack with cooking spray; place on grill over medium-hot coals (350° to 400°). Place salmon on rack; grill, uncovered, 5 to 6 minutes on each side or until fish flakes easily when tested with a fork, basting frequently with reserved marinade.

3 Combine mayonnaise and next 3 ingredients, stirring well. Top each salmon steak with 1 tablespoon mayonnaise mixture. Garnish with cilantro sprigs, if desired. Yield: 2 servings.

BASIL-CRUSTED SALMON

EXCHANGES PER
SERVING:
3 Lean Meat
½ Starch

PER SERVING:
Calories 193
Carbohydrate 6.8g
Protein 25.2g
Fat 6.6g
Cholesterol 64mg
Fiber 0.3g
Sodium 193mg

✎ For 1½ cups of soft breadcrumbs, you'll need about 3 slices of bread. Tear the bread into pieces, and process in a mini-food chopper until the bread is in fine crumbs. Broil the crumbs in a pan on the middle oven rack for about 3 minutes.

Olive-oil flavored vegetable cooking
 spray
1 teaspoon olive oil
2 teaspoons minced garlic
3 tablespoons finely chopped fresh basil
1 tablespoon fresh lemon juice
1½ cups soft breadcrumbs, lightly toasted
¼ cup freshly grated Romano cheese
½ teaspoon freshly ground pepper
6 (4-ounce) salmon fillets
 Lemon wedges (optional)
 Fresh basil sprigs (optional)

1 Coat a large nonstick skillet with cooking spray; add oil. Place over medium-high heat until hot. Add garlic; sauté 30 seconds. Add basil and lemon juice; sauté 1 minute. Add breadcrumbs, cheese, and pepper; toss well.

2 Place fish in a single layer in a 13- x 9- x 2-inch baking dish coated with cooking spray. Spoon breadcrumb mixture evenly over fish. Cover and bake at 350° for 25 minutes or until fish flakes easily when tested with a fork. Broil 5½ inches from heat (with electric oven door partially opened) 3 to 5 minutes or until topping is lightly browned. Serve with lemon wedges, and garnish with basil, if desired. Yield: 6 servings.

POACHED SALMON ON ZUCCHINI

YIELD: 4 servings

EXCHANGES PER
SERVING:
3 Lean Meat
1 Vegetable

PER SERVING:
Calories 216
Carbohydrate 3.7g
Protein 25.8g
Fat 10.5g
Cholesterol 77mg
Fiber 0.6g
Sodium 221mg

4 (4-ounce) salmon steaks (½ inch thick)
   Vegetable cooking spray
½ cup skim milk
2 tablespoons water
¼ teaspoon chicken-flavored bouillon
   granules
3 medium zucchini (about 1 pound)
¼ teaspoon salt
¾ teaspoon minced fresh basil
1 teaspoon poppy seeds
   Fresh basil sprigs (optional)

1 Place salmon in a large nonstick skillet coated with cooking spray. Combine milk, water, and bouillon granules; pour over salmon. Bring to a boil; cover, reduce heat, and simmer 8 minutes or until fish flakes easily when tested with a fork. Remove fish from skillet; set aside, and keep warm. Wipe skillet with a paper towel.

2 Using a vegetable peeler, cut zucchini lengthwise into thin strips. Coat skillet with cooking spray. Place over medium-high heat until hot. Add zucchini, salt, and minced basil; sauté until tender. Add poppy seeds; toss lightly.

3 Transfer zucchini to a serving platter. Top with salmon. Garnish with basil sprigs, if desired. Yield: 4 servings.

CREOLE RED SNAPPER

YIELD: 4 servings

EXCHANGES PER
SERVING:
3 Very Lean Meat
1 Vegetable

PER SERVING:
Calories 173
Carbohydrate 6.9g
Protein 24.3g
Fat 5.0g
Cholesterol 42mg
Fiber 1.1g
Sodium 243mg

Serve the snapper with French bread, if desired.
(Bread is not included in analysis.)

1 tablespoon olive oil
¼ cup chopped onion
¼ cup chopped green pepper
1 clove garlic, minced
1 (14½-ounce) can no-salt-added whole
   tomatoes, undrained and chopped
2 teaspoons low-sodium Worcestershire
   sauce
2 teaspoons red wine vinegar
½ teaspoon dried basil
¼ teaspoon salt
¼ teaspoon freshly ground pepper
   Dash of hot sauce
4 (4-ounce) red snapper fillets
   Fresh basil sprigs (optional)

1 Heat oil in a large nonstick skillet over
medium-high heat until hot. Add onion,
green pepper, and garlic; sauté until tender.

2 Add tomato and next 6 ingredients. Bring to
a boil; add fillets, spooning tomato mixture
over fish. Reduce heat; cover and simmer 12
minutes or until fish flakes easily when tested
with a fork. Garnish with basil sprigs, if desired.
Yield: 4 servings.

GRECIAN SNAPPER

YIELD: 6 servings

Vegetable cooking spray
1 teaspoon olive oil
1 cup chopped onion
1 clove garlic, minced
3 medium tomatoes, peeled, seeded, and chopped
¼ cup dry white wine
1 teaspoon dried oregano
¼ teaspoon salt
⅛ teaspoon pepper
6 (4-ounce) snapper fillets
2 ounces feta cheese, crumbled
2 tablespoons chopped fresh parsley
1 tablespoon chopped ripe olives
Lemon twists (optional)
Fresh parsley sprigs (optional)

EXCHANGES PER SERVING:
4 Very Lean Meat
1 Vegetable

PER SERVING:
Calories 206
Carbohydrate 6.3g
Protein 32.2g
Fat 5.3g
Cholesterol 62mg
Fiber 1.5g
Sodium 288mg

1 Coat a large nonstick skillet with cooking spray; add olive oil, and place over medium heat until hot. Add onion and garlic; sauté until tender. Stir in tomato and next 4 ingredients. Bring to a boil; reduce heat, and simmer, uncovered, 20 minutes.

2 Rinse fillets with cold water, and pat dry. Place in a 13- x 9- x 2-inch baking dish coated with cooking spray; spoon tomato mixture over fillets. Bake, uncovered, at 350° for 15 minutes or until fish flakes easily when tested with a fork.

3 Sprinkle cheese, parsley, and olives over fillets, and serve immediately. If desired, garnish with lemon twists and parsley. Yield: 6 servings.

SALSA SNAPPER

EXCHANGES PER
SERVING:
4 Very Lean Meat
1 Starch
1 Vegetable

PER SERVING:
Calories 240
Carbohydrate 19.8g
Protein 34.5g
Fat 3.0g
Cholesterol 54mg
Fiber 3.5g
Sodium 288mg

3 medium ears fresh corn
　Vegetable cooking spray
1 cup seeded, chopped tomato
½ cup chopped purple onion
½ cup minced fresh cilantro
1 tablespoon lime juice
½ teaspoon hot sauce
1 (4½-ounce) can chopped green chiles
4 (4-ounce) red snapper fillets
½ cup plain nonfat yogurt
½ teaspoon garlic powder
¼ teaspoon salt

1 Remove husks and silks from corn. Coat 3 large pieces of heavy-duty aluminum foil with cooking spray. Wrap each ear in a piece of foil. Twist foil at each end. Bake at 500° for 20 minutes. Remove from oven, and let cool slightly. Cut corn from cob, and place corn in a medium bowl. Add tomato and next 5 ingredients; stir well.

2 Place 1 fish fillet on each of 4 additional large pieces of heavy-duty foil coated with cooking spray. Combine yogurt, garlic powder, and salt; spread evenly on both sides of fillets. Let stand 15 minutes.

3 Spoon corn mixture evenly onto fillets. Wrap each fillet securely, sealing edges. Bake at 450° for 20 to 25 minutes or until fish flakes easily when tested with a fork. To serve, remove from foil, and transfer to serving plates. Yield: 4 servings.

SNAPPER VERACRUZ

If snapper isn't available, grouper,
redfish, or halibut will work just as well
in this Mexican seafood dish.

4 (4-ounce) red snapper fillets
½ cup lime juice
   Vegetable cooking spray
½ cup chopped onion
2 cups chopped tomato
1 (2-ounce) jar diced pimiento, drained
2 tablespoons canned chopped green
   chiles
1 teaspoon dried parsley flakes
¼ teaspoon salt
   Dash of hot sauce
   Lime slices (optional)
   Flat-leaf parsley sprigs (optional)

1 Place fillets in a shallow dish; pour lime juice over fillets. Cover and marinate in refrigerator 15 minutes.

2 Coat a large nonstick skillet with cooking spray; place over medium-high heat until hot. Add onion, and cook until tender. Add tomato and next 5 ingredients. Cover and cook over medium heat 7 minutes or until thoroughly heated.

3 Remove fillets from lime juice; discard lime juice. Place fillets in skillet with tomato mixture. Cover and cook 6 to 8 minutes or until fish flakes easily when tested with a fork. Transfer fillets to individual serving plates, and keep warm.

4 Continue cooking tomato mixture, uncovered, 10 minutes or until liquid evaporates. Spoon tomato mixture evenly over fillets. If desired, garnish with lime slices and parsley sprigs. Yield: 4 servings.

YIELD: 4 servings

**EXCHANGES PER
SERVING:**
3 Very Lean Meat
1 Vegetable

PER SERVING:
Calories 149
Carbohydrate 7.9g
Protein 24.6g
Fat 2.1g
Cholesterol 42mg
Fiber 1.7g
Sodium 242mg

Fresh fish is best cooked the day it's purchased. If you need to keep it overnight, rinse fish under cold water, pat dry, and wrap in wax paper. Seal fish in a zip-top plastic bag; place bag in a bowl of ice cubes, and store in the refrigerator.

SWORDFISH BROCHETTES

For only a slight difference in calories, you can substitute another firm-flesh fish like tuna or mahimahi for swordfish.

EXCHANGES PER
SERVING:
3 Lean Meat

PER SERVING:
Calories 167
Carbohydrate 5.3g
Protein 24.1g
Fat 5.3g
Cholesterol 44mg
Fiber 1.2g
Sodium 156mg

1 tablespoon coarse-grained mustard
1 pound swordfish steaks (¾ inch thick)
1 large zucchini, cut into 8 slices
1 large sweet red pepper, seeded and cut
   into 8 (1½-inch) cubes
2 small purple onions, quartered
8 medium-size fresh mushroom caps
   Vegetable cooking spray
   Lemon wedges (optional)

✒ Timing is critical when cooking fish because it's so delicate. Perfectly cooked fish will be moist and tender; overcooked fish will be dry and tough. As fish cooks, its translucent flesh turns opaque (or solid) in appearance.

1 Spread mustard over swordfish steaks. Cut steaks into 12 (1¼-inch) pieces. Arrange swordfish, zucchini, pepper, onion, and mushrooms alternately on 4 (12-inch) skewers.

2 Place kabobs on rack of a broiler pan coated with cooking spray. Broil 5½ inches from heat (with electric oven door partially opened) 10 to 12 minutes or until fish flakes easily when tested with a fork, turning occasionally. Serve kabobs with lemon wedges, if desired. Yield: 4 servings.

Grilling Instructions: Coat grill rack with cooking spray; place on grill over medium-hot coals (350° to 400°). Place kabobs on rack; grill 10 to 12 minutes or until fish flakes easily when tested with a fork, turning occasionally.

SWORDFISH SANTA FE

YIELD: 6 servings

6 (4-ounce) swordfish steaks (¾ inch thick)
⅓ cup lime juice
⅓ cup beer
1½ tablespoons vegetable oil
1 tablespoon ground cumin
1 tablespoon Dijon mustard
¼ teaspoon salt
2 cloves garlic, minced
  Vegetable cooking spray
  Salsa Fresca

EXCHANGES PER SERVING:
3 Lean Meat
1 Vegetable

PER SERVING:
Calories 179
Carbohydrate 6.1g
Protein 20.4g
Fat 8.0g
Cholesterol 38mg
Fiber 0.8g
Sodium 366mg

1 Place steaks in a shallow dish. Combine lime juice and next 6 ingredients; pour over steaks. Cover; marinate in refrigerator at least 30 minutes, turning once.

2 Remove steaks from marinade, reserving marinade. Bring marinade to a boil in a saucepan; boil 2 minutes. Remove from heat.

3 Coat grill rack with cooking spray; place on grill over medium-hot coals (350° to 400°). Place steaks on rack; grill, covered, 4 to 6 minutes on each side or until fish flakes easily with a fork, basting frequently with marinade. Serve with Salsa Fresca. Yield: 6 servings.

SALSA FRESCA

1 cup coarsely chopped tomato
⅓ cup chopped onion
¼ cup chopped green pepper
1½ tablespoons lime juice
4 teaspoons dried cilantro
1 teaspoon seeded, chopped jalapeño pepper
1 clove garlic, minced
¼ cup no-salt-added tomato juice
¼ teaspoon salt
⅛ teaspoon ground cumin

1 Position knife blade in food processor bowl; add first 7 ingredients. Process 10 seconds. Add tomato juice, salt, and cumin. Process 10 seconds. Cover and chill. Yield: 1½ cups.

Island Swordfish

EXCHANGES PER
SERVING:
3 Lean Meat
½ Fruit

PER SERVING:
Calories 178
Carbohydrate 8.2g
Protein 22.8g
Fat 5.3g
Cholesterol 44mg
Fiber 0.8g
Sodium 459mg

½ cup chopped ripe mango
¼ cup peeled, seeded, and chopped
   papaya
2 tablespoons finely chopped celery
1 tablespoon minced fresh parsley
1 tablespoon lime juice
2 teaspoons finely chopped purple onion
1 teaspoon grated fresh ginger
1 teaspoon seeded, minced jalapeño
   pepper
2 tablespoons rice vinegar
2 tablespoons Dijon mustard
1 tablespoon plus 1 teaspoon low-sodium
   soy sauce
4 (4-ounce) swordfish steaks (¾ inch
   thick)
   Vegetable cooking spray
   Fresh parsley sprigs (optional)

1 Combine first 8 ingredients in a small bowl, tossing gently.

2 Combine vinegar, mustard, and soy sauce in a small bowl; stir with a wire whisk until well blended. Brush over steaks.

3 Coat a grill rack with cooking spray; place on grill over medium-hot coals (350° to 400°). Place steaks on rack, and grill, covered, 5 minutes on each side or until fish flakes easily when tested with a fork. Serve with mango mixture. Garnish with parsley sprigs, if desired. Yield: 4 servings.

BLACKENED TUNA

YIELD: 6 servings

1 tablespoon onion powder
1 tablespoon dried basil
2 teaspoons dried thyme
½ teaspoon ground white pepper
½ teaspoon black pepper
⅛ to ¼ teaspoon ground red pepper
6 (4-ounce) tuna steaks (½ inch thick)
  Vegetable cooking spray
1½ tablespoons margarine, melted
  Fresh thyme sprigs (optional)
  Lime wedges (optional)

**EXCHANGES PER
SERVING:**
4 Lean Meat

PER SERVING:
Calories 191
Carbohydrate 1.8g
Protein 25.7g
Fat 8.4g
Cholesterol 42mg
Fiber 0.3g
Sodium 77mg

1 Combine first 6 ingredients in a small bowl, and stir well. Rub tuna steaks with pepper mixture.

2 Coat grill rack with cooking spray; place on grill over medium-hot (350° to 400°) coals. Place tuna on rack; drizzle with margarine, and grill 4 to 5 minutes on each side or until tuna flakes easily when tested with a fork. If desired, garnish with thyme sprigs and lime wedges (not included in analysis). Yield: 6 servings.

TROUT AMANDINE

EXCHANGES PER
SERVING:
3 Lean Meat
1 Fat

PER SERVING:
Calories 231
Carbohydrate 2.0g
Protein 24.4g
Fat 14.2g
Cholesterol 64mg
Fiber 0.8g
Sodium 288mg

Serve with a fresh vegetable like steamed green beans (beans not included in analysis).

¼ cup reduced-calorie margarine, melted
1 tablespoon chopped onion
1 tablespoon lemon juice
¼ cup sliced almonds, toasted
1 tablespoon chopped fresh parsley
4 (4-ounce) rainbow trout fillets
2 teaspoons lemon juice
¼ teaspoon salt
⅛ teaspoon black pepper
⅛ teaspoon ground red pepper
Lemon slices (optional)

1 Combine first 3 ingredients in a small saucepan; cook over medium heat 5 minutes or until onion is tender, stirring occasionally. Stir in almonds and parsley. Set aside, and keep warm.

2 Line an 11- x 7- x 1½-inch baking dish with aluminum foil. Place fish in dish; sprinkle with lemon juice and next 3 ingredients. Broil 5½ inches from heat (with electric oven door partially opened) 8 minutes or until fish flakes easily when tested with a fork. Transfer fish to individual serving plates, and top with almond mixture. Garnish with lemon slices, if desired. Yield: 4 servings.

Clams With Angel Hair Pasta

1 dozen littleneck clams
2 teaspoons cornmeal
  Olive oil-flavored vegetable cooking
  spray
1½ teaspoons minced garlic
2 cups peeled, seeded, and chopped
  tomato
¼ cup clam juice
¼ cup dry white wine
⅛ teaspoon dried crushed red pepper
2 ounces capellini (angel hair pasta),
  uncooked
1½ teaspoons chopped flat-leaf parsley

YIELD: 2 servings

EXCHANGES PER
SERVING:
2 Very Lean Meat
2 Starch
1 Vegetable

PER SERVING:
Calories 236
Carbohydrate 34.3g
Protein 19.6g
Fat 2.5g
Cholesterol 36mg
Fiber 3.3g
Sodium 149mg

1 Scrub clams thoroughly, discarding any that are cracked or open. Place remaining clams in a large bowl; cover with cold water, and sprinkle with cornmeal. Let clams stand 30 minutes. Drain and rinse clams; set aside. Discard cornmeal.

2 Coat a medium nonstick skillet with cooking spray. Place over medium-high heat until hot. Add garlic, and sauté 30 seconds. Add tomato and next 3 ingredients. Bring to a boil; reduce heat, and simmer, uncovered, 15 minutes, stirring occasionally.

3 Place clams on top of tomato mixture. Cover and cook 8 to 10 minutes or until clams open. Remove and discard any unopened clams.

4 Cook pasta according to package directions, omitting salt and fat. Drain. Remove clams from tomato mixture; set aside. Toss pasta with tomato mixture, and transfer to serving plates. Arrange clams evenly over pasta. Sprinkle with parsley. Yield: 2 servings.

🍃 Cook pasta until al dente; this means pliable, but firm to the bite and no longer starchy.

LINGUINE WITH RED CLAM SAUCE

Vegetable cooking spray
¼ cup chopped onion
1 (14½-ounce) can no-salt-added whole tomatoes, undrained and chopped
1 (6-ounce) can no-salt-added tomato paste
¼ cup dry white wine
¼ cup no-salt-added tomato juice
1 teaspoon dried basil
½ teaspoon garlic powder
⅛ teaspoon dried crushed red pepper
1 (10-ounce) can whole baby clams, drained
8 ounces linguine, uncooked
¼ cup grated Parmesan cheese
Fresh basil sprigs (optional)

1 Coat a large nonstick skillet with cooking spray; place over medium-high heat until hot. Add onion, and sauté until tender. Add tomato and next 6 ingredients; bring to a boil. Reduce heat, and simmer, uncovered, 10 minutes or until sauce is slightly thickened, stirring occasionally. Stir in clams, and cook until thoroughly heated.

2 Cook linguine according to package directions, omitting salt and fat; drain well.

3 To serve, place linguine evenly on 6 plates; top evenly with clam sauce. Sprinkle each serving with ½ tablespoon Parmesan cheese. Garnish each serving with a basil sprig, if desired. Yield: 6 (1-cup) servings.

FAR EAST CRAB CAKES

YIELD: 4 servings

If you'd like to serve this as an appetizer, divide the crab mixture evenly into 16 small patties. These smaller versions will have about 31 calories each.

2 (6-ounce) cans lump crabmeat, drained
½ cup finely chopped water chestnuts
¼ cup soft breadcrumbs
1 tablespoon plus 1 teaspoon dried
   parsley flakes
½ teaspoon pepper
½ teaspoon dark sesame oil
3 tablespoons reduced-calorie mayonnaise
   Vegetable cooking spray
   Lemon wedges (optional)
   Green onion fan (optional)

1 Combine first 7 ingredients in a small bowl; stir well. Shape into 8 patties.

2 Coat a large nonstick skillet with cooking spray; place over medium-high heat until hot. Add crabmeat patties, and cook 6 to 8 minutes or until lightly browned on both sides, turning once. Transfer to a serving platter. If desired, garnish with lemon wedges and a green onion fan. Yield: 4 servings.

EXCHANGES PER SERVING:
2 Lean Meat
½ Starch

PER SERVING:
Calories 129
Carbohydrate 6.6g
Protein 13.7g
Fat 5.0g
Cholesterol 68mg
Fiber 0.3g
Sodium 283mg

✎ To make a green onion fan, slice off the root and most of the onion's top portion. Cut the onion into 3- or 4-inch lengths, and place on a cutting board. Using a sharp knife, cut several slits at the end of the piece of onion, cutting almost to, but not through, the center. Place in ice water, and chill about 10 minutes or until fan curls.

CRAB MORNAY

YIELD: 4 servings

EXCHANGES PER
SERVING:
3 Very Lean Meat
1 Vegetable

PER SERVING:
Calories 146
Carbohydrate 5.5g
Protein 21.5g
Fat 4.0g
Cholesterol 85mg
Fiber 0.4g
Sodium 478mg

½ cup dry white wine
¼ cup water
1 teaspoon chicken-flavored bouillon
    granules
    Dash of white pepper
1 cup sliced fresh mushrooms
2 tablespoons sliced green onions
¼ cup skim milk
1 tablespoon cornstarch
½ cup (2 ounces) shredded reduced-fat
    Swiss cheese
⅔ pound fresh lump crabmeat, drained
1 (2-ounce) jar chopped pimiento,
    drained
    Vegetable cooking spray
    Sliced green onions (optional)

1 Combine first 4 ingredients in a small saucepan; bring to a boil. Add mushrooms and 2 tablespoons green onions. Cover, reduce heat, and simmer 1 minute or until mushrooms are tender.

2 Combine milk and cornstarch; add to mushroom mixture. Bring to a boil over medium heat; boil 1 minute, stirring constantly. Remove from heat; add cheese, and stir until melted. Stir in crabmeat and pimiento.

3 Spoon crabmeat mixture into 4 baking shells or 4 (6-ounce) ramekins coated with cooking spray. Broil 3 inches from heat (with electric oven door partially opened) 2 minutes or until hot and bubbly. Garnish with green onions, if desired. Yield: 4 servings.

CRABMEAT CASSEROLE

YIELD: 4 servings

1 cup fusilli (corkscrew pasta), uncooked
½ pound fresh asparagus
  Vegetable cooking spray
1 tablespoon plus 1 teaspoon reduced-calorie margarine, melted and divided
2 small carrots, scraped and cut into very thin strips
½ medium-size green pepper, chopped
1 green onion, cut into ½-inch pieces
3 tablespoons dry white wine
1½ tablespoons all-purpose flour
1½ cups skim milk
1½ tablespoons grated Parmesan cheese
1 teaspoon chicken-flavored bouillon granules
½ pound fresh lump crabmeat, drained

EXCHANGES PER SERVING:
2 Very Lean Meat
2 Starch

PER SERVING:
Calories 237
Carbohydrate 28.0g
Protein 20.0g
Fat 5.1g
Cholesterol 60mg
Fiber 2.5g
Sodium 494mg

1 Cook fusilli according to package directions, omitting salt and fat. Drain; set aside.

2 Snap off tough ends of asparagus. Remove scales with a vegetable peeler, if desired. Cut asparagus into 1½-inch pieces.

3 Coat a large skillet with cooking spray; place over medium-high heat. Add 1 teaspoon margarine. Add asparagus, carrot, pepper, and onion; sauté 3 minutes. Add wine. Cook over medium heat until liquid evaporates. Remove from skillet; set aside.

4 Add margarine to skillet; place over low heat. Add flour, stirring until smooth. Cook 1 minute, stirring constantly. Add milk; cook over medium heat, stirring constantly with a wire whisk, until thickened. Add cheese and bouillon granules; stir well.

5 Coat an 11- x 7- x 1½-inch baking dish with cooking spray. Combine pasta, vegetables, cheese sauce, and crabmeat. Spoon into baking dish. Cover and bake at 350° for 20 to 25 minutes. Serve immediately. Yield: 4 servings.

SEAFOOD NEWBURG

EXCHANGES PER
SERVING:
3 Lean Meat
2 Starch
2 Vegetable

PER SERVING:
Calories 372
Carbohydrate 40.6g
Protein 31.7g
Fat 8.5g
Cholesterol 145mg
Fiber 2.4g
Sodium 607mg

Vegetable cooking spray
⅔ cup sliced fresh mushrooms
½ cup chopped onion
¼ cup plus 2 tablespoons all-purpose flour
1 teaspoon vegetable oil
3 cups skim milk
1 egg yolk, lightly beaten
3 ounces Neufchâtel cheese, cubed
¼ cup dry sherry
1 tablespoon lemon juice
¼ teaspoon salt
¼ teaspoon pepper
⅛ teaspoon dry mustard
⅛ teaspoon paprika
Dash of ground red pepper
1 cup coarsely chopped lobster
½ pound fresh lump crabmeat, drained
2½ cups cooked long-grain brown rice
(cooked without salt or fat)

1 Coat a large nonstick skillet with cooking spray. Place over medium-high heat until hot. Add mushrooms and onion; sauté until tender. Remove from skillet, and set aside.

2 Add flour and oil to skillet; cook 1 minute, stirring constantly with a wire whisk. (Mixture will be dry and crumbly.)

3 Combine milk and egg yolk; stir well. Gradually add milk mixture to flour mixture, stirring well. Cook over medium heat, stirring constantly, 15 minutes or until thickened. Add cheese; stir until cheese melts and mixture is smooth.

4 Stir in mushroom mixture, sherry, and next 6 ingredients. Reduce heat; simmer 3 minutes, stirring constantly. Add lobster and crabmeat; simmer 8 minutes or until lobster is done, stirring often. Spoon ½ cup rice onto each plate; top with lobster mixture. Yield: 5 servings.

EASY COASTAL PAELLA

YIELD: 4 servings

12 fresh mussels
  Olive oil-flavored vegetable cooking
    spray
 2 teaspoons olive oil
 1 cup chopped onion
 1 cup chopped leeks
 ⅔ cup chopped celery
 1 tablespoon minced garlic
 1 teaspoon threads of saffron
 2 cups peeled, seeded, and chopped
    tomato
 ½ cup dry white wine
 ½ cup canned low-sodium chicken broth,
    undiluted
 2 (4-ounce) red snapper fillets, skinned
    and cut into bite-size pieces
 1 (4-ounce) monkfish fillet, cut into bite-
    size pieces
 2 cups cooked long-grain rice (cooked
    without salt or fat)
 1 tablespoon plus 1 teaspoon chopped
    fresh parsley

**EXCHANGES PER
SERVING:**
2 Lean Meat
2 Starch
2 Vegetable

PER SERVING:
Calories 283
Carbohydrate 38.2g
Protein 21.8g
Fat 4.7g
Cholesterol 32mg
Fiber 3.1g
Sodium 128mg

1 Scrub mussels with a brush, removing beards. Discard opened, cracked, or heavy mussels (they're filled with sand).

2 Coat a large nonstick skillet with cooking spray; add olive oil. Place over medium-high heat until hot. Add onion and next 4 ingredients; sauté 3 minutes or until vegetables are tender.

3 Add tomato, wine, and chicken broth; cook, uncovered, 10 minutes, stirring occasionally. Add fish and mussels to tomato mixture; cover and cook 5 minutes or until mussels are open and fish flakes easily when tested with a fork.

4 Place ½ cup rice in each individual serving bowl; spoon 1 cup fish mixture over each serving. Sprinkle with parsley. Yield: 4 servings.

ITALIAN SCALLOP KABOBS

**EXCHANGES PER
SERVING:**
3 Very Lean Meat

PER SERVING:
Calories 103
Carbohydrate 3.4g
Protein 17.4g
Fat 1.9g
Cholesterol 36mg
Fiber 0.1g
Sodium 460mg

36 sea scallops (about 1 pound)
 1 (5-ounce) package lean, smoked sliced
      ham, cut into 36 (½-inch-wide) strips
      Vegetable cooking spray
 2 cloves garlic, minced
¼ cup lemon juice
 2 tablespoons minced fresh parsley
¾ teaspoon dried oregano
      Fresh oregano sprigs (optional)
      Lemon rind strips (optional)

1 Wrap each scallop with a strip of ham; thread 6 scallops onto each of 6 (12-inch) skewers. Set aside.

2 Coat a small nonstick skillet with cooking spray; place over medium heat until hot. Add garlic; sauté until golden. Remove from heat, and stir in lemon juice, parsley, and oregano.

3 Coat grill rack with cooking spray; place on grill over medium-hot coals (350° to 400°). Place kabobs on rack, and grill, uncovered, 9 to 10 minutes or until scallops are opaque, turning and basting often with lemon juice mixture. If desired, garnish with oregano sprigs and lemon rind strips. Yield: 6 servings.

Scallop-Vegetable Stir-Fry

YIELD: 2 servings

Try serving this stir-fry with Oriental bean thread noodles instead of rice. After cooking, the brittle, wire-thin strands become translucent. Look for bean thread noodles in the international foods section of most supermarkets or in Oriental food stores.

EXCHANGES PER SERVING:
2 Lean Meat
3 Vegetable

PER SERVING:
Calories 276
Carbohydrate 26.5g
Protein 23.7g
Fat 7.5g
Cholesterol 37mg
Fiber 6.1g
Sodium 516mg

¾ cup canned low-sodium chicken broth, undiluted
1½ tablespoons low-sodium soy sauce
1 tablespoon cornstarch
½ teaspoon sesame oil
  Vegetable cooking spray
2 teaspoons vegetable oil
1¼ cups diagonally sliced carrot
1 cup sliced fresh mushrooms
1 (6-ounce) package frozen snow pea pods, thawed
½ cup diagonally sliced green onions
1 tablespoon peeled, minced ginger
½ pound fresh bay scallops

1 Combine first 4 ingredients in a small bowl, stirring well. Set aside.

2 Coat a wok or nonstick skillet with cooking spray; drizzle vegetable oil around top of wok, coating sides. Heat at medium-high (375°) until hot. Add carrot; stir-fry 1 minute. Add mushrooms; stir-fry 1 minute. Add snow peas; stir-fry 1 minute. Remove vegetables from wok; set aside, and keep warm. Wipe drippings from wok with a paper towel.

3 Coat wok with cooking spray. Add green onions and ginger; stir-fry 30 seconds. Add scallops; stir-fry 1 to 2 minutes or until scallops are opaque. Add vegetables to wok; stir well. Pour broth mixture over vegetable mixture. Cook, stirring constantly, 1 minute or until slightly thickened and thoroughly heated. Yield: 2 servings.

✄ When purchasing fresh bay scallops, count on about 40 to the pound. Since they're highly perishable, cook scallops within two days of purchase. Before cooking, always rinse the scallops well to remove sand and grit.

SWEET-AND-SOUR SCALLOPS

EXCHANGES PER SERVING:
3 Very Lean Meat
1 Starch
2 Fruit

PER SERVING:
Calories 298
Carbohydrate 45.0g
Protein 21.5g
Fat 2.7g
Cholesterol 37mg
Fiber 1.5g
Sodium 486mg

✍ Scallops are generally classified into two groups—bay scallops and sea scallops. Bay scallops are smaller and sweeter than sea scallops. Bay scallops are more expensive because they're less plentiful. Sea scallops are chewier, but the meat is still sweet and moist.

1 (8-ounce) can pineapple chunks in juice
2 tablespoons cornstarch
1 tablespoon granulated brown sugar substitute
2 tablespoons cider vinegar
2 tablespoons low-sodium soy sauce
½ teaspoon chicken-flavored bouillon granules
⅛ teaspoon ground ginger
  Vegetable cooking spray
1 teaspoon vegetable oil
1 medium-size green pepper, cut into ¾-inch pieces
1 pound fresh sea scallops
½ cup seedless red grapes, halved
2 cups cooked long-grain rice (cooked without salt or fat)

1 Drain pineapple chunks, reserving juice. Set pineapple aside. Add water to juice to make ½ cup liquid.

2 Combine cornstarch and next 5 ingredients in a small bowl; stir well. Add pineapple juice mixture; stir well. Set aside.

3 Coat a large nonstick skillet with cooking spray; add oil. Place over medium-high heat until hot. Add green pepper; sauté 1 minute. Add scallops and cornstarch mixture; sauté 3 to 4 minutes or until scallops are opaque and mixture is slightly thickened. Stir in grapes and pineapple chunks.

4 To serve, spoon ½ cup rice onto each serving plate; spoon scallop mixture evenly over rice. Yield: 4 servings.

BROILED SHRIMP KABOBS

YIELD: 8 servings

4 pounds large fresh unpeeled shrimp
1 cup chopped onion
4 cloves garlic, minced
⅓ cup commercial oil-free Italian dressing
¼ cup lemon juice
¼ cup low-sodium soy sauce
2 teaspoons ground ginger
  Vegetable cooking spray
  Fresh basil sprigs (optional)

EXCHANGES PER SERVING:
3 Very Lean Meat
1 Vegetable

PER SERVING:
Calories 132
Carbohydrate 4.0g
Protein 24.1g
Fat 1.4g
Cholesterol 221mg
Fiber 0.4g
Sodium 482mg

1 Peel shrimp, leaving tails intact. Place shrimp in a large heavy-duty, zip-top plastic bag. Combine onion and next 5 ingredients in a small bowl; pour over shrimp. Seal bag securely, and shake well. Marinate shrimp in refrigerator at least 40 minutes, turning bag occasionally.

2 Remove shrimp from marinade, reserving marinade. Place marinade in a small saucepan; bring to a boil. Reduce heat; simmer 3 minutes.

3 Thread shrimp evenly onto eight 12-inch skewers.

4 Coat grill rack with cooking spray. Place rack over medium-hot coals (350° to 400°). Place skewers on rack; grill, covered, 3 minutes on each side or until shrimp are done, turning and basting frequently with marinade. Garnish with basil sprigs, if desired. Yield: 8 servings.

Broiling Instructions: Complete steps 1 and 2 as directed. Place kabobs on rack of a broiler pan coated with cooking spray. Broil 5½ inches from heat (with electric oven door partially opened) 3 to 4 minutes on each side or until shrimp are done, turning and basting frequently with marinade.

SHRIMP MONTEREY

EXCHANGES PER
SERVING:
4 Very Lean Meat
½ Starch

PER SERVING:
Calories 217
Carbohydrate 7.3g
Protein 31.3g
Fat 6.4g
Cholesterol 201mg
Fiber 0.2g
Sodium 322mg

2¼ pounds unpeeled medium-size fresh
    shrimp
    Vegetable cooking spray
1½ tablespoons chopped fresh cilantro
  3 tablespoons all-purpose flour
1¼ cups skim milk, divided
1½ tablespoons reduced-calorie margarine
  ½ cup (2 ounces) shredded reduced-fat
    Monterey Jack cheese
  1 jalapeño pepper, seeded and chopped
  1 tablespoon grated Parmesan cheese
    Fresh cilantro sprigs (optional)

1 Peel and devein shrimp; arrange shrimp in a steamer basket over boiling water. Cover and steam 3 minutes or until shrimp turn pink. Divide shrimp among 6 (1½-cup) baking dishes coated with cooking spray. Sprinkle with chopped cilantro; set aside.

2 Combine flour and ¼ cup milk in a small saucepan; stir until smooth. Add remaining 1 cup milk and margarine to flour mixture, stirring well. Cook over medium heat, stirring constantly, until mixture is thickened and bubbly. Remove from heat; add Monterey Jack cheese and jalapeño pepper, stirring until cheese melts.

3 Pour sauce evenly over shrimp; sprinkle evenly with Parmesan cheese. Broil 5½ inches from heat (with electric oven door partially opened) 3 to 5 minutes or until lightly browned. Garnish with cilantro sprigs, if desired. Yield: 6 servings.

Shrimp Stir-Fry

YIELD: 6 servings

1¼ pounds unpeeled medium-size fresh shrimp
    Vegetable cooking spray
4 cups sliced yellow squash
1 cup sliced zucchini
⅔ cup chopped sweet red pepper
½ cup diagonally sliced celery
½ pound sliced fresh mushrooms
2 tablespoons cornstarch
1 tablespoon granulated brown sugar substitute
3 tablespoons low-sodium soy sauce
1 (10½-ounce) can low-sodium chicken broth
⅛ teaspoon ground ginger
2 cloves garlic, minced
3 cups cooked rice (cooked without salt or fat)

EXCHANGES PER SERVING:
2 Very Lean Meat
2 Starch
1 Vegetable

PER SERVING:
Calories 244
Carbohydrate 36.4g
Protein 19.6g
Fat 2.2g
Cholesterol 108mg
Fiber 3.0g
Sodium 379mg

1 Peel shrimp, and devein, if desired. Coat a wok or large nonstick skillet with cooking spray; heat at medium-high (375°) until hot. Add shrimp; stir-fry 2 minutes or until shrimp turn pink. Remove from wok, and set aside.

2 Combine yellow squash and next 4 ingredients; add half of vegetable mixture to wok. Stir-fry 3 minutes; remove from wok, and set aside. Add remaining vegetables to wok; stir-fry 3 minutes, and set aside.

3 Combine cornstarch and next 3 ingredients, stirring well. Add ginger and garlic to wok; stir-fry 30 seconds. Add cornstarch mixture; bring to a boil, and cook, stirring constantly, 1 minute or until thickened.

4 Stir in shrimp and vegetables; cook 1 minute or until thoroughly heated. To serve, spoon 1 cup shrimp mixture over ½ cup rice.
Yield: 6 servings.

YIELD: 4 servings

EXCHANGES PER SERVING:
2 Lean Meat
2 Starch
1 Vegetable

PER SERVING:
Calories 279
Carbohydrate 35.7g
Protein 22.1g
Fat 4.7g
Cholesterol 130mg
Fiber 1.3g
Sodium 215mg

SHRIMP IN SHERRY CREAM SAUCE

1 pound unpeeled medium-size fresh shrimp
2 tablespoons reduced-calorie margarine
1½ cups sliced fresh mushrooms
¼ cup chopped green onions
¼ cup all-purpose flour
⅛ teaspoon ground red pepper
½ cup skim milk
¼ cup dry sherry
2 cups cooked long-grain rice (cooked without salt or fat)
1 teaspoon minced fresh parsley

1 Peel shrimp, and devein, if desired. Set shrimp aside.

2 Melt margarine in a medium nonstick skillet; add mushrooms and green onions, and sauté 2 to 3 minutes or until tender.

3 Combine flour and next 3 ingredients in a medium saucepan; add mushroom mixture, and cook over medium heat until thickened, stirring often. Add shrimp. Cook 3 to 5 minutes or until shrimp turn pink, stirring often.

4 To serve, spoon shrimp mixture over rice, and sprinkle with parsley. Serve with thin breadsticks, if desired (breadsticks not included in analysis). Yield: 4 servings.

CAJUN GUMBO AND RICE

YIELD: 9 servings

1 tablespoon vegetable oil
1 cup chopped onion
1 cup chopped celery
¾ cup chopped green pepper
¾ cup chopped sweet red pepper
4 ounces Canadian bacon, chopped
2 cloves garlic, minced
2 (13¾-ounce) cans no-salt-added chicken broth, undiluted
1 (14½-ounce) can no-salt-added whole tomatoes, undrained and chopped
¼ cup chopped fresh parsley
½ teaspoon salt
½ teaspoon dried basil
½ teaspoon dried thyme
¼ teaspoon ground red pepper
2 bay leaves
1 (10-ounce) package frozen sliced okra, thawed
1 tablespoon plus 1 teaspoon cornstarch
¼ cup water
2 pounds medium-size fresh shrimp, peeled and deveined
2 tablespoons gumbo filé
4½ cups cooked long-grain rice (cooked without salt or fat)
Hot sauce (optional)

EXCHANGES PER SERVING:
2 Lean Meat
2 Starch
1 Vegetable

PER SERVING:
Calories 295
Carbohydrate 35.7g
Protein 22.5g
Fat 6.3g
Cholesterol 121mg
Fiber 1.8g
Sodium 494mg

✍ This gumbo gets its rich flavor from salt-free seasonings, vegetables, and shrimp instead of from a traditional fat-laden roux (a mixture of half flour and half fat).

1 Heat oil in a Dutch oven over medium-high heat until hot. Add onion and next 5 ingredients; sauté until tender. Add chicken broth and next 7 ingredients; stir. Bring to a boil. Cover, reduce heat, and simmer 20 minutes.

2 Stir in okra; cover and cook 5 minutes. Combine cornstarch and water; add to hot mixture. Stir in shrimp and filé; cook 5 minutes or until shrimp turn pink. Remove and discard bay leaves.

3 Place ½ cup rice in individual serving bowls. Ladle 1 cup gumbo over each; sprinkle with hot sauce, if desired. Yield: 9 servings.

SEAFOOD-ARTICHOKE CASSEROLE

EXCHANGES PER
SERVING:
3 Very Lean Meat
1 Starch
1 Vegetable

PER SERVING:
Calories 219
Carbohydrate 20.4g
Protein 29.5g
Fat 2.1g
Cholesterol 202mg
Fiber 0.5g
Sodium 815mg

8 cups water
2 pounds medium-size fresh shrimp, peeled
    and deveined
1 (14-ounce) can artichoke hearts, drained
    and quartered
1 (6-ounce) can lump crabmeat, drained
¼ cup chopped celery
2 tablespoons chopped green onions
½ cup plain nonfat yogurt
½ cup nonfat mayonnaise
1 teaspoon low-sodium Worcestershire sauce
¼ teaspoon ground white pepper
¼ cup fine, dry breadcrumbs
¼ teaspoon paprika
    Lemon slices
    Green onion curls (optional)

1 Bring water to a boil; add shrimp, and cook 3 to 5 minutes or until shrimp turn pink. Drain well.

2 Place shrimp in a large bowl; add artichokes and next 3 ingredients, tossing gently.

3 Combine yogurt and next 3 ingredients. Stir yogurt mixture into shrimp mixture; spoon into a 1-quart casserole. Combine breadcrumbs and paprika; sprinkle over shrimp mixture.

4 Bake at 350° for 30 minutes or until golden. If desired, garnish with lemon slices and green onion curls. Serve immediately.
Yield: 4 servings.

Meatless
Main Dishes

BREAKFAST SCRAMBLE

YIELD: 6 servings

EXCHANGES PER
SERVING:
1½ Lean Meat

PER SERVING:
Calories 92
Carbohydrate 3.2g
Protein 10.9g
Fat 3.7g
Cholesterol 114mg
Fiber 0.4g
Sodium 161mg

Vegetable cooking spray
¾ cup seeded, chopped tomato
¼ cup chopped green pepper
¼ cup sliced green onions
3 eggs
1½ cups frozen egg substitute, thawed
¼ cup skim milk
¼ cup (1 ounce) shredded reduced-fat
    Cheddar cheese
⅛ teaspoon pepper
⅛ teaspoon hot sauce

1 Coat a large nonstick skillet with cooking spray; place over medium-high heat until hot. Add tomato, green pepper, and green onions; sauté until tender. Remove mixture from skillet, and set aside.

2 Combine eggs and next 5 ingredients in a large bowl; beat well with a wire whisk. Pour mixture into skillet, and cook over low heat, stirring gently. Cook until mixture is firm, but still moist. Remove from heat. Stir in vegetable mixture. Serve immediately. Yield: 6 servings.

CHEDDAR-POTATO FRITTATA

YIELD: 6 servings

1½ cups coarsely chopped round red potato
    Vegetable cooking spray
 1 cup chopped tomato
 ¼ cup chopped green onions
 ½ teaspoon pepper
 ¼ teaspoon salt
1½ cups egg substitute
 ½ cup (2 ounces) shredded reduced-fat
    sharp Cheddar cheese
    Green onions (optional)

1 Cook potato in a medium saucepan in boiling water to cover 10 to 12 minutes or until tender. Drain well.

2 Coat a large nonstick skillet with cooking spray; place over medium-high heat until hot. Add potato, tomato, and next 3 ingredients; sauté until onion is tender. Pour egg substitute over vegetable mixture. Cover and cook over medium-low heat 15 minutes or until egg is set. Sprinkle with shredded cheese; cover and cook 2 additional minutes or until cheese melts.

3 Remove from heat; cut into 6 wedges, and serve immediately. Garnish with green onions, if desired. Yield: 6 servings.

EXCHANGES PER SERVING:
1 Lean Meat
½ Starch
1 Vegetable

PER SERVING:
Calories 100
Carbohydrate 10.5g
Protein 10.1g
Fat 2.1g
Cholesterol 6mg
Fiber 1.4g
Sodium 263mg

EXCHANGES PER
SERVING:
1 Medium-Fat Meat
2 Vegetable

PER SERVING:
Calories 130
Carbohydrate 10.4g
Protein 13.5g
Fat 4.2g
Cholesterol 12mg
Fiber 1.6g
Sodium 294mg

CORN AND TOMATO FRITTATA

Vegetable cooking spray
1¼ cups fresh corn cut from cob (about 3 ears)
¼ cup chopped green onions
1½ cups egg substitute
⅓ cup skim milk
1½ teaspoons minced fresh basil
⅛ teaspoon salt
⅛ teaspoon pepper
2 small tomatoes, each cut into 6 wedges
1 cup (4 ounces) shredded reduced-fat Cheddar cheese
Fresh basil sprigs (optional)

1 Coat a medium nonstick skillet with vegetable cooking spray, and place over medium-high heat until hot. Add corn and green onions; sauté until vegetables are tender.

2 Combine egg substitute and next 4 ingredients in a bowl, and stir well. Pour egg mixture over vegetables in skillet. Cover and cook over medium-low heat 15 minutes or until almost set.

3 Arrange tomato wedges on top of egg mixture, and sprinkle with cheese. Cover and cook 5 additional minutes or until cheese melts. Cut into 6 wedges, and serve immediately. Garnish with basil sprigs, if desired. Yield: 6 servings.

VEGETABLE SWISS OMELET

YIELD: 2 servings

Vegetable cooking spray
⅓ cup finely chopped zucchini
¼ cup chopped green onions
¼ cup peeled, seeded, and chopped tomato
Dash of pepper
2 egg whites
¾ cup frozen egg substitute, thawed
2 tablespoons water
¼ teaspoon dried basil
¼ teaspoon celery seeds
⅛ teaspoon salt
⅛ teaspoon pepper
¼ cup (1 ounce) shredded reduced-fat
Swiss cheese

EXCHANGES PER SERVING:
3 Very Lean Meat
1 Vegetable

PER SERVING:
Calories 124
Carbohydrate 5.3g
Protein 17.7g
Fat 3.4g
Cholesterol 9mg
Fiber 0.8g
Sodium 362mg

1 Coat a 6-inch heavy skillet with cooking spray; place over medium heat until hot. Add zucchini, green onions, and tomato; sauté 2 to 3 minutes or until vegetables are tender. Stir in dash of pepper. Remove vegetables from skillet; set aside, and keep warm. Wipe skillet dry with a paper towel.

2 Beat egg whites until stiff peaks form; set aside.

3 Combine egg substitute and next 5 ingredients in a small bowl; stir well. Gently fold egg whites into egg substitute mixture.

4 Coat skillet with cooking spray; place over medium heat until hot enough to sizzle a drop of water. Spread half of egg mixture in skillet. Cover, reduce heat to low, and cook 5 minutes or until puffy and golden on bottom, gently lifting omelet at edge to judge color. Turn omelet, and cook 3 minutes or until golden. Carefully slide omelet onto a warm plate. Spoon half of vegetable mixture over half of omelet; sprinkle with 2 tablespoons cheese, and carefully fold in half. Repeat procedure with remaining egg mixture, vegetable mixture, and cheese. Yield: 2 servings.

HUEVOS RANCHEROS

This Mexican-style egg and bean dish is great for brunch or a casual supper.

EXCHANGES PER
SERVING:
1 Medium-Fat Meat
2 Starch
1 Vegetable

PER SERVING:
Calories 265
Carbohydrate 35.1g
Protein 16.2g
Fat 6.4g
Cholesterol 221mg
Fiber 4.7g
Sodium 585mg

1 (8-inch) pita bread round
    Butter-flavored vegetable cooking spray
½ teaspoon dried basil
½ teaspoon garlic powder
½ teaspoon ground cumin
1 (16-ounce) can red beans, drained
1 (14½-ounce) can Mexican-style stewed
    tomatoes, undrained
2 tablespoons sliced green onions
4 eggs
¼ cup salsa
¼ cup nonfat sour cream
    Fresh cilantro sprigs (optional)

1 Separate pita bread into 2 rounds; cut each round into 8 wedges. Place on an ungreased baking sheet; coat with cooking spray. Combine basil, garlic powder, and cumin; sprinkle over wedges. Bake at 400° for 5 minutes or until crisp and lightly browned.

2 Combine beans, tomato, and green onions in a saucepan. Cook, uncovered, over medium heat 10 minutes, stirring occasionally. Set aside; keep warm.

3 Add water to a large saucepan to depth of 2 inches. Bring to a boil; reduce heat, and maintain at a simmer. Break eggs, one at a time, into water. Simmer 7 to 9 minutes or until internal temperature of egg reaches 160°. Remove eggs with a slotted spoon.

4 To serve, arrange 4 pita wedges around edge of each plate; top evenly with bean mixture. Top each serving with 1 egg, 1 tablespoon salsa, and 1 tablespoon sour cream. Garnish with cilantro sprig, if desired. Serve immediately. Yield: 4 servings.

VEGETABLE-SWISS QUICHE

YIELD: 4 servings

1 cup thinly sliced leek
2 cups thinly sliced zucchini
2 cups thinly sliced yellow squash
1 cup thinly sliced sweet red pepper
1⅓ cups all-purpose flour
¼ cup margarine
2 to 3 tablespoons cold water
2 eggs
1 egg white
2 tablespoons 1% low-fat milk
1 teaspoon dried Italian seasoning
½ teaspoon salt
¼ teaspoon black pepper
¼ cup (1 ounce) finely shredded reduced-
 fat Swiss cheese

EXCHANGES PER
SERVING:
1 High-Fat Meat
3 Starch
1 Fat

PER SERVING:
Calories 384
Carbohydrate 46.8g
Protein 14.0g
Fat 16.3g
Cholesterol 115mg
Fiber 4.2g
Sodium 501mg

1 Add water to a Dutch oven to depth of 2 inches; bring to a boil. Add leek; cover and simmer 5 minutes. Add zucchini, squash, and red pepper; cover and simmer 5 minutes. Drain; pat dry.

2 Place flour in a bowl; cut in margarine with pastry blender until mixture resembles coarse meal. Sprinkle cold water over surface; stir until dry ingredients are moistened. Shape into a ball. Place between 2 sheets of plastic wrap; press into a 4-inch circle. Chill 20 minutes. Roll into a 12-inch circle. Freeze 5 minutes. Remove top sheet of plastic. Invert and fit pastry into a 9-inch pieplate; remove remaining plastic. Fold edges of pastry under, and flute; seal to edge of pieplate. Bake at 450° for 5 minutes. Add vegetable mixture to pastry.

3 Combine eggs and next 5 ingredients; stir well. Pour over vegetable mixture. Bake at 375° for 30 minutes; sprinkle with cheese. Bake 5 minutes or until cheese melts. Let stand 5 minutes. Yield: 4 servings.

TOMATO-BASIL QUICHE

**EXCHANGES PER
SERVING:**
1 Medium-Fat Meat
1 Starch
2 Vegetable

PER SERVING:
Calories 218
Carbohydrate 25.3g
Protein 12.6g
Fat 7.2g
Cholesterol 84mg
Fiber 1.1g
Sodium 391mg

1 (7-ounce) package refrigerated
   breadstick dough
   Vegetable cooking spray
1 teaspoon olive oil
1 cup chopped onion
1 clove garlic, minced
¾ cup (3 ounces) shredded part-skim
   mozzarella cheese
1 cup sliced plum tomato
¼ cup shredded fresh basil
1 cup evaporated skimmed milk
1½ teaspoons cornstarch
¼ teaspoon freshly ground pepper
2 large eggs
1 egg white

1 Unroll breadstick dough, separating into strips. Coil 1 strip of dough. Add a second strip to end of first, pinching ends together; continue coiling. Repeat procedure with remaining strips to make an 8-inch-round coil. Press coiled dough into a 13-inch circle, and place in a 9-inch pieplate coated with cooking spray. Fold edges under, and set aside.

2 Coat a nonstick skillet with cooking spray; add oil, and place over medium heat until hot. Add onion and garlic; sauté 8 minutes or until lightly browned. Spread onion mixture in bottom of prepared crust; sprinkle with cheese. Arrange tomato over cheese; top with basil.

3 Combine milk and remaining 4 ingredients in container of an electric blender; cover and process until smooth. Pour over tomato slices. Bake at 350° for 45 minutes or until a knife inserted 1 inch from center comes out clean; let stand 10 minutes. Yield: 6 servings.

VEGETABLE STRATA

This make-ahead dish is great
for breakfast or brunch.

1½ cups chopped fresh broccoli
4 (1-ounce) slices white bread, cubed
Butter-flavored vegetable cooking spray
1 cup (4 ounces) shredded reduced-fat
Swiss cheese
¼ cup coarsely shredded carrot
2 tablespoons chopped sweet red pepper
2 tablespoons chopped green onions
1½ cups 1% low-fat milk
1 cup egg substitute
½ teaspoon dry mustard
½ teaspoon hot sauce
½ teaspoon low-sodium Worcestershire
sauce
¼ teaspoon pepper
⅛ teaspoon salt

1 Arrange broccoli in a steamer basket over boiling water. Cover and steam 3 minutes or until crisp-tender. Set aside.

2 Place bread cubes in a 2-quart baking dish coated with cooking spray; sprinkle with cheese. Top with broccoli, carrot, red pepper, and green onions. Combine milk and remaining 6 ingredients in a small bowl, stirring well; pour over broccoli mixture. Cover and chill at least 8 hours.

3 Remove from refrigerator, and let stand, covered, at room temperature 30 minutes. Bake, uncovered, at 350° for 40 to 45 minutes or until set. Let stand 10 minutes before serving. Yield: 4 servings.

YIELD: 4 servings

EXCHANGES PER
SERVING:
2 Medium-Fat Meat
1 Starch
2 Vegetable

PER SERVING:
Calories 262
Carbohydrate 26.0g
Protein 23.1g
Fat 7.5g
Cholesterol 22mg
Fiber 3.2g
Sodium 427mg

MACARONI AND CHEESE

YIELD: 8 servings

EXCHANGES PER
SERVING:
1 Medium-Fat Meat
2 Starch

PER SERVING:
Calories 228
Carbohydrate 32.5g
Protein 12.5g
Fat 5.1g
Cholesterol 12mg
Fiber 1.0g
Sodium 353mg

If you're cooking for a small household, you can easily halve the ingredients for 4 servings.

2 cups elbow macaroni, uncooked
1 tablespoon plus 1 teaspoon reduced-calorie margarine
¼ cup all-purpose flour
½ teaspoon dry mustard
¼ teaspoon ground red pepper
3 cups skim milk
1 cup (4 ounces) shredded reduced-fat Cheddar cheese
2 tablespoons grated Parmesan cheese
½ teaspoon salt
¼ teaspoon black pepper
   Vegetable cooking spray
1 tablespoon plus 1 teaspoon fine, dry breadcrumbs

1 Cook macaroni according to package directions, omitting salt; drain and set aside.

2 Melt margarine in a large saucepan over low heat; add flour, mustard, and red pepper. Cook 1 minute, stirring constantly with a wire whisk. Gradually add milk, stirring constantly. Cook over medium heat 20 minutes or until thickened and bubbly. Remove from heat; add cheeses, salt, and black pepper, stirring until cheese melts. Add macaroni; stir well.

3 Spoon macaroni mixture into a 1-quart baking dish coated with cooking spray. Top with breadcrumbs. Cover and bake at 400° for 30 minutes. Yield: 8 (¾-cup) servings.

SPICY CHILI MAC

YIELD: 7 servings

Vegetable cooking spray
1½ cups finely chopped onion
1⅓ cups finely chopped green pepper
2 cloves garlic, minced
1 tablespoon chili powder
1 teaspoon ground cumin
½ teaspoon garlic powder
½ teaspoon dried crushed red pepper
½ pound firm tofu, drained and crumbled
1 (28-ounce) can crushed tomatoes with puree, undrained
2 (15-ounce) cans red kidney beans, drained
7 ounces wagon wheel pasta, uncooked
¼ cup plus 3 tablespoons (1¾ ounces) shredded reduced-fat Cheddar cheese

EXCHANGES PER
SERVING:
3 Starch
2 Vegetable
1 Fat

PER SERVING:
Calories 281
Carbohydrate 53.2g
Protein 10.9g
Fat 4.1g
Cholesterol 1mg
Fiber 5.2g
Sodium 228mg

1 Coat a Dutch oven with cooking spray; place over medium-high heat until hot. Add onion, green pepper, and garlic; sauté until tender.

2 Add chili powder and next 3 ingredients; sauté 1 minute. Stir in tofu and tomato. Bring mixture to a boil; reduce heat, and simmer, uncovered, 15 minutes. Add kidney beans, and cook 10 additional minutes or until thoroughly heated.

3 Cook pasta according to package directions, omitting salt and fat; drain.

4 To serve, place ½ cup pasta in each of 7 bowls, and spoon 1 cup bean mixture over each serving. Top each with 1 tablespoon cheese. Yield: 7 servings.

MACARONI CASSEROLE

Please your family with this hearty
pasta casserole. Serve a tossed salad and
fresh fruit to complete the meal.

EXCHANGES PER
SERVING:
2 Very Lean Meat
2 Starch
1 Vegetable

PER SERVING:
Calories 228
Carbohydrate 34.3g
Protein 15.5g
Fat 3.2g
Cholesterol 8mg
Fiber 1.2g
Sodium 548mg

1 (8-ounce) package elbow macaroni,
   uncooked
2 cups 1% low-fat cottage cheese
¼ cup skim milk
2 tablespoons minced fresh parsley
1 tablespoon minced fresh chives
2 teaspoons dried oregano
½ teaspoon salt
½ teaspoon pepper
   Vegetable cooking spray
½ cup (2 ounces) shredded 40% less-fat
   Cheddar cheese
1 (8-ounce) can no-salt-added tomato
   sauce
¼ cup fine, dry breadcrumbs
2 tablespoons freshly grated Parmesan
   cheese

1 Cook macaroni according to package directions, omitting salt and fat. Drain; set aside.

2 Place cottage cheese and milk in container of an electric blender; cover and process until smooth. Transfer to a large bowl; stir in parsley and next 4 ingredients. Add macaroni, and toss to combine.

3 Spoon half of macaroni mixture into a 1½-quart baking dish coated with cooking spray. Sprinkle with half of Cheddar cheese; top with half of tomato sauce. Repeat layers. Sprinkle with breadcrumbs and Parmesan cheese.

4 Bake at 375° for 30 minutes or until bubbly and golden. Yield: 7 (1-cup) servings.

PASTA PRIMAVERA

YIELD: 4 servings

¼ pound fresh asparagus spears, diagonally
    sliced into 1-inch pieces
½ cup broccoli flowerets
½ cup fresh snow pea pods, trimmed and
    diagonally sliced into 1-inch pieces
½ cup sliced yellow squash
½ cup sliced zucchini
    Vegetable cooking spray
¼ pound fresh mushrooms, sliced
1 clove garlic, minced
1 tablespoon chopped fresh chives
8 ounces fresh linguine, uncooked
¼ cup canned vegetable broth
2 tablespoons dry white wine
¾ cup skim milk
1 tablespoon all-purpose flour
⅓ cup grated Parmesan cheese, divided
1 tablespoon chopped fresh parsley
1½ teaspoons chopped fresh basil
⅛ teaspoon salt

**EXCHANGES PER
SERVING:**
1 Lean Meat
3 Starch
1 Vegetable

PER SERVING:
Calories 294
Carbohydrate 51.8g
Protein 14.0g
Fat 3.5g
Cholesterol 6mg
Fiber 3.3g
Sodium 274mg

1 Arrange first 5 ingredients in a vegetable steamer over boiling water. Cover and steam 15 minutes or until crisp-tender.

2 Coat a nonstick skillet with cooking spray; place over medium-high heat until hot. Add mushrooms and garlic; sauté 5 minutes. Add steamed vegetables and chives. Reduce heat; simmer, uncovered, 5 minutes.

3 Cook linguine according to package directions, omitting salt and fat. Drain.

4 Combine vegetable broth and wine in a saucepan. Bring to a boil; cook until reduced to 2 tablespoons. Combine milk and flour. Add to broth mixture. Cook over medium heat 5 minutes, stirring constantly. Pour over pasta; toss. Add ¼ cup cheese and next 3 ingredients; toss. Top with vegetable mixture; sprinkle with remaining cheese. Yield: 4 servings.

MUSHROOM MARINARA

YIELD: 2 servings

EXCHANGES PER
SERVING:
3 Starch
2 Vegetable
1 Fat

PER SERVING:
Calories 281
Carbohydrate 53.2g
Protein 10.9g
Fat 4.1g
Cholesterol 1mg
Fiber 5.2g
Sodium 228mg

Vegetable cooking spray
1 teaspoon olive oil
2 cups sliced fresh mushrooms
1 (14½-ounce) can no-salt-added stewed
    tomatoes, undrained and coarsely
    chopped
¼ cup no-salt-added tomato paste
1 tablespoon dried parsley flakes
1 tablespoon dry red wine
½ teaspoon dried oregano
½ teaspoon dried basil
¼ teaspoon dried thyme
¼ teaspoon pepper
⅛ teaspoon garlic powder
⅛ teaspoon salt
1½ cups cooked cappellini (angel hair pasta)
    (cooked without salt or fat)
2 teaspoons grated Parmesan cheese

1 Coat a saucepan with cooking spray; add olive oil. Place over medium-high heat until hot; add mushrooms, and sauté until tender.

2 Add tomato and next 9 ingredients; stir well. Bring mixture to a boil; reduce heat and simmer, uncovered, 5 to 10 minutes or until slightly thickened, stirring occasionally. Set aside, and keep warm.

3 Cook pasta according to package directions, omitting salt and fat. Drain.

4 To serve, place pasta evenly on 2 plates; top evenly with mushroom mixture. Sprinkle each serving with 1 teaspoon Parmesan cheese. Yield: 2 servings.

Pesto-Stuffed Shells

YIELD: 6 servings

EXCHANGES PER
SERVING:
1 High-Fat Meat
2 Starch

PER SERVING:
Calories 233
Carbohydrate 29.0g
Protein 13.8g
Fat 7.1g
Cholesterol 17mg
Fiber 3.3g
Sodium 246mg

Vegetable cooking spray
1¾ cups finely chopped sweet red pepper
½ cup chopped onion
2 cloves garlic, minced
1 (14½-ounce) can no-salt-added whole
   tomatoes, undrained
1 (8-ounce) can no-salt-added tomato sauce
½ teaspoon dried Italian seasoning
¼ teaspoon salt
¼ teaspoon ground white pepper
12 jumbo pasta shells, uncooked
½ pound firm tofu
1¼ cups part-skim ricotta cheese
¼ cup grated Parmesan cheese
½ cup minced fresh basil
½ cup minced fresh parsley

1 Coat a nonstick skillet with cooking spray;
place over medium-high heat until hot. Add
red pepper, onion, and garlic; sauté until tender.

2 Place pepper mixture and tomatoes in container of an electric blender or food processor; cover and process until smooth. Transfer to
a saucepan. Add tomato sauce and next 3 ingredients; stir. Bring to a boil; reduce heat, and simmer 20 minutes.

3 Spread ½ cup sauce mixture in an 11- x 7- x
1½-inch baking dish coated with cooking spray.

4 Cook pasta according to package directions,
omitting salt and fat; drain and set aside.

5 Wrap tofu in paper towels. Remove towels;
crumble tofu. Position knife blade in food
processor bowl; add tofu, ricotta cheese, and
next 3 ingredients. Process 1 minute.

6 Spoon mixture into shells; place in baking
dish. Top with remaining sauce mixture.
Cover and bake at 400° for 40 minutes.
Yield: 6 servings.

OVERNIGHT BROCCOLI LASAGNA

EXCHANGES PER
SERVING:
2 Very Lean Meat
1½ Starch
1 Vegetable

PER SERVING:
Calories 209
Carbohydrate 25.4g
Protein 18.2g
Fat 4.9g
Cholesterol 58mg
Fiber 3.3g
Sodium 462mg

Vegetable cooking spray
½ cup chopped green pepper
2 tablespoons chopped onion
1 clove garlic, minced
1 (4-ounce) can mushroom pieces, drained
2 tablespoons all-purpose flour
1 teaspoon dried parsley flakes
1 teaspoon dried oregano
¼ teaspoon pepper
⅛ teaspoon salt
¾ cup plus 1 tablespoon skim milk, divided
2 (10-ounce) packages frozen chopped broccoli, thawed
1½ cups 1% low-fat cottage cheese
1 egg
4 lasagna noodles, uncooked
1 cup curd-style farmer cheese
2 tablespoons grated Parmesan cheese

1 Coat a nonstick skillet with cooking spray; place over medium-high heat until hot. Add green pepper and next 3 ingredients; sauté until tender. Add flour and next 4 ingredients. Cook over medium heat 1 minute, stirring constantly. Gradually add ¾ cup milk; cook 10 minutes, stirring constantly. Stir in broccoli.

2 Combine cottage cheese, egg, and 1 tablespoon milk in container of an electric blender; cover and process until smooth.

3 Coat an 8-inch square baking dish with cooking spray. Spoon one-third of broccoli into dish. Break noodles in half crosswise. Place 4 halves over broccoli. Spread half of cottage cheese over noodles; top with half of farmer cheese. Repeat layers, ending with broccoli. Cover and chill at least 8 hours.

4 Sprinkle with Parmesan cheese. Bake at 375° for 40 minutes. Remove from oven; let stand 10 minutes before serving. Yield: 6 servings.

Vegetable Lasagna

YIELD: 8 servings

2 cups broccoli flowerets
1 cup thinly sliced zucchini
1 cup thinly sliced yellow squash
1 cup thinly sliced carrot
   Vegetable cooking spray
1½ cups thinly sliced fresh mushrooms
1 cup chopped onion
1 (16-ounce) carton 1% low-fat cottage
   cheese
½ cup frozen egg substitute, thawed
3 cups fat-free spaghetti sauce
8 cooked lasagna noodles (cooked
   without salt or fat)
1 cup (4 ounces) shredded part-skim
   mozzarella cheese

EXCHANGES PER
SERVING:
1½ Lean Meat
1½ Starch
2 Vegetable

PER SERVING:
Calories 237
Carbohydrate 33.1g
Protein 18.2g
Fat 3.9g
Cholesterol 10mg
Fiber 4.0g
Sodium 625mg

1 Arrange first 4 ingredients in a vegetable steamer over boiling water. Cover and steam 4 to 5 minutes or until vegetables are crisp-tender; drain. Transfer to a bowl; set aside.

2 Coat a nonstick skillet with cooking spray. Place over medium-high heat until hot. Add mushrooms and onion; sauté until tender. Add to broccoli mixture.

3 Combine cottage cheese and egg substitute, stirring well.

4 Spread ½ cup spaghetti sauce over bottom of a 13- x 9- x 2-inch baking dish coated with cooking spray. Place 4 lasagna noodles over sauce; top with vegetable mixture. Spoon cottage cheese mixture over vegetable mixture. Top with remaining 4 noodles and spaghetti sauce.

5 Cover and bake at 350° for 40 minutes. Uncover and sprinkle with mozzarella cheese. Bake, uncovered, 10 additional minutes or until cheese melts. Let stand 15 minutes before serving. Yield: 8 servings.

GREEK VEGETABLE LASAGNA

**EXCHANGES PER
SERVING:**
1 Medium-Fat Meat
2 Starch
1 Vegetable

PER SERVING:
Calories 253
Carbohydrate 35.2g
Protein 14.5g
Fat 6.5g
Cholesterol 21mg
Fiber 4.9g
Sodium 737mg

1 (4-ounce) package feta cheese, crumbled
2 egg whites, lightly beaten
½ teaspoon freshly ground pepper
2 (16-ounce) packages frozen broccoli,
   red pepper, onion, and mushroom
   blend, thawed
4½ cups fat-free chunky spaghetti sauce
   with mushrooms and sweet peppers
¼ cup pitted kalamata olives, finely
   chopped
   Olive oil-flavored vegetable cooking
   spray
9 cooked lasagna noodles (cooked
   without salt or fat)
1 cup (4 ounces) shredded part-skim
   mozzarella cheese

1 Combine first 3 ingredients; stir well. Set aside. Press broccoli mixture between paper towels to remove excess moisture; set aside.

2 Position knife blade in food processor bowl; add spaghetti sauce and olives. Process until smooth, stopping once to scrape down sides.

3 Spread 1 cup spaghetti sauce mixture over bottom of a 13- x 9- x 2-inch baking dish coated with cooking spray. Place 3 noodles over sauce; spoon half of feta cheese mixture over noodles. Top with half of broccoli mixture; spoon 1 cup spaghetti sauce over broccoli mixture. Repeat procedure with 3 noodles, remaining feta cheese mixture, broccoli mixture, and 1 cup spaghetti sauce. Top with remaining 3 noodles and spaghetti sauce.

4 Cover and bake at 375° for 35 to 40 minutes or until thoroughly heated. Uncover and sprinkle with mozzarella cheese. Bake, uncovered, 5 additional minutes or until cheese melts. Let stand 15 minutes before serving. Yield: 8 servings.

GOURMET PIZZAS

YIELD: 4 servings

3 tablespoons no-salt-added tomato paste
1 teaspoon dried oregano
1 teaspoon chopped fresh garlic
¼ teaspoon dried basil
¼ teaspoon dried crushed red pepper
2 (4-ounce) Italian cheese-flavored pizza
  crusts (such as Boboli)
1½ tablespoons pitted and coarsely chopped
  kalamata olives
½ cup canned artichoke hearts, drained
  and cut into eighths
2 tablespoons crumbled goat cheese

EXCHANGES PER SERVING:
2 Starch
1 Fat

PER SERVING:
Calories 197
Carbohydrate 30.0g
Protein 9.0g
Fat 4.5g
Cholesterol 8mg
Fiber 1.5g
Sodium 390mg

1 Combine first 5 ingredients in a small bowl, stirring well.

2 Spread tomato paste mixture evenly over pizza crusts, leaving a ½-inch border around sides. Sprinkle evenly with olives; top evenly with artichoke. Bake at 450° for 5 minutes. Sprinkle evenly with cheese; bake 5 additional minutes or until cheese melts. Yield: 4 servings (serving size: ½ pizza).

PIZZA IN A SKILLET

EXCHANGES PER
SERVING:
1 Medium-Fat Meat
2 Starch
1 Vegetable

PER SERVING:
Calories 246
Carbohydrate 38.2g
Protein 12.0g
Fat 5.7g
Cholesterol 11mg
Fiber 3.2g
Sodium 637mg

1 (3-ounce) package sun-dried tomatoes
  Vegetable cooking spray
2 small onions, thinly sliced and separated
  into rings
4 cloves garlic, minced
4 cups finely chopped fresh spinach
½ (32-ounce) package frozen bread dough,
  thawed
¼ cup plus 2 tablespoons no-salt-added
  tomato sauce
1 cup (4 ounces) shredded part-skim
  mozzarella cheese
¼ cup grated Parmesan cheese

1 Place tomatoes in a medium bowl. Cover with hot water to depth of 2 inches above tomatoes; let stand 15 minutes. Drain; coarsely chop tomatoes, and set aside.

2 Coat an electric skillet with cooking spray. Heat at 375° until hot. Add onion and garlic; sauté until tender. Add chopped tomato and spinach; cook 1 minute or until spinach is wilted. Remove from skillet, and set aside. Wipe skillet dry with a paper towel.

3 Divide bread dough into 2 equal portions. Roll each portion of bread dough into a 10-inch circle on a lightly floured surface.

4 Coat electric skillet with cooking spray. Heat at 275° until hot. Place 1 portion of dough in skillet, and prick dough with a fork. Cover and cook 10 minutes or until lightly browned on bottom. Spread half of tomato sauce over dough; sprinkle with half of mozzarella cheese. Spread half of spinach mixture over cheese; sprinkle with half of Parmesan cheese. Cover and cook an additional 5 minutes or until cheese melts. Transfer to a large serving platter. Repeat procedure with remaining dough, sauce, spinach mixture, and cheese. Yield: 8 servings.

CARAMELIZED ONION PIZZA

YIELD: 6 servings

2 tablespoons reduced-calorie margarine
2 cups thinly sliced yellow onion (about 2 medium)
2 tablespoons granulated sugar substitute (such as Sugar Twin)
1¼ cups lite ricotta cheese
2 teaspoons Italian seasoning, divided
¾ cup (3 ounces) shredded part-skim mozzarella cheese
¼ cup grated Parmesan cheese
⅛ teaspoon pepper
1 (11-ounce) package refrigerated French bread dough
Vegetable cooking spray
1 large unpeeled tomato, seeded and thinly sliced
¼ cup chopped fresh parsley

EXCHANGES PER SERVING:
1 High-Fat Meat
2 Starch
1 Vegetable

PER SERVING:
Calories 268
Carbohydrate 32.2g
Protein 15.7g
Fat 9.5g
Cholesterol 19mg
Fiber 1.3g
Sodium 485mg

1 Melt margarine in a large skillet over medium-high heat. Add sliced onion and sugar substitute; sauté 5 minutes or until onion is deep golden. Set aside.

2 Combine ricotta cheese, 1 teaspoon Italian seasoning, and next 3 ingredients; stir well.

3 Unroll bread dough, and pat into a 13- x 9- x 2-inch baking pan coated with cooking spray. Spread ricotta cheese mixture evenly over dough; top with tomato. Sprinkle with remaining 1 teaspoon Italian seasoning and parsley. Bake at 450° for 13 minutes. Top with onion mixture, and bake 5 additional minutes. Yield: 6 servings.

GARDEN MEDLEY PIZZA

YIELD: 6 servings

EXCHANGES PER
SERVING:
1 High-Fat Meat
2 Starch
3 Vegetable

PER SERVING:
Calories 320
Carbohydrate 47.1g
Protein 17.1g
Fat 8.1g
Cholesterol 17mg
Fiber 4.3g
Sodium 646mg

Vegetable cooking spray
1 teaspoon olive oil
2 cups sliced fresh mushrooms
1 cup thinly sliced broccoli flowerets
1 cup thinly sliced broccoli stalks
½ cup diagonally sliced green onions
2 yellow squash, sliced and quartered
1 small green pepper, seeded and sliced
1 small sweet red pepper, seeded and sliced
1 (8-ounce) can no-salt-added tomato
    sauce
1 (6-ounce) can no-salt-added tomato
    paste
2 tablespoons red wine vinegar
¾ teaspoon dried basil
½ teaspoon dried oregano
3 cloves garlic, minced
1 (10-ounce) can refrigerated pizza dough
¾ cup (3 ounces) finely shredded part-skim
    mozzarella cheese
¾ cup (3 ounces) finely shredded reduced-
    fat Cheddar cheese

1 Coat a large nonstick skillet with cooking spray; add oil. Place over medium-high heat until hot. Add mushrooms and next 6 ingredients; sauté until crisp-tender. Drain; set aside.

2 Combine tomato sauce and next 5 ingredients in a saucepan. Bring to a boil, stirring constantly. Reduce heat, and simmer, uncovered, 15 to 20 minutes or until thickened.

3 Unroll dough; pat into a 10-inch pizza pan coated with cooking spray. Spread tomato sauce mixture over dough. Arrange vegetable mixture over sauce. Bake at 350° for 25 minutes or until crust is lightly browned. Combine cheeses; sprinkle over pizza. Bake 5 minutes or until cheese melts. Yield: 6 servings.

BEAN BURRITOS

YIELD: 2 servings

Vegetable cooking spray
2 tablespoons chopped onion
1 clove garlic, minced
½ cup drained canned pinto beans
Dash of ground cumin
2 tablespoons reduced-calorie chili sauce
1 tablespoon chopped green chiles
2 (6-inch) flour tortillas
¼ cup plus 2 tablespoons (1½ ounces)
    shredded reduced-fat Monterey
    Jack cheese
¼ cup seeded, chopped tomato
¼ cup alfalfa sprouts

EXCHANGES PER SERVING:
1 High-Fat Meat
2 Starch

PER SERVING:
Calories 245
Carbohydrate 32.4g
Protein 12.3g
Fat 7.5g
Cholesterol 14mg
Fiber 4.4g
Sodium 502mg

1 Coat a nonstick skillet with cooking spray; place over medium heat until hot.

2 Add onion and garlic; sauté 3 minutes or until tender. Stir in beans and cumin. Reduce heat; cook, uncovered, 5 minutes or until bean mixture is a thick paste, mashing beans with a wooden spoon. Add chili sauce and green chiles. Cook 1 minute or until thoroughly heated, stirring occasionally. Set aside, and keep warm.

3 Wrap tortillas in aluminum foil, and bake at 350° for 5 minutes.

4 Spread ¼ cup bean mixture in center of each tortilla; top each with 3 tablespoons cheese and 2 tablespoons tomato. Place 2 tablespoons alfalfa sprouts in each burrito. Fold bottom half of each tortilla over filling; fold sides over filling, securing with wooden picks. Yield: 2 servings.

CORN AND RICE BURRITOS

EXCHANGES PER
SERVING:
1 Medium-Fat Meat
2 Starch
1 Vegetable

PER SERVING:
Calories 263
Carbohydrate 38.9g
Protein 11.6g
Fat 6.7g
Cholesterol 11mg
Fiber 3.1g
Sodium 442mg

If you don't want to heat up your oven,
wrap tortillas in wax paper or paper towels,
and warm in the microwave at HIGH for
about 20 seconds.

1 (4.4-ounce) package Spanish rice
1 cup no-salt-added pinto beans, drained
1 cup frozen whole-kernel corn, thawed
¾ cup chopped tomato
8 (6-inch) flour tortillas
1 cup (4 ounces) shredded Monterey Jack
    cheese with peppers
½ cup plus 2 tablespoons nonfat sour
    cream
Fresh chile peppers (optional)

❧ Fresh chile peppers
are extremely hot, so
be very careful if you
eat one.

1 Cook rice mix according to package directions, omitting fat. Combine beans, corn, and
tomato in a saucepan. Cook over low heat until
thoroughly heated. Add to rice.

2 Wrap tortillas in heavy-duty aluminum foil.
Bake at 350° for 5 minutes or until thoroughly heated. Spoon rice mixture evenly down
center of each tortilla. Top each with 2 tablespoons cheese and 1 tablespoon sour cream; roll
up. Garnish with chile peppers, if desired. Serve
immediately. Yield: 8 servings.

CHILE-BEAN BURRITOS

YIELD: 4 servings

This Tex-Mex favorite is tailor-made for healthful eating. It features texture, color, and intense flavor, but very little fat.

Vegetable cooking spray
½ cup sliced green onions
1 (15-ounce) can black beans, drained
2 tablespoons canned chopped green chiles
¼ teaspoon garlic powder
¼ teaspoon ground cumin
¼ teaspoon chili powder
Dash of hot sauce
4 (8-inch) fat-free flour tortillas
3 cups shredded green leaf lettuce
½ cup no-salt-added salsa
½ cup (2 ounces) shredded 40% less-fat Cheddar cheese
Jalapeño pepper slices (optional)

EXCHANGES PER SERVING:
1 Lean Meat
2 Starch
1 Vegetable

PER SERVING:
Calories 246
Carbohydrate 39.4g
Protein 11.4g
Fat 2.9g
Cholesterol 8mg
Fiber 4.2g
Sodium 541mg

◄ To increase the number of meat exchanges in a serving of Chile-Bean Burritos, use an additional ounce of cheese per serving. (One ounce of cheese is 1 Meat Exchange.)

1 Coat a large nonstick skillet with cooking spray; place over medium-high heat until hot. Add green onions; cook until tender. Set aside.

2 Mash beans with a potato masher; add to onions. Stir in chiles and next 4 ingredients. Cook over medium heat, stirring constantly, 6 to 7 minutes or until thickened.

3 Wrap tortillas in aluminum foil, and heat at 350° for 10 minutes or until softened. Spread bean mixture evenly over tortillas. Roll up jellyroll fashion.

4 To serve, arrange shredded lettuce on a serving platter; place tortillas, seam side down, on lettuce. Top burritos evenly with salsa and cheese. Garnish with jalapeño pepper slices, if desired. Yield: 4 servings.

BLACK-EYED PEA QUESADILLAS

EXCHANGES PER
SERVING:
1 High-Fat Meat
2 Starch

PER SERVING:
Calories 246
Carbohydrate 29.2g
Protein 14.4g
Fat 8.7g
Cholesterol 18mg
Fiber 2.6g
Sodium 375mg

1 cup canned drained black-eyed peas
1 cup seeded, diced tomato
½ cup water
¼ cup peeled, diced avocado
2½ tablespoons minced fresh cilantro
2 tablespoons minced purple onion
1 tablespoon seeded, minced jalapeño
    pepper
2 tablespoons fresh lime juice
¼ teaspoon ground cumin
⅛ teaspoon garlic powder
    Vegetable cooking spray
1 cup thinly sliced zucchini
1 cup frozen whole kernel corn, thawed
4 (8-inch) flour tortillas
¾ cup (3 ounces) shredded reduced-fat
    Cheddar cheese
¾ cup (3 ounces) shredded reduced-fat
    Monterey Jack cheese
    Fresh cilantro sprigs (optional)

1 Place peas in a saucepan. Cook over medium-high heat until thoroughly heated. Set aside, and keep warm.

2 Combine tomato and next 8 ingredients in a medium bowl; stir well. Set aside.

3 Coat a large nonstick skillet with cooking spray; place over medium-high heat until hot. Add zucchini; sauté 3 minutes or until tender. Add corn; sauté 2 minutes. Remove from heat; stir in peas.

4 Place 2 tortillas on a baking sheet coated with cooking spray; top tortillas with cheeses and pea mixture. Top with remaining tortillas. Bake at 400° for 8 minutes or just until tortillas are crisp and cheese melts. Cut each into thirds. Place on individual serving plates; top with tomato mixture. Garnish with cilantro sprigs, if desired. Yield: 6 servings.

Tortilla Stacks

YIELD: 8 servings

1 cup (4 ounces) shredded farmer cheese
1 cup part-skim ricotta cheese
1 cup shredded carrot
½ cup chopped radish
¼ cup chopped ripe olives
1 (15-ounce) can garbanzo beans, drained
3 cloves garlic, halved
½ cup firmly packed parsley sprigs
3 green onions, cut into ½-inch pieces
1 tablespoon lemon juice
½ teaspoon ground cumin
12 (6-inch) corn tortillas
½ cup (2 ounces) shredded farmer cheese
  Red Chile Sauce

EXCHANGES PER SERVING:
1 Medium-Fat Meat
2 Starch
1 Vegetable

PER SERVING:
Calories 247
Carbohydrate 36.5g
Protein 12.9g
Fat 7.1g
Cholesterol 13mg
Fiber 4.5g
Sodium 405mg

1 Combine first 5 ingredients, and stir well.

2 Position knife blade in food processor bowl; add beans and garlic. Process 1 minute. Add parsley and next 3 ingredients; process 10 seconds.

3 Place 4 tortillas on a baking sheet. Layer each with one-eighth bean mixture and one-eighth cheese mixture. Repeat with tortillas, bean mixture, and cheese mixture; top with 4 tortillas. Sprinkle with ½ cup cheese. Bake at 375° for 15 minutes. Cut each in half. Serve with Red Chile Sauce. Yield: 8 servings.

🖝 A pasilla pepper has a long, slender shape with wrinkled brown-black skin. For a milder flavor, substitute an ancho pepper.

RED CHILE SAUCE

1 large dried pasilla chile pepper, seeded
1 medium onion, quartered
4 cloves garlic, halved
1 (28-ounce) can plum tomatoes, drained
½ teaspoon ground cumin
¼ teaspoon hot sauce

1 Rinse chile; add boiling water to cover. Let stand 15 minutes. Drain; coarsely chop. Combine chile, onion, and garlic in food processor; pulse 4 times. Add tomato, cumin, and hot sauce; process until smooth. Yield: 2 cups.

CUBAN BLACK BEANS

EXCHANGES PER SERVING:
½ High-Fat Meat
3 Starch
2 Vegetable

PER SERVING:
Calories 325
Carbohydrate 56.5g
Protein 16.0g
Fat 4.8g
Cholesterol 9mg
Fiber 5.9g
Sodium 432mg

Vegetable cooking spray
2 teaspoons olive oil
1 cup chopped onion
¾ cup chopped green pepper
2 cups no-salt-added tomato juice
1 cup water
3 (15-ounce) cans black beans, rinsed and drained
1 (14½-ounce) can no-salt-added whole tomatoes, undrained and chopped
1 (8-ounce) can no-salt-added tomato sauce
1 (4-ounce) jar diced pimiento, drained
1 teaspoon pepper
½ teaspoon garlic powder
¼ teaspoon salt
4 cups cooked rice (cooked without salt or fat)
1 cup (4 ounces) shredded reduced-fat Monterey Jack cheese

1 Coat a large Dutch oven with cooking spray; add oil. Place over medium-high heat until hot. Add onion and green pepper; sauté until tender.

2 Add tomato juice and next 8 ingredients; bring to a boil. Cover, reduce heat, and simmer 20 to 25 minutes or until vegetables are tender, stirring occasionally.

3 To serve, spoon ½ cup rice into each of 8 individual bowls. Ladle 1 cup bean mixture over each serving. Sprinkle each with 2 tablespoons cheese. Yield: 8 servings.

RED BEANS AND RICE

YIELD: 6 servings

Vegetable cooking spray
2 teaspoons olive oil
1 cup chopped onion
2 (15-ounce) cans red kidney beans,
  rinsed and drained
3½ cups canned vegetable broth, undiluted
1½ cups instant rice, uncooked
3 bay leaves
¼ teaspoon ground red pepper
⅛ teaspoon paprika
1 cup seeded, chopped tomato
3 tablespoons sliced green onions

EXCHANGES PER SERVING:
3 Starch
2 Vegetable

PER SERVING:
Calories 296
Carbohydrate 56.4g
Protein 11.9g
Fat 2.8g
Cholesterol 0mg
Fiber 4.8g
Sodium 419mg

1 Coat a Dutch oven with cooking spray; add oil. Place over medium-high heat until hot. Add onion; sauté until tender.

2 Add kidney beans and next 5 ingredients. Bring mixture to a boil; cover, reduce heat, and simmer 15 minutes or until rice is tender. Remove and discard bay leaves.

3 To serve, ladle into individual bowls, and top evenly with tomato and green onions. Yield: 6 (1⅓-cup) servings.

EXCHANGES PER
SERVING:
1 Medium-Fat Meat
1 Starch
1 Vegetable

PER SERVING:
Calories 181
Carbohydrate 22.8g
Protein 10.9g
Fat 5.8g
Cholesterol 10mg
Fiber 4.4g
Sodium 268mg

Spaghetti Squash With Garden Vegetables

1 (3-pound) spaghetti squash
¾ cup freshly grated Parmesan cheese
   Vegetable cooking spray
2 teaspoons olive oil
1 cup diagonally sliced carrot
½ cup diagonally sliced celery
1 cup preshredded cabbage
1 small zucchini, cut into thin strips
1 (16-ounce) can kidney beans, rinsed and
   drained
1 (14½-ounce) can no-salt-added whole
   tomatoes, drained and chopped
⅓ cup dry white wine
1 teaspoon dried thyme
1 teaspoon dried parsley flakes
½ teaspoon garlic powder
⅛ teaspoon pepper

1 Cut squash in half lengthwise; remove and discard seeds. Place squash, cut side down, in a Dutch oven; add water to depth of 2 inches. Bring to a boil; cover, reduce heat, and simmer 20 to 25 minutes or until tender. Drain.

2 Using a fork, remove 3 cups spaghetti-like strands from squash; reserve remaining squash for another use. Discard squash shells. Combine strands and cheese; toss. Set aside; keep warm.

3 Coat a nonstick skillet with cooking spray; add oil. Place over medium heat until hot. Add carrot and celery; sauté 5 minutes. Add cabbage and zucchini; sauté 5 minutes. Add beans and remaining 6 ingredients. Cook over medium heat 5 minutes, stirring often.

4 Place ½ cup squash mixture on each plate. Top evenly with vegetables. Yield: 6 servings.

VEGETARIAN CASSEROLE

YIELD: 6 servings

1½ cups water
¼ teaspoon salt
1 cup couscous, uncooked
1 (15-ounce) can black beans, drained
1 (8¾-ounce) can no-salt-added whole
    kernel corn, drained
1 (8-ounce) can sliced water chestnuts,
    drained
1 (7-ounce) jar roasted red peppers in
    water, drained and cut into strips
⅓ cup minced green onions
2 tablespoons minced pickled jalapeño
    pepper
1 cup part-skim ricotta cheese
2 tablespoons balsamic vinegar
2 teaspoons sesame oil
1 teaspoon ground cumin
    Vegetable cooking spray
6 cups fresh spinach leaves

**EXCHANGES PER
SERVING:**
1 Medium-Fat Meat
3 Starch

PER SERVING:
Calories 291
Carbohydrate 46.0g
Protein 15.2g
Fat 6.1g
Cholesterol 13mg
Fiber 5.5g
Sodium 208mg

1 Combine water and salt in a large saucepan; bring to a boil. Remove from heat. Add to couscous; stir well. Cover and let stand 5 minutes or until couscous is tender and liquid is absorbed. Add black beans and next 5 ingredients; stir gently.

2 Combine ricotta cheese and next 3 ingredients; stir into couscous mixture. Spoon mixture into an 11- x 7- x 1½-inch baking dish coated with cooking spray. Bake, uncovered, at 350° for 25 minutes or until thoroughly heated.

3 Cut spinach leaves into thin strips. Place 1 cup spinach on each serving plate; spoon couscous mixture evenly over spinach. Yield: 6 servings.

BEAN AND RICE STUFFED PEPPERS

EXCHANGES PER
SERVING:
1 Medium-Fat Meat
2 Starch
1 Vegetable

PER SERVING:
Calories 257
Carbohydrate 36.8g
Protein 15.4g
Fat 6.3g
Cholesterol 19mg
Fiber 4.6g
Sodium 334mg

6 medium-size sweet red, yellow, or
    orange peppers
1½ cups cooked long-grain rice (cooked
    without salt or fat)
½ cup chopped onion
1 (15-ounce) can red kidney beans, rinsed
    and drained
1 (14½-ounce) can no-salt-added stewed
    tomatoes, undrained
1 (4½-ounce) can chopped green chiles,
    drained
1 teaspoon chili powder
1½ cups (6 ounces) shredded reduced-fat
    sharp Cheddar cheese, divided

1 Cut tops off peppers, and remove seeds. Cook tops and bottoms of peppers in boiling water 5 minutes. Drain peppers; set aside.

2 Combine rice and next 5 ingredients in a medium bowl; stir in 1 cup cheese. Spoon rice mixture evenly into peppers, and replace pepper tops; place peppers in an 11- x 7- x 1½-inch baking dish.

3 Add hot water to dish to depth of ½ inch. Bake, uncovered, at 350° for 25 minutes. Remove pepper tops, and sprinkle remaining ½ cup cheese evenly over rice mixture. Bake 5 additional minutes or until cheese melts. Yield: 6 servings.

VEGETABLE-STUFFED PEPPERS

YIELD: 6 servings

This recipe is a healthy one with emphasis on grains, fresh vegetables, and low-fat cheese.

⅔ cup boiling water
⅔ cup bulgur (cracked wheat), uncooked
6 small green peppers
  Vegetable cooking spray
½ cup diced carrot
½ cup diced onion
½ cup diced celery
1 egg, lightly beaten
½ cup raisins
⅓ cup pine nuts, toasted
½ cup part-skim ricotta cheese
¼ cup lemon juice
½ teaspoon salt
½ teaspoon dried mint flakes
½ cup canned vegetable broth, undiluted

EXCHANGES PER SERVING:
1 Medium-Fat Meat
2 Starch
1 Vegetable

PER SERVING:
Calories 243
Carbohydrate 36.3g
Protein 10.3g
Fat 8.8g
Cholesterol 45mg
Fiber 6.5g
Sodium 332mg

1 Pour ⅔ cup boiling water over bulgur in a large bowl; cover and let stand 15 minutes or until bulgur is tender and water is absorbed.

2 Cut tops off peppers; remove and discard seeds and membranes, and reserve tops. Cook peppers and tops in a small amount of boiling water 10 minutes. Drain and set peppers aside.

3 Coat a nonstick skillet with cooking spray; place over medium-high heat until hot. Add carrot, onion, and celery; sauté until crisp-tender. Add bulgur mixture, egg, and next 6 ingredients; stir well. Spoon mixture into peppers. Cover with reserved tops. Place peppers in a shallow baking dish. Pour broth over peppers. Bake at 350° for 30 minutes or until thoroughly heated. Yield: 6 servings.

SHEPHERD'S PIE

EXCHANGES PER
SERVING:
2 Starch
2 Vegetable

PER SERVING:
Calories 218
Carbohydrate 40.6g
Protein 11.4g
Fat 2.0g
Cholesterol 4mg
Fiber 3.7g
Sodium 302mg

3 cups frozen peas and carrots, thawed
1 cup frozen chopped onion, thawed
1 cup frozen chopped green pepper, thawed
2 teaspoons dried thyme
2 teaspoons paprika
  Olive oil-flavored vegetable cooking spray
4 cups frozen shredded hash brown potatoes, thawed
⅔ cup lite ricotta cheese
¼ teaspoon salt
2 cups drained canned black-eyed peas
1 cup diced tomato
1 (8-ounce) can no-salt-added tomato sauce
2 teaspoons low-sodium Worcestershire sauce
¼ teaspoon salt
  Paprika

1 Combine first 5 ingredients; stir well. Spoon mixture into a 15- x 10- x 1-inch jellyroll pan coated with cooking spray; coat vegetables with cooking spray. Bake, uncovered, at 400° for 20 minutes, stirring after 10 minutes; set vegetable mixture aside.

2 Cook potato in boiling water to cover 10 minutes or until tender. Drain and mash. Stir in ricotta cheese and salt; set aside.

3 Combine vegetable mixture, black-eyed peas, and next 4 ingredients, stirring well. Spoon into a 2½-quart shallow baking dish coated with cooking spray.

4 Spoon potato mixture in a border around edge of dish; spoon remaining potato mixture over center of dish. Sprinkle additional paprika over top of potato mixture. Bake, uncovered, at 350° for 20 minutes. Yield: 6 servings.

POTATO LASAGNA

YIELD: 8 servings

1 (10-ounce) package frozen chopped
   broccoli, thawed
1 (15-ounce) carton nonfat ricotta cheese
1 cup shredded carrot
½ cup minced green onions
1 teaspoon dried marjoram
½ teaspoon freshly ground pepper
   Vegetable cooking spray
5 large round red potatoes, peeled and
   thinly sliced (about 2¼ pounds)
1½ cups (6 ounces) shredded part-skim
   mozzarella cheese
½ cup freshly grated Parmesan cheese

**EXCHANGES PER
SERVING:**
2 Lean Meat
2 Starch

PER SERVING:
Calories 227
Carbohydrate 28.5g
Protein 18.8g
Fat 5.6g
Cholesterol 23mg
Fiber 3.3g
Sodium 262mg

1 Press broccoli between paper towels until barely moist. Combine broccoli, ricotta cheese, and next 4 ingredients in a medium bowl; stir well. Set aside.

2 Coat an 11- x 7- x 1½-inch baking dish with cooking spray. Place one-third of potato slices in bottom of dish. Top with half of broccoli mixture; sprinkle with half of mozzarella cheese. Repeat layers. Top with remaining potato slices, and sprinkle with Parmesan cheese.

3 Cover and bake at 375° for 30 minutes; uncover and bake 55 additional minutes or until potato is tender and golden. Let stand 10 minutes before serving. Yield: 8 servings.

ITALIAN POLENTA

EXCHANGES PER
SERVING:
1 Lean Meat
2 Starch
1 Vegetable

PER SERVING:
Calories 227
Carbohydrate 34.8g
Protein 11.3g
Fat 5.9g
Cholesterol 16mg
Fiber 4.3g
Sodium 232mg

🌿 Polenta is a corn-meal specialty from northern Italy sold dry or precooked. Cooking dry polenta produces a warm cereal similar to cream of wheat. When cooled, polenta can be sliced and served with a variety of toppings. Precooked polenta is ready to slice. Look for it in the refrigerated vegetable section of the super-market.

If you can't find precooked polenta, cook ¾ cup dry polenta in 2¼ cups water for about 30 minutes to make the amount for this recipe.

Vegetable cooking spray
1 cup finely chopped zucchini (about 1 small)
1 cup frozen whole kernel corn, thawed
1 (8-ounce) can no-salt-added tomato sauce
¾ cup finely chopped onion
1 teaspoon dried sage
1 teaspoon dried Italian seasoning
⅛ teaspoon salt
⅛ teaspoon garlic powder
2 teaspoons balsamic vinegar
½ (32-ounce) package precooked polenta (yellow cornmeal)
1 cup (4 ounces) shredded part-skim mozzarella cheese

1 Coat a nonstick skillet with cooking spray; place over medium-high heat until hot. Add zucchini and next 7 ingredients. Reduce heat, and cook 5 minutes or until vegetables are tender. Stir in vinegar. Set aside, and keep warm.

2 Cut precooked polenta crosswise into 12 even slices; place on a baking sheet, and bake at 350° for 10 to 15 minutes or until thoroughly heated. Arrange 3 polenta slices on each serving plate. Top each serving with ⅓ cup sauce and ¼ cup mozzarella cheese. Yield: 4 servings.

CHINESE VEGETABLE STIR-FRY

YIELD: 5 servings

Tofu is a protein-rich soybean product with a very mild flavor. It absorbs the flavors of the recipe and adds texture.

¼ cup fresh lemon juice
¼ cup low-sodium soy sauce
1 tablespoon peeled, grated gingerroot
1½ teaspoons granulated sugar substitute
2 cloves garlic, minced
1 cup chopped onion
1 (10-ounce) package firm tofu, drained and cubed
1½ tablespoons vegetable oil
2 cups shredded Chinese cabbage
1 cup fresh bean sprouts
1 cup diced sweet red pepper
1 cup sliced fresh mushrooms
¼ cup sliced green onions
2 teaspoons cornstarch
3¾ cups cooked brown rice (cooked without salt or fat)

EXCHANGES PER SERVING:
1 Medium-Fat Meat
2 Starch
2 Vegetable

PER SERVING:
Calories 291
Carbohydrate 44.6g
Protein 10.5g
Fat 8.5g
Cholesterol 0mg
Fiber 5.0g
Sodium 350mg

1 Combine first 5 ingredients. Add onion and tofu. Cover and marinate in refrigerator 2 to 3 hours. Drain, reserving marinade.

2 Drizzle oil around top of wok, coating sides. Heat at medium (350°) until hot. Add tofu mixture; stir-fry 5 minutes or until tofu starts to brown and onion is tender. Remove from wok; set aside, and keep warm.

3 Add cabbage and next 4 ingredients to wok; stir-fry 2 to 3 minutes or until crisp-tender.

4 Combine reserved marinade and cornstarch, stirring well. Add marinade mixture to vegetables; stir-fry 3 minutes or until thickened. Add tofu mixture, and stir-fry 30 seconds or until thoroughly heated. To serve, spoon ¾ cup rice onto each serving plate. Top evenly with vegetable mixture. Yield: 5 servings.

CHEESY BROCCOLI-CORN STRUDEL

YIELD: 7 servings

EXCHANGES PER
SERVING:
2 Medium-Fat Meat
2 Starch

PER SERVING:
Calories 267
Carbohydrate 29.0g
Protein 14.3g
Fat 10.9g
Cholesterol 27mg
Fiber 2.5g
Sodium 345mg

1 cup part-skim ricotta cheese
3 ounces light process cream cheese, softened
1 (10-ounce) package frozen chopped broccoli, thawed and drained
1 cup frozen whole kernel corn, thawed
½ cup (2 ounces) shredded fontina cheese
½ cup frozen egg substitute, thawed
¼ cup sliced green onions
1 (2-ounce) jar diced pimiento, drained
½ teaspoon dried basil
¼ teaspoon pepper
12 sheets frozen phyllo pastry, thawed
   Butter-flavored vegetable cooking spray
¼ cup toasted wheat germ
1 teaspoon reduced-calorie margarine, melted

1 Combine cheeses, stirring well. Add broccoli and next 7 ingredients; stir well.

2 Place 4 sheets phyllo pastry on wax paper, keeping remaining phyllo pastry covered with a slightly damp towel. Coat phyllo with cooking spray, and sprinkle with 2 tablespoons wheat germ. Top with 4 more sheets; coat with cooking spray, and sprinkle with remaining 2 tablespoons wheat germ. Top with remaining 4 phyllo sheets; coat with cooking spray.

3 Spoon cheese mixture lengthwise down half of phyllo stack, leaving a 1-inch margin on long side and a 1½-inch margin on short sides. Roll up phyllo, jellyroll fashion, starting with longest side. Tuck ends under, and place diagonally, seam side down, on a 15- x 10- x 1-inch jellyroll pan coated with cooking spray. Brush with margarine. Make diagonal slits about ¼ inch deep, 2 inches apart, across top of pastry, using a sharp knife. Bake at 375° for 30 minutes. Let stand 10 minutes before serving. Yield: 7 servings.

VEGETARIAN DUTCH BABY

YIELD: 4 servings

Vegetable cooking spray
1 cup sliced fresh mushrooms
½ cup thinly sliced and quartered yellow squash
½ cup thinly sliced and quartered zucchini
½ (16-ounce) package commercial slaw mix
¾ cup canned black beans, rinsed and drained
½ teaspoon dried basil
¼ teaspoon dried thyme
¼ teaspoon onion powder
¼ teaspoon garlic powder
⅛ teaspoon salt
⅛ teaspoon pepper
1 tablespoon reduced-calorie margarine
½ cup all-purpose flour
½ cup skim milk
2 eggs, lightly beaten
½ cup (2 ounces) shredded provolone cheese

EXCHANGES PER SERVING:
1 High-Fat Meat
1 Starch
3 Vegetable

PER SERVING:
Calories 248
Carbohydrate 28.6g
Protein 14.3g
Fat 9.0g
Cholesterol 121mg
Fiber 4.1g
Sodium 287mg

1 Coat a large nonstick skillet with cooking spray; place over medium-high heat until hot. Add mushrooms and next 3 ingredients; sauté 5 to 7 minutes or until vegetables are tender, stirring often. Stir in black beans and next 6 ingredients. Set aside, and keep warm.

2 Coat a 9-inch pieplate with cooking spray; add margarine. Place in 425° oven 1 minute or until margarine melts. Combine flour, milk, and eggs in a medium bowl; stir well with a wire whisk. Pour mixture into prepared pieplate (do not stir).

3 Bake at 425° for 15 to 20 minutes or until puffed and browned. Spoon vegetable mixture into shell; sprinkle with cheese. Bake 1 to 2 additional minutes or until cheese melts. Serve immediately. Yield: 4 servings.

MEXICAN VEGETABLES IN PASTRY BOWL

EXCHANGES PER
SERVING:
1½ Lean Meat
2 Starch
2 Vegetable

PER SERVING:
Calories 279
Carbohydrate 39.7g
Protein 16.6g
Fat 6.4g
Cholesterol 120mg
Fiber 4.4g
Sodium 493mg

Vegetable cooking spray
¾ cup sliced green onions
¼ cup chopped green pepper
1 clove garlic, minced
1 (15-ounce) can pinto beans, rinsed and
    drained
¾ cup frozen whole kernel corn
¾ cup seeded, chopped tomato
¼ cup chunky picante sauce
1 tablespoon lime juice
1 tablespoon minced fresh cilantro
½ cup skim milk
¼ cup all-purpose flour
¼ cup yellow cornmeal
⅛ to ¼ teaspoon chili powder
2 eggs, lightly beaten
¼ cup (1 ounce) shredded reduced-fat
    Monterey Jack cheese
¼ cup (1 ounce) shredded reduced-fat
    Cheddar cheese

1 Coat a large nonstick skillet with cooking spray; place over medium-high heat until hot. Add green onions, pepper, and garlic; sauté 3 to 4 minutes or until tender.

2 Stir in pinto beans and next 5 ingredients; cook until thoroughly heated. Remove from heat; set aside, and keep warm.

3 Combine milk and next 4 ingredients in a medium bowl; stir well with a wire whisk. Pour mixture into a 9-inch pieplate coated with cooking spray. (Do not stir.) Bake at 475° for 10 minutes or until puffed and browned.

4 Spoon bean mixture into shell; sprinkle with cheeses. Bake 1 to 2 minutes or until cheese melts. Serve immediately. Yield: 4 servings.

Meats

Beefy Tortilla Pie

YIELD: 6 servings

EXCHANGES PER
SERVING:
2 Lean Meat
1 Starch
2 Vegetable

PER SERVING:
Calories 255
Carbohydrate 24.4g
Protein 22.3g
Fat 7.6g
Cholesterol 44mg
Fiber 3.3g
Sodium 297mg

¾ pound ground round
1½ teaspoons chili powder
1 clove garlic, minced
1½ cups canned red kidney beans, rinsed
  and drained
½ cup sliced green onions
2 tablespoons red wine vinegar
2 tablespoons tomato paste
5 (6-inch) corn tortillas
1¼ cups canned no-salt-added chicken
  broth, undiluted
1 tablespoon plus 2 teaspoons
  all-purpose flour
½ teaspoon ground cumin
1 (4½-ounce) can chopped green chiles
  Vegetable cooking spray
¾ cup (3 ounces) shredded reduced-fat
  Cheddar cheese

1 Combine first 3 ingredients in a nonstick skillet. Cook over medium-high heat until browned, stirring until meat crumbles. Drain. Return meat mixture to skillet. Stir in kidney beans and next 3 ingredients.

2 Cut each tortilla into 6 wedges. Wrap in aluminum foil; bake at 350° for 8 minutes.

3 Bring broth to a boil in a saucepan. Reduce heat to low; add flour and cumin. Cook, stirring constantly, until slightly thickened. Remove from heat; stir in chiles. Set aside.

4 Coat a 9-inch pieplate with cooking spray; line with 14 tortilla wedges. Top with one-third of meat mixture. Spoon one-third of broth mixture over meat. Repeat layers twice, using 10 tortilla wedges on second layer, and 6 on third layer. Top with cheese.

5 Bake at 375° for 10 minutes or until cheese melts. Let stand 5 minutes on a wire rack. Yield: 6 servings.

Saucy Meatballs

1 pound ground round
1½ cups plus 2 tablespoons canned
    no-salt-added beef broth, undiluted
    and divided
2 tablespoons low-sodium Worcestershire
    sauce
¼ teaspoon garlic powder
    Vegetable cooking spray
½ cup frozen small whole onions, thawed
½ teaspoon dried thyme
¼ teaspoon pepper
⅛ teaspoon salt
¼ cup water
2 tablespoons cornstarch

YIELD: 4 servings

EXCHANGES PER
SERVING:
3 Lean Meat
½ Starch

PER SERVING:
Calories 214
Carbohydrate 8.9g
Protein 24.8g
Fat 7.1g
Cholesterol 70mg
Fiber 0.2g
Sodium 161mg

1 Combine ground round, 2 tablespoons broth, Worcestershire sauce, and garlic powder. Shape into 28 meatballs, using 1 tablespoon meat mixture for each meatball.

2 Place meatballs on rack of a broiler pan coated with cooking spray. Broil 5½ inches from heat (with electric oven door partially opened) 10 to 12 minutes or until browned, turning occasionally. Drain and pat dry with paper towels; set aside.

3 Coat a large nonstick skillet with cooking spray; place over medium-high heat until hot. Add onions, and sauté 2 minutes or until tender. Stir in meatballs, remaining 1½ cups broth, thyme, pepper, and salt. Bring to a boil; cover, reduce heat, and simmer 20 minutes.

4 Combine water and cornstarch in a small bowl, stirring well. Add cornstarch mixture to meatball mixture. Cook 3 to 4 minutes or until thickened and bubbly, stirring constantly. Yield: 4 servings.

SALISBURY STEAK

YIELD: 4 servings

EXCHANGES PER SERVING:
3 Lean Meat
½ Starch
1 Vegetable

PER SERVING:
Calories 244
Carbohydrate 12.8g
Protein 26.7g
Fat 8.5g
Cholesterol 70mg
Fiber 0.9g
Sodium 332mg

1 pound ground round
¼ cup finely chopped onion
3 tablespoons fine, dry breadcrumbs
1 egg white
2 tablespoons water
¼ teaspoon beef-flavored bouillon granules
¼ teaspoon pepper
⅛ teaspoon salt
   Vegetable cooking spray
1 teaspoon margarine, melted
¾ cup sliced fresh mushrooms
1 small onion, sliced and separated into rings
1 (13¾-ounce) can no-salt-added beef broth, undiluted
2 tablespoons low-sodium Worcestershire sauce
1 tablespoon cornstarch
2 tablespoons water

1 Combine first 8 ingredients in a bowl; stir well. Shape into 4 (¾-inch-thick) patties.

2 Coat a large nonstick skillet with cooking spray; place over medium-high heat until hot. Add patties; cook 5 minutes on each side. Drain and pat dry with paper towels. Wipe drippings from skillet with a paper towel.

3 Coat skillet with cooking spray; add margarine. Add mushrooms and onion; cook over medium-high heat until tender. Add beef broth and Worcestershire sauce; cook 5 minutes.

4 Return patties to skillet. Cover, reduce heat, and simmer 10 minutes. Remove patties from liquid, using a slotted spoon, and place patties on a platter; set aside, and keep warm.

5 Combine cornstarch and water in a small bowl; stir well. Add cornstarch mixture to broth mixture. Bring to a boil, and cook, stirring constantly, 1 minute or until thickened. Spoon evenly over patties. Yield: 4 servings.

REUBEN MEAT ROLL

YIELD: 6 servings

1 pound ground round
1 cup soft rye breadcrumbs
1 egg, lightly beaten
¼ cup chopped onion
¼ cup finely chopped dill pickles
2 tablespoons commercial reduced-calorie
   Russian dressing
1 tablespoon low-sodium Worcestershire
   sauce
½ teaspoon pepper
   Vegetable cooking spray
1 (10-ounce) can chopped sauerkraut,
   drained
½ cup (2 ounces) shredded reduced-fat
   Swiss cheese
1 (2-ounce) jar sliced pimiento, drained

EXCHANGES PER SERVING:
3 Lean Meat
½ Starch

PER SERVING:
Calories 208
Carbohydrate 9.5g
Protein 23.3g
Fat 8.2g
Cholesterol 95mg
Fiber 1.2g
Sodium 501mg

1 Combine first 8 ingredients in a bowl; stir well. Shape mixture into a 12- x 10-inch rectangle on heavy-duty plastic wrap coated with cooking spray.

2 Combine sauerkraut, cheese, and pimiento; spread over meat mixture, leaving a 1-inch margin on all sides.

3 Carefully roll meat, jellyroll fashion, starting at narrow end, using plastic wrap to support meat. Pinch edges and seam of meat to seal. Remove from plastic wrap, and place roll, seam side down, on a rack in a roasting pan that has been coated with cooking spray. Cover and bake at 350° for 10 minutes. Uncover and bake 35 to 40 additional minutes. Let stand 10 minutes before slicing. Yield: 6 servings.

PICANTE MEAT LOAF

YIELD: 6 servings

EXCHANGES PER
SERVING:
3 Medium-Fat Meat
1 Vegetable

PER SERVING:
Calories 234
Carbohydrate 5.6g
Protein 20.2g
Fat 14.1g
Cholesterol 59mg
Fiber 0.6g
Sodium 410mg

1 pound ground chuck
⅔ cup soft whole wheat breadcrumbs
½ cup chopped onion
¼ cup coarsely chopped carrot
2 egg whites, lightly beaten
¼ teaspoon salt
¼ teaspoon rubbed sage
¼ teaspoon pepper
    Vegetable cooking spray
½ cup picante sauce
    Cherry tomatoes (optional)

1 Combine first 8 ingredients in a medium bowl. Shape mixture into a 6- x 4- x 2-inch loaf, and place on a rack in a shallow roasting pan coated with cooking spray.

2 Bake at 400° for 35 minutes. Brush picante sauce over meat loaf. Return to oven, and bake 5 additional minutes. Let stand 5 minutes before slicing. Garnish with cherry tomatoes, if desired. Yield: 6 servings.

Teriyaki Beef and Sweet Peppers

¼ cup low-sodium soy sauce
2 tablespoons unsweetened pineapple juice
2 teaspoons cornstarch
1 teaspoon instant minced garlic
¾ pound lean round steak
    Vegetable cooking spray
2 teaspoons vegetable oil
1 medium-size sweet red pepper, seeded and cut into thin strips
1 medium-size sweet yellow pepper, seeded and cut into thin strips
1 medium-size green pepper, seeded and cut into thin strips
2 cups cooked rice (cooked without salt or fat)

1 Combine first 4 ingredients in a small bowl; set aside.

2 Trim excess fat from steak. Slice steak diagonally across grain into ¼-inch-wide strips.

3 Coat a wok or large nonstick skillet with cooking spray; drizzle oil around top of wok, coating sides. Heat at medium-high (375°) until hot. Add steak; stir-fry 2 minutes. Add peppers, and stir-fry 4 minutes or until steak is browned. Add cornstarch mixture to steak mixture. Stir-fry 3 minutes or until thickened. Serve over rice. Yield: 4 servings.

YIELD: 4 servings

EXCHANGES PER SERVING:
2 Lean Meat
2 Starch

PER SERVING:
Calories 284
Carbohydrate 30.8g
Protein 21.4g
Fat 7.1g
Cholesterol 49mg
Fiber 1.8g
Sodium 440mg

❧ There is a difference in low-sodium and lite soy sauce. Lite has 200 milligrams of sodium per teaspoon, while low-sodium brands have 130 milligrams per teaspoon. One teaspoon of regular soy sauce contains about 343 milligrams of sodium.

**EXCHANGES PER
SERVING:**
3 Lean Meat
½ Starch

PER SERVING:
Calories 206
Carbohydrate 6.6g
Protein 27.2g
Fat 7.2g
Cholesterol 120mg
Fiber 0.4g
Sodium 254mg

LEMON-PEPPER
STEAK CUTLETS

These steak cutlets are a lower fat
alternative to country-fried steak. Be sure
to use enough cooking spray in the nonstick
skillet so that the cutlets won't stick.

1 pound lean round steak
1 egg
1 teaspoon grated lemon rind
2 tablespoons lemon juice
1 tablespoon water
½ cup soft whole wheat breadcrumbs
2 tablespoons all-purpose flour
½ teaspoon pepper
¼ teaspoon salt
   Vegetable cooking spray
   Lemon slices (optional)
   Fresh tarragon (optional)

1 Trim excess fat from steak; place steak
between 2 sheets of heavy-duty plastic wrap,
and flatten to ¼-inch thickness, using a meat
mallet or rolling pin. Cut into 4 equal pieces.

2 Combine egg and next 3 ingredients in
a small bowl, stirring well. Combine breadcrumbs and next 3 ingredients in a medium
bowl, stirring well. Dip steak pieces in egg
mixture, and dredge in breadcrumb mixture.

3 Coat a large nonstick skillet with cooking
spray; place over medium-high heat until
hot. Add steak, and cook 2½ minutes on
each side or to desired degree of doneness. If
desired, garnish with lemon slices and tarragon.
Yield: 4 servings.

ORIENTAL BEEF AND VEGETABLES

YIELD: 8 servings

EXCHANGES PER
SERVING:
2 Medium-Fat Meat
2 Starch

PER SERVING:
Calories 279
Carbohydrate 32.7g
Protein 15.9g
Fat 9.2g
Cholesterol 28mg
Fiber 3.1g
Sodium 218mg

1 (1-pound) lean flank steak
½ cup canned no-salt added beef broth,
    undiluted
3 tablespoons low-sodium soy sauce
1 teaspoon cornstarch
½ pound fresh broccoli
2 tablespoons peanut oil
2 cups sliced leek
1 (8-ounce) package presliced fresh
    mushrooms
½ cup thinly sliced onion
8 cups torn fresh spinach
4 cups cooked long-grain rice (cooked
    without salt or fat)

1 Trim fat from steak; partially freeze steak. Slice diagonally across grain into ¼-inch strips.

2 Combine broth, soy sauce, and cornstarch in a bowl; stir well.

3 Trim off large leaves of broccoli, and remove tough ends of lower stalks. Wash broccoli thoroughly, and separate into flowerets. Cut stalks into ½-inch pieces.

4 Drizzle oil around top of a wok or large nonstick skillet; heat at medium (325°) until hot. Add steak, and stir-fry 1 minute. Add broth mixture; cover and simmer 2 minutes. Add broccoli, leek, mushrooms, and onion; stir well. Place spinach on top of mixture; cover and cook 10 minutes or until spinach wilts and other vegetables are crisp-tender. Serve over rice. Yield: 8 servings.

❧ Because stir-frying requires little fat or oil, the amount of calories from fat is significantly lower than frying. If you do use oil for stir-frying, choose peanut, safflower, olive, or corn oil because none of them smokes at high cooking temperatures.

FLANK STEAK WITH HORSERADISH CREAM

EXCHANGES PER
SERVING:
3 Medium-Fat Meat

PER SERVING:
Calories 253
Carbohydrate 5.2g
Protein 23.7g
Fat 14.4g
Cholesterol 60mg
Fiber 0.1g
Sodium 251mg

¼ cup light olive oil vinaigrette
1 teaspoon dried Italian seasoning
1 small onion, quartered
1 (1-pound) flank steak
  Vegetable cooking spray
½ cup nonfat sour cream
2 tablespoons nonfat mayonnaise
1½ tablespoons prepared horseradish
  Fresh oregano sprigs (optional)

1 Position knife blade in food processor bowl; add first 3 ingredients. Cover and process until onion is minced.

2 Place steak in a heavy-duty, zip-top plastic bag. Pour onion mixture over steak; seal bag, and shake until steak is well coated. Marinate in refrigerator 8 hours, turning bag occasionally.

3 Remove steak from marinade; discard marinade. Coat grill rack with cooking spray; place on grill over medium-hot coals (350° to 400°). Place steak on rack; grill, covered, 10 to 12 minutes or to desired degree of doneness. Let steak stand 5 minutes.

4 Combine sour cream, mayonnaise, and horseradish, stirring well. Cut steak diagonally across grain into thin slices. Garnish with fresh oregano, if desired. Serve with horseradish mixture. Yield: 4 servings.

Spicy Skillet Steaks

YIELD: 4 servings

2 tablespoons cornmeal
¼ teaspoon garlic powder
¼ teaspoon ground cumin
¼ teaspoon dried oregano
⅛ teaspoon salt
⅛ teaspoon onion powder
⅛ teaspoon ground red pepper
4 (4-ounce) lean cubed sirloin steaks
  Vegetable cooking spray
¼ cup plus 2 tablespoons no-salt-added
  tomato sauce
1 (4½-ounce) can chopped green chiles,
  drained
1 large ripe tomato, cut into 16 wedges

EXCHANGES PER SERVING:
3 Lean Meat
2 Vegetable

PER SERVING:
Calories 219
Carbohydrate 9.5g
Protein 28.6g
Fat 6.9g
Cholesterol 80mg
Fiber 1.3g
Sodium 213mg

1 Combine first 7 ingredients in a shallow bowl; stir well. Dredge steaks in cornmeal mixture. Coat a large nonstick skillet with cooking spray; place over medium heat until hot. Add steaks, and cook 5 minutes on each side or until browned.

2 Remove steaks from skillet. Drain and pat dry with paper towels. Wipe drippings from skillet with a paper towel.

3 Combine tomato sauce and chiles in skillet, stirring well; bring to a boil. Return steaks to skillet. Cover, reduce heat, and simmer 6 minutes or until steaks are tender. Add tomato wedges; cover and simmer 2 minutes or until thoroughly heated. Yield: 4 servings.

SAVORY SIRLOIN STEAK

YIELD: 4 servings

EXCHANGES PER
SERVING:
4 Lean Meat

PER SERVING:
Calories 193
Carbohydrate 1.5g
Protein 26.1g
Fat 8.4g
Cholesterol 76mg
Fiber 0.1g
Sodium 213mg

1 (1-pound) lean boneless beef sirloin
    steak (¾ inch thick)
¾ teaspoon fresh rosemary, minced
¼ teaspoon pepper
    Vegetable cooking spray
1 tablespoon reduced-calorie margarine
1 tablespoon plain nonfat yogurt
1 tablespoon Dijon mustard
1 tablespoon low-sodium Worcestershire
    sauce
1 tablespoon chopped fresh parsley
    Fresh rosemary sprigs (optional)
    Lemon wedges (optional)

1 Trim fat from steak. Combine rosemary and pepper; sprinkle over steak.

2 Coat a large nonstick skillet with cooking spray; add margarine, and place over medium heat until margarine melts. Add steak, and cook 6 minutes on each side or to desired degree of doneness. Remove steak from skillet; transfer to a serving platter, and keep warm.

3 Combine yogurt, mustard, and Worcestershire sauce in a small saucepan. Cook over low heat, stirring constantly, until thoroughly heated. (Do not boil.) Spoon sauce over steak. Sprinkle with parsley. If desired, garnish with rosemary sprigs and lemon wedges. Yield: 4 servings.

Skillet Beef Casserole

YIELD: 6 servings

2 (8-ounce) baking potatoes, peeled and
   cut into ⅛-inch slices
1 pound lean boneless beef sirloin steak
   Vegetable cooking spray
½ cup thinly sliced carrot
1 cup thinly sliced onion
½ cup thinly sliced celery
2 cloves garlic, minced
2 tablespoons all-purpose flour
1 teaspoon coarsely ground pepper
¾ teaspoon dried thyme
1 (16-ounce) can no-salt-added green
   beans, drained
1 (14-ounce) can no-salt-added whole
   tomatoes, drained and chopped
1 (5½-ounce) can no-salt-added
   vegetable juice
2 teaspoons reduced-calorie margarine,
   melted

**EXCHANGES PER
SERVING:**
2 Lean Meat
1 Starch
1 Vegetable

PER SERVING:
Calories 191
Carbohydrate 19.4g
Protein 18.4g
Fat 4.8g
Cholesterol 43mg
Fiber 3.4g
Sodium 77mg

1 Cook potato in boiling water to cover 3 minutes or until crisp-tender. Drain.

2 Trim fat from steak; cut steak into 1-inch pieces. Coat a 10-inch ovenproof skillet with cooking spray; place over medium-high heat until hot. Add steak; cook 8 minutes or until browned on all sides. Remove from skillet, and set aside. Wipe drippings from skillet.

3 Coat skillet with cooking spray. Add carrot; sauté 5 minutes. Add onion, celery, and garlic; sauté until tender. Combine flour, pepper, and thyme; stir well. Stir flour mixture into vegetable mixture; cook 1 minute, stirring constantly. Add steak, beans, tomato, and vegetable juice. Bring to a boil; reduce heat, and simmer 5 minutes, stirring occasionally.

4 Remove skillet from heat; arrange potato over steak mixture to cover. Brush potato with margarine. Broil 5½ inches from heat (with electric oven door partially opened) 15 minutes or until golden. Yield: 6 servings.

STEAK DIANE

YIELD: 4 servings

EXCHANGES PER
SERVING:
3 Lean Meat
2 Vegetable

PER SERVING:
Calories 249
Carbohydrate 11.0g
Protein 25.9g
Fat 10.6g
Cholesterol 70mg
Fiber 2.0g
Sodium 569mg

If you prefer not to use brandy, replace it with ¼ cup no-salt-added canned beef broth.

  1 tablespoon reduced-calorie margarine, melted
  2 tablespoons low-sodium Worcestershire sauce
  ¾ pound fresh mushrooms, sliced
  1 cup chopped onion
  4 (4-ounce) beef tenderloin steaks (1 inch thick)
  ¼ cup Dijon mustard, divided
  ¼ cup brandy

1 Combine margarine and Worcestershire sauce in a large nonstick skillet; place over medium heat until hot. Add mushrooms and onions; sauté until tender.

2 Place steaks between 2 sheets of heavy-duty plastic wrap, and flatten to ¼-inch thickness, using a meat mallet or rolling pin. Spread 1½ teaspoons mustard on 1 side of each steak.

3 Move mushroom mixture to one side of skillet; add steaks, mustard side down. Cook steaks over medium heat 3 minutes. Stir mushroom mixture occasionally. Spread 1½ teaspoons mustard on top side of each steak; turn and cook 3 to 4 minutes or to desired degree of doneness.

4 Lightly pierce steaks in several places with a fork. Pour brandy over steaks; cover, reduce heat, and simmer 1 minute. Remove steaks to a serving platter; spoon mushroom mixture over steaks. Yield: 4 servings.

Beef Tenderloin Stroganoff

YIELD: 6 servings

EXCHANGES PER
SERVING:
3 Lean Meat
1 Vegetable

PER SERVING:
Calories 225
Carbohydrate 5.7g
Protein 25.8g
Fat 10.6g
Cholesterol 79mg
Fiber 0.9g
Sodium 148mg

6 (4-ounce) beef tenderloin steaks
¼ teaspoon garlic powder
¼ teaspoon pepper
   Vegetable cooking spray
2 cups sliced fresh mushrooms
1 small onion, sliced and separated into
   rings
⅓ cup water
3 tablespoons dry red wine
1 tablespoon all-purpose flour
½ teaspoon dry mustard
½ teaspoon beef-flavored bouillon
   granules
¼ teaspoon dried dillweed
½ cup low-fat sour cream
   Fresh dill sprigs (optional)

1 Trim fat from steaks. Combine garlic powder and pepper; sprinkle over steaks.

2 Coat a large nonstick skillet with cooking spray; place over medium-high heat until hot. Add steaks, and cook 5 to 6 minutes on each side or to desired degree of doneness. Remove steaks from skillet. Drain steaks; keep warm. Wipe drippings from skillet with a paper towel.

3 Coat skillet with cooking spray; place over medium-high heat until hot. Add mushrooms and onion; sauté until tender. Combine water and next 5 ingredients, stirring well with a wire whisk. Add to mushroom mixture. Cook 1 minute, stirring constantly. Remove from heat; stir in sour cream.

4 Transfer steaks to a serving platter, and spoon mushroom mixture over steaks. Garnish with dill sprigs, if desired. Yield: 6 servings.

EXCHANGES PER SERVING:
2½ Lean Meat

PER SERVING:
Calories 142
Carbohydrate 1.3g
Protein 16.7g
Fat 7.3g
Cholesterol 49mg
Fiber 0g
Sodium 258mg

✄ Use a meat thermometer or a kitchen timer when roasting meat as a fail-safe way to prevent overcooking.

BEEF TENDERLOIN WITH TARRAGON SAUCE

1 (2-pound) beef tenderloin, trimmed
¼ teaspoon salt
¼ teaspoon pepper
  Vegetable cooking spray
2 tablespoons reduced-calorie margarine, softened
2 tablespoons coarse-grained mustard
¾ cup dry white wine
3 tablespoons minced shallots
1½ teaspoons dried tarragon
1 tablespoon skim milk
  Assorted steamed baby vegetables (optional)

1 Sprinkle tenderloin with salt and pepper. Place tenderloin on rack coated with cooking spray; place rack in a roasting pan coated with cooking spray. Insert meat thermometer into thickest portion of tenderloin. Bake at 425° for 35 minutes or until meat thermometer registers 160° (medium). Cover and let stand.

2 Combine margarine and mustard; stir well, and set aside.

3 Combine wine, shallot, and tarragon in a small saucepan. Cook over medium heat 5 minutes or until reduced to about 3 tablespoons. Remove from heat; stir in milk. Add reserved margarine mixture, stirring until smooth. Cook tarragon sauce over low heat until thoroughly heated. (Do not boil.)

4 To serve, transfer tenderloin to a serving platter. Garnish with baby vegetables, if desired. Serve with tarragon sauce.
Yield: 8 servings.

SAVORY POT ROAST

YIELD: 10 servings

1 (2½-pound) lean bottom round roast
  Vegetable cooking spray
2 teaspoons vegetable oil
2 cups canned no-salt-added beef broth
2 tablespoons minced garlic
2 tablespoons lemon juice
1 teaspoon pepper
1 (8-ounce) can no-salt-added tomato
    sauce
2 bay leaves
2 large carrots, scraped and cut into
    fourths
2 stalks celery, cut into fourths
1 large onion, peeled and cut into fourths

**EXCHANGES PER
SERVING:**
3 Lean Meat
1 Vegetable

PER SERVING:
Calories 196
Carbohydrate 7.6g
Protein 26.9g
Fat 5.6g
Cholesterol 65mg
Fiber 1.7g
Sodium 81mg

1 Trim fat from roast. Coat a Dutch oven with cooking spray; add oil. Place over medium-high heat until hot. Add roast; cook until browned on all sides.

2 Add beef broth and next 5 ingredients; bring to a boil. Cover, reduce heat, and simmer 1 hour and 45 minutes.

3 Add carrot, celery, and onion; cook 45 minutes or until meat is tender. Remove and discard bay leaves. Yield: 10 servings.

VEAL-ASPARAGUS STIR-FRY

EXCHANGES PER
SERVING:
3 Very Lean Meat
1 Vegetable

PER SERVING:
Calories 168
Carbohydrate 6.6g
Protein 24.3g
Fat 4.8g
Cholesterol 94mg
Fiber 1.8g
Sodium 248mg

½ pound fresh asparagus spears
1 pound veal cutlets (¼ inch thick)
  Vegetable cooking spray
1 teaspoon vegetable oil
1 small onion, thinly sliced
1 small sweet red pepper, seeded and cut
  into thin strips
¼ teaspoon salt
¼ teaspoon fennel seeds, crushed
⅛ teaspoon garlic powder
⅛ teaspoon dried crushed red pepper
2 tablespoons dry sherry
1 teaspoon lemon zest

1 Snap off tough ends of asparagus. Remove scales with a vegetable peeler, if desired. Cut asparagus into 2-inch pieces. Set aside.

2 Cut veal into thin strips. Coat a large non-stick skillet with cooking spray; add oil. Place over medium-high heat until hot. Add veal; stir-fry 5 minutes or until browned. Remove veal from skillet with a slotted spoon; set aside.

3 Add asparagus, onion, and next 5 ingredients to skillet; stir-fry 3 to 4 minutes or until vegetables are crisp-tender. Return veal to skillet. Add sherry, and stir-fry 1 minute or until thoroughly heated. Transfer to a serving platter, and sprinkle with lemon zest. Yield: 4 servings.

APPLE VEAL CHOPS

Try this autumn-accented entrée with
sweet potatoes and steamed brussels sprouts.

4 (6-ounce) loin veal chops (1 inch thick)
¼ cup all-purpose flour, divided
½ teaspoon dried marjoram
¼ teaspoon salt
    Vegetable cooking spray
1 tablespoon olive oil
½ cup chopped onion
½ cup canned no-salt-added chicken
    broth, undiluted
¼ cup unsweetened apple juice
2 small cooking apples, cored and thinly
    sliced
4 fresh marjoram sprigs (optional)

1 Trim fat from veal chops. Combine 3 tablespoons flour, dried marjoram, and salt in a
small bowl; sprinkle over chops.

2 Coat a large nonstick skillet with cooking
spray; add oil. Place over medium-high heat
until hot. Add chops, and cook 3 to 4 minutes on
each side or until lightly browned. Remove chops
from skillet. Drain chops; set aside, and keep
warm.

3 Add onion to skillet; cook 2 minutes or until
tender. Stir in remaining 1 tablespoon flour,
and cook over medium heat, stirring constantly,
until thickened. Gradually stir in chicken broth
and apple juice.

4 Return chops to skillet; top with apple slices.
Bring to a boil; cover, reduce heat, and
simmer 15 to 20 minutes or until veal is tender.
Transfer to a serving platter. Garnish with
marjoram sprigs, if desired. Yield: 4 servings.

YIELD: 4 servings

EXCHANGES PER
SERVING:
3 Medium-Fat Meat
1½ Fruit

PER SERVING:
Calories 306
Carbohydrate 24.5g
Protein 20.8g
Fat 13.9g
Cholesterol 80mg
Fiber 3.7g
Sodium 237mg

❧ There are several
varieties of cooking
apples. Look for
Baldwin, Cortland,
Granny Smith,
Northern Spy, Rome
Beauty, Winesap, or
York Imperial.

YIELD: 4 servings

EXCHANGES PER
SERVING:
2 Lean Meat
1½ Starch

PER SERVING:
Calories 232
Carbohydrate 26.8g
Protein 17.6g
Fat 5.7g
Cholesterol 67mg
Fiber 3.0g
Sodium 63mg

BRAISED LAMB WITH YOGURT SAUCE

½ pound lean boneless lamb, cut into
    1-inch cubes
1 medium onion, thinly sliced and
    separated into rings
½ cup canned no-salt-added beef broth,
    undiluted
2 teaspoons peeled, grated ginger
2 teaspoons ground coriander
½ teaspoon ground cumin
⅛ teaspoon pepper
    Dash of ground turmeric
1 medium-size sweet red pepper, seeded
    and cut into thin strips
2 cups cooked medium egg noodles
    (cooked without salt or fat)
    Yogurt Sauce

1 Combine first 8 ingredients in a Dutch oven; bring to a boil. Cover, reduce heat, and simmer 20 to 25 minutes or until lamb is tender, stirring occasionally.

2 Add red pepper strips; cover and cook 5 additional minutes.

3 To serve, place ½ cup noodles onto each of 4 individual serving plates; spoon lamb mixture over noodles and serve with 2 tablespoons Yogurt Sauce. Yield: 4 servings.

YOGURT SAUCE

¼ cup plain nonfat yogurt
2 tablespoons low-fat sour cream
¼ cup peeled, seeded and chopped
    cucumber

1 Combine yogurt and sour cream in a small bowl; stir well. Stir in cucumber. Yield: ½ cup.

Lamb Kabobs With Caraway Sauce

YIELD: 6 servings

EXCHANGES PER SERVING:
3½ Lean Meat
1 Vegetable

PER SERVING:
Calories 233
Carbohydrate 7.1g
Protein 26.8g
Fat 10.0g
Cholesterol 82mg
Fiber 1.5g
Sodium 145mg

¾ cup dry red wine
1 tablespoon chopped fresh parsley
1 clove garlic, minced
1 teaspoon Worcestershire sauce
½ teaspoon freshly ground pepper
¼ teaspoon dried thyme
1 bay leaf, crumbled
1½ pounds lean boneless lamb, cubed
2 sweet red peppers, cut into 1-inch strips
3 yellow squash, cut into 1-inch pieces
½ pound fresh mushrooms
 Vegetable cooking spray
2 tablespoons finely chopped onion
½ teaspoon caraway seeds
⅓ cup plain nonfat yogurt
⅓ cup low-fat sour cream
1 tablespoon brandy
¼ teaspoon freshly ground pepper
⅛ teaspoon salt

1 Combine first 7 ingredients in a shallow dish. Add lamb; cover and marinate in refrigerator 8 hours, turning occasionally.

2 Remove lamb from marinade; reserving marinade. Place marinade in a saucepan; bring to a boil. Reduce heat; simmer 5 minutes.

3 Arrange pepper strips, squash, mushrooms, and lamb onto six 12-inch skewers.

4 Coat a nonstick skillet with cooking spray. Add onion and seeds; sauté until onion is tender. Add yogurt and remaining ingredients; stir well. Cook until heated (do not boil).

5 Coat grill rack with cooking spray; place on grill over medium-hot coals (350° to 400°). Place kabobs on rack; grill, covered, 12 minutes or to desired degree of doneness, turning and basting occasionally with marinade. Serve with Caraway Sauce. Yield: 6 servings.

LAMB CHOPS WITH PARSLEY

YIELD: 4 servings

EXCHANGES PER SERVING:
4 Lean Meat

PER SERVING:
Calories 215
Carbohydrate 5.0g
Protein 26.4g
Fat 9.4g
Cholesterol 81mg
Fiber 1.3g
Sodium 429mg

Despite the lack of marbling, the leanest cuts of lamb are tender. Most of the fat is on the outside and should be trimmed.

4 (6-ounce) lean lamb loin chops (1¼ inch thick)
1 lemon, cut in half
¼ teaspoon garlic powder
¼ teaspoon pepper
¾ cup chopped fresh parsley
3 tablespoons Dijon mustard
2 tablespoons unprocessed wheat bran
Vegetable cooking spray
Fresh parsley sprigs (optional)
Cherry tomatoes (optional)

1 Trim fat from chops. Rub both sides of each chop with lemon, squeezing juice over chops; sprinkle with garlic powder and pepper.

2 Combine chopped parsley, mustard, and bran; press mixture on all sides of chops. Place chops in an 11- x 7- x 1½-inch baking dish coated with cooking spray.

3 Bake, uncovered, at 500° for 4 minutes. Reduce heat to 350°, and bake 15 additional minutes or to desired degree of doneness. Transfer to a serving platter. If desired, garnish with parsley sprigs and cherry tomatoes. Yield: 4 servings.

GRILLED LAMB CHOPS

YIELD: 4 servings

4 (5-ounce) lean lamb loin chops (1 inch
   thick)
½ cup frozen unsweetened apple juice
   concentrate, thawed and undiluted
½ teaspoon curry powder
½ teaspoon ground cumin
¼ teaspoon garlic powder
   Vegetable cooking spray

**EXCHANGES PER
SERVING:**
3 Lean Meat
1 Starch

PER SERVING:
Calories 250
Carbohydrate 14.8g
Protein 26.3g
Fat 8.8g
Cholesterol 82mg
Fiber 0.1g
Sodium 82mg

1 Trim fat from lamb. Place lamb in a large
heavy-duty, zip-top plastic bag. Combine
apple juice concentrate and next 3 ingredients;
stir well. Pour mixture over lamb; seal bag, and
shake until lamb is well coated. Marinate lamb
in refrigerator at least 8 hours, turning bag
occasionally.

2 Remove lamb from marinade. Place marinade
in a small saucepan. Bring to a boil, and remove from heat.

3 Coat grill rack with cooking spray; place
rack on grill over medium-hot coals (350° to
400°). Place lamb chops on rack, and cook 7
to 9 minutes on each side or to desired degree
of doneness, basting often with marinade.
Yield: 4 servings.

MEDITERRANEAN LEG OF LAMB

YIELD: 10 servings

EXCHANGES PER SERVING:
3 Lean Meat
1 Starch
1 Vegetable

PER SERVING:
Calories 251
Carbohydrate 18.3g
Protein 26.3g
Fat 8.4g
Cholesterol 72mg
Fiber 3.6g
Sodium 71mg

1 (3½-pound) leg of lamb, trimmed
5 cloves garlic, thinly sliced and divided
2 teaspoons dried rosemary, divided
1 teaspoon freshly ground black pepper, divided
  Vegetable cooking spray
1 pound small round red potatoes, halved
1 pound fresh mushrooms
12 plum tomatoes, halved
1 small eggplant, peeled and cut into 1-inch cubes
1 medium-size sweet red pepper, cut into 1-inch pieces
1 medium-size sweet yellow pepper, cut into 1-inch pieces
1 large purple onion, cut into wedges
¼ cup canned low-sodium chicken broth
2 tablespoons balsamic vinegar
1 tablespoon olive oil

1 Cut 1-inch lengthwise slits in meat; insert half of garlic slices into slits, reserving remaining garlic. Rub meat with 1 teaspoon dried rosemary and ½ teaspoon ground pepper; place on a rack in a large roasting pan coated with cooking spray. Insert meat thermometer into thickest part of meat, if desired. Add potato to pan. Bake at 325° for 1 hour.

2 Remove stems from mushrooms; reserve stems for another use. Add mushroom caps, tomato, eggplant, red pepper, yellow pepper, and onion to pan.

3 Combine remaining garlic, 1 teaspoon dried rosemary, ½ teaspoon ground pepper, chicken broth, vinegar, and oil; stir well. Pour broth mixture over vegetables in pan. Bake at 325° for 50 minutes or until thermometer registers 150°. Let stand 10 minutes before serving. Yield: 10 servings.

PORK PAPRIKASH

YIELD: 6 servings

Vegetable cooking spray
1½ pounds lean pork loin, cubed
1 medium onion, coarsely chopped
1 cup canned no-salt-added chicken
   broth
1 (10¾-ounce) can reduced-fat, reduced-
   sodium cream of mushroom soup,
   undiluted
2 teaspoons paprika
¼ teaspoon salt
⅓ cup low-fat sour cream
3 cups cooked egg noodles (cooked
   without salt or fat)
Chopped fresh parsley (optional)

**EXCHANGES PER
SERVING:**
3 Medium-Fat Meat
2 Starch

PER SERVING:
Calories 346
Carbohydrate 27.0g
Protein 29.0g
Fat 12.8g
Cholesterol 104mg
Fiber 2.8g
Sodium 383mg

1 Coat a large nonstick skillet with cooking
  spray; place over medium-high heat until hot.
Add pork and onion; cook until pork is browned
on all sides, stirring often. Add broth; bring to a
boil. Cover, reduce heat, and simmer 20 minutes
or until pork is tender.

2 Add soup, paprika, and salt to skillet,
  stirring well; bring to a boil. Reduce heat,
and simmer, uncovered, 10 minutes. Remove
from heat; stir in sour cream. Serve over
cooked noodles; sprinkle with parsley, if desired.
Yield: 6 servings.

PORK CHOW MEIN

YIELD: 4 servings

EXCHANGES PER
SERVING:
2 Lean Meat
3 Vegetable

PER SERVING:
Calories 227
Carbohydrate 15.3g
Protein 21.8g
Fat 7.9g
Cholesterol 55mg
Fiber 4.0g
Sodium 548mg

1 pound lean boneless pork loin
1 cup canned no-salt-added chicken
    broth, undiluted
¼ cup low-sodium soy sauce
3 tablespoons cornstarch
1 teaspoon ground ginger
    Vegetable cooking spray
1 clove garlic, minced
2½ cups shredded fresh spinach, divided
1 cup thinly sliced carrot
1 cup thinly sliced celery
1 cup chopped onion
1 cup coarsely chopped cabbage

1 Trim fat from pork; slice pork diagonally across grain into 2- x ¼-inch strips.

2 Combine broth and next 3 ingredients in a small bowl; set aside.

3 Coat a wok or nonstick skillet with cooking spray; place over medium-high (375°) until hot. Add pork and garlic; stir-fry 5 minutes or until pork is browned. Add 1 cup spinach, carrot, celery, onion, and cabbage; stir-fry 3 minutes.

4 Add broth mixture; cover and cook 3 minutes or until vegetables are crisp-tender, stirring occasionally. To serve, spoon pork mixture over remaining shredded spinach. Yield: 4 servings.

Pork Bundles

YIELD: 4 servings

1 pound lean boneless pork loin
¼ cup unsweetened orange juice
¼ cup low-sodium soy sauce
1 teaspoon peeled, grated gingerroot
1 teaspoon honey
1 large carrot, scraped and cut lengthwise
    into very thin 3-inch strips
1 medium zucchini, cut lengthwise into
    very thin 3-inch strips
1 medium yellow squash, cut lengthwise
    into very thin 3-inch strips
    Vegetable cooking spray

EXCHANGES PER
SERVING:
3 Lean Meat
1 Vegetable

PER SERVING:
Calories 221
Carbohydrate 8.2g
Protein 21.1g
Fat 10.6g
Cholesterol 67mg
Fiber 1.5g
Sodium 451mg

1 Slice pork diagonally across grain into 12
(3- x ¼-inch) strips. Place between two pieces
of heavy-duty plastic wrap; flatten to ⅛-inch
thickness, using a meat mallet or rolling pin.

2 Combine orange juice and next 3 ingredients
in an 11- x 7- x 1½-inch dish; add pork,
turning to coat. Cover and marinate in refrigerator at least 15 minutes.

3 Arrange carrot in a vegetable steamer over
boiling water. Cover and steam 5 minutes or
until tender. Set aside.

4 Remove pork from marinade; reserve marinade. Place marinade in a suacepan. Bring to
a boil; reduce heat, and simmer 5 minutes.

5 Wrap 1 pork strip around 9 vegetable strips
(3 strips of each vegetable). Thread onto two
(10-inch) metal skewers, placing 3 bundles on
each pair. Repeat with remaining ingredients.

6 Place on rack of a broiler pan coated with
cooking spray. Brush with one-half of marinade. Broil 5½ inches from heat (with electric
oven door partially opened) 7 minutes, turning
once and brushing with remaining marinade.
Yield: 4 servings.

EXCHANGES PER
SERVING:
3 Lean Meat
1 Starch

PER SERVING:
Calories 276
Carbohydrate 18.5g
Protein 26.4g
Fat 9.9g
Cholesterol 71mg
Fiber 0.6g
Sodium 447mg

PORK CHOPS WITH MUSTARD SAUCE

8 (2-ounce) lean boned center-loin
    pork chops
2 tablespoons all-purpose flour
¼ teaspoon salt
⅛ teaspoon pepper
    Vegetable cooking spray
1 teaspoon olive oil
½ cup frozen orange juice concentrate,
    thawed and undiluted
2 tablespoons lemon juice
2 tablespoons minced green onions
2 tablespoons Dijon mustard
1 teaspoon granulated brown sugar
    substitute
1 teaspoon dried basil
¼ teaspoon curry powder
    Dash of red pepper

1 Trim fat from pork chops. Combine flour, salt, and pepper in a small bowl; stir well. Dredge pork chops in flour mixture.

2 Coat a large nonstick skillet with cooking spray; add oil. Place over medium-high heat until hot. Add pork chops, and cook 3 to 5 minutes on each side or until browned. Add orange juice concentrate and lemon juice; cook 4 to 5 minutes or until pork chops are tender. Transfer to serving plates, and keep warm.

3 Add green onions and next 5 ingredients to orange juice mixture; cook over medium heat 1 minute or until thickened, stirring frequently. Spoon sauce evenly over pork chops. Yield: 4 servings.

Pork Chops With Jalapeño-Apricot Sauce

YIELD: 4 servings

EXCHANGES PER
SERVING:
4 Lean Meat
1 Fruit

PER SERVING:
Calories 251
Carbohydrate 16.1g
Protein 26.6g
Fat 8.6g
Cholesterol 71mg
Fiber 2.0g
Sodium 254mg

1 (16-ounce) can apricot halves in juice,
    undrained
1½ teaspoons white wine vinegar
¾ teaspoon cornstarch
1 tablespoon thinly sliced canned jalapeño
    peppers
4 (6-ounce) lean center-cut loin pork
    chops (½ inch thick)
2 tablespoons Italian-seasoned
    breadcrumbs
¼ teaspoon salt
⅛ teaspoon garlic powder
⅛ teaspoon paprika
    Vegetable cooking spray

1 Drain apricot halves, reserving ½ cup juice and ½ cup apricot halves; quarter apricot halves, and set aside. (Reserve remaining apricot halves and juice for another use.)

2 Combine ½ cup apricot juice, vinegar, and cornstarch in a small saucepan. Cook over medium heat, stirring constantly, until mixture is slightly thickened. Stir in jalapeño peppers and quartered apricots; set sauce aside.

3 Trim fat from chops. Combine breadcrumbs and next 3 ingredients in a shallow bowl. Dredge chops in breadcrumb mixture. Coat a nonstick skillet with cooking spray; place over medium-high heat until hot. Place chops in skillet, and cook 2 to 3 minutes on each side or until lightly browned. Reduce heat to medium-low; cook 8 minutes on each side or until chops are tender and no longer pink.

4 Transfer chops to a serving platter, and spoon sauce evenly over chops. Yield: 4 servings.

PORK AND VEGETABLE PICCATA

EXCHANGES PER
SERVING:
4 Very Lean Meat
2 Vegetable

PER SERVING:
Calories 218
Carbohydrate 11.4g
Protein 30.0g
Fat 6.5g
Cholesterol 83mg
Fiber 4.0g
Sodium 343mg

1 pound pork tenderloin
   Vegetable cooking spray
1 teaspoon olive oil
3 cups small fresh broccoli flowerets
3 cups sliced yellow squash
¼ cup chopped fresh parsley
½ teaspoon ground white pepper
⅛ teaspoon salt
2 cloves garlic, crushed
¼ cup fresh lemon juice, divided
1 cup canned low-sodium chicken broth
1 teaspoon grated lemon rind
2 cloves garlic, crushed
1 tablespoon drained capers
½ teaspoon paprika

1 Trim fat from pork; cut pork into 16 pieces. Place pork between 2 sheets of heavy-duty plastic wrap; flatten to ¼-inch thickness.

2 Coat a large nonstick skillet with cooking spray; add oil, and place over medium-high heat until hot. Add broccoli and next 5 ingredients; sauté 6 minutes or until crisp-tender. Add 2 tablespoons lemon juice; toss well. Transfer vegetable mixture to a platter; keep warm.

3 Coat skillet with cooking spray; place over medium-high heat until hot. Add one-third of pork; cook 2 minutes on each side or until done. Drain on paper towels; place on platter with vegetables, and keep warm. Repeat with remaining pork. Wipe drippings from skillet.

4 Add broth, lemon rind, and garlic to skillet; scrape bottom of skillet with a wooden spoon to loosen browned bits. Bring to a boil; cook 2½ minutes. Remove from heat; stir in remaining 2 tablespoons lemon juice, capers, and paprika. Spoon over vegetables and pork. Yield: 4 servings.

CUMIN-SCENTED PORK TENDERLOINS

¼ cup lime juice
2 tablespoons dry white wine
1 tablespoon minced fresh cilantro
1 teaspoon coarsely ground pepper
¾ teaspoon garlic powder
¼ teaspoon ground cumin
1 small jalapeño pepper, seeded and finely chopped
2 (¾-pound) pork tenderloins
Vegetable cooking spray
Lime wedges (optional)
Fresh cilantro sprigs (optional)

1 Combine first 7 ingredients in a large heavy-duty, zip-top plastic bag; seal bag, and shake well. Trim fat from pork tenderloins. Add pork to bag; seal bag, and shake until pork is well coated. Marinate in refrigerator 8 hours, turning bag occasionally.

2 Remove pork from marinade, reserving marinade. Place marinade in a small saucepan; bring to a boil. Remove from heat; set aside.

3 Place pork on a rack in a roasting pan coated with cooking spray. Insert meat thermometer into thickest part of tenderloin, if desired. Bake at 400° for 40 to 45 minutes or until thermometer registers 160°, basting often with reserved marinade.

4 Let pork stand at room temperature 10 minutes before slicing diagonally across grain into thin slices. If desired, garnish with lime wedges and cilantro sprigs. Yield: 6 servings.

YIELD: 6 servings

EXCHANGES PER SERVING:
4 Very Lean Meat

PER SERVING:
Calories 156
Carbohydrate 1.7g
Protein 26.1g
Fat 4.5g
Cholesterol 83mg
Fiber 0.2g
Sodium 62mg

CHESTNUT-SAGE STUFFED PORK TENDERLOINS

EXCHANGES PER
SERVING:
3 Very Lean Meat
1 Starch

PER SERVING:
Calories 201
Carbohydrate 13.2g
Protein 25.4g
Fat 4.8g
Cholesterol 77mg
Fiber 2.0g
Sodium 250mg

2 (½-pound) pork tenderloins
½ cup soft whole wheat breadcrumbs
⅓ cup coarsely chopped chestnuts
½ teaspoon rubbed sage
2 cloves garlic, minced
1 tablespoon frozen orange juice
    concentrate, thawed and undiluted
½ teaspoon coarsely ground pepper
¼ teaspoon salt
¼ teaspoon poultry seasoning
¼ teaspoon rubbed sage
    Vegetable cooking spray

1 Trim fat from pork. Cut each tenderloin lengthwise down center, cutting to, but not through, bottom. Place each tenderloin between 2 sheets of heavy-duty plastic wrap, and flatten to ¼-inch-thick rectangle, using a meat mallet or rolling pin.

2 Combine breadcrumbs and next 3 ingredients; stir well. Spoon one-half of mixture over 1 tenderloin; spread to within 1/2 inch of sides. Roll up tenderloin, jellyroll fashion, starting at narrow end. Tie with heavy string at 2-inch intervals. Repeat procedure with remaining tenderloin and breadcrumb mixture.

3 Combine orange juice concentrate and next 4 ingredients in a small bowl; rub mixture over entire surface of each tenderloin.

4 Place tenderloins on a rack in a roasting pan coated with cooking spray. Bake, uncovered, at 400° for 45 minutes. Let stand 10 minutes; slice and arrange on a serving platter. Yield: 4 servings.

ORANGE-GLAZED PORK

YIELD: 6 servings

2 (¾-pound) pork tenderloins
  Vegetable cooking spray
1 cup water
2 tablespoons honey
1½ teaspoons ground cinnamon
2 teaspoons peeled, grated gingerroot
1 teaspoon grated orange rind
¼ teaspoon salt
⅛ teaspoon pepper
1 teaspoon cornstarch
¼ cup unsweetened orange juice
1 cup orange sections (about 3 oranges)
  Orange leaves (optional)

EXCHANGES PER SERVING:
3 Very Lean Meat
1 Fruit

PER SERVING:
Calories 189
Carbohydrate 15.7g
Protein 24.5g
Fat 3.0g
Cholesterol 74mg
Fiber 3.1g
Sodium 154mg

1 Trim fat from tenderloins; place tenderloins on a rack in a shallow roasting pan coated with cooking spray. Pour 1 cup water into roasting pan. Combine honey and next 5 ingredients, and brush over tenderloins. Insert a meat thermometer into the thickest part of 1 tenderloin, if desired.

2 Bake at 400° for 30 minutes or until meat thermometer registers 160°. Remove tenderloins from rack; set aside, and keep warm. Skim fat from pan drippings.

3 Place cornstarch and orange juice in a small saucepan, stirring with a wire whisk until blended. Pour pan drippings into saucepan; bring to a boil, and cook 1 minute. Remove from heat, and gently stir in orange sections. Cut pork into ½-inch-thick slices. Serve with orange sauce. Garnish with orange leaves, if desired. Yield: 6 servings.

EXCHANGES PER
SERVING:
3 Very Lean Meat
1½ Starch

PER SERVING:
Calories 249
Carbohydrate 25.3g
Protein 23.6g
Fat 5.0g
Cholesterol 69mg
Fiber 0.6g
Sodium 102mg

ORIENTAL PORK MEDAILLONS

Pork medaillons are cut from the tenderloin, the leanest and tenderest cut of pork. Ask your butcher to cut a tenderloin into medaillons.

> Vegetable cooking spray
> 1 teaspoon dark sesame oil
> ⅛ teaspoon dried crushed red pepper
> 1 clove garlic, minced
> 1 pound pork medaillons (½ inch thick)
> 2 tablespoons water
> 2 tablespoons dry sherry
> 1½ teaspoons granulated brown sugar substitute
> 1½ teaspoons low-sodium soy sauce
> Dash of garlic powder
> 1 teaspoon dried cilantro (coriander)
> 2 cups cooked long-grain rice (cooked without salt or fat)
> ¼ cup sliced green onions

1 Coat a large nonstick skillet with cooking spray; add sesame oil. Place over medium-high heat until hot. Add red pepper and garlic; sauté 1 minute. Add pork, and cook 4 to 5 minutes on each side or until browned. Transfer to a serving platter, and keep warm. Wipe pan drippings from skillet with a paper towel.

2 Add water and next 5 ingredients to skillet; stir well. Cook over medium heat, stirring constantly, 1 minute or until slightly thickened.

3 To serve, spoon ½ cup rice on each individual plate; place pork over rice. Spoon sauce evenly over each serving. Sprinkle evenly with green onions. Yield: 4 servings.

PIZZA ON THE GRILL

YIELD: 4 servings

Instead of grilling the pizza, you can prebake the crust in the oven at 425° for 5 minutes. Add the toppings, and bake 5 additional minutes or until cheese melts.

Vegetable cooking spray
¾ cup peeled, seeded, and chopped plum tomato (about 3 medium)
3 tablespoons evaporated skimmed milk
⅛ teaspoon garlic powder
1 (10-ounce) package refrigerated pizza crust dough
¼ cup torn fresh basil leaves
4 (¾-ounce) slices Canadian bacon, cut into thin strips
¾ cup (3 ounces) shredded part-skim mozzarella cheese

EXCHANGES PER SERVING:
1 High-Fat Meat
2 Starch
1 Vegetable

PER SERVING:
Calories 287
Carbohydrate 37.0g
Protein 16.8g
Fat 7.9g
Cholesterol 23mg
Fiber 1.4g
Sodium 806mg

1 Coat a nonstick skillet with cooking spray; place over medium-high heat until hot. Add tomato; sauté 2 minutes. Add milk. Bring mixture to a boil; reduce heat, and simmer 1 minute, stirring occasionally. Remove from heat, and stir in garlic powder. Set aside.

2 Roll dough into a 12- x 10-inch rectangle on a large piece of aluminum foil. Lightly coat pizza dough with cooking spray. Coat grill rack with cooking spray; place on grill over medium-hot coals (350° to 400°). Place dough, sprayed side down, on rack; remove foil. Grill, uncovered, 2 to 3 minutes or until top of crust is slightly set and bottom is lightly browned. (Pierce any air bubbles with a fork.)

3 Remove crust from grill. Lightly coat top of crust with cooking spray, and turn crust over. Spread tomato mixture over dough. Sprinkle with basil, and top with bacon. Sprinkle with cheese. Grill 3 to 5 additional minutes or until bottom is browned and cheese melts. Yield: 4 servings.

Vegetable-Ham Frittata

YIELD: 4 servings

EXCHANGES PER
SERVING:
1 Medium-Fat Meat
1 Vegetable

PER SERVING:
Calories 114
Carbohydrate 9.3g
Protein 10.9g
Fat 4.1g
Cholesterol 12mg
Fiber 1.8g
Sodium 349mg

Vegetable cooking spray
1 small sweet red pepper, cut into
   ¼-inch rings
1 cup frozen broccoli flowerets, thawed
½ cup frozen sliced yellow squash,
   thawed
⅓ cup frozen whole kernel corn, thawed
2 ounces lean cooked ham, chopped
½ cup frozen egg substitute, thawed
¼ cup evaporated skimmed milk
1 teaspoon freeze-dried chives
¼ teaspoon dried dillweed
⅛ teaspoon salt
⅛ teaspoon ground red pepper
¼ cup (1 ounce) shredded reduced-fat
   Swiss cheese

1 Coat an ovenproof 8-inch skillet with cooking spray, and place over medium-high heat until hot. Add pepper rings; sauté 2 minutes or until crisp-tender. Remove from skillet, and set aside.

2 Arrange broccoli, squash, and corn in a steamer basket over boiling water. Cover and steam 3 minutes or until crisp-tender. Drain well. Place broccoli mixture and ham in skillet.

3 Combine egg substitute and next 5 ingredients in a bowl; stir with a wire whisk. Pour over broccoli mixture. Cover and cook over medium-low heat 7 minutes or until almost set.

4 Sprinkle frittata with cheese. Broil 5½ inches from heat (with electric oven door partially opened) 1 minute or until cheese melts. Let stand 5 minutes. Top with pepper rings. Yield: 4 servings.

Fettuccine With Vegetables and Ham

8 ounces fettuccine, uncooked
¼ cup water
1 (16-ounce) package frozen broccoli, cauliflower, and carrots
1 cup skim milk
½ cup grated Romano cheese
8 (¾-ounce) slices ham, cut into ½-inch squares
½ teaspoon pepper

1 Cook fettuccine according to package directions, omitting salt and fat; drain. Place in a large bowl, and keep warm.

2 Bring ¼ cup water to a boil in a medium saucepan. Add vegetables; cook, uncovered, 3 minutes or until vegetables are crisp-tender. Drain vegetables. Set aside, and keep warm.

3 Place milk in a small saucepan; cook over low heat until warm. Add warm milk and cheese to pasta; stir until thoroughly heated. Stir in vegetables, ham, and pepper. Serve warm. Yield: 7 (1-cup) servings.

YIELD: 7 servings

EXCHANGES PER SERVING:
1 Medium-Fat Meat
2 Starch
1 Vegetable

PER SERVING:
Calories 239
Carbohydrate 35.0g
Protein 14.7g
Fat 4.3g
Cholesterol 24mg
Fiber 3.3g
Sodium 489mg

HAWAIIAN HAM KABOBS

YIELD: 6 servings

EXCHANGES PER
SERVING:
2 Very Lean Meat
1 Starch
2 Vegetable
1 Fruit

PER SERVING:
Calories 269
Carbohydrate 40.5g
Protein 16.1g
Fat 4.2g
Cholesterol 37mg
Fiber 1.1g
Sodium 874mg

1 (15¼-ounce) can pineapple chunks in
    juice, undrained
¼ cup low-sodium soy sauce
1 tablespoon granulated brown sugar
    substitute
1 tablespoon balsamic vinegar
2 teaspoons ground ginger
1 teaspoon garlic powder
1 teaspoon Dijon mustard
¼ teaspoon pepper
1 pound reduced-fat, low-salt cooked
    ham, cut into 1-inch cubes
1 medium-size green pepper, cut into
    1-inch pieces
1 medium-size sweet red pepper, cut into
    1-inch pieces
    Vegetable cooking spray
3 cups cooked long-grain rice (cooked
    without salt or fat)

1 Drain pineapple chunks, reserving juice. Set pineapple aside.

2 Combine juice, soy sauce, and next 6 ingredients in a shallow dish; stir well. Add ham and pineapple; stir lightly to coat. Cover and marinate in refrigerator at least 15 minutes, stirring occasionally.

3 Remove ham and pineapple from marinade, reserving marinade. Place marinade in a small saucepan. Bring to a boil; remove from heat, and set aside.

4 Thread ham, pineapple, and peppers alternately on 12 (10-inch) skewers. Coat grill rack with cooking spray; place on grill over medium-hot coals (350° to 400°). Place kabobs on rack, and grill, uncovered, 8 to 10 minutes or until thoroughly heated, turning and basting often with marinade. Serve kabobs over rice. Yield: 6 servings.

Poultry

CHICKEN ENCHILADA CASSEROLE

YIELD: 6 servings

EXCHANGES PER
SERVING:
4½ Lean Meat
3 Starch
1 Vegetable

PER SERVING:
Calories 502
Carbohydrate 47.1g
Protein 44.4g
Fat 15.6g
Cholesterol 103mg
Fiber 6.6g
Sodium 741mg

½ cup no-salt-added salsa
½ cup canned low-sodium chicken broth
1 teaspoon ground cumin
3 (8-ounce) cans no-salt-added tomato
sauce
3 cups cubed cooked chicken breast
(skinned before cooking and cooked
without salt)
3 tablespoons chopped pickled jalapeño
pepper
1 (15-ounce) can no-salt-added black
beans, rinsed and drained
12 (6-inch) corn tortillas
1½ cups (6 ounces) shredded reduced-fat
sharp Cheddar cheese
½ cup (2 ounces) shredded reduced-fat
Monterey Jack cheese
¾ cup low-fat sour cream
½ cup chopped green onions

1 Combine first 4 ingredients; stir well. Spread ¾ cup mixture in bottom of a 13- x 9- x 2-inch baking dish.

2 Combine chicken, pepper, black beans, and ½ cup tomato sauce mixture in a medium bowl. Stir well. Spoon chicken mixture evenly down center of each tortilla. Roll up tortillas; place, seam side down, on sauce mixture in baking dish. Top with remaining sauce mixture and cheeses.

3 Cover and bake at 350° for 25 minutes or until thoroughly heated. Top with sour cream, and sprinkle with green onions. Yield: 6 servings.

CHICKEN DIVAN

YIELD: 8 servings

2 (10-ounce) packages frozen broccoli
spears, thawed
3 cups chopped cooked chicken breast
½ cup (2 ounces) shredded reduced-fat
sharp Cheddar cheese
1½ cups skim milk
1 (10¾-ounce) can reduced-fat, reduced-
sodium cream of mushroom soup,
undiluted
1 teaspoon lemon juice
⅛ teaspoon salt
⅛ teaspoon black pepper
3 tablespoons all-purpose flour
3 tablespoons water
½ cup finely crushed onion-flavored Melba
toast rounds (about 19)
1 tablespoon margarine, melted

**EXCHANGES PER
SERVING:**
4 Lean Meat
1 Starch

PER SERVING:
Calories 269
Carbohydrate 15.7g
Protein 33.9g
Fat 7.6g
Cholesterol 81mg
Fiber 1.9g
Sodium 410mg

1 Arrange broccoli spears horizontally in 2 rows in a 13- x 9- x 2-inch baking dish with stalks facing each other in center of dish. Spoon chicken on top of stalk ends, and top with cheese; set aside.

2 Combine milk and next 4 ingredients in a heavy saucepan; stir well. Combine flour and water; stir well. Add flour mixture to soup mixture; stir well. Bring to a boil over medium heat, stirring constantly with a wire whisk. Cook, stirring constantly, 8 minutes or until thickened and bubbly.

3 Pour soup mixture over chicken. Combine Melba toast crumbs and margarine; sprinkle over soup mixture.

4 Cover and bake at 350° for 20 minutes. Uncover; bake 15 additional minutes or until thoroughly heated. Let stand 10 minutes before serving. Yield: 8 servings.

CHICKEN JAMBALAYA

YIELD: 4 servings

EXCHANGES PER
SERVING:
2 Lean Meat
2 Starch
1 Vegetable

PER SERVING:
Calories 272
Carbohydrate 37.2g
Protein 19.7g
Fat 4.3g
Cholesterol 44mg
Fiber 2.0g
Sodium 614mg

Vegetable cooking spray
1 teaspoon vegetable oil
¾ cup coarsely chopped lean cooked ham
   (about ¼ pound)
¾ cup chopped green pepper
½ cup chopped onion
½ cup chopped celery
2 cloves garlic, minced
2 cups canned low-sodium chicken broth,
   undiluted
1 cup chopped cooked chicken breast
   (skinned before cooking and cooked
   without salt)
⅔ cup long-grain rice, uncooked
1 teaspoon dried basil
½ teaspoon dried thyme
½ teaspoon chili powder
¼ teaspoon salt
¼ teaspoon pepper
½ teaspoon hot sauce
1 bay leaf
1 (14½-ounce) can no-salt-added stewed
   tomatoes, undrained and chopped

1 Coat a large nonstick skillet with cooking spray; add oil. Place over medium heat until hot. Add ham and next 4 ingredients; sauté 5 minutes.

2 Stir in chicken broth and remaining ingredients. Bring to a boil; cover, reduce heat, and simmer 15 minutes.

3 Uncover and cook 15 additional minutes or until rice is tender, stirring occasionally. Remove and discard bayleaf.
Yield: 4 (1-cup) servings.

CHICKEN LINGUINE

YIELD: 12 servings

1 pound sliced fresh mushrooms
½ cup dry sherry
2 tablespoons reduced-calorie margarine,
    melted and divided
1 pound skinned, boned chicken breasts
    Vegetable cooking spray
½ cup chopped onion
¼ cup plus 2 tablespoons all-purpose flour
3 cups canned no-salt-added chicken
    broth, undiluted
1 (8-ounce) carton nonfat sour cream
1 (16-ounce) package linguine, uncooked
½ cup (2 ounces) shredded reduced-fat
    Monterey Jack cheese
¼ cup plus 2 tablespoons freshly grated
    Parmesan cheese, divided
⅛ teaspoon freshly ground black pepper
¼ cup fine, dry breadcrumbs

EXCHANGES PER SERVING:
2 Lean Meat
2 Starch
1 Vegetable

PER SERVING:
Calories 292
Carbohydrate 36.9g
Protein 19.4g
Fat 5.5g
Cholesterol 29mg
Fiber 1.7g
Sodium 197mg

1 Sauté mushrooms and sherry in 1 tablespoon margarine in a nonstick skillet over high heat.

2 Place chicken in a saucepan; add water to cover. Bring to a boil; cover, reduce heat, and simmer 20 minutes. Drain, cool, and shred.

3 Coat pan with cooking spray; add onion, and sauté over medium heat until tender. Combine flour and ½ cup broth. Add remaining broth and flour mixture. Cook until thickened. Remove from heat; stir in sour cream.

4 Cook linguine; drain. Combine mushrooms, chicken, sour cream mixture, Monterey Jack cheese, ¼ cup Parmesan cheese, and pepper. Stir in pasta. Spoon into a 13- x 9- x 2-inch baking dish coated with cooking spray.

5 Combine breadcrumbs, 1 tablespoon margarine, and remaining 2 tablespoons Parmesan cheese; sprinkle over chicken. Bake at 350° for 30 minutes. Yield: 12 servings.

CORNBREAD CHICKEN PIE

YIELD: 8 servings

EXCHANGES PER
SERVING:
2 Lean Meat
2 Starch
1 Vegetable

PER SERVING:
Calories 310
Carbohydrate 36.3g
Protein 23.5g
Fat 6.2g
Cholesterol 82mg
Fiber 3.0g
Sodium 391mg

1 (3-pound) broiler-fryer, skinned
3 quarts water
2 cups peeled, cubed sweet potato
1 tablespoon cornstarch
1 tablespoon water
  Vegetable cooking spray
1 cup chopped onion
1 cup frozen whole kernel corn, thawed
2 cloves garlic, minced
¾ cup self-rising flour
¾ cup self-rising cornmeal
1 teaspoon sugar
¾ teaspoon chili powder
¾ cup nonfat buttermilk
1 egg, lightly beaten

1 Place chicken and 3 quarts water in a Dutch oven. Bring to a boil; cover, reduce heat, and simmer 45 minutes. Remove chicken from broth. Reserve 4 cups broth. Bone and chop chicken; cover and chill. Cover and chill broth.

2 Skim and discard fat from broth; bring broth to a boil. Add potato; cook 13 minutes. Remove potato with a slotted spoon. Cook broth 20 minutes or until reduced to 1 cup.

3 Combine cornstarch and 1 tablespoon water; stir well. Add to broth; cook, stirring constantly, until thickened and bubbly.

4 Coat a nonstick skillet with cooking spray; place over medium-high heat until hot. Add onion, corn, and garlic; sauté until tender. Add chicken, potato, and broth mixture; stir well. Spoon into an 11- x 7- x 1½-inch baking dish coated with cooking spray.

5 Combine flour and next 3 ingredients; make a well in center. Combine buttermilk and egg; add to dry ingredients, stirring just until moistened. Spoon over chicken mixture. Bake at 425° for 15 minutes. Yield: 8 servings.

Sweet-and-Sour Chicken

YIELD: 6 servings

2 tablespoons cornstarch
2 tablespoons granulated brown sugar
   substitute
1½ teaspoons low-sodium Worcestershire
   sauce
¾ teaspoon ground ginger
¼ teaspoon garlic powder
1½ cups unsweetened pineapple juice
¼ cup low-sodium soy sauce
¼ cup white wine vinegar
¼ cup reduced-calorie ketchup
   Vegetable cooking spray
1½ pounds skinned, boned chicken breast
   halves, cut into 1½-inch pieces
½ cup sliced sweet red pepper
½ cup sliced green pepper
½ cup sliced sweet yellow pepper
3 cups cooked rice (cooked without salt
   or fat)

EXCHANGES PER SERVING:
3 Very Lean Meat
2 Starch
1 Vegetable

PER SERVING:
Calories 294
Carbohydrate 36.4g
Protein 28.7g
Fat 1.9g
Cholesterol 66mg
Fiber 1.0g
Sodium 351mg

1 Combine first 9 ingredients in a medium bowl; stir well.

2 Coat a large nonstick skillet with cooking spray; place over medium-high heat until hot. Add chicken, and cook 5 minutes or until browned. Add peppers, and cook 2 minutes. Gradually stir in cornstarch mixture. Cook over medium heat, stirring constantly, until mixture is thickened and bubbly. Serve over rice. Yield: 6 servings.

CHICKEN STIR-FRY

YIELD: 2 servings

EXCHANGES PER
SERVING:
3 Very Lean Meat
2 Starch
2 Vegetable

PER SERVING:
Calories 338
Carbohydrate 39.0g
Protein 33.4g
Fat 4.9g
Cholesterol 66mg
Fiber 3.4g
Sodium 449mg

½ cup canned low-sodium chicken broth, undiluted
1 tablespoon dry sherry
1 tablespoon low-sodium soy sauce
1 teaspoon cornstarch
⅛ teaspoon salt
2 (4-ounce) skinned, boned chicken breast halves
   Vegetable cooking spray
1 teaspoon sesame oil
1 cup fresh broccoli flowerets
1 cup sliced fresh mushrooms
¼ cup chopped green onions
2 teaspoons minced garlic
¾ cup fresh bean sprouts
¾ cup fresh snow pea pods
¼ cup canned, sliced water chestnuts, drained
1 cup cooked long-grain rice (cooked without salt or fat)

1 Combine first 5 ingredients, stirring until smooth. Set aside.

2 Cut chicken into ¼-inch-thick strips. Coat a medium nonstick skillet or stir-fry pan with cooking spray; add oil. Place over medium-high heat until hot; add chicken, and stir-fry 2 minutes. Add broccoli and next 3 ingredients; stir-fry 2 minutes. Add bean sprouts, snow peas, and water chestnuts; stir-fry 1 minute.

3 Add broth mixture to chicken mixture. Cook, stirring constantly, until mixture is slightly thickened and thoroughly heated. Spoon over cooked rice. Yield: 2 servings.

Chicken Kabobs
With Salsa

YIELD: 2 servings

EXCHANGES PER
SERVING:
3 Lean Meat
2 Vegetable

PER SERVING:
Calories 218
Carbohydrate 9.5g
Protein 27.3g
Fat 8.0g
Cholesterol 70mg
Fiber 1.8g
Sodium 204mg

¾ cup seeded, chopped tomato
¼ cup chopped avocado
2 tablespoons fresh lime juice
1 tablespoon chopped green onions
1 tablespoon chopped fresh cilantro
1 teaspoon finely chopped jalapeño
  pepper
¼ teaspoon minced garlic
2 (4-ounce) skinned, boned chicken breast
  halves, cut into 1-inch pieces
2 tablespoons fresh lime juice
2 teaspoons low-sodium soy sauce
1 teaspoon minced garlic
  Vegetable cooking spray
  Fresh jalapeño pepper (optional)
  Lime slices (optional)
  Fresh cilantro sprig (optional)

1 Combine first 7 ingredients. Cover and chill. Place chicken in a shallow dish. Combine 2 tablespoons lime juice, soy sauce, and garlic. Pour over chicken. Cover and marinate in refrigerator 1 hour.

2 Remove chicken from marinade, reserving marinade. Place marinade in a small saucepan; bring to a boil, and remove from heat. Thread chicken onto 2 (10-inch) skewers. Coat grill rack with cooking spray; place on grill over medium-hot coals (350° to 400°). Place chicken on rack; grill, covered, 6 to 8 minutes or until chicken is done, turning occasionally, and basting with reserved marinade.

3 To serve, spoon tomato mixture onto a serving plate; place chicken kabobs over tomato mixture. If desired, garnish with a jalapeño pepper, lime slices, and cilantro sprig. Yield: 2 servings.

SANTA FE GRILLED CHICKEN

YIELD: 4 servings

EXCHANGES PER
SERVING:
3 Very Lean Meat
1 Vegetable

PER SERVING:
Calories 185
Carbohydrate 6.2g
Protein 26.7g
Fat 5.7g
Cholesterol 70mg
Fiber 1.5g
Sodium 218mg

  4 (4-ounce) skinned, boned chicken
      breast halves
 ¼ teaspoon salt
 ¼ teaspoon pepper
 ⅓ cup lime juice
  2 teaspoons olive oil
1¾ cups diced plum tomato (about ¾
      pound)
 ⅓ cup chopped onion
  3 tablespoons minced fresh cilantro
  2 tablespoons red wine vinegar
  1 tablespoon seeded, minced jalapeño
      pepper
     Vegetable cooking spray

1 Place chicken between two sheets heavy-duty plastic wrap, and flatten to ½-inch thickness, using a meat mallet or rolling pin. Sprinkle chicken with salt and pepper; place in a shallow dish.

2 Combine lime juice and olive oil in a small bowl; stir well, and pour over chicken. Cover chicken, and marinate in refrigerator 3 hours, turning occasionally.

3 Combine tomato and next 4 ingredients in a small bowl. Cover and chill thoroughly.

4 Remove chicken from marinade, discarding marinade. Coat grill rack with cooking spray; place on grill over medium-hot coals. Place chicken on rack, and grill, covered, 5 to 6 minutes on each side or until done. Serve with chilled tomato mixture. Yield: 4 servings.

CHICKEN BREAST FRICASSEE

YIELD: 4 servings

4 (4-ounce) skinned, boned chicken breast
   halves
⅛ teaspoon pepper
   Vegetable cooking spray
1⅓ cups diagonally sliced carrot
1 cup coarsely chopped onion
1 cup frozen whole kernel corn
½ pound sliced fresh mushrooms
1½ cups water
¼ cup dry white wine
½ teaspoon chicken-flavored bouillon
   granules
½ teaspoon dried tarragon
½ teaspoon dried thyme
1 bay leaf
2 tablespoons cornstarch
½ cup evaporated skimmed milk
1 teaspoon lemon juice
   Fresh tarragon sprigs (optional)

**EXCHANGES PER
SERVING:**
3 Very Lean Meat
1 Starch
2 Vegetable

PER SERVING:
Calories 251
Carbohydrate 26.6g
Protein 32.0g
Fat 2.2g
Cholesterol 67mg
Fiber 4.2g
Sodium 235mg

1 Sprinkle chicken with pepper. Coat a Dutch oven with cooking spray; place over medium-high heat until hot. Add chicken, and cook 2 minutes on each side or until browned. Add carrot and next 9 ingredients; bring to a boil. Cover, reduce heat, and simmer 15 minutes or until chicken is tender. Remove chicken from Dutch oven; transfer to a serving platter, and keep warm. Reserve vegetable mixture in Dutch oven.

2 Combine cornstarch and milk, stirring until smooth; add to vegetable mixture, stirring constantly. Bring to a boil; reduce heat, and simmer, stirring constantly, until thickened and bubbly. Remove from heat; stir in lemon juice. Remove and discard bay leaf.

3 Spoon vegetable mixture around chicken on platter. Garnish with tarragon sprigs, if desired. Yield: 4 servings.

GREEK-SEASONED CHICKEN WITH ORZO

¼ cup fresh lemon juice
3 tablespoons water
1 teaspoon olive oil
½ teaspoon dried oregano
½ teaspoon Greek-style seasoning
¼ teaspoon pepper
2 cloves garlic, crushed
4 (6-ounce) skinned chicken breast halves
1 cup orzo, uncooked
¼ cup sliced ripe olives
1½ tablespoons chopped fresh chives
1 tablespoon reduced-calorie margarine, melted
¾ teaspoon Greek-style seasoning
    Vegetable cooking spray
    Fresh oregano sprigs (optional)

1 Combine first 7 ingredients in a large heavy-duty, zip-top plastic bag; add chicken. Seal bag, and shake until chicken is well coated. Marinate in refrigerator 30 minutes, turning bag occasionally.

2 Cook orzo according to package directions, omitting salt and fat; drain. Combine orzo, olives, and next 3 ingredients, tossing gently. Set aside, and keep warm.

3 Remove chicken from marinade, reserving marinade. Bring marinade to a boil in a small saucepan; reduce heat, and simmer 2 minutes.

4 Coat grill rack with cooking spray; place on grill over medium-hot coals (350° to 400°). Place chicken on rack; grill, covered, 10 minutes on each side or until chicken is done, basting occasionally with marinade. Serve over orzo mixture. Garnish with oregano sprigs, if desired. Yield: 4 servings.

Chicken Parmesan

6 (4-ounce) skinned, boned chicken breast halves
½ teaspoon pepper
  Vegetable cooking spray
1 tablespoon reduced-calorie margarine
½ cup sliced fresh mushrooms
1 tablespoon sliced green onions
1 tablespoon all-purpose flour
1 cup skim milk
3 tablespoons grated Parmesan cheese
⅛ teaspoon pepper
  Green onion tops (optional)

YIELD: 6 servings

EXCHANGES PER SERVING:
4 Very Lean Meat

PER SERVING:
Calories 180
Carbohydrate 3.6g
Protein 28.4g
Fat 5.1g
Cholesterol 73mg
Fiber 0.2g
Sodium 148mg

1 Place chicken between two pieces of heavy-duty plastic wrap; flatten to ¼-inch thickness, using a meat mallet or rolling pin. Sprinkle chicken with ½ teaspoon pepper.

2 Coat a large nonstick skillet with cooking spray; place over medium-high heat until hot. Add chicken, and cook 8 minutes or until done, turning once. Transfer to a serving platter; set aside, and keep warm. Wipe skillet dry with a paper towel.

3 Add margarine, mushrooms, and sliced green onions to skillet; sauté until tender. Add flour; stir well. Gradually add milk; cook, stirring constantly, 1 minute or until thickened. Add cheese and ⅛ teaspoon pepper; stir well. Spoon sauce over chicken. Garnish with green onion tops, if desired. Yield: 6 servings.

CHICKEN PICCATA

YIELD: 4 servings

EXCHANGES PER
SERVING:
4 Very Lean Meat

PER SERVING:
Calories 154
Carbohydrate 4.2g
Protein 26.8g
Fat 2.9g
Cholesterol 66mg
Fiber 0.3g
Sodium 194mg

2 tablespoons dry white wine
2 tablespoons lemon juice
2 teaspoons reduced-calorie margarine
½ teaspoon chicken-flavored bouillon
    granules
4 (4-ounce) skinned, boned chicken breast
    halves
2 tablespoons all-purpose flour
1 teaspoon paprika
⅛ teaspoon ground red pepper
    Vegetable cooking spray
1 tablespoon chopped fresh parsley
    Lemon slices (optional)

1 Combine first 4 ingredients in a small saucepan; cook over medium heat until margarine melts, stirring often. Set aside, and keep warm.

2 Place chicken between 2 sheets of heavy-duty plastic wrap, and flatten to ½-inch thickness, using a meat mallet or rolling pen.

3 Combine flour, paprika, and red pepper in a shallow bowl; dredge chicken in flour mixture.

4 Coat a large nonstick skillet with cooking spray; place over medium heat until hot. Add chicken, and cook 4 to 5 minutes on each side or until chicken is lightly browned.

5 To serve, transfer chicken to a serving plate, and drizzle with wine mixture. Sprinkle with chopped parsley, and garnish with lemon slices, if desired. Yield: 4 servings.

Apple-Stuffed Chicken Rolls

Vegetable cooking spray
¼ cup finely chopped green onions
1 cup unsweetened apple juice, divided
½ cup finely chopped, peeled apple
½ cup soft rye breadcrumbs
2 tablespoons minced fresh parsley
⅛ teaspoon salt
⅛ teaspoon caraway seeds
4 (4-ounce) skinned, boned chicken breast
  halves
2 teaspoons reduced-calorie margarine
2 tablespoons brandy
1 tablespoon cornstarch

YIELD: 4 servings

EXCHANGES PER
SERVING:
4 Very Lean Meat
1 Starch

PER SERVING:
Calories 203
Carbohydrate 15.8g
Protein 27.1g
Fat 3.1g
Cholesterol 66mg
Fiber 1.2g
Sodium 210mg

1 Coat a nonstick skillet with cooking spray; place over medium-high heat until hot. Add onions; sauté until tender. Remove from heat. Stir in 2 tablespoons apple juice and next 5 ingredients. Remove from skillet.

2 Place chicken between 2 sheets of wax paper; flatten to ¼-inch thickness, using a meat mallet. Spoon breadcrumb mixture onto center of each chicken breast half. Roll up lengthwise, tucking ends under. Secure with wooden picks.

3 Coat skillet with cooking spray; add margarine, and place over medium-high heat until hot. Add chicken rolls, and cook until browned on all sides. Add 2 tablespoons apple juice and brandy. Cover, reduce heat, and simmer 45 minutes or until chicken is tender. Transfer chicken to a serving platter; remove wooden picks, and keep warm.

4 Add cornstarch to pan juices in skillet; stir until smooth. Stir in remaining ¾ cup apple juice. Bring to a boil; cook 1 minute. Spoon juice mixture over chicken rolls. Yield: 4 servings.

YIELD: 6 servings

EXCHANGES PER
SERVING:
4 Very Lean Meat
1 Starch

PER SERVING:
Calories 248
Carbohydrate 13.5g
Protein 36.1g
Fat 5.2g
Cholesterol 66mg
Fiber 1.1g
Sodium 489mg

VEGETABLE-FILLED CHICKEN BREASTS

6 (4-ounce) skinned, boned chicken breast
   halves
12 small fresh asparagus spears
1 cup plus 2 tablespoons (4½ ounces)
   shredded nonfat mozzarella cheese
¾ cup sliced fresh mushrooms
1 cup frozen artichoke hearts, thawed,
   drained, and chopped
1 tablespoon diced pimiento
¼ teaspoon salt
¼ teaspoon pepper
½ cup frozen egg substitute, thawed
¾ cup fine, dry breadcrumbs
2 tablespoons reduced-calorie margarine
   Vegetable cooking spray
   Dash of paprika

1 Place chicken breasts between 2 sheets of
heavy-duty plastic wrap; flatten to ¼-inch
thickness, using a meat mallet or rolling pin.

2 Snap off tough ends of asparagus. Remove
scales from stalks with a knife or vegetable
peeler, if desired. Arrange asparagus, cheese, and
mushrooms on chicken breasts. Top with artichoke and pimiento; sprinkle with salt and pepper. Fold chicken over vegetable mixture, and
secure with wooden picks. Dip chicken in egg
substitute, and dredge in breadcrumbs.

3 Melt margarine in a large nonstick skillet
over medium heat. Add chicken, and cook
6 to 8 minutes on each side or until browned.
Remove chicken from skillet, and place on a
baking sheet. Coat chicken with cooking spray;
sprinkle with paprika.

4 Bake at 350° for 15 to 18 minutes or until
golden. Transfer chicken to a serving platter,
and remove wooden picks. Yield: 6 servings.

Chicken Breasts With Marmalade

Vegetable cooking spray
1 teaspoon margarine
½ cup finely chopped onion
4 fresh mushrooms, sliced
⅛ teaspoon salt
⅛ teaspoon pepper
4 (6-ounce) skinned chicken breast halves
¼ cup water
¼ cup low-sodium teriyaki sauce
2 tablespoons low-sugar orange marmalade
2 cups cooked couscous (cooked without salt or fat)
Fresh orange slices (optional)
Flat-leaf parsley sprigs (optional)

YIELD: 4 servings

EXCHANGES PER SERVING:
4 Very Lean Meat
2 Starch

PER SERVING:
Calories 293
Carbohydrate 32.2g
Protein 31.9g
Fat 3.0g
Cholesterol 66mg
Fiber 2.1g
Sodium 551mg

1 Coat a large nonstick skillet with cooking spray; add margarine. Place over medium-high heat until margarine melts. Add onion and mushrooms; sauté until tender. Transfer mushroom mixture to a small bowl. Stir in salt and pepper; set aside.

2 Coat skillet with cooking spray; place over medium-high heat until hot. Add chicken, and cook 2 minutes on each side or until browned. Combine water, teriyaki sauce, and orange marmalade; pour over chicken in skillet. Bring to a boil; cover, reduce heat, and simmer 20 minutes or until chicken is done, turning occasionally. Add mushroom mixture to skillet; bring to a boil. Reduce heat, and simmer, uncovered, 3 minutes.

3 To serve, place ½ cup couscous on each plate. Top with chicken. Spoon mushroom mixture evenly over chicken. If desired, garnish with orange slices and parsley sprigs. Yield: 4 servings.

EXCHANGES PER
SERVING:
3 Very Lean Meat
2 Vegetable

PER SERVING:
Calories 181
Carbohydrate 11.9g
Protein 28.4g
Fat 2.1g
Cholesterol 66mg
Fiber 1.4g
Sodium 102mg

✖ Fines herbes,
pronounced "FEEN
erb," is a mixture of
very finely chopped
herbs, usually chervil,
chives, parsley, and
tarragon.

CHICKEN WITH TOMATO-VINEGAR SAUCE

2 cups peeled, coarsely chopped tomato
1 cup red wine vinegar
¾ cup canned low-sodium chicken broth, undiluted
2 tablespoons no-salt-added tomato paste
15 cloves garlic
4 (6-ounce) skinned chicken breast halves
1 teaspoon fines herbes
1 bay leaf
Fresh thyme sprigs (optional)
Fresh oregano sprigs (optional)

1 Combine first 5 ingredients in a medium saucepan; stir well. Cover and simmer over medium-low heat 20 minutes. Add chicken, fines herbes, and bay leaf. Cover and simmer 25 additional minutes or until chicken is tender. Transfer to a serving platter, and keep warm.

2 Bring tomato mixture to a boil; cook, uncovered, over medium heat 20 minutes or until mixture is reduced to 1⅓ cups. Remove and discard bay leaf. Remove and discard garlic, if desired.

3 To serve, spoon tomato mixture over chicken. If desired, garnish with thyme and oregano sprigs. Yield: 4 servings.

ZESTY BARBECUED CHICKEN

YIELD: 6 servings

1½ cups no-salt-added tomato sauce
¼ cup plus 2 tablespoons lemon juice
1½ tablespoons granulated brown sugar
     substitute
3 tablespoons cider vinegar
2 tablespoons low-sodium Worcestershire
     sauce
2 teaspoons minced garlic
1½ teaspoons prepared mustard
¾ teaspoon ground red pepper
¼ teaspoon black pepper
6 (6-ounce) skinned chicken breast halves
     Vegetable cooking spray

**EXCHANGES PER
SERVING:**
3 Very Lean Meat
1 Vegetable

PER SERVING:
Calories 150
Carbohydrate 3.7g
Protein 25.4g
Fat 3.0g
Cholesterol 69mg
Fiber 0.4g
Sodium 81mg

1 Combine first 9 ingredients in a medium saucepan. Bring to a boil; cover, reduce heat, and simmer 20 minutes.

2 Pour 1 cup tomato sauce mixture into a heavy-duty, zip-top plastic bag. Set aside remaining tomato sauce mixture. Add chicken to bag; seal bag, and shake until chicken is well coated. Marinate in refrigerator 8 hours, turning occasionally.

3 Remove chicken from marinade, discarding marinade. Coat grill rack with cooking spray; place on grill over medium-hot coals (350° to 400°). Place chicken on rack; grill, covered, 8 minutes on each side or until chicken is done, basting frequently with reserved tomato sauce mixture. Transfer chicken to a large serving platter. Yield: 6 servings.

YIELD: 4 servings

EXCHANGES PER
SERVING:
3 Very Lean Meat
1 Starch
1 Fat

PER SERVING:
Calories 198
Carbohydrate 12.1g
Protein 24.6g
Fat 5.2g
Cholesterol 88mg
Fiber 1.3g
Sodium 202mg

CHIPPER CHICKEN DRUMSTICKS

1   teaspoon chili powder
¼   teaspoon garlic powder
¼   teaspoon ground thyme
¼   teaspoon ground oregano
⅛   teaspoon pepper
8   chicken drumsticks, skinned
      (about 1½ pounds)
      Olive oil-flavored vegetable cooking
      spray
1   cup crushed low-fat barbecue potato
      chips
      Fresh thyme sprigs (optional)
      Fresh oregano sprigs (optional)

1 Combine first 5 ingredients in a small bowl, stirring well. Coat drumsticks with cooking spray; sprinkle evenly with chili powder mixture. Cover and chill 30 minutes.

2 Dredge drumsticks in crushed potato chips. Place drumsticks on a rack in a roasting pan. Bake at 400° for 20 minutes. Turn drumsticks, and bake 15 additional minutes or until done. If desired, garnish with thyme and oregano sprigs. Yield: 4 servings.

CRISPY OVEN-FRIED CHICKEN

YIELD: 6 servings

¼ cup plus 2 tablespoons frozen egg
    substitute, thawed
1 tablespoon water
1 cup crispy rice cereal, crushed
⅓ cup toasted wheat germ
1 tablespoon instant minced onion
½ teaspoon salt-free herb-and-spice blend
¼ teaspoon garlic powder
¼ teaspoon salt
¼ teaspoon pepper
1 (3-pound) broiler-fryer, cut up and
    skinned
¼ cup all-purpose flour
    Vegetable cooking spray

**EXCHANGES PER
SERVING:**
3 Very Lean Meat
1 Starch

PER SERVING:
Calories 209
Carbohydrate 14.0g
Protein 27.3g
Fat 4.2g
Cholesterol 76mg
Fiber 1.3g
Sodium 253mg

1 Combine egg substitute and water in a shallow dish; stir well. Combine cereal and next 6 ingredients in a shallow dish; stir well.

2 Place chicken pieces and flour in a large heavy-duty, zip-top plastic bag; seal bag, and shake until chicken is well coated.

3 Dip chicken in egg substitute mixture; dredge in cereal mixture. Place chicken on rack of a broiler pan coated with cooking spray. Bake, uncovered, at 350° for 1 hour or until chicken is tender and golden. Yield: 6 servings.

ROASTED CHICKEN AND VEGETABLES

EXCHANGES PER
SERVING:
3 Very Lean Meat
1 Starch
2 Vegetable

PER SERVING:
Calories 257
Carbohydrate 25.4g
Protein 27.9g
Fat 4.6g
Cholesterol 76mg
Fiber 3.4g
Sodium 296mg

1 (3-pound) broiler-fryer, skinned
1 teaspoon olive oil
  Vegetable cooking spray
12 small round red potatoes
2 cups thinly sliced leek
1 cup Sugar Snap peas, trimmed
6 small squash, cut into 1-inch-thick slices
6 small zucchini, cut into 1-inch-thick slices
3 heads Belgian endive, sliced lengthwise
1 cup canned low-sodium chicken broth
¼ cup dry white wine
½ teaspoon salt
½ teaspoon pepper
½ teaspoon minced fresh thyme
3 tablespoons all-purpose flour
¼ cup water
  Fresh thyme sprigs (optional)

1 Trim fat from chicken. Remove giblets and neck from chicken; reserve for another use. Rinse chicken with cold water; pat dry. Brush chicken with olive oil. Place chicken, breast side up, on a rack in a large roasting pan coated with cooking spray. Insert meat thermometer into meaty part of thigh, making sure it does not touch bone.

2 Add potatoes to pan. Bake at 350° for 1 hour. Add leek and next 4 ingredients. Combine broth and next 4 ingredients; pour over chicken and vegetables. Bake 45 additional minutes or until meat thermometer registers 180° to 185°, basting occasionally with pan juices.

3 Transfer chicken and vegetables to a platter. Pour pan juices through a wire-mesh strainer into a saucepan, discarding solids. Combine flour and water, stirring until smooth; stir into pan juices. Cook over medium-high heat, stirring constantly, until thickened. Serve sauce with chicken and vegetables. Garnish with thyme sprigs, if desired. Yield: 6 servings.

Cornish Hens With Mushroom-Wine Sauce

Vegetable cooking spray
1 teaspoon vegetable oil
½ cup minced green onions
¼ cup minced carrot
1 tablespoon all-purpose flour
½ pound fresh mushrooms, halved
¾ cup dry white wine
¾ cup water
½ teaspoon chicken-flavored bouillon granules
½ teaspoon dried rosemary
¼ teaspoon dried thyme
¼ teaspoon garlic powder
1 bay leaf
4 (1¼-pound) Cornish hens, skinned
1 teaspoon coarsely ground pepper
1 (12-ounce) package baby carrots, scraped
2 stalks celery, cut into 1-inch pieces
Fresh thyme and rosemary (optional)

1 Coat a large nonstick skillet with cooking spray; add oil. Place skillet over medium-high heat until hot. Add green onions and minced carrot; sauté until crisp-tender. Stir in flour. Cook over medium heat 1 minute, stirring constantly. Stir in mushrooms and next 7 ingredients. Bring to a boil. Reduce heat; simmer 8 minutes, stirring often.

2 Remove giblets from hens; reserve for another use. Rinse hens with cold running water; pat dry. Split in half lengthwise, using an electric knife. Sprinkle with pepper.

3 Coat a roasting pan with cooking spray. Place hens, cut side down, in pan. Spoon mushroom mixture over hens. Cover and bake at 350° for 45 minutes, basting frequently. Add baby carrots and celery. Cover; bake 20 additional minutes. Discard bay leaf. Garnish with rosemary and thyme sprigs, if desired. Yield: 8 servings.

YIELD: 8 servings

EXCHANGES PER SERVING:
4 Very Lean Meat
½ Starch

PER SERVING:
Calories 206
Carbohydrate 8.2g
Protein 30.6g
Fat 5.2g
Cholesterol 95mg
Fiber 2.3g
Sodium 185mg

TROPICAL CORNISH HENS

YIELD: 4 servings

EXCHANGES PER
SERVING:
4 Very Lean Meat
1 Fruit

PER SERVING:
Calories 273
Carbohydrate 23.5g
Protein 28.0g
Fat 7.3g
Cholesterol 83mg
Fiber 1.5g
Sodium 82mg

2 (1-pound) Cornish hens, skinned
½ teaspoon coarsely ground pepper
  Vegetable cooking spray
¼ cup frozen orange juice concentrate,
    thawed and undiluted
⅛ teaspoon garlic powder
½ cup peeled, diced fresh mango
½ cup unsweetened pineapple chunks
1 firm ripe banana, peeled and coarsely
    chopped
  Orange slices (optional)
  Orange curls (optional)

1 Remove and discard giblets from hens. Rinse hens under cold water, and pat dry with paper towels. Split each hen in half lengthwise, using an electric knife. Sprinkle with pepper. Place hens, cut side down, on a rack in a roasting pan coated with cooking spray.

2 Combine orange juice concentrate and garlic powder; brush over hens. Bake at 350° for 45 minutes, basting frequently with orange juice mixture.

3 Add mango, pineapple, and banana to pan. Drizzle with remaining orange juice mixture. Bake 20 minutes or until fruit is thoroughly heated and hens are done. If desired, garnish with orange slices and orange curls (not included in analysis). Yield: 4 servings.

Cornish Hens Provençal

Tomatoes, garlic, and olive oil, the primary ingredients of provençal cooking, add an international flavor to this entrée. Serve with a favorite steamed vegetable and French bread.

EXCHANGES PER
SERVING:
3 Lean Meat
2 Vegetable

PER SERVING:
Calories 230
Carbohydrate 12.3g
Protein 25.0g
Fat 8.8g
Cholesterol 76mg
Fiber 1.8g
Sodium 393mg

2 (1-pound) Cornish hens, skinned
  Vegetable cooking spray
1 tablespoon olive oil
1¾ cups chopped leek
1 (14½-ounce) can no-salt-added whole
  tomatoes, drained and chopped
½ cup canned no-salt-added chicken
  broth, undiluted
¼ cup dry white wine
1 (2¼-ounce) can sliced ripe olives, drained
1 teaspoon dried thyme
1 teaspoon ground turmeric
½ teaspoon garlic powder
¼ teaspoon salt
¼ teaspoon pepper
1 bay leaf
  Fresh thyme sprigs (optional)

1 Remove giblets from hens; reserve for another use. Rinse hens under cold water, and pat dry with paper towels. Split each hen in half lengthwise, using an electric knife.

2 Coat a large nonstick skillet with cooking spray; add olive oil. Place over medium-high heat until hot. Add hens; cook until hens are lightly browned on both sides, turning occasionally. Remove hens from skillet. Add leek; sauté until tender.

3 Place leek and hens, skinned side up, in an 11- x 7- x 1½-inch baking dish. Combine tomatoes and next 9 ingredients; pour over hens. Cover and bake at 375° for 20 minutes. Uncover and bake 10 additional minutes or until done. Remove and discard bay leaf. Transfer to a serving platter. Garnish with thyme sprigs, if desired. Yield: 4 servings.

EXCHANGES PER
SERVING:
4 Lean Meat
1 Starch
1 Fruit

PER SERVING:
Calories 313
Carbohydrate 30.2g
Protein 30.2g
Fat 8.6g
Cholesterol 81mg
Fiber 3.7g
Sodium 208mg

🌿 Look for parchment paper at the grocery store, bakery shops, or specialty kitchen shops. If you can't find it, use aluminum foil.

CORNISH HENS WITH FRUITED WILD RICE

¼ cup chopped dried figs
¼ cup chopped dried apricot halves
2 tablespoons apricot nectar
¼ cup canned low-sodium chicken broth
½ cup chopped fresh mushrooms
¼ cup minced onion
1⅓ cups cooked wild rice (cooked without salt or fat)
¼ cup chopped lean cooked ham
3 tablespoons chopped walnuts, toasted
2 (1-pound) Cornish hens, skinned
1 teaspoon olive oil
1 teaspoon paprika
1 teaspoon pepper

1 Combine chopped figs and apricots. Bring nectar to a simmer in a saucepan; pour over fruit. Cover; let stand 15 minutes. Bring broth to a boil in a skillet over medium-high heat. Add mushrooms and onion; sauté 5 minutes.

2 Cut 4 (18- x 15-inch) rectangles of parchment paper; fold each in half lengthwise, and trim each into a heart shape. Place on 2 large baking sheets, and open out flat. Combine fig and mushroom mixtures, rice, ham, and walnuts. Spoon one-fourth of mixture on 1 side of each parchment heart near the crease.

3 Remove and discard giblets from hens. Rinse hens under cold water; pat dry. Split each hen in half lengthwise. Place hen halves, cut side down, on rice mixture. Rub hens with oil; sprinkle with paprika and pepper.

4 Fold paper edges over hens. Starting with rounded edges, pleat and crimp edges to seal. Bake at 325° for 40 minutes. Remove from paper. Yield: 4 servings.

TURKEY SAUSAGE QUICHE IN CRÊPE CUPS

Vegetable cooking spray
4 ounces smoked turkey sausage, chopped
½ cup chopped green pepper
½ cup chopped onion
1 (8-ounce) carton egg substitute
½ cup skim milk
2 tablespoons instant nonfat dry milk powder
1 tablespoon all-purpose flour
⅛ teaspoon garlic powder
4 (9-inch) refrigerated crêpes
¾ cup frozen broccoli flowerets, thawed and cut into bite-size pieces
½ cup (2 ounces) shredded reduced-fat sharp Cheddar cheese

YIELD: 4 servings

EXCHANGES PER SERVING:
2 Medium-Fat Meat
1 Starch

PER SERVING:
Calories 216
Carbohydrate 14.3g
Protein 18.2g
Fat 9.5g
Cholesterol 41mg
Fiber 1.3g
Sodium 494mg

1 Coat a large nonstick skillet with cooking spray; place over medium-high heat until hot. Add sausage, green pepper, and onion; sauté 5 to 7 minutes or until vegetables are tender. Remove from heat.

2 Combine egg substitute and next 4 ingredients in a small bowl; stir until smooth.

3 Coat 4 (10-ounce) custard cups with cooking spray. Place 1 crêpe in each cup, pressing in center to form a cup. Spoon sausage mixture and broccoli into crêpe cups. Sprinkle with cheese. Pour ¼ cup egg substitute mixture into each cup.

4 Place custard cups on a baking sheet; bake, uncovered, at 400° for 15 minutes. Cover and bake 15 minutes or until a knife inserted in center comes out clean. Remove from oven; let stand 5 minutes. Run a knife around sides of crêpe cups, and carefully lift out of custard cups. Yield: 4 servings.

EXCHANGES PER
SERVING:
1 High-Fat Meat
1 Starch
2 Vegetable

PER SERVING:
Calories 268
Carbohydrate 25.2g
Protein 12.4g
Fat 12.9g
Cholesterol 32mg
Fiber 2.1g
Sodium 621mg

ITALIAN SAUSAGE WITH PEPPERS AND ONIONS

Olive oil-flavored vegetable cooking
    spray
¾ pound smoked Italian turkey sausage,
    cut into ¾-inch-thick slices
2 cups sliced onion
1 cup sliced green pepper
1 cup sliced sweet yellow pepper
1 cup fat-free no-salt-added spaghetti
    sauce
1 (8-ounce) can no-salt-added tomato
    sauce
½ cup water
1 tablespoon minced garlic
1 teaspoon dried Italian seasoning
6 (1-inch-thick) slices French bread,
    toasted
Hot sauce (optional)

1 Coat a large nonstick skillet with cooking spray; place over medium heat until hot. Add sausage and next 3 ingredients; cook 10 minutes, stirring occasionally.

2 Add spaghetti sauce and next 4 ingredients to skillet; bring to a boil. Reduce heat; simmer, uncovered, 10 minutes. Spoon turkey mixture evenly over bread slices. Sprinkle with hot sauce, if desired. Yield: 6 servings.

Spaghetti With Savory Sauce

Vegetable cooking spray
1 pound freshly ground raw turkey
3 tablespoons minced onion
2 cups plus 3 tablespoons water
2 teaspoons dried Italian seasoning
¼ teaspoon garlic powder
¼ teaspoon salt
1½ (6-ounce) cans no-salt-added tomato paste
6 ounces spaghetti, uncooked
1 tablespoon freshly grated Parmesan cheese

YIELD: 6 servings

EXCHANGES PER SERVING:
3 Very Lean Meat
2 Starch

PER SERVING:
Calories 237
Carbohydrate 28.6g
Protein 22.0g
Fat 3.8g
Cholesterol 44mg
Fiber 1.4g
Sodium 173mg

1 Coat a large nonstick skillet with cooking spray; place over medium-high heat until hot. Add turkey and onion; cook over medium heat until turkey is lightly browned, stirring to crumble. Drain and pat dry with paper towels. Wipe drippings from skillet with a paper towel.

2 Add turkey mixture, water, and next 4 ingredients to skillet. Bring to a boil. Reduce heat, and simmer 10 minutes or until thickened, stirring occasionally.

3 Cook spaghetti according to package directions, omitting salt and fat; drain. Place on serving platter; top with sauce. Sprinkle with cheese. Yield: 6 (1½-cup) servings.

TURKEY-NOODLE CASSEROLE

YIELD: 6 servings

EXCHANGES PER
SERVING:
3 Medium-Fat Meat
2 Starch

PER SERVING:
Calories 358
Carbohydrate 30.5g
Protein 26.0g
Fat 14.7g
Cholesterol 102mg
Fiber 2.2g
Sodium 268mg

6 ounces wide egg noodles, uncooked
  Vegetable cooking spray
1 pound freshly ground raw turkey
½ cup sliced fresh mushrooms
¼ cup chopped onion
2 (8-ounce) cans no-salt-added tomato
  sauce
¼ teaspoon garlic powder
¼ teaspoon pepper
¼ teaspoon dried oregano
⅛ teaspoon salt
1 cup part-skim ricotta cheese
3 tablespoons skim milk
½ (8-ounce) package Neufchâtel cheese,
  cut into ½-inch cubes and softened
2 teaspoons poppy seeds

1 Cook noodles according to package directions, omitting salt and fat; drain well.

2 Coat a nonstick skillet with cooking spray; place over medium-high heat. Add turkey, mushrooms, and onion; cook until turkey is browned and onion is tender, stirring until meat crumbles. Drain.

3 Add tomato sauce and next 4 ingredients. Bring to a boil; reduce heat, and simmer, uncovered, 3 minutes, stirring occasionally.

4 Combine ricotta and milk in container of an electric blender; cover and process until smooth. Transfer to a bowl; stir in Neufchâtel cheese and poppy seeds. Add noodles; toss well.

5 Layer two-thirds of noodle mixture in an 11- x 7- x 1½-inch baking dish. Spread turkey mixture over noodle mixture, leaving a 1-inch border. Top with remaining noodle mixture, leaving a 1-inch border of the turkey mixture. Cover and bake at 400° for 25 minutes. Yield: 6 servings.

Turkey-Avocado-Cheese Melts

¼ cup reduced-calorie no-salt-added chili sauce
3 tablespoons reduced-calorie mayonnaise
2 tablespoons, chopped green onions
8 (1-ounce) slices lean turkey breast
4 (¾-ounce) slices French bread, toasted
1 small avocado, peeled and cut into 8 slices
4 (1-ounce) slices fontina cheese
2 tablespoons chopped green onions
    Dash of ground red pepper

YIELD: 4 servings

EXCHANGES PER SERVING:
3 Lean Meat
1 Starch
1 Vegetable
1 Fat

PER SERVING:
Calories 333
Carbohydrate 20.4g
Protein 26.9g
Fat 15.7g
Cholesterol 73mg
Fiber 1.1g
Sodium 438mg

1 Combine first 3 ingredients in a small bowl, stirring well.

2 Place 2 slices turkey on each bread slice; spread half of mayonnaise mixture over turkey. Top each with 2 slices avocado and remaining mayonnaise mixture. Top each with 1 slice cheese.

3 Broil 5½ inches from heat (with electric oven door partially opened) 5 minutes or until cheese melts.

4 Sprinkle with green onions and red pepper. Serve warm. Yield: 4 servings.

TURKEY POT PIES

YIELD: 4 servings

EXCHANGES PER
SERVING:
3 Very Lean Meat
2 Starch

PER SERVING:
Calories 273
Carbohydrate 28.9g
Protein 24.7g
Fat 5.8g
Cholesterol 44mg
Fiber 2.9g
Sodium 418mg

2 cups diced cooked turkey
¾ cup sliced fresh mushrooms
1 (10-ounce) package frozen mixed
    vegetables, thawed
1 (10¾-ounce) can low-sodium cream of
    chicken soup
1 cup water
¾ teaspoon poultry seasoning
    Vegetable cooking spray
¾ cup self-rising flour
1 tablespoon margarine
¼ cup plus 2 tablespoons skim milk

1 Combine first 3 ingredients in a medium
bowl, stirring well.

2 Combine soup, water, and poultry seasoning
in a medium bowl; stir well. Add soup mixture to turkey mixture, stirring well to combine.

3 Spoon turkey mixture evenly into 4 (10-
ounce) baking dishes coated with cooking
spray.

4 Place flour in a small bowl; cut in margarine
with pastry blender until mixture is crumbly.
Stir in milk. Pinch off dough into 1½-inch
pieces; drop over each serving. Bake at 450° for
12 minutes or until golden. Yield: 4 servings.

Turkey Fajitas

YIELD: 2 servings

½ pound turkey breast cutlets
2 tablespoons low-sodium soy sauce
1 tablespoon fresh lime juice
1 tablespoon water
2 teaspoons minced garlic
1 teaspoon olive oil
½ teaspoon cracked pepper
¼ teaspoon ground cumin
2 tablespoons chopped avocado
1 tablespoon tomatillo salsa
1 tablespoon low-fat sour cream
1 teaspoon minced onion
¾ teaspoon minced fresh cilantro
½ teaspoon minced jalapeño pepper
   Olive oil-flavored vegetable cooking
      spray
1 cup thinly sliced sweet red pepper
½ cup thinly sliced onion
2 (8-inch) flour tortillas

EXCHANGES PER SERVING:
3 Lean Meat
1 Starch
2 Vegetable

PER SERVING:
Calories 328
Carbohydrate 27.5g
Protein 31.3g
Fat 9.3g
Cholesterol 71mg
Fiber 2.9g
Sodium 657mg

1 Cut turkey into strips; place in a small shallow dish. Combine soy sauce and next 6 ingredients; pour over turkey. Cover and marinate in refrigerator 2 hours.

2 Place avocado in a small bowl, and mash; stir in salsa and next 4 ingredients. Set aside.

3 Remove turkey from marinade, discarding marinade. Coat a nonstick skillet with cooking spray; place over medium-high heat until hot. Add turkey; sauté 2 minutes. Add red pepper and onion; sauté 6 minutes or until turkey is done and vegetables are tender. Spoon mixture evenly down center of tortillas. Roll up tortillas, folding in sides. Serve with avocado mixture. Yield: 2 servings.

SOUTHWESTERN TURKEY

YIELD: 4 servings

EXCHANGES PER
SERVING:
4 Very Lean Meat
1 Starch

PER SERVING:
Calories 193
Carbohydrate 15.5g
Protein 27.7g
Fat 2.7g
Cholesterol 70mg
Fiber 3.3g
Sodium 181mg

You can substitute skinned, boned chicken
breasts for turkey breast cutlets.

Vegetable cooking spray
1 pound (¼-inch-thick) turkey breast
   cutlets, cut into 2½- x ½-inch strips
1¼ teaspoons chili powder
¼ teaspoon ground cumin
1 teaspoon vegetable oil
1¼ cups green pepper strips
1 cup thinly sliced onion, separated into
   rings
1 cup frozen whole kernel corn
¾ cup thick and chunky salsa

1 Coat a large nonstick skillet with cooking
spray; place over high heat until hot. Add
turkey; sauté 3 minutes. Stir in chili powder and
cumin. Remove turkey from skillet, and
set aside.

2 Add oil to skillet; place over medium-high
heat. Add pepper strips and onion; sauté 3
minutes.

3 Return turkey to skillet. Stir in corn and
salsa; sauté 2 minutes or until thoroughly
heated. Yield: 4 (1-cup) servings.

Holiday Turkey Cutlets

YIELD: 4 servings

1 pound turkey breast cutlets, cut into
   8 pieces
3 tablespoons all-purpose flour
2 teaspoons vegetable oil
   Vegetable cooking spray
¾ cup chopped onion
¾ cup fresh cranberries
½ cup canned low-sodium chicken broth,
   undiluted
2 tablespoons granulated sugar substitute
2 tablespoons red wine vinegar
2 tablespoons fat-free Catalina dressing
¼ teaspoon salt
   Fresh sage sprigs (optional)
   Orange slices (optional)

EXCHANGES PER SERVING:
4 Very Lean Meat
1 Fruit

PER SERVING:
Calories 203
Carbohydrate 11.6g
Protein 27.6g
Fat 4.1g
Cholesterol 68mg
Fiber 0.5g
Sodium 317mg

1 Place turkey breast cutlets between 2 sheets of heavy-duty plastic wrap, and flatten to ⅛-inch thickness, using a meat mallet or rolling pin. Dredge turkey cutlets in flour.

2 Heat oil in a large nonstick skillet over medium heat. Add cutlets, and cook 2 minutes on each side or until browned. Transfer to a platter, and keep warm. Wipe drippings from skillet with a paper towel.

3 Coat skillet with cooking spray; place skillet over medium-high heat until hot. Add onion, and sauté until tender. Add cranberries and next 5 ingredients; bring to a boil. Cook over medium-high heat 4 to 5 minutes or until cranberry skins pop and sauce is slightly thickened. Spoon sauce over cutlets; serve immediately. If desired, garnish with sage sprigs and orange slices (not included in analysis). Yield: 4 servings.

TURKEY ROMANO

YIELD: 4 servings

EXCHANGES PER
SERVING:
4 Very Lean Meat
1 Starch
1 Fat

PER SERVING:
Calories 253
Carbohydrate 13.5g
Protein 29.7g
Fat 8.1g
Cholesterol 63mg
Fiber 0.8g
Sodium 204mg

1 pound turkey breast cutlets, cut into 8
  pieces
⅓ cup all-purpose flour
½ teaspoon freshly ground pepper
1 tablespoon vegetable oil, divided
  Vegetable cooking spray
1 teaspoon reduced-calorie margarine
⅓ cup sliced fresh mushrooms
1 tablespoon sliced green onions
¾ cup skim milk, divided
1 tablespoon all-purpose flour
2 tablespoons grated Romano cheese
1 teaspoon lemon juice
⅛ teaspoon salt
⅛ teaspoon freshly ground pepper
⅛ teaspoon paprika
½ cup sliced green onions

1 Place cutlets between 2 sheets of plastic wrap; flatten to ¼-inch thickness. Combine ⅓ cup flour and ½ teaspoon pepper; dredge cutlets in flour mixture.

2 Heat 1½ teaspoons oil in a nonstick skillet over medium-high heat until hot. Add half of cutlets, and cook 3 minutes on each side or until browned. Drain. Repeat with remaining oil and cutlets.

3 Coat a saucepan with cooking spray; add margarine. Place over medium heat until margarine melts. Add mushrooms and 1 tablespoon green onions; sauté until tender.

4 Combine 1 tablespoon milk and 1 tablespoon flour; stir until smooth. Add remaining milk to vegetable mixture. Stir in flour mixture. Cook over medium heat, stirring constantly, until slightly thickened. Add cheese and next 3 ingredients; stir well. Spoon cheese mixture over cutlets. Sprinkle with paprika. Top with ½ cup green onions. Yield: 4 servings.

Lemon Turkey Cutlets

8 (2-ounce) turkey breast cutlets
2½ tablespoons all-purpose flour
2 teaspoons olive oil, divided
¼ teaspoon salt
¼ teaspoon freshly ground pepper
2 tablespoons lemon juice
1 lemon, sliced (optional)
  Fresh sage sprigs (optional)

1 Place cutlets between 2 sheets of heavy-duty plastic wrap; flatten to ⅛-inch thickness, using a meat mallet or rolling pin. Dredge in flour; set aside.

2 Heat 1 teaspoon oil in a large nonstick skillet over medium heat until hot. Add half of cutlets, and cook 3 minutes on each side or until browned. Transfer cutlets to a serving platter; keep warm.

3 Repeat procedure with remaining 1 teaspoon oil and cutlets. Sprinkle cutlets with salt, pepper, and lemon juice. If desired, garnish with lemon slices and sage sprigs. Yield: 4 servings.

YIELD: 4 servings

EXCHANGES PER SERVING:
4 Very Lean Meat
½ Fat

PER SERVING:
Calories 179
Carbohydrate 4.5g
Protein 26.8g
Fat 5.2g
Cholesterol 61mg
Fiber 0.0g
Sodium 203mg

YIELD: 4 servings

EXCHANGES PER
SERVING:
4 Very Lean Meat
½ Starch

PER SERVING:
Calories 173
Carbohydrate 9.6g
Protein 27.5g
Fat 2.1g
Cholesterol 71mg
Fiber 0.5g
Sodium 330mg

TURKEY CUTLETS WITH CAPER SAUCE

1½ tablespoons lemon juice
  4 (4-ounce) turkey breast cutlets
  3 tablespoons all-purpose flour
  2 teaspoons paprika
  ¼ teaspoon ground white pepper
    Vegetable cooking spray
  ½ teaspoon olive oil
  2 tablespoons all-purpose flour
  1 cup canned no-salt-added chicken
    broth, undiluted
  2 tablespoons lemon juice
1½ tablespoons capers
  2 teaspoons chopped fresh parsley

1 Drizzle 1½ tablespoons lemon juice over cutlets. Combine 3 tablespoons flour, paprika, and pepper. Dredge cutlets in flour mixture.

2 Coat a large nonstick skillet with cooking spray; add oil. Place over medium-high heat until hot. Add cutlets, and cook 2 to 3 minutes on each side or until browned. Transfer to a serving platter, and keep warm.

3 Combine 2 tablespoons flour and broth, stirring until smooth. Place in a small heavy saucepan over medium heat; cook 3 minutes, stirring constantly. Stir in 2 tablespoons lemon juice; cook, stirring constantly, until mixture is thickened and bubbly. Remove from heat; stir in capers. Spoon sauce over cutlets; sprinkle with parsley. Serve warm. Yield: 4 servings.

STUFFED TURKEY BREAST

YIELD: 12 servings

1 (3-pound) boneless turkey breast,
    skinned and trimmed of fat
Vegetable cooking spray
1 teaspoon reduced-calorie margarine
½ cup finely chopped onion
½ cup chopped fresh mushrooms
½ cup shredded carrot
1 cup soft whole wheat breadcrumbs
¼ cup chopped fresh parsley
½ teaspoon dried thyme
½ teaspoon grated lemon rind
¼ teaspoon pepper
¼ cup canned low-sodium chicken broth,
    undiluted
1 egg, lightly beaten
2 teaspoons lemon juice
2 tablespoons reduced-calorie margarine
1 tablespoon white wine Worcestershire
    sauce

EXCHANGES PER SERVING:
3 Very Lean Meat
1 Vegetable

PER SERVING:
Calories 129
Carbohydrate 3.9g
Protein 21.8g
Fat 2.6g
Cholesterol 74mg
Fiber 0.5g
Sodium 98mg

1 Place turkey breast on heavy-duty plastic wrap. From center, slice horizontally through thickest part of each side almost to outer edge; flip each cut piece. Flatten to ½-inch thickness, using a meat mallet or rolling pin.

2 Coat a large nonstick skillet with cooking spray; add 1 teaspoon margarine. Place over medium-high heat until hot. Add onion, mushrooms, and carrot; cook until crisp-tender. Stir in breadcrumbs and next 7 ingredients. Spoon over turkey, leaving a 2-inch border at sides; roll up, jellyroll fashion, starting at short side. Tie at 2-inch intervals with string. Place, seam side down, on a rack in a roasting pan coated with cooking spray. Insert meat thermometer.

3 Bake at 325° for 45 minutes. Combine 2 tablespoons margarine and Worcestershire sauce; brush over turkey. Bake an additional 1½ hours or until meat thermometer registers 170°, brushing with margarine mixture after 1 hour. Remove string; let stand 10 minutes before slicing. Yield: 12 servings.

ROASTED TURKEY BREAST

EXCHANGES PER
SERVING:
4 Very Lean Meat

PER SERVING:
Calories 153
Carbohydrate 0.2g
Protein 26.4g
Fat 4.3g
Cholesterol 61mg
Fiber 0.0g
Sodium 116mg

1 (4½-pound) turkey breast
⅓ cup chopped onion
⅓ cup chopped celery
2 teaspoons lemon juice
1 tablespoon minced fresh basil
2 teaspoons minced fresh oregano
  Vegetable cooking spray
1 tablespoon olive oil
½ teaspoon garlic powder
¼ teaspoon salt
  Fresh basil sprigs (optional)
  Fresh oregano sprigs (optional)
  Fresh rosemary sprigs (optional)

1 Trim fat from turkey. Rinse turkey under cold water, and pat dry. Wrap onion and celery in a single layer of wet cheesecloth; place in cavity of turkey.

2 Combine lemon juice, minced basil, and minced oregano; set aside.

3 Place turkey on a rack in a roasting pan coated with cooking spray. Insert meat thermometer into meaty part of breast, making sure it does not touch bone. Brush with olive oil, and sprinkle with garlic powder and salt.

4 Bake at 325° for 2 to 2½ hours or until meat thermometer registers 170°, brushing with lemon juice mixture after 1½ hours. Remove and discard onion and celery.

5 Transfer turkey to a serving platter, and, if desired, garnish with basil, oregano, and rosemary sprigs. (Remove skin from turkey slices before serving.) Yield: 10 servings.

Salads &
Salad Dressings

THREE-LAYER CONGEALED SALAD

EXCHANGES PER
SERVING:
½ Fruit

PER SERVING:
Calories 50
Carbohydrate 7.6g
Protein 2.3g
Fat 1.4g
Cholesterol 4mg
Fiber 0.2g
Sodium 34mg

1 (0.3-ounce) package sugar-free
  strawberry-flavored gelatin
1 cup boiling water
1½ cups frozen unsweetened strawberries,
  thawed and halved
  Vegetable cooking spray
1 (0.3-ounce) package sugar-free
  lemon-flavored gelatin
1 cup boiling water
3 ounces Neufchâtel cheese, softened
1 cup skim milk
1 (0.3-ounce) package sugar-free
  lime-flavored gelatin
1 cup boiling water
1 (20-ounce) can crushed pineapple
  in juice, undrained

1 Combine strawberry gelatin and 1 cup boiling water, stirring 2 minutes or until gelatin dissolves. Stir in strawberries, and pour into a 10-cup mold coated with cooking spray. Cover and chill 1 hour.

2 Combine lemon gelatin and 1 cup boiling water, stirring 2 minutes or until gelatin dissolves; set aside.

3 Beat Neufchâtel cheese in a medium bowl at medium speed of an electric mixer until smooth. Gradually add milk, beating well. Add lemon gelatin to cheese mixture, beating at low speed until smooth. Gently pour into mold over strawberry layer. Cover and chill 1 hour.

4 Combine lime gelatin and 1 cup boiling water, stirring 2 minutes or until gelatin dissolves; chill until the consistency of unbeaten egg white. Stir in pineapple. Pour over lemon layer. Cover and chill 1 hour. Unmold onto a serving plate. Yield: 16 servings.

Jewel Salad

1 (0.3-ounce) package sugar-free cherry-
flavored gelatin
3 cups boiling water, divided
3 cups cold water, divided
Vegetable cooking spray
1 (0.3-ounce) package sugar-free lemon-
flavored gelatin
1 (0.3-ounce) package sugar-free lime-
flavored gelatin
2 (0.3-ounce) packages sugar-free orange-
flavored gelatin
3 cups boiling water
⅔ cup unsweetened pineapple juice
½ envelope reduced-calorie whipped
topping mix sweetened with aspartame
Green leaf lettuce leaves (optional)

YIELD: 10 servings

EXCHANGES PER
SERVING:
Free

PER SERVING:
Calories 27
Carbohydrate 2.6g
Protein 2.9g
Fat 0.4g
Cholesterol 0mg
Fiber 0g
Sodium 17mg

1 Combine cherry gelatin and 1 cup boiling water, stirring 2 minutes or until gelatin
dissolves. Add 1 cup cold water; pour into an 8-
inch square pan coated with cooking spray.
Cover and chill 1 hour or until set. Repeat procedure with lemon and lime gelatins, using 1 cup
boiling water and 1 cup cold water for each.

2 Cut cherry, lemon, and lime gelatin into
½-inch cubes. Place 1 cup of each in a
medium bowl; reserve remaining gelatin cubes
for another use.

3 Combine orange gelatin and 3 cups boiling
water, stirring 2 minutes or until gelatin
dissolves. Add pineapple juice; cover and chill
until the consistency of unbeaten egg white.

4 Beat orange gelatin at medium speed of an
electric mixer until foamy. Prepare whipped
topping mix according to package directions.

5 Fold orange gelatin into whipped topping;
fold in gelatin cubes. Spoon mixture into a
11- x 7- x 1½-inch baking dish; cover and chill
until set. Serve on lettuce-lined salad plates, if
desired. Yield: 10 servings.

FROZEN FRUIT CUPS

YIELD: 12 servings

EXCHANGES PER
SERVING:
1 Very Lean Meat
1 Fruit

PER SERVING:
Calories 82
Carbohydrate 12.1g
Protein 4.8g
Fat 1.9g
Cholesterol 3.2mg
Fiber 1.6g
Sodium 165mg

1 (12-ounce) carton 1% low-fat
   cottage cheese
1 (8-ounce) carton strawberry nonfat
   yogurt sweetened with aspartame
¼ cup reduced-fat mayonnaise
2 tablespoons granulated sugar substitute
   with aspartame (such as Equal
   Spoonful)
1¼ cups sliced fresh strawberries
2 medium-size ripe bananas, peeled and
   sliced
1 (15¼-ounce) can pineapple tidbits in
   juice, drained
   Curly leaf lettuce leaves
   Fresh mint sprigs (optional)

1 Position knife blade in food processor bowl;
add first 4 ingredients. Process until smooth,
stopping twice to scrape down sides.

2 Combine strawberries, banana, and pineapple in a large bowl. Fold cottage cheese
mixture into fruit mixture. Spoon mixture
evenly into muffin cups lined with foil liners.
Cover and freeze until firm.

3 To serve, remove from freezer, and let soften
slightly. Remove from foil liners, and place
each fruit cup on a lettuce-lined salad plate.
Garnish with mint sprigs, if desired.
Yield: 12 servings.

MIXED GREENS WITH TARRAGON DRESSING

YIELD: 10 servings

EXCHANGES PER
SERVING:
1 Vegetable
½ Fat

PER SERVING:
Calories 44
Carbohydrate 4.2g
Protein 2.1g
Fat 2.3g
Cholesterol 7mg
Fiber 0.4g
Sodium 97mg

½ cup light process cream cheese product
2 tablespoons freeze-dried chives
2 tablespoons skim milk
1 teaspoon dried tarragon
   Olive oil-flavored vegetable
      cooking spray
¼ teaspoon olive oil
¼ teaspoon garlic powder
2 (1-ounce) slices whole wheat bread,
   cut into ½-inch cubes
8 cups torn leaf lettuce
2 cups torn curly endive
   Dash of coarsely ground pepper

1 Combine first 4 ingredients in container of an electric blender; cover and process until smooth. Transfer to a small bowl; cover and chill.

2 Coat a small nonstick skillet with cooking spray; add olive oil. Place over medium heat until hot; add garlic powder and bread cubes. Cook 5 minutes or until bread is lightly browned, stirring often. Set aside.

3 Combine leaf lettuce and curly endive in a large bowl. Add croutons, and sprinkle with pepper. Arrange lettuce mixture on individual salad plates. Drizzle cream cheese mixture over each salad. Yield: 10 (1-cup) servings.

GREEK SALAD

This salad combines all the traditional ingredients of a Greek salad with a lighter vinaigrette dressing made of red wine vinegar, olive oil, oregano, and pepper.

EXCHANGES PER SERVING:
1 Vegetable
1 Fat

PER SERVING:
Calories 67
Carbohydrate 6.4g
Protein 2.0g
Fat 4.3g
Cholesterol 5mg
Fiber 1.7g
Sodium 73mg

🌿 Romaine lettuce is also called Cos after the Greek island where it originated. It has crisp, oblong leaves that are dark green with a thick white rib down the center. The inner leaves are usually pale yellow-green and more tender than the outer ones.

4 cups torn romaine lettuce
2 medium tomatoes, cut into wedges
1 small cucumber, sliced
1 small purple onion, thinly sliced
1 small green pepper, seeded and cut into strips
²/₃ cup sliced radishes
½ cup crumbled feta cheese
3 tablespoons red wine vinegar
2 tablespoons olive oil
½ teaspoon dried oregano
¼ teaspoon pepper

1 Combine first 7 ingredients in a large bowl; toss well. Combine vinegar, oil, oregano, and pepper in a small bowl, stirring well.

2 Pour vinegar mixture over lettuce mixture, tossing well. Yield: 10 (1-cup) servings.

Antipasto Salad

YIELD: 9 servings

1 (14-ounce) can artichoke hearts, drained
   and halved
1 (8-ounce) package presliced fresh
   mushrooms
1 medium zucchini, cut into thin strips
¼ cup sliced green onions
½ cup commercial fat-free Italian dressing
¼ cup balsamic vinegar
4 cups torn leaf lettuce
1 cup cherry tomatoes, halved
4 ounces part-skim mozzarella cheese, cut
   into ½-inch cubes
¼ cup sliced ripe olives
2 tablespoons grated Parmesan cheese

EXCHANGES PER SERVING:
2 Vegetable
½ Fat

PER SERVING:
Calories 79
Carbohydrate 8.5g
Protein 5.7g
Fat 3.1g
Cholesterol 8mg
Fiber 1.4g
Sodium 294mg

1 Combine first 4 ingredients in a shallow dish. Pour Italian dressing and balsamic vinegar over vegetable mixture; toss lightly to coat. Cover and marinate in refrigerator at least 4 hours.

2 Combine vegetable mixture, lettuce, and next 3 ingredients in a large bowl; toss lightly to coat. Sprinkle with Parmesan cheese. Yield: 9 (1-cup) servings.

❧ Balsamic vinegar is an Italian vinegar made from white Trebbiano grape juice. This dark vinegar has a pungent sweetness that adds a distinctive flavor to salads, vegetables, and meats. Look for balsamic vinegar on the grocery shelves along with other vinegars.

BACON, LETTUCE, AND TOMATO SALAD

EXCHANGES PER
SERVING:
1 Medium-Fat Meat
1 Starch
1 Vegetable

PER SERVING:
Calories 187
Carbohydrate 23.4g
Protein 11.0g
Fat 5.4g
Cholesterol 24mg
Fiber 1.5g
Sodium 822mg

This salad is higher in sodium than some of the other salads in the chapter because of the Canadian bacon, turkey bacon, salad dressing, and cheese. Use reduced-sodium versions of these products if you need to decrease your sodium intake.

8 cups tightly packed torn red leaf lettuce
4 small tomatoes, cut into wedges
6 ounces Canadian bacon, coarsely chopped
4 (1-ounce) slices French bread, cubed and toasted
¾ cup (3 ounces) shredded reduced-fat sharp Cheddar cheese
4 slices turkey bacon, cooked and coarsely crumbled
¾ cup fat-free French dressing
3 tablespoons cider vinegar
1 tablespoon low-sodium Worcestershire sauce

1 Combine lettuce, tomato, and Canadian bacon in a large bowl; toss well. Place lettuce mixture evenly on 8 salad plates.

2 Top salads evenly with toasted bread cubes, and sprinkle evenly with cheese and turkey bacon.

3 Combine French dressing, vinegar, and Worcestershire sauce, stirring well. Drizzle 2 tablespoons dressing over each salad. Yield: 8 (1¼-cup) servings.

TOSSED GREENS AND GRILLED VEGETABLES

YIELD: 4 servings

EXCHANGES PER SERVING:
2 Vegetable
½ Fat

PER SERVING:
Calories 79
Carbohydrate 12.5g
Protein 2.7g
Fat 3.1g
Cholesterol 0mg
Fiber 3.3g
Sodium 152mg

2 tablespoons white wine vinegar
1 tablespoon water
1 teaspoon dried basil
2 teaspoons olive oil
1 teaspoon Dijon mustard
½ teaspoon chicken-flavored bouillon granules
½ teaspoon dried oregano
¼ teaspoon pepper
1 large yellow squash, halved lengthwise
1 small eggplant, halved lengthwise
Vegetable cooking spray
3 cups torn Bibb lettuce
2 cups torn curly endive
8 cherry tomatoes, halved

1 Combine first 8 ingredients in a small bowl; stir well. Brush 1 tablespoon vinegar mixture over squash halves and eggplant halves.

2 Coat grill rack with cooking spray; place on grill over medium-hot coals (350° to 400°). Place squash and eggplant on rack; grill, uncovered, 8 to 10 minutes or until vegetables are tender, turning often. Remove from grill, and set aside until cool enough to handle.

3 Cut squash and eggplant into 1-inch pieces; place in a large salad bowl. Add lettuce, endive, and tomatoes. Drizzle remaining vinegar mixture over salad, and toss lightly. Yield: 4 (1½-cup) servings.

ORANGE-AVOCADO SALAD

YIELD: 6 servings

EXCHANGES PER SERVING:
1 Vegetable
1 Fat

PER SERVING:
Calories 60
Carbohydrate 5.1g
Protein 1.1g
Fat 4.5g
Cholesterol 0mg
Fiber 1.9g
Sodium 63mg

2 tablespoons unsweetened orange juice
2 tablespoons red wine vinegar
2 teaspoons olive oil
¼ teaspoon grated orange rind
⅛ teaspoon salt
⅛ teaspoon pepper
2 cups torn fresh watercress
1 cup torn fresh spinach
2 oranges, peeled and sectioned
1 small avocado, peeled and sliced
  Fresh chives (optional)

1 Combine first 6 ingredients in a small bowl, stirring well with a wire whisk.

2 Combine watercress and spinach in a bowl. Pour orange juice mixture over greens; toss gently.

3 Place watercress mixture evenly onto individual salad plates. Arrange orange sections and avocado slices over each salad. Garnish with chives, if desired. Yield: 6 servings.

Strawberry-Spinach Salad

YIELD: 8 servings

⅓ cup reduced-calorie mayonnaise
¼ cup unsweetened orange juice
1 teaspoon granulated sugar substitute
  (such as Sugar Twin)
1 teaspoon poppy seeds
½ pound torn fresh spinach
2 cups sliced fresh strawberries

**EXCHANGES PER
SERVING:**
1 Vegetable
½ Fat

PER SERVING:
Calories 47
Carbohydrate 4.8g
Protein 1.0g
Fat 3.0g
Cholesterol 3mg
Fiber 1.7g
Sodium 89mg

1 Combine first 4 ingredients in a small bowl, stirring well.

2 Combine spinach and strawberries; toss. Arrange on salad plates. Drizzle 1 tablespoon mayonnaise mixture over each. Yield: 8 servings.

Fruited Spinach Salad

YIELD: 6 servings

1 (11-ounce) can mandarin oranges in
  water, undrained
¼ teaspoon unflavored gelatin
1 teaspoon lemon juice, divided
1 teaspoon poppy seeds
½ pound torn fresh spinach
1½ cups chopped red apple
½ cup thinly sliced celery
⅓ cup raisins
2 tablespoons unsalted sunflower kernels

**EXCHANGES PER
SERVING:**
1 Vegetable
1 Fruit
½ Fat

PER SERVING:
Calories 101
Carbohydrate 19.7g
Protein 3.0g
Fat 2.0g
Cholesterol 0mg
Fiber 3.5g
Sodium 48mg

1 Drain oranges, reserving ½ cup liquid; set oranges aside. Combine liquid and gelatin in a saucepan; let stand 1 minute. Place over medium heat; cook, stirring constantly, 2 minutes or until gelatin dissolves. Remove from heat; stir in ½ teaspoon lemon juice and poppy seeds. Pour into a glass bowl. Cover and chill.

2 Combine oranges, ½ teaspoon lemon juice, spinach, and next 3 ingredients. Top with dressing, and sprinkle with sunflower kernels. Yield: 6 servings.

super·quick
SPINACH-ONION SALAD

YIELD: 4 servings

EXCHANGES PER
SERVING:
1 Vegetable

PER SERVING:
Calories 41
Carbohydrate 8.2g
Protein 2.2g
Fat 0.3g
Cholesterol 0mg
Fiber 3.1g
Sodium 277mg

1 (10-ounce) package torn fresh spinach
   leaves
½ purple onion, thinly sliced
¼ cup fat-free red wine vinaigrette

1 Combine spinach leaves and onion. Add vinaigrette, and toss.
Yield: 4 (1½-cup) servings.

super·quick
SWEET-AND-SOUR
SPINACH SALAD

YIELD: 6 servings

EXCHANGES PER
SERVING:
1 Starch

PER SERVING:
Calories 77
Carbohydrate 13.5g
Protein 2.9g
Fat 1.5g
Cholesterol 2mg
Fiber 2.1g
Sodium 476mg

1 (10-ounce) package torn fresh spinach
1 cup croutons
1 tablespoons crumbled bacon bits
½ cup fat-free sweet-and-sour dressing

1 Combine spinach, croutons, and bacon bits in a large bowl. Add dressing, and toss well.
Yield: 6 (1½-cup) servings.

Fruited Green Salad

YIELD: 8 servings

A combination of soft and crunchy textures and a zesty dressing makes this salad a robust accompaniment to grilled chicken (chicken not included in analysis).

1½ cups torn Boston lettuce
1½ cups torn red leaf lettuce
1 (½-pound) jicama, peeled and cut into very thin strips
1½ cups sliced celery
1 large pink grapefruit, peeled and sectioned
2 medium kiwifruit, peeled and sliced
1 small purple onion, thinly sliced
¼ cup sliced green onions
½ cup unsweetened grapefruit juice
2 tablespoons lime juice
¼ teaspoon salt
¼ teaspoon pepper
1½ tablespoons vegetable oil

1 Combine first 8 ingredients in a large bowl, and toss well.

2 Combine grapefruit juice and next 3 ingredients in a bowl. Add oil, and stir with a wire whisk to combine. Pour over lettuce mixture, tossing gently. Yield: 8 (1-cup) servings.

EXCHANGES PER SERVING:
½ Fruit
½ Fat

PER SERVING:
Calories 65
Carbohydrate 9.6g
Protein 1.1g
Fat 2.8g
Cholesterol 0mg
Fiber 1.3g
Sodium 88mg

🍃 Jicama, a large, bulbous root vegetable, has a thin brown skin and white crunchy flesh with a sweet, nutty flavor. Often referred to as the Mexican potato, jicama is good raw or cooked. Store jicama in the refrigerator and peel before using.

EXCHANGES PER
SERVING:
1 Fruit
½ Fat

PER SERVING:
Calories 84
Carbohydrate 15.6g
Protein 1.5g
Fat 2.4g
Cholesterol 3mg
Fiber 1.7g
Sodium 98mg

❧ Feta is a white,
crumbly Greek cheese
with a sharp, salty
flavor. Look for it in
the grocery store's
dairy case or with
the specialty cheeses.

TROPICAL FRUIT AND FETA SALAD

In this fruit and cheese combination,
the feta cheese adds a savory accent to
the flavors of the fruits.

2½ cups torn Boston lettuce
2½ cups torn Bibb lettuce
1¾ cups peeled, cubed mango (about 1
    small)
1 cup seedless red grapes, halved
2 kiwifruit, peeled and sliced
1 medium starfruit, sliced
1 small purple onion, sliced and
    separated into rings
⅓ cup unsweetened orange juice
1 tablespoon lemon juice
1 tablespoon Dijon mustard
2 teaspoons vegetable oil
½ teaspoon ground ginger
¼ teaspoon grated orange rind
  Dash of pepper
¼ cup crumbled feta cheese

1 Combine first 7 ingredients in a large bowl,
tossing well.

2 Combine orange juice and next 6 ingredients
in a small jar; cover tightly, and shake
vigorously to combine. Pour over lettuce mixture; toss gently to coat. Sprinkle evenly with
feta cheese, and serve immediately.
Yield: 8 (1-cup) servings.

super·quick

QUICK VEGGIE SLAW

YIELD: 9 servings

1 (16-ounce) package broccoli slaw
1 Red Delicious apple, chopped
1 green onion, chopped
½ cup cider vinegar
¼ cup apple juice
⅓ cup sugar
¼ teaspoon salt
¼ teaspoon pepper

EXCHANGES PER SERVING:
1 Fruit

PER SERVING:
Calories 60
Carbohydrate 14.7g
Protein 0.7g
Fat 0.1g
Cholesterol 0mg
Fiber 0.1g
Sodium 74mg

1 Combine first 3 ingredients in a large bowl. Combine cider and remaining 4 ingredients, stirring well.

2 Pour vinegar mixture over slaw mixture, and toss. Serve immediately, or cover and chill. Yield: 9 (1-cup) servings.

super·quick

ZESTY COLESLAW

YIELD: 4 servings

4 cups coleslaw mix
⅓ cup fat-free vinaigrette

EXCHANGES PER SERVING:
1 Vegetable

PER SERVING:
Calories 27
Carbohydrate 6.1g
Protein 0.9g
Fat 0.1g
Cholesterol 0mg
Fiber 1.7g
Sodium 228mg

1 Combine coleslaw mix and vinaigrette, tossing well. Yield: 4 (1-cup) servings.

MEXICALI COLESLAW

EXCHANGES PER
SERVING:
2 Vegetable
½ Fat

PER SERVING:
Calories 69
Carbohydrate 9.0g
Protein 3.9g
Fat 2.4g
Cholesterol 7mg
Fiber 1.1g
Sodium 65mg

1 small green cabbage, untrimmed
¼ cup coarsely shredded red cabbage
¼ cup no-salt-added whole kernel corn, drained
2 tablespoons seeded, chopped tomato
1 tablespoon chopped green pepper
1 tablespoon shredded reduced-fat Cheddar cheese
1 teaspoon minced jalapeño pepper
1 tablespoon plain low-fat yogurt
1 tablespoon low-fat sour cream
⅛ teaspoon chili powder
Dash of ground cumin
Dash of hot sauce

1 Remove 2 large outer leaves of cabbage; set leaves aside. Coarsely shred inner leaves to measure ½ cup; reserve remaining cabbage for another use.

2 Combine ½ cup shredded cabbage, red cabbage, and next 5 ingredients in a medium bowl; toss well, and set aside.

3 Combine yogurt and next 4 ingredients in a small bowl, stirring well. Add yogurt mixture to shredded cabbage mixture, tossing lightly. Cover and chill.

4 To serve, spoon coleslaw into reserved cabbage leaves. Yield: 2 (¾-cup) servings.

Asparagus-Beet Salad

YIELD: 2 servings

8 fresh asparagus spears
1 tablespoon water
1 tablespoon red wine vinegar
1½ teaspoons vegetable oil
1 teaspoon lemon juice
⅛ teaspoon granulated sugar substitute
    (such as Sugar Twin)
2 Boston lettuce leaves
1 (8¼-ounce) can sliced beets, drained
¼ cup seasoned croutons
1 tablespoon crumbled blue cheese

EXCHANGES PER SERVING:
3 Vegetable
1 Fat

PER SERVING:
Calories 121
Carbohydrate 14.5g
Protein 4.0g
Fat 5.9g
Cholesterol 3mg
Fiber 2.6g
Sodium 207mg

1 Snap off tough ends of asparagus. Remove scales with a vegetable peeler, if desired. Arrange asparagus in a steamer basket over boiling water. Cover and steam 4 minutes or until crisp-tender. Drain. Place asparagus in freezer 10 to 15 minutes or until chilled.

2 Combine 1 tablespoon water and next 4 ingredients in a jar. Cover tightly, and shake vigorously to combine.

3 Place 1 lettuce leaf on each salad plate. Arrange chilled asparagus and beets over lettuce. Spoon 2 tablespoons vinegar mixture over each salad; top evenly with croutons and blue cheese. Yield: 2 servings.

LAYERED CABBAGE SALAD

EXCHANGES PER
SERVING:
2 Vegetable
1 Fruit

PER SERVING:
Calories 123
Carbohydrate 23.1g
Protein 5.8g
Fat 0.3g
Cholesterol 0mg
Fiber 3.3g
Sodium 206mg

You can assemble this layered
salad up to 8 hours ahead, and
then chill until serving time.

2 cups preshredded cabbage
1 (10-ounce) package frozen English peas,
    thawed and drained
¼ teaspoon salt
1 (8-ounce) can sliced water chestnuts,
    drained
1 cup chopped Red Delicious apple
    (about 1 large)
2 teaspoons lemon juice
¾ cup chopped celery
½ cup nonfat sour cream
½ cup plain nonfat yogurt
1 teaspoon granulated sugar substitute
    with aspartame (such as Equal
    Spoonful)
2 tablespoons shredded carrot
    Fresh parsley sprigs (optional)

1 Layer cabbage and peas in a 6-cup glass
  bowl; sprinkle with salt, and top with water
chestnuts.

2 Combine apple and lemon juice, tossing
  well. Arrange apple over water chestnuts,
and top with celery.

3 Combine sour cream, yogurt, and sugar
  substitute; stir well. Spread mixture over
top of salad. Sprinkle with carrot. Cover
and chill. Garnish with parsley, if desired.
Yield: 6 (1-cup) servings.

Seven-Layer Italian Salad

YIELD: 8 servings

3 cups shredded iceberg lettuce
1 medium-size sweet red pepper, cut into strips
1 medium cucumber, sliced
2 cups yellow or red teardrop tomatoes, halved
1 medium-size sweet yellow pepper, cut into ½-inch pieces
1 cup thinly sliced celery
¾ cup sliced green onions
¼ cup red wine vinegar
¼ cup water
1 tablespoon vegetable oil
2 teaspoons Dijon mustard
1 teaspoon dried Italian seasoning
1 teaspoon minced fresh garlic
½ teaspoon black pepper
¼ teaspoon hot sauce
½ cup (2 ounces) shredded nonfat mozzarella cheese
Sweet red pepper rings (optional)

EXCHANGES PER SERVING:
3 Vegetable

PER SERVING:
Calories 70
Carbohydrate 14.4g
Protein 5.1g
Fat 2.3g
Cholesterol 2mg
Fiber 2.2g
Sodium 187mg

1 Layer shredded lettuce and next 6 ingredients in a 3-quart bowl.

2 Combine vinegar and next 7 ingredients in a small bowl, stirring with a wire whisk. Pour vinegar mixture over vegetable layers. Sprinkle with cheese. Cover and chill. Garnish with red pepper rings, if desired. Yield: 8 servings.

CARROT-RAISIN SALAD

YIELD: 6 servings

EXCHANGES PER
SERVING:
1 Vegetable
½ Fruit

PER SERVING:
Calories 43
Carbohydrate 10.6g
Protein 0.4g
Fat 0.1g
Cholesterol 0mg
Fiber 1.3g
Sodium 14mg

¼ cup raisins
2 tablespoons cider vinegar
2 cups coarsely shredded carrot
1 cup drained pineapple tidbits in juice
¼ cup unsweetened pineapple juice
⅛ teaspoon ground cinnamon
⅛ teaspoon ground nutmeg

1 Combine raisins and vinegar in a medium bowl; let stand 15 minutes.

2 Add carrot and pineapple tidbits; stir well. Combine pineapple juice, cinnamon, and nutmeg in a bowl; pour over carrot mixture, and toss well. Cover and chill. Yield: 6 (½-cup) servings.

CARROT-FRUIT SALAD

YIELD: 4 servings

EXCHANGES PER
SERVING:
2 Vegetable
1 Fruit
½ Fat

PER SERVING:
Calories 115
Carbohydrate 24.5g
Protein 1.4g
Fat 2.3g
Cholesterol 2mg
Fiber 5.7g
Sodium 74mg

2 medium oranges, peeled, sectioned, and seeded
2 medium carrots, scraped and shredded
1 medium-size Red Delicious apple, chopped
½ stalk celery, thinly sliced
¼ cup raisins
2 tablespoons reduced-fat mayonnaise
½ teaspoon lemon juice

1 Combine first 5 ingredients in a medium bowl; toss lightly. Add mayonnaise and lemon juice, stirring until well blended. Cover and chill. Yield: 4 (½-cup) servings.

super·quick

TEX-MEX SALAD

1 (15-ounce) can no-salt-added black
   beans, drained and rinsed
¼ cup chopped green onions
¼ cup whole kernel corn, thawed
½ cup salsa
2 cups shredded romaine lettuce

1 Combine first 3 ingredients, and stir. Spoon
mixture over shredded lettuce.
Yield: 4 servings.

YIELD: 4 servings

**EXCHANGES PER
SERVING:**
1 Starch
1 Vegetable

PER SERVING:
Calories 111
Carbohydrate 21.3g
Protein 6.9g
Fat 0.6g
Cholesterol 0mg
Fiber 4.3g
Sodium 103mg

super·quick

BLACK BEAN-RICE SALAD

2 cups cooked long-grain rice (cooked
   without salt or fat)
1 (15-ounce) can no-salt-added black
   beans, drained
¾ cup salsa

1 Combine all 3 ingredients, stirring well.
Cover and chill. Yield: 4 (¾-cup servings).

YIELD: 4 servings

**EXCHANGES PER
SERVING:**
3 Starch
1 Vegetable

PER SERVING:
Calories 259
Carbohydrate 51.6g
Protein 11.9g
Fat 0.8g
Cholesterol 0mg
Fiber 5.6g
Sodium 141mg

YIELD: 10 servings

EXCHANGES PER
SERVING:
1 Starch

PER SERVING:
Calories 77
Carbohydrate 14.4g
Protein 4.9g
Fat 0.5g
Cholesterol 0mg
Fiber 4.5g
Sodium 146mg

BLACK AND WHITE BEAN SALAD

1 (15-ounce) can Great Northern beans, rinsed and drained
1 (15-ounce) can black beans, rinsed and drained
1¼ cups peeled, seeded, and chopped tomato
¾ cup diced sweet red pepper
¾ cup diced sweet yellow pepper
¾ cup thinly sliced green onions
½ cup commercial salsa
¼ cup red wine vinegar
2 tablespoons chopped fresh cilantro
¼ teaspoon salt
⅛ teaspoon freshly ground pepper
10 cups finely shredded romaine lettuce (about 1 head)

1 Combine beans and chopped tomato in a large bowl, tossing gently. Add red pepper, yellow pepper, and green onions, tossing to combine.

2 Combine salsa and next 4 ingredients; stir with a wire whisk until well blended. Pour over bean mixture, and toss gently.

3 Line a large serving bowl with shredded lettuce; top with bean mixture.
Yield: 10 servings.

SOUTHWESTERN SUCCOTASH SALAD

YIELD: 11 servings

EXCHANGES PER SERVING:
1 Starch

PER SERVING:
Calories 74
Carbohydrate 15.7g
Protein 3.3g
Fat 0.4g
Cholesterol 0mg
Fiber 1.7g
Sodium 122mg

1   (10-ounce) package frozen baby lima beans
1¾ cups frozen whole kernel corn, thawed
1   cup quartered cherry tomatoes
½   cup diced green pepper
½   cup thinly sliced celery
½   cup thinly sliced green onions
¼   cup minced fresh cilantro
2   tablespoons finely chopped jalapeño pepper
⅓   cup fat-free Ranch-style dressing
2   tablespoons lime juice
½   teaspoon ground cumin
½   teaspoon ground oregano
¼   teaspoon garlic powder
¼   teaspoon ground red pepper
    Red cabbage leaves (optional)

1 Cook lima beans in boiling water to cover 5 to 6 minutes or until crisp-tender. Drain.

2 Combine lima beans, corn, and next 6 ingredients in a large bowl; toss lightly, and set aside. Combine Ranch dressing and next 5 ingredients; pour over vegetable mixture, and toss lightly. Cover and chill 2 hours, stirring occasionally.

3 To serve, spoon vegetable mixture into a cabbage leaf-lined serving bowl, if desired. Yield: 11 (½-cup) servings.

Calico Corn Salad

YIELD: 8 servings

EXCHANGES PER
SERVING:
1 Starch

PER SERVING:
Calories 55
Carbohydrate 11.0g
Protein 1.5g
Fat 0.7g
Cholesterol 0mg
Fiber 0.7g
Sodium 79mg

If no-salt-added corn isn't available,
use 2 cups frozen corn instead.

2 (11-ounce) cans no-salt-added whole
  kernel corn, drained
⅓ cup canned no-salt-added chicken
  broth, undiluted
¾ cup chopped green pepper
½ cup chopped purple onion
2 tablespoons chopped fresh cilantro
2 tablespoons rice wine vinegar
2 teaspoons lime juice
¼ teaspoon salt
¼ teaspoon garlic powder
¼ teaspoon ground red pepper
1 (4-ounce) jar diced pimiento, drained
  Lettuce leaves (optional)

1 Combine corn and broth in a large nonstick
skillet; cook over medium-high heat 3 to 5
minutes or until liquid evaporates.

2 Remove from heat; add green pepper and
next 8 ingredients, stirring well. If desired,
serve corn mixture in a lettuce-lined bowl.
Yield: 8 (½-cup) servings.

Marinated Bean Salad

YIELD: 13 servings

1 cup chopped green pepper
1 cup thinly sliced purple onion
1 teaspoon minced garlic
1 (16-ounce) can no-salt-added green
  beans, drained
1 (16-ounce) can yellow wax beans,
  drained
1 (10-ounce) package frozen English peas,
  thawed
1 (2-ounce) jar diced pimiento, drained
¾ cup white vinegar
1 teaspoon vegetable oil
½ teaspoon salt
½ teaspoon pepper
16 packets sugar substitute with
  aspartame (such as Equal)
  Curly leaf lettuce leaves (optional)

EXCHANGES PER SERVING:
1 Vegetable

PER SERVING:
Calories 41
Carbohydrate 8.0g
Protein 1.9g
Fat 0.6g
Cholesterol 0mg
Fiber 1.7g
Sodium 171mg

1 Combine first 7 ingredients in a large bowl; set aside.

2 Combine vinegar and next 3 ingredients in a saucepan; bring to a boil. Remove from heat; stir in sugar substitute. Pour vinegar mixture over vegetable mixture; toss lightly. Cover and chill at least 3 hours, stirring occasionally.

3 Serve with a slotted spoon. Serve on lettuce leaves, if desired (lettuce not included in analysis). Yield: 13 (½-cup) servings.

SNOW PEA SALAD

YIELD: 2 servings

EXCHANGES PER
SERVING:
1 Starch

PER SERVING:
Calories 72
Carbohydrate 14.2g
Protein 3.0g
Fat 0.2g
Cholesterol 0mg
Fiber 2.5g
Sodium 209mg

2 tablespoons rice wine vinegar
1 tablespoon low-sodium soy sauce
¼ teaspoon ground ginger
¼ teaspoon garlic powder
1 cup fresh snow pea pods, trimmed
1 (8-ounce) can sliced water chestnuts, drained
1 tablespoon chopped fresh parsley
Green onion fans (optional)

1 Combine first 4 ingredients in a jar; cover tightly, and shake vigorously.

2 Wash snow peas; arrange in a steamer basket over boiling water. Cover and steam 3 minutes; drain and rinse with cold water.

3 Combine snow peas, water chestnuts, and parsley in a small bowl. Pour vinegar mixture over snow pea mixture, and toss lightly. Garnish with green onion fans, if desired. Yield: 2 servings.

Dilled Vegetable Salad

YIELD: 14 servings

- 2 cups fresh or frozen broccoli flowerets, thawed
- 2 cups fresh or frozen cauliflower flowerets, thawed
- 1 cup diagonally sliced carrot
- ½ cup low-fat sour cream
- ¼ cup nonfat buttermilk
- 3 tablespoons reduced-calorie mayonnaise
- 2 tablespoons water
- 2 teaspoons granulated sugar substitute (such as Sugar Twin)
- 1 teaspoon celery seeds
- 1 teaspoon dried dillweed
- ½ teaspoon garlic powder
- ¼ teaspoon salt
- ⅛ teaspoon ground white pepper
- 2 teaspoons white wine vinegar
- 2 cups diagonally sliced celery
- ½ cup chopped green onions
- Fresh dill sprigs (optional)

1 Arrange first 3 ingredients in a vegetable steamer over boiling water. Cover and steam 2 to 3 minutes or until crisp-tender; rinse with cold water, and drain well.

2 Combine sour cream and next 10 ingredients in a small bowl; stir well.

3 Combine broccoli mixture, sour cream mixture, celery, and green onions in a large bowl; toss gently. Cover and chill thoroughly. Garnish with dill sprigs, if desired.
Yield: 14 (½-cup) servings.

EXCHANGES PER SERVING:
1 Vegetable

PER SERVING:
Calories 44
Carbohydrate 5.2g
Protein 2.0g
Fat 2.2g
Cholesterol 4mg
Fiber 1.7g
Sodium 99mg

You can substitute sour milk for buttermilk in most recipes. To make sour milk, add 1 tablespoon lemon juice or vinegar to 1 cup skim milk. Let stand about 15 minutes before using.

SEA SHELL SALAD

To add a twist to this pasta salad, try serving it in whole wheat pita bread halves with shredded lettuce. One pita bread half has about 61 calories.

EXCHANGES PER
SERVING:
1 Lean Meat
1½ Starch
1 Vegetable

PER SERVING:
Calories 189
Carbohydrate 28.5g
Protein 10.1g
Fat 3.4g
Cholesterol 9mg
Fiber 1.3g
Sodium 236mg

❧ Use your imagination to create variations of this pasta salad. Substitute 8 ounces of uncooked elbow or corkscrew macaroni for the shell macaroni. Add diced sweet red or yellow pepper instead of green. Replace the tuna with canned lump crabmeat or canned salmon.

8 ounces small shell macaroni, uncooked
1 cup shredded carrot
¾ cup diced green pepper
⅔ cup sliced celery
½ cup minced green onions
1 (6⅛-ounce) can tuna in water, drained and flaked
¼ cup plus 2 tablespoons plain low-fat yogurt
¼ cup reduced-calorie mayonnaise
¼ teaspoon celery seeds
¼ teaspoon salt
¼ teaspoon pepper
Curly leaf lettuce leaves

1 Cook macaroni according to package directions, omitting salt and fat; drain. Rinse with cold water, and drain well.

2 Combine macaroni, carrot, and next 4 ingredients; toss gently. Combine yogurt and next 4 ingredients; stir well. Add to pasta mixture, tossing gently. Cover and chill thoroughly.

3 To serve, spoon pasta mixture onto lettuce-lined salad plates. Yield: 7 (1-cup) servings.

Country Garden Tortellini

This pasta salad is perfect for a crowd. You can toss the salad together early in the day or the day before, and chill it until time to serve.

2 (9-ounce) packages fresh cheese-filled tortellini
1 cup sliced carrot
1 cup cherry tomatoes, halved
1 (8-ounce) package frozen asparagus spears, thawed and cut into 1-inch pieces
1 (6-ounce) package frozen snow pea pods, thawed
2/3 cup sliced radishes
1 small purple onion, thinly sliced and separated into rings
3 tablespoons water
2 tablespoons lemon juice
2 tablespoons cider vinegar
1½ tablespoons olive oil
1 teaspoon dried basil
½ teaspoon pepper
¼ teaspoon salt

1 Cook tortellini according to package directions, omitting salt and fat; drain. Rinse with cold water; drain well, and set aside.

2 Arrange carrot in a vegetable steamer over boiling water. Cover and steam 3 to 5 minutes or until crisp-tender.

3 Combine tortellini, carrot, tomato, and next 4 ingredients in a large bowl.

4 Combine water and remaining 6 ingredients; stir well. Pour over tortellini mixture, and toss gently. Cover and chill.
Yield: 11 (1-cup) servings.

YIELD: 11 servings

EXCHANGES PER SERVING:
½ Medium-Fat Meat
1½ Starch
1 Vegetable

PER SERVING:
Calories 179
Carbohydrate 27.2g
Protein 9.1g
Fat 4.3g
Cholesterol 0mg
Fiber 1.5g
Sodium 235mg

❧ Tortellini is bite-size pasta stuffed with a variety of fillings and shaped into a ring. Look for fresh tortellini in the refrigerated section of the supermarket. If you don't use fresh tortellini within a week of purchase, freeze it to retain maximum freshness.

POTATO SALAD WITH ASPARAGUS

YIELD: 2 servings

EXCHANGES PER SERVING:
1 Starch

PER SERVING:
Calories 98
Carbohydrate 16.5g
Protein 2.9g
Fat 2.5g
Cholesterol 0mg
Fiber 2.5g
Sodium 117mg

2 medium-size round red potatoes
  (about 6 ounces)
¼ pound fresh asparagus spears (about 5
  spears)
1 tablespoon sliced green onions
2 tablespoons white wine vinegar
1 teaspoon olive oil
½ teaspoon Dijon mustard
  Dash of salt
  Dash of ground white pepper
2 Bibb lettuce leaves

1 Wash potatoes. Cook in boiling water to cover 20 to 25 minutes or until tender; drain and cool slightly. Cut each potato into 6 wedges. Set aside.

2 Snap off tough ends of asparagus. Remove scales from spears with a vegetable peeler, if desired. Cut asparagus into 1-inch pieces. Arrange asparagus in a steamer basket over boiling water. Cover and steam 4 to 5 minutes or until crisp-tender. Rinse with cold water.

3 Combine potato wedges, asparagus, and green onions in a shallow dish. Combine vinegar and next 4 ingredients; pour over potato mixture, and toss lightly. Cover and chill at least 1 hour, stirring occasionally. Spoon potato mixture evenly onto 2 lettuce-lined salad plates. Yield: 2 servings.

Warm Potato Salad

YIELD: 4 servings

2 cups cubed round red potatoes
2 tablespoons finely chopped purple onion
1½ tablespoons white wine vinegar
1 tablespoon freeze-dried chives
1 teaspoon olive oil
¼ teaspoon granulated sugar substitute
   (such as Sugar Twin)
¼ teaspoon salt
¼ teaspoon pepper

EXCHANGES PER SERVING:
1 Starch

PER SERVING:
Calories 69
Carbohydrate 13.0g
Protein 1.7g
Fat 1.2g
Cholesterol 0mg
Fiber 1.5g
Sodium 153mg

1 Place potato in a saucepan; add water to cover. Bring to a boil; cover, reduce heat, and simmer 10 minutes. Drain; add onion.

2 Combine vinegar and remaining ingredients; stir well. Add to potato mixture; toss lightly to coat. Serve warm. Yield: 4 (½-cup) servings.

Potato-Vegetable Salad

YIELD: 8 servings

1 pound round red potatoes, quartered
1 (10-ounce) package frozen Brussels
   sprouts, thawed
1½ cups cherry tomatoes, halved
⅓ cup white wine vinegar
1 tablespoon olive oil
½ teaspoon granulated sugar substitute
¼ teaspoon onion powder
¼ teaspoon dried dillweed
⅛ teaspoon salt

EXCHANGES PER SERVING:
1 Starch

PER SERVING:
Calories 80
Carbohydrate 13.9g
Protein 2.7g
Fat 1.9g
Cholesterol 0mg
Fiber 2.9g
Sodium 52mg

1 Cook potatoes in boiling water to cover 12 minutes. Drain. Set aside; keep warm.

2 Cut Brussels sprouts in half lengthwise. Cook according to package directions. Combine potatoes, sprouts, and tomatoes. Combine vinegar and remaining 5 ingredients. Add to potato mixture; toss. Serve warm.
Yield: 8 (¾-cup) servings.

CURRIED RICE SALAD

YIELD: 4 servings

EXCHANGES PER
SERVING:
1 Starch

PER SERVING:
Calories 96
Carbohydrate 16.8g
Protein 2.4g
Fat 2.4g
Cholesterol 0mg
Fiber 1.5g
Sodium 153mg

1 cup cooked long-grain rice (cooked
   without salt or fat)
½ cup chopped celery
¼ cup minced fresh chives
¼ cup chopped sweet red pepper
¼ cup commercial fat-free Italian dressing
2 teaspoons vinegar
1 teaspoon curry powder
2 tablespoons slivered almonds, toasted
4 leaves Bibb lettuce (optional)

1 Combine first 4 ingredients in a medium bowl, stirring well.

2 Combine dressing, vinegar, and curry powder; add to rice mixture, and toss well. Cover and chill.

3 To serve, stir in almonds, and spoon mixture over lettuce leaves, if desired.
Yield: 4 servings.

TACO SALAD FOR TWO

YIELD: 2 servings

1 (8-inch) flour tortilla
   Vegetable cooking spray
⅓ pound ground round
½ cup water
2 tablespoons chopped green onions
2 teaspoons chili powder
⅛ teaspoon ground cumin
2 cups shredded iceberg lettuce
¾ cup seeded, chopped tomato
2 tablespoons (½ ounce) reduced-fat
   shredded Cheddar cheese
2 tablespoons nonfat sour cream
½ cup no-salt-added salsa

EXCHANGES PER SERVING:
3 Lean Meat
1 Starch
1 Vegetable

PER SERVING:
Calories 272
Carbohydrate 24.3g
Protein 23.8g
Fat 8.9g
Cholesterol 51mg
Fiber 3.1g
Sodium 394mg

1 Cut tortilla into 8 wedges; place on a baking sheet. Bake at 350° for 7 to 8 minutes or until lightly browned.

2 Coat a large nonstick skillet with cooking spray; place over medium-high heat until hot. Add ground round, and cook over medium heat until browned, stirring until meat crumbles. Drain and pat dry with paper towels. Wipe drippings from skillet with a paper towel.

3 Return meat to skillet; add water and next 3 ingredients, stirring well to combine. Bring to a boil; reduce heat, and simmer 10 minutes.

4 Layer 4 tortilla wedges, 1 cup shredded lettuce, and one-half of meat mixture and chopped tomato on each of 2 serving plates. Top each with 1 tablespoon shredded cheese and 1 tablespoon sour cream. Serve with salsa. Yield: 2 servings.

STEAK SALAD WITH CREAMY MUSTARD DRESSING

EXCHANGES PER
SERVING:
3 Lean Meat
2 Vegetable
½ Fruit

PER SERVING:
Calories 268
Carbohydrate 15.9g
Protein 26.4g
Fat 11.4g
Cholesterol 63mg
Fiber 4.3g
Sodium 382mg

2 tablespoons plain nonfat yogurt
2 teaspoons reduced-fat mayonnaise
2 teaspoons Dijon mustard
1 teaspoon white wine vinegar
1 small cucumber
   Vegetable cooking spray
6 ounces lean boneless sirloin steak, cut
   into thin strips
2 green onions, coarsely chopped
1 tablespoon chopped walnuts
½ teaspoon dried basil
¼ teaspoon garlic powder
2 cups torn red leaf lettuce
1 cup torn fresh spinach
1 medium-size ripe nectarine, cut into
   wedges
¼ cup (1 ounce) shredded reduced-fat
   Edam cheese

1 Combine first 4 ingredients in a small bowl, stirring well. Set yogurt mixture aside.

2 Slice cucumber lengthwise into thin strips, using a vegetable peeler and applying firm pressure. Reserve center core of cucumber for another use. Set cucumber strips aside.

3 Coat a small nonstick skillet with cooking spray; place over medium heat until hot. Add steak and next 4 ingredients; sauté 3 to 4 minutes or until steak is done.

4 Combine lettuce and spinach; place evenly on 2 salad plates. Arrange cucumber strips, steak mixture, and nectarine wedges over lettuce mixture. Drizzle yogurt mixture evenly over salads, and sprinkle with cheese. Yield: 2 servings.

TOSTADA SALAD

YIELD: 6 servings

4 (4-ounce) skinned, boned chicken
   breast halves
2 bay leaves
¼ teaspoon salt
¼ teaspoon pepper
6 (6-inch) corn tortillas
   Vegetable cooking spray
⅓ cup hot water
¾ teaspoon chicken-flavored bouillon
   granules
⅓ cup water
¼ cup plus 2 tablespoons cider vinegar
1 tablespoon olive oil
1 teaspoon granulated sugar substitute
   (such as Sugar Twin)
½ teaspoon salt
1 teaspoon dry mustard
¼ teaspoon pepper
2 heads romaine lettuce, torn
¾ cup chopped tomato
⅓ cup chopped fresh cilantro
1 large avocado, peeled and cut into cubes
1 large green pepper, diced
1 small purple onion, thinly sliced

EXCHANGES PER
SERVING:
2 Medium-Fat Meat
1 Starch

PER SERVING:
Calories 238
Carbohydrate 17.6g
Protein 21.5g
Fat 9.9g
Cholesterol 47mg
Fiber 4.6g
Sodium 481mg

1 Place chicken in a nonstick skillet; cover with water. Add bay leaves, salt, and pepper. Bring to a boil; cover, reduce heat, and simmer 15 minutes. Discard bay leaves. Drain.

2 Cut each tortilla into 8 wedges; place on a baking sheet coated with cooking spray. Bake at 350° for 15 minutes, turning once.

3 Combine hot water and bouillon granules, stirring until granules dissolve. Add ⅓ cup water and next 6 ingredients; stir well.

4 Shred chicken. Combine chicken, lettuce, and next 5 ingredients. Pour ½ cup dressing over salad; toss. Serve with tortilla wedges and remaining dressing. Yield: 6 (1-cup) servings.

YIELD: 8 servings

EXCHANGES PER
SERVING:
2 Lean Meat
1 Starch
1 Vegetable

PER SERVING:
Calories 196
Carbohydrate 22.2g
Protein 17.6g
Fat 4.6g
Cholesterol 39mg
Fiber 3.7g
Sodium 236mg

CHICKEN AND FETTUCCINE SALAD

6 ounces fettuccine, uncooked and broken
   in half
2½ cups broccoli flowerets
1 cup diagonally sliced carrot
¾ cup diagonally sliced celery
⅓ cup fat-free Italian dressing
⅓ cup reduced-fat mayonnaise
2½ tablespoons prepared horseradish
½ teaspoon freshly ground pepper
12 cherry tomatoes, halved
4 (3-ounce) cooked, boned chicken breast
   halves (skinned before cooking and
   cooked without salt)

1 Cook pasta according to package directions, omitting salt and fat. Drain and rinse under cold water; drain again. Set aside.

2 Arrange broccoli, carrot, and celery in a steamer basket over boiling water. Cover and steam 6 minutes or until crisp-tender. Drain; plunge into ice water, and drain again.

3 Combine cooked pasta and broccoli mixture in a large bowl. Combine Italian dressing and next 3 ingredients; stir well. Add to pasta mixture; toss lightly. Stir in tomato.

4 Cut chicken into ½-inch-wide strips. Arrange evenly over salad. Yield: 8 (1-cup) servings.

Grilled Chicken and Pasta Salad

YIELD: 6 servings

EXCHANGES PER
SERVING:
2 Lean Meat
1½ Starch
1 Vegetable

PER SERVING:
Calories 243
Carbohydrate 27.4g
Protein 20.2g
Fat 5.3g
Cholesterol 36mg
Fiber 2.4g
Sodium 225mg

½ cup canned low-sodium chicken broth
3 tablespoons dry white wine
1 tablespoon olive oil
2 cloves garlic, minced
3 (4-ounce) skinned, boned chicken breast
  halves
  Vegetable cooking spray
2 medium-size sweet red peppers
2 medium-size sweet yellow peppers
10 ounces fresh mushrooms, thinly sliced
1 jalapeño pepper, seeded and chopped
¼ cup diagonally sliced green onions
6 ounces bow tie pasta, uncooked
¼ cup freshly grated Parmesan cheese
¼ teaspoon salt
⅛ teaspoon freshly ground pepper
½ cup chopped fresh cilantro
12 green lettuce leaves

1 Combine first 4 ingredients in a zip-top plastic bag; add chicken. Seal and shake well. Marinate in refrigerator at least 2 hours.

2 Remove chicken from marinade; reserve marinade. Coat grill rack with cooking spray; place on grill over medium-hot coals. Grill chicken, covered, 4 minutes on each side. Cut into 1-inch pieces.

3 Cut sweet peppers in half lengthwise; remove seeds. Flatten with palm; grill, covered, 10 minutes, turning often. Cut into 1-inch pieces.

4 Coat a nonstick skillet with cooking spray; sauté mushrooms over medium-high heat until tender. Stir in marinade, jalapeño pepper, and onions. Bring to a boil; cook 2 minutes.

5 Cook pasta, omitting salt and fat; drain. Add chicken, peppers, mushroom mixture, cheese, and next 3 ingredients. Serve warm or chilled on lettuce. Yield: 6 (1½-cup) servings.

CHINESE CHICKEN SALAD

YIELD: 4 servings

EXCHANGES PER
SERVING:
3 Very Lean Meat
1 Fruit

PER SERVING:
Calories 194
Carbohydrate 16.3g
Protein 21.5g
Fat 5.2g
Cholesterol 48mg
Fiber 2.4g
Sodium 346mg

    2 (4-ounce) skinned, boned chicken breast
      halves
    1 (10-ounce) package frozen broccoli
      flowerets, thawed
  ½ cup sliced water chestnuts, drained
  ½ cup mandarin oranges in light syrup,
      drained
  ⅓ cup unsweetened orange juice
    3 tablespoons cider vinegar
    1 tablespoon low-sodium soy sauce
    2 teaspoons granulated sugar substitute
      (such as Sugar Twin)
1½ teaspoons dark sesame oil
    1 teaspoon grated orange rind
  ¼ teaspoon salt
  ¼ teaspoon ground ginger
  ⅛ teaspoon dried crushed red pepper
    4 cups shredded Chinese cabbage
    2 tablespoons chow mein noodles
    1 tablespoon sesame seeds, toasted

1 Place chicken in a nonstick skillet; add water
to cover. Bring to a boil; cover, reduce heat,
and simmer 15 minutes or until chicken is tender. Cut chicken into strips.

2 Combine chicken strips, broccoli, water
chestnuts, and mandarin oranges. Combine
orange juice and next 8 ingredients. Pour juice
mixture over chicken mixture; toss lightly.

3 To serve, arrange 1 cup cabbage on each of 4
serving plates, and top evenly with chicken
mixture. Sprinkle evenly with noodles and
sesame seeds. Yield: 4 servings.

MEXICAN TURKEY AND BEAN SALAD

Instead of crackers, serve this main-dish salad with toasted pita bread rounds (bread not included in analysis).

¼ cup plus 2 tablespoons salsa
¼ cup plus 2 tablespoons vinegar
    Vegetable cooking spray
½ pound freshly ground raw turkey
½ teaspoon chili powder
¼ teaspoon dried oregano
⅛ teaspoon pepper
1 (15-ounce) can dark red kidney beans, drained
⅓ cup thinly sliced green onions
⅓ cup chopped sweet yellow pepper
8 cherry tomatoes, quartered
3 cups torn iceberg lettuce
3 cups torn curly endive
1 cup frozen green beans, thawed and drained

1 Combine salsa and vinegar in a small jar; cover tightly, and shake vigorously. Set aside.

2 Coat a skillet with cooking spray; place over medium heat until hot. Add turkey and next 3 ingredients; cook until turkey is browned, stirring until it crumbles. Drain, if necessary.

3 Combine turkey mixture, kidney beans, and next 3 ingredients in a large bowl; toss lightly. Add ⅓ cup salsa mixture, and toss.

4 Place lettuce and endive in a large bowl; spoon turkey mixture over lettuce mixture. Top with green beans, and drizzle with remaining salsa mixture. Yield: 5 servings.

YIELD: 5 servings

EXCHANGES PER SERVING:
2 Very Lean Meat
1 Starch

PER SERVING:
Calories 134
Carbohydrate 15.0g
Protein 14.0g
Fat 2.3g
Cholesterol 26mg
Fiber 4.8g
Sodium 376mg

FRUITED TURKEY SALAD

YIELD: 6 servings

EXCHANGES PER
SERVING:
2 Lean Meat
1 Starch
1 Fruit

PER SERVING:
Calories 230
Carbohydrate 29.4g
Protein 19.8g
Fat 4.2g
Cholesterol 44mg
Fiber 3.7g
Sodium 160mg

2½ cups chopped fresh pear (about 2
    medium)
2 cups chopped apple (about 2 small)
2 tablespoons lemon juice
1 cup coarsely chopped celery
½ cup jellied whole-berry cranberry sauce
⅓ cup nonfat mayonnaise
½ teaspoon ground ginger
2½ cups chopped cooked turkey breast
2 tablespoons chopped pecans, toasted

1 Combine first 3 ingredients in a medium
bowl; toss well. Stir in celery; set aside.

2 Combine cranberry sauce, mayonnaise, and
ginger in a bowl; stir well. Add to pear mixture, and toss lightly.

3 Stir in turkey; cover and chill thoroughly.
Sprinkle with pecans before serving.
Yield: 6 (1½-cup) servings.

SALAD NIÇOISE

YIELD: 2 servings

EXCHANGES PER
SERVING:
3 Lean Meat
1 Starch

PER SERVING:
Calories 239
Carbohydrate 18.1g
Protein 24.1g
Fat 7.9g
Cholesterol 32mg
Fiber 5.2g
Sodium 238mg

3 tablespoons white wine vinegar
2 tablespoons water
1½ teaspoons Dijon mustard
½ teaspoon olive oil
⅛ teaspoon freshly ground pepper
¼ pound fresh green beans
2 small round red potatoes
2 tablespoons thinly sliced sweet red pepper
1 tablespoon chopped purple onion
1 (6-ounce) tuna steak (¾ inch thick)
½ teaspoon olive oil
   Vegetable cooking spray
2 cups torn fresh spinach
4 cherry tomatoes, quartered
1 tablespoon sliced ripe olives

1 Combine first 5 ingredients in a small jar; cover tightly, and shake vigorously. Set aside.

2 Wash beans; trim ends, and remove strings. Arrange beans in a steamer basket over boiling water. Cover and steam 5 minutes or until crisp-tender. Drain.

3 Wash potatoes. Cook in boiling water to cover 20 minutes or just until tender. Drain and cool slightly. Cut into ¼-inch-thick slices.

4 Combine green beans, potato, red pepper, and onion; toss lightly. Add half of vinegar mixture; toss lightly. Chill 2 hours.

5 Brush tuna steak with ½ teaspoon olive oil. Place on a rack of broiler pan coated with cooking spray. Broil 5½ inches from heat (with electric oven door partially opened) 3 to 4 minutes on each side or until fish flakes easily when tested with a fork. Flake fish into pieces.

6 Place spinach on a serving plate. Arrange green bean mixture, tuna, tomato, and olives over spinach. Drizzle remaining vinegar mixture over salad. Yield: 2 servings.

EXCHANGES PER
SERVING:
1 Lean Meat
2 Vegetable

PER SERVING:
Calories 100
Carbohydrate 9.7g
Protein 10.3g
Fat 2.4g
Cholesterol 69mg
Fiber 2.8g
Sodium 207mg

SHRIMP AND VEGETABLE SALAD

²/₃ cup water
½ cup chopped onion
⅓ cup dry white wine
¼ teaspoon dried crushed red pepper
1½ pounds medium-size fresh shrimp,
   peeled and deveined
3 carrots
1 small sweet red pepper, seeded
1 small sweet yellow pepper, seeded
1 small green pepper, seeded
1 small zucchini
1 small yellow squash
   Vegetable cooking spray
1 clove garlic, minced
¾ cup plain nonfat yogurt
¼ cup reduced-calorie mayonnaise
2 tablespoons chopped fresh dill
1 tablespoon lemon juice
¼ teaspoon salt
¼ teaspoon freshly ground black pepper
7½ cups shredded romaine lettuce
½ pound snow pea pods, trimmed

1 Combine first 4 ingredients in a skillet; bring to a boil. Boil 5 minutes. Add shrimp; cook 3 minutes. Remove shrimp; reserve liquid in skillet. Rinse shrimp with cold water; drain. Boil liquid 3 minutes. Set aside 2 tablespoons liquid; discard remaining liquid.

2 Cut carrots, peppers, zucchini, and squash into strips. Coat a nonstick skillet with cooking spray; place over medium-high heat until hot. Add carrot and garlic; sauté 2 minutes. Add remaining vegetables; sauté 3 minutes.

3 Combine 2 tablespoons liquid, yogurt, and next 5 ingredients. Arrange lettuce on plate; top with vegetable mixture, peas, and shrimp. Serve with yogurt mixture. Yield: 6 servings.

Creamy Blue Cheese Dressing

½ cup plain nonfat yogurt
½ cup nonfat mayonnaise
¼ cup plus 3 tablespoons skim milk
¼ cup crumbled blue cheese
2 tablespoons lemon juice
½ teaspoon minced fresh garlic
⅛ teaspoon freshly ground pepper
Dash of hot sauce

1 Combine all ingredients in a small bowl, stirring well. Cover and chill.

2 Serve with assorted salad greens (salad greens not included in analysis). Yield: 1½ cups.

YIELD: 1½ cups

EXCHANGES PER SERVING: Free

PER SERVING:
Calories 13
Carbohydrate 1.7g
Protein 0.7g
Fat 0.4g
Cholesterol 1mg
Fiber 0.0g
Sodium 86mg

Rosy Italian Dressing

½ cup plus 1 tablespoon nonfat buttermilk
¼ cup plus 1 tablespoon nonfat mayonnaise
¼ cup no-salt-added tomato juice
1 tablespoon grated onion
¼ teaspoon dried oregano
¼ teaspoon dried basil
¼ teaspoon pepper
¼ teaspoon paprika
1 clove garlic, crushed

1 Combine all ingredients in a small bowl, stirring well with a wire whisk. Cover and chill.

2 Serve with assorted salad greens (salad greens not included in analysis).
Yield: 1 cup plus 2 tablespoons.

YIELD: 1 cup plus 2 tablespoons

EXCHANGES PER SERVING: Free

PER SERVING:
Calories 8
Carbohydrate 1.6g
Protein 0.4g
Fat 0.0g
Cholesterol 0mg
Fiber 0.0g
Sodium 62mg

ZESTY YOGURT DRESSING

YIELD: ¾ cup

EXCHANGES PER
SERVING: Free

PER SERVING:
Calories 8
Carbohydrate 1.4g
Protein 0.6g
Fat 0.0g
Cholesterol 0mg
Fiber 0g
Sodium 11mg

½ plain nonfat yogurt
1 tablespoon minced fresh parsley
1 tablespoon skim milk
1 tablespoon lemon juice
2 teaspoons granulated sugar substitute
   with aspartame (such as Equal
   Spoonful)
1 teaspoon honey-mustard
   Dash of hot sauce

1 Combine all ingredients in a small bowl; stir well. Store in the refrigerator up to 3 days. Serve with salad greens. Yield: ¾ cup.

CREAMY BUTTERMILK DRESSING

YIELD: ¾ cup plus
2 tablespoons

EXCHANGES PER
SERVING:
Free

PER SERVING:
Calories 11
Carbohydrate 1.9g
Protein 0.5g
Fat 0.1g
Cholesterol 1mg
Fiber 0g
Sodium 98mg

½ cup nonfat buttermilk
¼ cup plus 2 tablespoons nonfat
   mayonnaise
1 tablespoon grated Parmesan cheese
1 teaspoon dried parsley flakes
¼ teaspoon cracked pepper
1 clove garlic, minced

1 Combine all ingredients in a small bowl; stir well. Store in the refrigerator up to 3 days. Serve with salad greens.
Yield: ¾ cup plus 2 tablespoons.

Soups &
Sandwiches

CHILLED BORSCHT

YIELD: 8 servings

EXCHANGES PER
SERVING:
1 Starch
1 Vegetable

PER SERVING:
Calories 83
Carbohydrate 18.6g
Protein 2.0g
Fat 0.2g
Cholesterol 0mg
Fiber 1.9g
Sodium 49mg

Borscht is a traditional Russian beet soup
that is served either warm or chilled.

1 cup peeled, coarsely chopped baking
    potato
1 cup coarsely chopped parsnip
1 cup coarsely chopped onion
2 (15-ounce) cans sliced beets, undrained
2 (10½-ounce) cans low-sodium chicken
    broth
¼ cup water
1 tablespoon granulated sugar substitute
1 tablespoon lemon juice
1 tablespoon red wine vinegar
½ teaspoon prepared horseradish
¼ teaspoon ground white pepper
½ cup shredded cucumber

1 Arrange first 3 ingredients in a steamer basket over boiling water. Cover and steam 6 to
8 minutes or until crisp-tender.

2 Position knife blade in food processor bowl;
add potato mixture and beets. Process 1½
minutes or until smooth. Transfer beet mixture
to a Dutch oven; add chicken broth and next
6 ingredients, stirring well. Bring mixture to
a boil. Reduce heat, and simmer, uncovered,
5 minutes or until thoroughly heated. Transfer
to a large bowl; cover and chill.

3 To serve, ladle soup into individual goblets.
Top each serving with 1 tablespoon shredded cucumber. Yield: 8 (1-cup) servings.

A BERRY COLD SOUP

Enjoy this soup as an appetizer or a dessert.

2 cups fresh or frozen blueberries
2 (6-ounce) cans frozen unsweetened
    apple juice concentrate, thawed and
    undiluted
¼ teaspoon ground cinnamon
    Dash of ground cloves
¼ cup water
1 tablespoon cornstarch
1 teaspoon vanilla extract
    Water crackers (optional)

1 Combine first 4 ingredients in a large saucepan. Bring to a boil, stirring constantly. Reduce heat, and simmer 5 minutes, stirring mixture occasionally.

2 Combine water and cornstarch, stirring until smooth. Add cornstarch mixture to blueberry mixture. Cook, stirring constantly, 1 minute or until thickened and bubbly. Remove from heat; stir in vanilla. Let cool. Cover and chill 8 hours.

3 To serve, ladle soup into 6 individual soup bowls. Serve with water crackers, if desired (crackers not included in analysis).
Yield: 6 (½-cup) servings.

Blackberry Soup: Substitute 2 cups fresh or frozen blackberries for blueberries. Substitute ground nutmeg for ground cloves.
Yield: 6 (½-cup) servings.

Raspberry Soup: Substitute 2 cups fresh or frozen raspberries for blueberries. Substitute framboise or other raspberry-flavored brandy for vanilla extract. Yield: 6 (½-cup) servings.

YIELD: 6 servings

EXCHANGES PER SERVING:
2 Fruit

PER SERVING:
Calories 128
Carbohydrate 31.0g
Protein 0.5g
Fat 0.5g
Cholesterol 0mg
Fiber 1.7g
Sodium 15mg

All three variations have about the same amount of carbohydrate, and each one counts as 2 Fruit Exchanges.

MINTED CANTALOUPE SOUP

YIELD: 6 servings

EXCHANGES PER
SERVING:
1 Fruit

PER SERVING:
Calories 71
Carbohydrate 13.8g
Protein 3.1g
Fat 0.9g
Cholesterol 2mg
Fiber 1.3g
Sodium 37mg

    5 cups cantaloupe chunks (1 medium)
  ⅓ cup unsweetened orange juice
    1 (8-ounce) carton plain low-fat yogurt
1½ teaspoons spoonable sugar alternative
    1 teaspoon minced fresh mint
        Fresh mint sprigs (optional)

1 Place cantaloupe and orange juice in food processor; process until smooth. Transfer to a medium bowl.

2 Combine yogurt, sugar alternative, and mint; add to cantaloupe mixture, and stir well. Cover and chill.

3 To serve, ladle into individual bowls, and garnish with mint sprigs, if desired.
Yield: 6 (¾-cup) servings.

CHILLED HONEYDEW SOUP

7 cups honeydew chunks (1 medium)
⅓ cup unsweetened orange juice
¼ cup Sauterne or other sweet white wine
2 tablespoons lime juice
1½ teaspoons spoonable sugar alternative
½ cup fresh raspberries
Fresh mint sprigs (optional)

1 Place half of honeydew in food processor; process until smooth. Transfer to a bowl. Repeat procedure with remaining honeydew.

2 Combine honeydew, orange juice, and next 3 ingredients; stir well. Cover and chill.

3 To serve, ladle into individual bowls, and top each with 1 tablespoon raspberries. Garnish with mint sprigs, if desired. Yield: 8 (¾-cup) servings.

YIELD: 8 servings

EXCHANGES PER SERVING:
1 Fruit

PER SERVING:
Calories 64
Carbohydrate 15.2g
Protein 0.8g
Fat 0.2g
Cholesterol 0mg
Fiber 1.8g
Sodium 15mg

SUMMER GAZPACHO

YIELD: 5 servings

EXCHANGES PER
SERVING:
1 Starch

PER SERVING:
Calories 76
Carbohydrate 15.3g
Protein 2.1g
Fat 1.4g
Cholesterol 0mg
Fiber 1.1g
Sodium 174mg

You can serve gazpacho as a refreshing
first course or with sandwiches and fresh
fruit for a complete light meal.

1 (10½-ounce) can low-sodium tomato
    soup
1¾ cups no-salt-added tomato juice
⅔ cup peeled, seeded, and finely chopped
    cucumber
½ cup finely chopped green pepper
½ cup finely chopped tomato
⅓ cup finely chopped onion
2 tablespoons red wine vinegar
1 tablespoon commercial fat-free Italian
    dressing
1 tablespoon lemon juice
1 clove garlic, minced
½ teaspoon pepper
¼ teaspoon salt
¼ teaspoon hot sauce
    Thinly sliced cucumber (optional)

1 Combine first 13 ingredients in a large bowl;
stir well. Cover and chill at least 8 hours.

2 To serve, ladle soup into individual bowls,
and garnish with cucumber slices, if desired.
Yield: 5 (1-cup) servings.

SAVORY CARROT SOUP

YIELD: 6 servings

EXCHANGES PER
SERVING:
1 Starch
1 Vegetable

PER SERVING:
Calories 112
Carbohydrate 20.6g
Protein 3.2g
Fat 2.1g
Cholesterol 0mg
Fiber 3.7g
Sodium 206mg

Vegetable cooking spray
2 teaspoons reduced-calorie margarine
1½ cups chopped onion
2¾ cups sliced carrot
1½ cups diced red potato
3 cups canned no-salt-added chicken broth
¾ cup unsweetened orange juice
½ teaspoon dried thyme
¼ teaspoon salt
¼ teaspoon pepper
Fresh thyme sprigs (optional)

1 Coat a large saucepan with cooking spray; add margarine, and place over medium-high heat until margarine melts. Add onion and carrot; sauté until crisp-tender. Add potato and broth; bring to a boil. Cover, reduce heat, and simmer 25 minutes or until carrot is tender.

2 Position knife blade in food processor; add carrot mixture in batches. Process 1 minute or until mixture is smooth, stopping once to scrape down sides.

3 Return carrot mixture to saucepan; add orange juice and next 3 ingredients. Cook, uncovered, until thoroughly heated. Serve warm or chilled. Garnish with thyme sprigs, if desired. Yield: 6 (1-cup) servings.

CHEDDAR CHEESE SOUP

Vegetable cooking spray
1 teaspoon reduced-calorie margarine
1 cup finely chopped onion
1 cup finely chopped celery
½ cup nonfat sour cream
¼ cup plain low-fat yogurt
⅓ cup all-purpose flour
2 (10½-ounce) cans low-sodium chicken
    broth, undiluted
¾ cup skim milk
1 teaspoon white wine Worcestershire
    sauce
¼ teaspoon garlic powder
⅛ teaspoon salt
⅛ teaspoon ground white pepper
⅛ teaspoon ground red pepper
6 (⅔-ounce) slices low-fat process
    Cheddar cheese
Celery leaves (optional)

1 Coat a nonstick skillet with cooking spray. Add margarine, and place over medium heat until margarine melts. Add onion and celery; sauté 5 minutes or until tender.

2 Combine sour cream, yogurt, and flour in a large saucepan; stir well with a wire whisk. Add broth and next 6 ingredients; stir well. Stir in onion mixture; cook over medium heat, stirring constantly, 15 to 20 minutes or until thickened and bubbly. (Mixture may appear curdled, but will smooth out as it cooks.)

3 Add cheese slices, and stir until cheese melts. To serve, ladle soup into individual bowls; garnish with celery leaves, if desired. Yield: 6 (1-cup) servings.

CHEESY POTATO CHOWDER

YIELD: 7 servings

Vegetable cooking spray
½ cup sliced green onions
½ cup chopped sweet red pepper
1 jalapeño pepper, seeded and diced
3 tablespoons cornstarch
4 cups water, divided
3¾ cups peeled, diced potato
2 teaspoons chicken-flavored bouillon
  granules
¼ teaspoon salt
⅛ teaspoon ground white pepper
1½ cups frozen whole kernel corn
1 cup (4 ounces) shredded reduced-fat
  Cheddar cheese, divided
2 tablespoons minced fresh parsley

EXCHANGES PER SERVING:
2 Starch
1 Fat

PER SERVING:
Calories 163
Carbohydrate 26.6g
Protein 7.9g
Fat 3.6g
Cholesterol 10mg
Fiber 2.6g
Sodium 446mg

1 Coat a Dutch oven with cooking spray; place over medium-high heat until hot. Add green onions, red pepper, and jalapeño pepper; sauté until tender.

2 Combine cornstarch and ¼ cup water; stir until smooth. Stir in remaining 3¾ cups water. Add cornstarch mixture to Dutch oven. Stir in potato and next 3 ingredients. Bring to a boil; reduce heat, and simmer, uncovered, 10 minutes, stirring constantly. Add corn, and cook 15 additional minutes, stirring occasionally. Add ¾ cup plus 2 tablespoons cheese; stir until cheese melts.

3 To serve, ladle chowder into individual bowls, and sprinkle evenly with remaining 2 tablespoons cheese and parsley.
Yield: 7 (1-cup) servings.

CORN AND PEPPER CHOWDER

YIELD: 5 servings

EXCHANGES PER
SERVING:
2 Starch

PER SERVING:
Calories 151
Carbohydrate 29.3g
Protein 6.9g
Fat 1.7g
Cholesterol 2mg
Fiber 2.8g
Sodium 239mg

🍃 Keep garnishes
for soup simple.
Add a sprinkling of
chopped fresh herbs
or green onions, a
slice of lemon, or a
little grated Parmesan
cheese for color.

Thickened with cubed potatoes, this
chowder captures the essence of a velvety,
luscious soup. Five unsalted crackers
add about 62 calories per serving.

Vegetable cooking spray
1 teaspoon olive oil
1 cup chopped onion
1 cup chopped sweet red pepper
1 tablespoon plus 2 teaspoons
   all-purpose flour
½ teaspoon ground cumin
2 cups water
1⅓ cups peeled, cubed round red potato
1 teaspoon chicken-flavored bouillon
   granules
2 cups frozen whole kernel corn, thawed
1 cup evaporated skimmed milk
2 tablespoons canned chopped green
   chiles, drained
¼ teaspoon pepper
⅛ teaspoon ground red pepper

1 Coat a large Dutch oven with cooking spray;
add oil. Place over medium-high heat until
hot. Add onion and chopped red pepper; cook
until tender.

2 Stir in flour and cumin; cook 1 minute. Add
water, potato, and bouillon granules. Bring
to a boil, stirring frequently. Cover, reduce heat,
and simmer 10 minutes or until potato is tender and liquid is thickened.

3 Add corn and next 4 ingredients; cook over
medium heat 5 additional minutes or until
thoroughly heated. Ladle chowder into soup
bowls. Yield: 5 (1-cup) servings.

French Onion Soup

Vegetable cooking spray
2 medium onions, sliced and separated
  into rings
3 cups canned no-salt-added beefbroth,
  undiluted
1 tablespoon low-sodium Worcestershire
  sauce
¼ teaspoon salt
¼ teaspoon pepper
4 (½-inch-thick) French baguette slices
¼ cup (1 ounce) shredded Gruyère
  cheese

YIELD: 4 servings

EXCHANGES PER
SERVING:
1 Starch
1 Vegetable
½ Fat

PER SERVING:
Calories 134
Carbohydrate 19.9g
Protein 5.1g
Fat 2.9g
Cholesterol 8mg
Fiber 2.5g
Sodium 276mg

1 Coat a large saucepan with cooking spray; place over medium-high heat until hot. Add onion, and sauté 2 minutes or until tender. Add beef broth and next 3 ingredients; bring to a boil. Reduce heat, and simmer, uncovered, 15 minutes.

2 Place baguette slices on a baking sheet, and broil 5½ inches from heat (with electric door partially opened) 1 minute or until lightly browned. Turn bread over; sprinkle evenly with cheese. Broil 1 minute or until cheese melts.

3 Ladle soup into 4 soup bowls; top each serving with a toasted bread slice. Serve immediately. Yield: 4 (1-cup) servings.

Microwave instructions: Coat a 2-quart casserole with cooking spray. Add onion, and microwave, uncovered, at HIGH 4 to 6 minutes or until onion is crisp-tender, stirring every 2 minutes. Add beef broth and next 3 ingredients. Microwave, uncovered, at HIGH 6 to 8 minutes or until boiling. Broil bread slices as directed above.

PASTA-VEGETABLE SOUP

YIELD: 9 servings

EXCHANGES PER
SERVING:
1 Starch
1 Vegetable

PER SERVING:
Calories 116
Carbohydrate 19.7g
Protein 5.7g
Fat 2.0g
Cholesterol 18mg
Fiber 2.0g
Sodium 222mg

4 cups canned no-salt-added chicken
   broth, undiluted
3 cups water
1 cup sun-dried tomatoes
6 ounces bow tie pasta, uncooked
4 green onions, sliced
1 tablespoon balsamic vinegar
1 clove garlic, minced
1 (10-ounce) package frozen leaf spinach,
   thawed and drained

1 Combine first 3 ingredients in a Dutch oven. Bring to a boil; cover, reduce heat, and simmer 10 minutes or until tomatoes are soft. Remove tomatoes from mixture. Let cool slightly; cut into thin strips.

2 Return tomatoes to pan. Stir in pasta and next 3 ingredients. Bring to a boil; cover, reduce heat, and simmer 15 minutes or until pasta is tender. Remove from heat; stir in spinach. Yield: 9 (1-cup) servings.

VEGETABLE-NOODLE SOUP

YIELD: 6 servings

If you don't have vermicelli on hand, substitute another pasta of similar shape like spaghetti, spaghettini, linguine, or fettuccine.

3 (10½-ounce) cans low-sodium chicken broth, undiluted
2 cups water
2 large carrots, scraped and cut into thin strips
1 large sweet red pepper, seeded and cut into thin strips
1 medium leek, sliced
2 ounces vermicelli, uncooked and broken in half
½ teaspoon salt
⅛ to ¼ teaspoon pepper
2 teaspoons dried parsley flakes

EXCHANGES PER SERVING:
1 Starch

PER SERVING:
Calories 82
Carbohydrate 14.7g
Protein 3.4g
Fat 1.3g
Cholesterol 0mg
Fiber 1.5g
Sodium 259mg

1 Combine chicken broth and water in a Dutch oven; bring to a boil. Add carrot, red pepper, and leek. Reduce heat, and simmer 4 minutes. Add pasta, salt, and pepper; cook 6 additional minutes or until pasta is done and vegetables are tender.

2 To serve, ladle soup into individual bowls, and sprinkle with parsley.
Yield: 6 (1-cup) servings.

BUTTERNUT SQUASH SOUP

YIELD: 6 servings

EXCHANGES PER
SERVING:
½ Starch
1 Vegetable

PER SERVING:
Calories 69
Carbohydrate 9.5g
Protein 3.6g
Fat 1.4g
Cholesterol 1mg
Fiber 0.5g
Sodium 213mg

4 cups canned no-salt-added chicken
      broth, undiluted
1 small butternut squash, peeled, seeded,
      and cubed
1 small apple, cored, peeled, and
      quartered
1 cup chopped onion
3 tablespoons long-grain rice, uncooked
½ teaspoon granulated sugar substitute
½ teaspoon curry powder
¼ teaspoon salt
¼ teaspoon pepper
½ cup evaporated skimmed milk
      Edible flowers (optional)

1 Combine first 9 ingredients in a saucepan;
  bring to a boil. Cover, reduce heat, and simmer 25 minutes or until squash is tender.

2 Transfer mixture, in batches, to container of
  an electric blender or food processor; cover
and process until smooth. Return soup to
saucepan; stir in milk. Cook over low heat until
thoroughly heated, stirring often. Garnish with
edible flowers, if desired.
Yield: 6 (1-cup) servings.

LAYERED VEGETABLE STEW

YIELD: 8 servings

Layer the vegetables in this flavorful stew so that all of the vegetables will get tender during cooking.

EXCHANGES PER SERVING:
1 Medium-Fat Meat
1 Starch

PER SERVING:
Calories 141
Carbohydrate 16.2g
Protein 7.2g
Fat 5.9g
Cholesterol 7mg
Fiber 2.1g
Sodium 326mg

1 (14½-ounce) can no-salt-added whole tomatoes, drained and coarsely chopped
2 cups sliced leeks
2 cups sliced zucchini (about ½ pound)
5 cups shredded romaine lettuce
1 clove garlic, minced
1 (9-ounce) package frozen artichoke hearts, thawed
¼ cup minced fresh parsley
1 teaspoon pepper
½ teaspoon salt
1 (10-ounce) package frozen baby lima beans, thawed
2 tablespoons olive oil
1 cup canned no-salt-added chicken broth
½ cup (2 ounces) grated Romano cheese

✿ Leeks are in the onion family, but are sweeter, milder, and more delicate in flavor than green onions. Leeks have straight, thick, white shanks instead of bulbs, and have flat green leaves.

1 Layer first 10 ingredients in a Dutch oven, beginning with tomato. Drizzle olive oil over vegetable mixture. Pour chicken broth over vegetables (do not stir). Bring mixture to a boil. Cover, reduce heat, and simmer, covered, 10 minutes.

2 Lightly stir vegetable mixture, and cook, covered, 20 additional minutes or until vegetables are tender, stirring often.

3 To serve, ladle stew into individual bowls, and sprinkle each with 1 tablespoon cheese. Yield: 8 (1-cup) servings.

BLACK BEAN SOUP OLÉ

YIELD: 8 servings

EXCHANGES PER
SERVING:
1 Starch

PER SERVING:
Calories 106
Carbohydrate 17.0g
Protein 4.8g
Fat 2.1g
Cholesterol 0mg
Fiber 4.1g
Sodium 251mg

1 tablespoon olive oil
1 cup chopped onion
½ cup chopped green pepper
½ cup sliced carrot
¼ cup chopped celery
2 (15-ounce) cans black beans, rinsed and
   drained
1 (14½-ounce) can no-salt-added
   tomatoes, undrained and chopped
1 (10-ounce) can tomatoes with chiles,
   undrained and chopped
1 cup water
½ cup low-sodium beef broth, undiluted
½ teaspoon ground cumin
½ teaspoon pepper
¼ teaspoon garlic powder

1 Heat oil in a large saucepan over medium-high heat. Add onion, green pepper, carrot, and celery; sauté until tender.

2 Add beans and remaining ingredients to vegetable mixture. Bring mixture to a boil. Cover, reduce heat, and simmer 30 minutes, stirring occasionally. Yield: 8 (1-cup) servings.

VEGETABLE CHILI

YIELD: 8 servings

2 cups chopped onion
1 cup chopped green pepper
1 (14¼-ounce) can no-salt-added beef
   broth
1 (2-pound) eggplant, cubed
2 (15-ounce) cans kidney beans, drained
2 (10¾-ounce) cans low-sodium tomato
   soup
¼ cup sliced ripe olives
2 tablespoons chili powder
1 teaspoon ground coriander
1 teaspoon dried oregano
1 teaspoon pepper
½ cup (2 ounces) finely shredded reduced-
   fat sharp Cheddar cheese

**EXCHANGES PER
SERVING:**
2 Starch
1 Vegetable
1 Fat

PER SERVING:
Calories 214
Carbohydrate 36.1g
Protein 10.5g
Fat 4.1g
Cholesterol 0mg
Fiber 5.9g
Sodium 248mg

1 Combine first 3 ingredients in a Dutch oven. Bring to a boil; cover, reduce heat, and simmer 15 minutes.

2 Add eggplant and next 7 ingredients; cover and cook 50 minutes or until vegetables are tender, stirring occasionally.

3 To serve, ladle chili into individual bowls. Sprinkle 1 tablespoon cheese over each serving. Yield: 8 (1½-cup) servings.

VEGETABLE-BEEF SOUP

YIELD: 10 servings

EXCHANGES PER
SERVING:
½ Medium-Fat Meat
1 Starch

PER SERVING:
Calories 114
Carbohydrate 13.8g
Protein 6.3g
Fat 3.6g
Cholesterol 13mg
Fiber 1.8g
Sodium 123mg

This recipe makes enough for two meals.
Measure out the needed portions, and freeze
the rest of the soup (up to two months)
to serve at another time.

Vegetable cooking spray
½ pound ground chuck
2⅓ cups chopped cabbage
2 cups chopped celery
1⅓ cups frozen sliced carrot, thawed
1 cup frozen chopped onion, thawed
½ cup frozen chopped green pepper,
thawed
4 cups canned no-salt-added beef broth,
undiluted
2 (14½-ounce) cans no-salt-added whole
tomatoes, undrained and chopped
1 (11-ounce) can no-salt-added whole
kernel corn, drained
1 teaspoon dried oregano
½ teaspoon dried thyme
½ teaspoon pepper
¼ teaspoon salt

1 Coat a Dutch oven with cooking spray; place
over medium-high heat until hot. Add
ground chuck; cook until meat is browned, stirring until it crumbles. Remove from Dutch
oven; drain and pat dry with paper towels.
Wipe drippings from pan with a paper towel.

2 Coat Dutch oven with cooking spray; place
over medium-high heat until hot. Add cabbage and next 4 ingredients; sauté 5 minutes or
until tender.

3 Return meat to Dutch oven. Add broth and
remaining ingredients. Bring to a boil; cover,
reduce heat, and simmer 20 to 25 minutes or
until vegetables are tender.
Yield: 10 (1-cup) servings.

CHUNKY BEEF STEW

YIELD: 6 servings

- 1 pound lean boneless top round steak
  Vegetable cooking spray
- 3½ cups water, divided
- ¾ cup chopped onion
- 2 teaspoons beef-flavored bouillon
  granules
- ½ teaspoon dried sage
- ¼ teaspoon dried thyme
- ⅛ teaspoon salt
- ⅛ teaspoon pepper
- 2 bay leaves
- ¾ pound round red potatoes, cut into
  1-inch pieces
- 3 large stalks celery, diagonally cut into
  1-inch pieces
- 2 large carrots, scraped and diagonally
  cut   into 1-inch pieces
- 2½ tablespoons all-purpose flour

**EXCHANGES PER
SERVING:**
2 Lean Meat
1 Starch
1 Vegetable

PER SERVING:
Calories 187
Carbohydrate 18.3g
Protein 19.6g
Fat 3.7g
Cholesterol 43mg
Fiber 3.1g
Sodium 442mg

1 Trim fat from steak. Cut meat into 1-inch cubes.

2 Coat a Dutch oven with cooking spray; place over medium-high heat until hot. Add meat, and cook 4 minutes on each side or until browned. Add 3¼ cups water, onion, and next 6 ingredients. Bring to a boil; cover, reduce heat, and simmer 45 minutes.

3 Add potato, celery, and carrot. Cover and simmer 45 minutes.

4 Combine flour and remaining ¼ cup water, stirring until smooth. Add to Dutch oven. Bring to a boil; reduce heat, and cook, uncovered, 10 additional minutes or until thickened, stirring often. Remove and discard bay leaves. Yield: 6 (1-cup) servings.

SPICY BEEF CHILI

YIELD: 6 servings

EXCHANGES PER
SERVING:
2 Lean Meat
1 Starch
1 Vegetable

PER SERVING:
Calories 216
Carbohydrate 20.9g
Protein 21.3g
Fat 5.7g
Cholesterol 46mg
Fiber 2.0g
Sodium 198mg

Vegetable cooking spray
1 pound ground round
1 cup chopped onion
2 cloves garlic, chopped
1 (16-ounce) can red kidney beans, rinsed and drained
1 (14½-ounce) can no-salt-added whole tomatoes, undrained and chopped
1½ cups no-salt-added tomato juice
1 teaspoon ground coriander
½ teaspoon ground cumin
¼ teaspoon salt
¼ teaspoon pepper
⅛ teaspoon ground red pepper
Dash of hot sauce
½ cup canned no-salt-added beef broth, undiluted
2 teaspoons cornstarch
¼ cup plus 2 tablespoons (1½ ounces) shredded 40% less-fat Cheddar cheese

1 Coat a Dutch oven with cooking spray; place over medium-high heat until hot. Add ground round; cook until meat is browned, stirring to crumble. Remove meat from pan; drain and pat dry with paper towels. Wipe drippings from pan with a paper towel.

2 Coat Dutch oven with cooking spray. Add onion and garlic; sauté 5 minutes or until onion is tender. Return meat to Dutch oven. Add beans and next 8 ingredients; bring to a boil over medium-high heat. Cover, reduce heat, and simmer 15 minutes, stirring occasionally.

3 Combine beef broth and cornstarch, stirring well; add to beef mixture. Bring to a boil, stirring constantly, and cook 1 minute or until thickened and bubbly. Ladle into individual bowls; sprinkle with cheese. Serve immediately. Yield: 6 (1-cup) servings.

CHICKEN-VEGETABLE SOUP

You can freeze this soup in airtight containers. Just defrost and reheat when you need a quick meal.

3½ cups water
1 tablespoon chicken-flavored bouillon granules
1 (14½-ounce) can no-salt-added whole tomatoes, undrained and chopped
¼ cup dried minced onion
1 teaspoon dried basil
1 teaspoon paprika
¾ teaspoon minced garlic
1 cup sliced carrot
1 (8-ounce) can mushroom stems and pieces, drained
1 cup diced zucchini
1 cup diced cooked chicken breast (skinned before cooking and cooked without salt or fat)
2 tablespoons dry red wine

1 Combine first 7 ingredients in a Dutch oven. Bring to a boil; cover, reduce heat, and simmer 10 minutes.

2 Add carrot; cover and simmer 10 minutes. Add mushrooms and remaining ingredients; simmer, uncovered, 8 minutes.
Yield: 7 (1-cup) servings.

YIELD: 7 servings

EXCHANGES PER SERVING:
1 Very Lean Meat
2 Vegetable

PER SERVING:
Calories 83
Carbohydrate 10.5g
Protein 7.5g
Fat 1.6g
Cholesterol 16mg
Fiber 1.2g
Sodium 492mg

To quickly prepare the chicken for this recipe, arrange 2 boned and skinned chicken breast halves in a baking dish. Microwave, covered, at HIGH 3 to 5 minutes or until done, turning dish once.

CHICKEN ENCHILADA SOUP

YIELD: 2 servings

EXCHANGES PER
SERVING:
2 Medium-Fat Meat
1 Starch
1 Vegetable

PER SERVING:
Calories 241
Carbohydrate 22.7g
Protein 20.6g
Fat 7.0g
Cholesterol 38mg
Fiber 2.9g
Sodium 416mg

1 (6-inch) corn tortilla
  Vegetable cooking spray
1 teaspoon vegetable oil
1 (4-ounce) skinned, boned chicken breast
  half, cubed
2 tablespoons all-purpose flour
¾ cup no-salt-added tomato sauce
¼ cup skim milk
1 (14¼-ounce) can no-salt-added chicken
  broth
¾ teaspoon chili powder
¼ teaspoon ground cumin
⅛ teaspoon salt
⅛ teaspoon garlic powder
  Dash of ground red pepper
¼ cup seeded, chopped tomato
2 tablespoons (½ ounce) shredded
  reduced-fat sharp Cheddar cheese
½ teaspoon minced jalapeño pepper
  (optional)
  Fresh jalapeño peppers (optional)

1 Cut tortilla into very thin strips; place on a baking sheet. Bake at 325° for 10 minutes or until crisp. Set aside.

2 Coat a medium saucepan with cooking spray; add oil. Place over medium-high heat until hot. Add chicken; sauté 4 minutes or until lightly browned. Add flour, and cook, stirring constantly, 1 minute. Gradually stir in tomato sauce, milk, and broth. Stir in chili powder and next 4 ingredients. Cover, reduce heat, and simmer 15 minutes, stirring occasionally.

3 To serve, ladle soup into individual bowls, and top each serving with half of tortilla strips, 2 tablespoons tomato, 1 tablespoon cheese, and ¼ teaspoon jalapeño pepper, if desired. Garnish each serving with a jalapeño pepper, if desired. Yield: 2 (1½-cup) servings.

CHUNKY CHICKEN-POTATO SOUP

3 medium-size baking potatoes, peeled and cubed
2 cups chopped onion
4 cups water
1 tablespoon chicken-flavored bouillon granules
¼ teaspoon salt
¼ teaspoon ground red pepper
⅛ teaspoon pepper
2 cups chopped cooked chicken breast (skinned before cooking and cooked without salt)
¼ cup skim milk
3 tablespoons chopped pimiento, undrained
⅓ cup low-fat sour cream
⅓ cup (1⅓ ounces) shredded reduced-fat Cheddar cheese
2 tablespoons plus 2 teaspoons chopped fresh chives

1 Combine first 7 ingredients in a large Dutch oven. Bring to a boil; cover; reduce heat, and simmer 30 minutes or until potato is tender.

2 Place half of potato mixture in container of an electric blender or food processor; cover and process until smooth. Add pureed mixture, chicken, and milk to remaining potato mixture in Dutch oven; cook over medium heat until thoroughly heated. Stir in pimiento.

3 To serve, ladle soup into serving bowls. Top each serving with 2 teaspoons sour cream, 2 teaspoons cheese, and 1 teaspoon chives. Yield: 8 (1-cup) servings.

YIELD: 8 servings

EXCHANGES PER SERVING:
2 Very Lean Meat
1 Starch

PER SERVING:
Calories 164
Carbohydrate 15.9g
Protein 18.0g
Fat 3.1g
Cholesterol 41mg
Fiber 1.7g
Sodium 463mg

TURKEY VEGETABLE STEW

YIELD: 9 servings

EXCHANGES PER
SERVING:
1 Very Lean Meat
3 Vegetable

PER SERVING:
Calories 127
Carbohydrate 13.5g
Protein 14.1g
Fat 1.3g
Cholesterol 25mg
Fiber 3.0g
Sodium 155mg

1¼ cups sliced carrot
1 cup sliced celery
¾ cup chopped onion
¾ cup water
1 tablespoon chopped fresh basil
2 tablespoons no-salt-added tomato paste
2 (10½-ounce) cans low-sodium chicken broth
1 (14½-ounce) can no-salt-added whole tomatoes, undrained and chopped
¼ teaspoon salt
¼ teaspoon pepper
¼ teaspoon hot sauce
2 cloves garlic, minced
2½ cups chopped cooked turkey breast (skinned before cooking and cooked without salt)
1 (10-ounce) package frozen English peas, thawed
1 (10-ounce) package frozen okra, thawed

1 Combine first 8 ingredients in a large Dutch oven. Add salt and next 3 ingredients, stirring well to combine. Bring to a boil; cover, reduce heat, and simmer 30 minutes.

2 Stir in turkey, peas, and okra; simmer, uncovered, 10 minutes or until thoroughly heated. Yield: 9 (1-cup) servings.

Shrimp-Celery Bisque

YIELD: 8 servings

2 cups peeled, diced potato
2 cups chopped celery
3½ cups skim milk, divided
½ cup chopped onion
½ teaspoon ground white pepper
¼ cup all-purpose flour
¾ pound medium-size frozen shrimp, thawed and drained
½ cup chopped fresh parsley
2 tablespoons reduced-calorie margarine
½ teaspoon dried thyme
⅛ teaspoon celery seeds
⅛ teaspoon salt
¼ cup dry sherry

EXCHANGES PER
SERVING:
1 Lean Meat
1 Starch
1 Vegetable

PER SERVING:
Calories 166
Carbohydrate 18.9g
Protein 14.1g
Fat 2.9g
Cholesterol 67mg
Fiber 1.8g
Sodium 221mg

1 Combine potato, celery, 2 cups milk, onion, and pepper in a large Dutch oven. Bring to a boil over medium-high heat. Cover, reduce heat, and simmer 10 to 12 minutes or until potato is tender.

2 Combine remaining 1½ cups milk and flour in a small bowl; stir well, and add to potato mixture, stirring constantly. Add shrimp and next 5 ingredients. Cover and cook over medium-high heat 10 minutes or until thickened and bubbly. Remove from heat, and stir in sherry. Yield: 8 (1-cup) servings.

CREAMY CLAM CHOWDER

Discarding the canned clam liquid lowers the sodium content of this chowder.

❧ Reduce calories, fat, and cholesterol in cream-based soups by using skim or low-fat milk in place of whipping cream or half-and-half.

1¼ cups peeled, diced potato
½ cup water
⅓ cup chopped celery
⅓ cup chopped onion
1 tablespoon reduced-calorie margarine
1 (12-ounce) can evaporated skimmed milk
1 cup skim milk
1 tablespoon cornstarch
1 (10-ounce) can whole shelled clams, drained
¼ teaspoon salt
⅛ teaspoon ground white pepper
Water crackers (optional)

1 Combine first 5 ingredients in a Dutch oven; place over medium-high heat, and bring to a boil. Cover, reduce heat, and simmer 15 minutes or until potato is tender.

2 Combine evaporated milk, skim milk, and cornstarch in a small bowl; add to potato mixture. Stir in clams, salt, and pepper. Cook over medium heat, stirring constantly, 10 minutes or until thickened and bubbly. To serve, ladle chowder into individual bowls, and serve with water crackers, if desired. Yield: 5 (1-cup) servings.

Fisherman's Wharf Cioppino

Vegetable cooking spray
1 teaspoon olive oil
1½ cups chopped onion
3 tablespoons chopped fresh parsley
2 cloves garlic, minced
2 cups canned no-salt-added chicken
  broth, undiluted
3 tablespoons dry sherry
½ teaspoon dried thyme
½ teaspoon pepper
¼ teaspoon hot sauce
1 (16-ounce) can tomato puree
2 (8-ounce) cans no-salt-added tomato
  sauce
2 bay leaves
12 fresh clams
1 cup water
½ pound large fresh shrimp, peeled and
  deveined
½ pound red snapper fillets, cut into
  2-inch pieces
½ pound fresh sea scallops

YIELD: 11 servings

EXCHANGES PER SERVING:
2 Very Lean Meat
½ Starch

PER SERVING:
Calories 117
Carbohydrate 10.8g
Protein 14.6g
Fat 1.7g
Cholesterol 43mg
Fiber 1.4g
Sodium 279mg

1 Coat a Dutch oven with cooking spray; add oil, and place over medium-high heat until hot. Add onion, parsley, and garlic; sauté until tender. Stir in broth and next 7 ingredients. Bring to a boil; cover, reduce heat, and simmer 20 minutes.

2 Scrub clams thoroughly, discarding any that are cracked or open. Bring water to a boil in a large saucepan; add clams. Cover, reduce heat, and steam 8 to 10 minutes or until shells open. Remove clams, using a slotted spoon. (Discard any unopened shells.)

3 Add clams, shrimp, snapper, and scallops to tomato sauce. Simmer 10 minutes or until fish flakes easily when tested with a fork. Discard bay leaves. Yield: 11 (1-cup) servings.

DILLED EGG SALAD SANDWICHES

EXCHANGES PER
SERVING:
½ High-Fat Meat
1 Starch
1 Vegetable

PER SERVING:
Calories 160
Carbohydrate 20.7g
Protein 8.0g
Fat 5.2g
Cholesterol 108mg
Fiber 1.1g
Sodium 314mg

2 hard-cooked eggs, peeled and chopped
2 ounces firm tofu, drained and diced
3 tablespoons chopped celery
2 tablespoons plain nonfat yogurt
1 tablespoon reduced-fat mayonnaise
1 tablespoon sliced green onions
¼ teaspoon dried dillweed
¼ teaspoon low-sodium Worcestershire
   sauce
⅛ teaspoon salt
⅛ teaspoon ground white pepper
4 (¼-inch-thick) slices tomato
2 (2-ounce) English muffins, split and
   toasted
1 cup alfalfa sprouts
2 tablespoons shredded cucumber, well
   drained

1 Combine first 10 ingredients in a small bowl; stir well. Cover and chill.

2 To serve, place 1 tomato slice on each muffin half; top each with ¼ cup alfalfa sprouts. Spoon egg mixture evenly over muffin halves. Top each with 1½ teaspoons cucumber. Yield: 4 servings.

Toasted Mozzarella Sandwiches

Vegetable cooking spray
¼ cup chopped onion
1 clove garlic, minced
1½ teaspoons dried Italian seasoning
⅛ teaspoon salt
Dash of freshly ground pepper
½ (14½-ounce) can no-salt-added whole
    tomatoes, undrained and chopped
¼ cup dry red wine
¼ cup water
1½ tablespoons no-salt-added tomato paste
½ cup egg substitute
½ cup skim milk
8 (1-ounce) slices part-skim mozzarella
    cheese
16 (½-ounce) slices French bread
¾ cup finely crushed shredded whole
    wheat cereal biscuits

YIELD: 8 servings

EXCHANGES PER
SERVING:
1 Medium-Fat Meat
2 Starch

PER SERVING:
Calories 214
Carbohydrate 27.7g
Protein 13.0g
Fat 5.5g
Cholesterol 18mg
Fiber 1.9g
Sodium 370mg

1 Coat a saucepan with cooking spray; place over medium-high heat until hot. Add onion and garlic; sauté until tender. Add Italian seasoning, salt, and pepper; sauté 30 seconds. Add tomato and next 3 ingredients, stirring to combine. Reduce heat, and simmer, uncovered, 20 to 30 minutes or until slightly thickened, stirring often.

2 Combine egg substitute and milk in a shallow bowl, beating well. Set aside.

3 Place 1 cheese slice on each of 8 bread slices; top with remaining 8 bread slices.

4 Dip sandwiches into egg substitute mixture, allowing excess to drip off. Sprinkle each sandwich with crushed cereal. Place sandwiches on a baking sheet coated with cooking spray. Bake at 400° for 3 minutes; turn sandwiches, and bake 4 to 6 additional minutes or until crisp and golden. Serve immediately with warm tomato sauce. Yield: 8 servings.

CELEBRATION SUBMARINE SANDWICH

EXCHANGES PER
SERVING:
2 Very Lean Meat
2 Starch

PER SERVING:
Calories 220
Carbohydrate 26.1g
Protein 17.5g
Fat 4.5g
Cholesterol 378mg
Fiber 1.5g
Sodium 644mg

1 (16-ounce) loaf French bread
⅔ cup 1% low-fat cottage cheese
3 tablespoons chopped fresh parsley
2 tablespoons chopped green onions
   Dash of ground white pepper
8 (1-ounce) slices smoked chicken
2 (1-ounce) slices reduced-fat Cheddar
   cheese, cut in half
2 (1-ounce) slices reduced-fat Swiss
   cheese, cut in half
4 small plum tomatoes, seeded and
   coarsely chopped
1 cup finely shredded green leaf lettuce

1 Using an electric or serrated knife, cut 8 (2-inch-wide) v-shaped wedges diagonally out of loaf, cutting to, but not through, bottom of loaf. Remove and reserve wedges of bread for another use. Set aside.

2 Position knife blade in food processor bowl; add cottage cheese. Process 1 minute or until smooth; transfer to a small bowl, and stir in parsley, green onions, and pepper. Spread mixture on cut surfaces of loaf.

3 Fold chicken slices in half; place 1 slice into each wedge in loaf. Add cheeses, alternating Cheddar and Swiss; top with tomato and lettuce. Cut into 8 sandwiches. Yield: 8 servings.

super·quick

GRILLED TUNA-CHEDDAR SANDWICHES

YIELD: 2 servings

1 (6½-ounce) can 60%-less-salt tuna
   in water, drained
¼ cup plus 2 tablespoons (1½ ounces)
   shredded reduced-fat Cheddar cheese
⅛ teaspoon pepper
1 tablespoon thinly sliced green onions
2 tablespoons plain nonfat yogurt
2 teaspoons diced pimiento
1 teaspoon Dijon mustard
¼ teaspoon low-sodium Worcestershire
   sauce
4 (1-ounce) slices whole wheat bread
Vegetable cooking spray

EXCHANGES PER
SERVING:
2 Lean Meat
2 Starch

PER SERVING:
Calories 282
Carbohydrate 34.0g
Protein 27.1g
Fat 5.6g
Cholesterol 21mg
Fiber 2.2g
Sodium 421mg

1 Combine first 8 ingredients in a bowl, and stir well.

2 Spread tuna mixture evenly over 2 slices of bread; top with remaining bread slices.

3 Transfer sandwiches to a sandwich press or hot griddle coated with cooking spray. Cook until bread is lightly browned and cheese is melted. Yield: 2 servings.

MIGHTY HERO

YIELD: 8 servings

**EXCHANGES PER
SERVING:**
2 Lean Meat
1 Starch
1½ Vegetable

PER SERVING:
Calories 232
Carbohydrate 24.1g
Protein 18.6g
Fat 7.1g
Cholesterol 32mg
Fiber 1.8g
Sodium 328mg

1 (16-ounce) round loaf sourdough bread
¼ cup balsamic vinegar
1 tablespoon olive oil
1 teaspoon dried oregano
1 teaspoon dried parsley flakes
¼ teaspoon pepper
2 cloves garlic, minced
1 cup sliced fresh mushrooms
6 (¼-inch-thick) tomato slices
2 (¼-inch-thick) purple onion slices,
    separated into rings
2 cups shredded zucchini
8 (1-ounce) slices lean turkey
6 (1-ounce) slices part-skim mozzarella
    cheese

1 Slice bread in half horizontally, using an electric or serrated knife. Carefully remove soft bread from inside each half, leaving ½-inch-thick shells. Set aside; reserve soft bread for another use.

2 Combine vinegar and next 5 ingredients in a shallow dish; add mushrooms, tomato slices, and onion rings. Let stand 15 to 20 minutes.

3 Drain vegetables with a slotted spoon, reserving marinade. Brush marinade evenly inside each bread cavity. Spoon 1 cup zucchini into bottom half of loaf; arrange half of mushroom mixture over zucchini. Layer with 4 turkey slices and 3 cheese slices. Repeat layers with remaining zucchini, mushroom mixture, turkey, and cheese. Top with remaining half of bread loaf.

4 Wrap loaf securely in heavy-duty aluminum foil, and chill until ready to serve. To serve, unwrap and slice loaf into wedges.
Yield: 8 servings.

GREEK SALAD HEROES

YIELD: 2 servings

¾ cup thinly sliced fresh mushrooms
½ cup thinly sliced cucumber
2 tablespoons sliced ripe olives
2 tablespoons crumbled feta cheese
1 tablespoon white balsamic vinegar
⅛ teaspoon dried oregano
4 cherry tomatoes, thinly sliced
1 clove garlic, minced
2 (2-ounce) submarine rolls
2 green leaf lettuce leaves
2 ounces thinly sliced reduced-fat, low-salt ham
2 ounces thinly sliced cooked turkey breast

EXCHANGES PER SERVING:
2 Medium-Fat Meat
2 Starch
2 Vegetable

PER SERVING:
Calories 345
Carbohydrate 39.1g
Protein 20.7g
Fat 12.0g
Cholesterol 58mg
Fiber 2.3g
Sodium 728mg

1 Combine first 8 ingredients in a small bowl, and toss lightly. Let stand 30 minutes, tossing occasionally.

2 Cut a thin slice off top of each roll; set tops aside. Cut a 2-inch-wide V-shaped wedge down length of each roll. Reserve bread wedges for another use.

3 Drain vegetable mixture. Line each roll with a lettuce leaf; top evenly with ham and turkey. Spoon vegetable mixture evenly over meat; cover with bread tops. Yield: 2 servings.

**EXCHANGES PER
SERVING:**
2 Lean Meat
1 Starch

PER SERVING:
Calories 149
Carbohydrate 9.2g
Protein 15.8g
Fat 5.8g
Cholesterol 25mg
Fiber 3.3g
Sodium 397mg

super·quick

TUNA-CHEESE MELT

1 small sweet red pepper
1 small sweet yellow pepper
1 (6-ounce) can white tuna in spring
    water, drained and flaked
4 (¾-ounce) slices reduced-calorie
    seven-grain bread, toasted
½ cup torn fresh watercress
2 teaspoons fat-free Italian salad dressing
¼ teaspoon coarsely ground pepper
2 (1-ounce) slices provolone cheese, cut
    into thin strips

1 Cut tops off peppers; remove and discard seeds and membranes. Cook peppers in boiling water 5 minutes; drain. Rinse with cold water until cool, and drain. Cut peppers into ¼-inch-wide slices. Set aside.

2 Spoon tuna evenly over toasted bread slices; arrange 2 tablespoons watercress over each. Drizzle ½ teaspoon Italian dressing over each sandwich. Top evenly with pepper slices, and sprinkle evenly with ground pepper. Top with cheese strips. Broil 5½ inches from heat (with electric oven door partially opened) 2 to 3 minutes or until cheese melts. Serve warm with assorted fresh vegetables, if desired (vegetables not included in analysis). Yield: 4 servings.

Chicken Caesar Sandwiches

YIELD: 4 servings

EXCHANGES PER SERVING:
4 Lean Meat
1½ Starch

PER SERVING:
Calories 296
Carbohydrate 22.7g
Protein 30.8g
Fat 8.0g
Cholesterol 74mg
Fiber 1.2g
Sodium 551mg

¼ cup lemon juice
1 tablespoon olive oil
1 teaspoon freshly ground pepper
2 teaspoons low-sodium Worcestershire sauce
1½ teaspoons anchovy paste
2 cloves garlic, minced
4 (4-ounce) skinned, boned chicken breast halves
1 clove garlic
8 (½-inch-thick) slices French bread
Butter-flavored vegetable cooking spray
1 cup shredded romaine lettuce
1½ teaspoons freshly grated Parmesan cheese

1 Combine first 6 ingredients. Pour half of mixture into a heavy-duty, zip-top plastic bag. Add chicken to bag; seal bag, and shake until chicken is well coated. Marinate in refrigerator 2 hours, turning occasionally.

2 Cut garlic in half; rub bread slices with cut side of garlic; coat bread with cooking spray.

3 Remove chicken from marinade, reserving marinade. Place marinade in a small microwave-safe bowl. Microwave at HIGH 45 seconds or until marinade comes to a boil.

4 Coat grill rack with cooking spray; place on grill over medium-hot coals (350° to 400°). Place chicken and bread slices on rack; grill, covered, 4 minutes on each side or until chicken is done and bread slices are toasted, basting chicken often with reserved marinade.

5 Combine lettuce and cheese; drizzle with reserved lemon juice mixture, and toss. Arrange lettuce over 4 slices of bread. Place chicken over lettuce mixture. Top with remaining bread. Yield: 4 servings.

GRILLED CHICKEN SANDWICH

YIELD: 6 servings

EXCHANGES PER
SERVING:
4 Very Lean Meat
1 Starch
1 Fat

PER SERVING:
Calories 268
Carbohydrate 19.2g
Protein 28.4g
Fat 7.8g
Cholesterol 73mg
Fiber 2.0g
Sodium 349mg

¼ cup fresh lime juice
2 tablespoons minced shallots
2 tablespoons dry white wine
1 teaspoon dried thyme
2 teaspoons vegetable oil
½ teaspoon dried marjoram
¼ teaspoon coarsely ground pepper
6 (4-ounce) skinned, boned chicken breast
   halves
   Vegetable cooking spray
3 tablespoons reduced-calorie mayonnaise
1 teaspoon spicy brown mustard
6 reduced-calorie whole wheat hamburger
   buns
6 green leaf lettuce leaves
1 small purple onion
6 tomato slices (¼ inch thick

1 Combine first 7 ingredients in a heavy-duty, zip-top plastic bag. Add chicken, turning to coat. Seal and marinate chicken in refrigerator at least 1 hour.

2 Remove chicken from marinade; place marinade in a small saucepan. Bring to a boil; reduce heat, and simmer 5 minutes.

3 Coat grill rack with cooking spray; place rack on grill over medium-hot coals (350° to 400°). Place chicken on rack, and grill, covered, 5 to 6 minutes on each side or until done, basting frequently with marinade. Set aside, and keep warm.

4 Combine mayonnaise and mustard; spread evenly over bottom halves of buns. Top each with a green lettuce leaf. Place chicken breasts on lettuce.

5 Cut onion into 6 slices, and separate into rings. Divide onion among sandwiches, and top with tomato and top halves of buns. Yield: 6 servings.

TURKEY REUBENS

YIELD: 6 servings

Look for bags of preshredded cabbage in the produce section of your grocery store.

1½ cups finely shredded cabbage
1½ tablespoons fat-free Thousand Island dressing
1 tablespoon reduced-fat mayonnaise
1 tablespoon Dijon mustard
12 (1-ounce) slices rye bread
6 ounces thinly sliced cooked turkey breast
6 (¾-ounce) slices reduced-fat Swiss cheese
   Butter-flavored vegetable cooking spray
   Cherry tomatoes (optional)

1 Combine first 3 ingredients in a medium bowl; toss well, and set aside.

2 Spread mustard evenly over 6 bread slices, and top with turkey. Top each with 1 cheese slice and ¼ cup cabbage mixture. Top with remaining bread slices.

3 Spray both sides of each sandwich with cooking spray; place on a hot griddle or in a skillet coated with cooking spray. Cook 2 minutes on each side or until bread is lightly browned and cheese melts. Garnish with cherry tomatoes, if desired. Serve immediately. Yield: 6 servings.

EXCHANGES PER SERVING:
2 Lean Meat
2 Starch

PER SERVING:
Calories 274
Carbohydrate 32.2g
Protein 21.3g
Fat 7.1g
Cholesterol 34mg
Fiber 3.9g
Sodium 560mg

TURKEY SLOPPY JOES

YIELD: 6 servings

EXCHANGES PER
SERVING:
2 Lean Meat
2 Starch

PER SERVING:
Calories 250
Carbohydrate 30.5g
Protein 15.8g
Fat 7.0g
Cholesterol 45mg
Fiber 1.2g
Sodium 292mg

Vegetable cooking spray
½ pound freshly ground raw turkey
¼ cup chopped celery
¼ cup chopped onion
1 (8-ounce) can no-salt-added tomato
    sauce
¾ cup water
2 tablespoons toasted wheat germ
2 tablespoons tomato paste
2 teaspoons chili powder
⅛ teaspoon salt
⅛ teaspoon garlic powder
⅛ teaspoon ground cumin
6 (1½-ounce) whole wheat hamburger
    buns
½ cup (2 ounces) shredded reduced-fat
    Cheddar cheese
½ cup shredded lettuce

1 Coat a nonstick skillet with cooking spray; place over medium heat until hot. Add turkey, celery, and onion; cook until turkey is browned, stirring to crumble.

2 Stir in tomato sauce and next 7 ingredients. Bring to a boil; cover, reduce heat, and simmer 10 minutes, stirring occasionally.

3 Divide turkey mixture evenly between bottom halves of buns; top with shredded cheese, lettuce, and tops of buns.
Yield: 6 servings.

TANGY BEEF POCKET SANDWICHES

YIELD: 6 servings

EXCHANGES PER SERVING:
3 Lean Meat
1 Starch
1 Vegetable

PER SERVING:
Calories 305
Carbohydrate 21.1g
Protein 26.3g
Fat 11.6g
Cholesterol 57mg
Fiber 3.9g
Sodium 273mg

1½ pounds lean flank steak
¼ cup lemon juice
2 tablespoons water
1¼ teaspoons ground cumin
1 teaspoon garlic powder
¼ teaspoon pepper
⅛ teaspoon ground ginger
½ cup plus 2 tablespoons plain nonfat yogurt
1 tablespoon chopped fresh parsley
2 teaspoons skim milk
Vegetable cooking spray
3 (6-inch) whole wheat pita bread rounds, cut in half crosswise
2 cups finely shredded romaine lettuce
1 cup seeded, chopped tomato (about 2 medium)

1 Trim fat from steak; slice steak diagonally across grain into ¼-inch-wide strips. Place steak in a large shallow dish. Combine lemon juice and next 5 ingredients; pour mixture over steak. Cover and marinate in refrigerator at least 15 minutes.

2 Combine yogurt, parsley, and milk in a small bowl; stir well, and set aside.

3 Remove steak from marinade, discarding marinade. Place steak on rack of a broiler pan coated with cooking spray. Broil 3 inches from heat (with electric oven door partially opened) 3 minutes on each side or to desired degree of doneness.

4 Wrap pita bread in aluminum foil, and bake at 350° for 10 minutes or until thoroughly heated. Line pita bread halves with lettuce, and top with steak, tomato, and yogurt mixture. Yield: 6 servings.

Triple-Treat Burgers

EXCHANGES PER
SERVING:
4 Lean Meat
2 Starch

PER SERVING:
Calories 373
Carbohydrate 33.5g
Protein 34.3g
Fat 10.5g
Cholesterol 76mg
Fiber 0.7g
Sodium 559mg

If your meal plan allows more starch servings, serve burgers with baked tortilla chips (chips not included in analysis).

1 pound ground round
2 tablespoons minced green pepper
1 tablespoon instant minced onion
2 teaspoons low-sodium Worcestershire sauce
¼ teaspoon pepper
1 teaspoon Dijon mustard
2 (¾-ounce) slices low-fat process Swiss cheese, quartered
2 (¾-ounce) slices lean cooked ham, quartered
Vegetable cooking spray
4 (2-ounce) onion buns
4 leaf lettuce leaves
4 (¼-inch-thick) tomato slices

1 Combine first 5 ingredients in a large bowl; stir well. Shape mixture into 8 (5-inch-round) patties.

2 Spread each of 4 patties with ¼ teaspoon mustard; top each with 2 pieces cheese and 2 pieces ham. Top with remaining 4 patties, pressing edges to seal.

3 Coat grill rack with cooking spray; place on grill over medium-hot coals (350° to 400°). Place patties on rack; grill, covered, 5 to 7 minutes on each side or until done. Place 1 patty on bottom half of each bun. Top each patty with 1 lettuce leaf, 1 tomato slice, and top half of bun. Yield: 4 servings.

ITALIAN MEATBALL SANDWICHES

Use a melon baller to make the meatballs.

6 (2-ounce) whole wheat submarine rolls
1 pound ground round
¼ cup finely chopped onion
3 tablespoons Italian-seasoned breadcrumbs
2 tablespoons water
¼ teaspoon pepper
1 egg white, lightly beaten
  Vegetable cooking spray
1½ cups no-salt-added meatless spaghetti
  sauce
¾ cup (3 ounces) shredded part-skim
  mozzarella cheese
  Fresh basil sprigs (optional)

1 Slanting knife at an angle, cut an oval piece out of top of each loaf; set loaves aside, reserving top pieces of loaves for another use.

2 Combine ground round and next 5 ingredients in a bowl; stir well. Shape mixture into 36 (1-inch) balls.

3 Coat a large skillet with cooking spray; place over medium heat until hot. Add meatballs, and cook 8 to 10 minutes or until browned on all sides, turning often. Remove from heat, and pat dry with paper towels. Wipe drippings from skillet with a paper towel.

4 Return meatballs to skillet; add spaghetti sauce, and cook over medium-low heat 10 minutes or until thoroughly heated.

5 Place submarine rolls on an ungreased baking sheet; top each with 6 meatballs. Spoon sauce evenly over meatballs. Sprinkle evenly with cheese. Bake at 400° for 5 minutes or until cheese melts. Garnish with basil sprigs, if desired. Serve immediately. Yield: 6 servings.

YIELD: 6 servings

EXCHANGES PER SERVING:
3 Lean Meat
2 Starch
1 Vegetable

PER SERVING:
Calories 365
Carbohydrate 37.7g
Protein 26.8g
Fat 12.1g
Cholesterol 72mg
Fiber 1.8g
Sodium 524mg

BARBECUE PORK SANDWICHES

YIELD: 4 servings

EXCHANGES PER
SERVING:
3 Lean Meat
1 Starch
1 Vegetable

PER SERVING:
Calories 257
Carbohydrate 19.2g
Protein 28.2g
Fat 6.7g
Cholesterol 83mg
Fiber 1.9g
Sodium 494mg

1 (1-pound) pork tenderloin
  Vegetable cooking spray
1 teaspoon vegetable oil
½ cup no-salt-added tomato sauce
1½ tablespoons granulated brown sugar
  substitute
2 tablespoons water
2 tablespoons vinegar
2 tablespoons low-sodium Worcestershire
  sauce
¼ teaspoon garlic powder
¼ teaspoon dry mustard
  Dash of hot sauce
4 reduced-calorie whole wheat hamburger
  buns, split and toasted

1 Trim fat from pork. Cut a slit lengthwise in each tenderloin to, but not through, bottom; place between 2 sheets of heavy-duty plastic wrap, and flatten to ¼-inch thickness, using a meat mallet or rolling pin. Cut into 4 cutlets.

2 Coat a large nonstick skillet with cooking spray; add oil. Place over medium-high heat until hot. Add cutlets, and cook 3 minutes on each side or until browned. Remove cutlets from skillet; drain and pat dry with paper towels. Set aside until cool enough to handle. Coarsely chop cutlets.

3 Wipe drippings from skillet with a paper towel. Add tomato sauce and next 7 ingredients to skillet. Bring to a boil; add chopped pork. Cover, reduce heat, and simmer 20 minutes, stirring often.

4 Spoon ½ cup pork mixture over bottom half of each bun. Top each with remaining half of bun. Serve sandwiches with carrot sticks, if desired (carrot sticks not included in analysis). Yield: 4 servings.

Starch
Side Dishes

CHEWY GRANOLA

YIELD: 20 servings

EXCHANGES PER
SERVING:
1 Starch
1 Fat

PER SERVING:
Calories 137
Carbohydrate 19.4g
Protein 3.9g
Fat 5.3g
Cholesterol 0mg
Fiber 2.5g
Sodium 19mg

3½ cups regular oats, uncooked
½ cup sliced almonds
⅓ cup nutlike cereal nuggets (like
    Grape Nuts)
¼ cup toasted wheat germ
3 tablespoons sesame seeds
1 teaspoon granulated sugar substitute
    (such as Sugar Twin)
½ teaspoon cinnamon
½ teaspoon nutmeg
1 (6-ounce) can frozen unsweetened
    apple juice concentrate, thawed and
    undiluted
¼ cup sugar-free maple syrup
2 tablespoons vegetable oil
2 teaspoons vanilla extract
½ cup dried cranberries

1 Combine first 8 ingredients in a large bowl; stir well.

2 Combine apple juice concentrate and next 3 ingredients; drizzle over oat mixture, tossing to coat. Spread oat mixture evenly in a 15- x 10- x 1-inch jellyroll pan. Bake at 350° for 25 minutes, stirring occasionally. Let cool in pan. Stir in cranberries. Store in an airtight container. Yield: 20 (¼-cup) servings.

TABBOULEH

YIELD: 10 servings

Bulgur, the main ingredient in this recipe, is similar to cracked wheat. Look for bulgur in the grains section of your supermarket or health food store.

EXCHANGES PER
SERVING:
1 Starch
½ Fat

PER SERVING:
Calories 96
Carbohydrate 16.3g
Protein 2.8g
Fat 3.1g
Cholesterol 0mg
Fiber 3.8g
Sodium 126mg

1 cup boiling water
1 cup bulgur, uncooked
1½ cups seeded, chopped tomato
1 cup chopped fresh mint
¾ cup minced fresh parsley
½ cup seeded, chopped cucumber
⅓ cup sliced green onions
½ cup lemon juice
2 tablespoons olive oil
½ teaspoon salt
½ teaspoon garlic powder
⅛ teaspoon ground red pepper
⅛ teaspoon black pepper
    Fresh mint sprigs (optional)

1 Pour water over bulgur in a large bowl; cover and let stand 5 to 10 minutes or until bulgur is tender and water is absorbed.

2 Add tomato and next 4 ingredients to bulgur mixture; toss well.

3 Combine lemon juice and next 5 ingredients in a small bowl; stir well with a wire whisk. Drizzle lemon juice mixture over bulgur mixture; toss well. Garnish with mint sprigs, if desired. Yield: 10 (½-cup) servings.

YIELD: 4 servings

EXCHANGES PER
SERVING:
1 Starch

PER SERVING:
Calories 70
Carbohydrate 13.2g
Protein 2.2g
Fat 1.6g
Cholesterol 0mg
Fiber 2.4g
Sodium 164mg

COUSCOUS WITH SUMMER VEGETABLES

Vegetable cooking spray
1 teaspoon olive oil
1¼ cups shredded zucchini
1¼ cups shredded carrot
½ cup chopped onion
1 small sweet red pepper, seeded and cut
  into ¼-inch strips
¼ cup chopped fresh parsley
1 tablespoon lemon juice
¼ teaspoon dried savory
¼ teaspoon dried rosemary, crumbled
¼ cup plus 2 tablespoons water
¼ teaspoon salt
½ cup couscous, uncooked

1 Coat a large nonstick skillet with cooking spray; add oil, and place over medium heat until hot. Add zucchini and next 3 ingredients; sauté until crisp-tender.

2 Transfer zucchini mixture to a large bowl; stir in parsley and next 3 ingredients. Set aside, and keep warm.

3 Bring water and salt to a boil in a small saucepan; remove from heat. Add couscous; cover and let stand 5 minutes or until liquid is absorbed and couscous is tender. Add couscous to vegetable mixture, and toss well. Yield: 4 (1-cup) servings.

VEGETABLE COUSCOUS

YIELD: 8 servings

You can serve this colorful dish
either warm or chilled.

**EXCHANGES PER
SERVING:**
1 Starch

PER SERVING:
Calories 77
Carbohydrate 16.2g
Protein 3.1g
Fat 0.4g
Cholesterol 0mg
Fiber 1.4g
Sodium 177mg

Vegetable cooking spray
1¼ cups diced yellow squash (about 2
    medium)
1 cup plus 2 tablespoons diced zucchini
    (about 1 medium)
8 small fresh mushrooms, sliced
⅔ cup seeded, diced sweet red pepper
    (about 1 small)
¼ cup plus 1 tablespoon oil-free Italian
    dressing, divided
¼ cup plus 2 tablespoons water
¼ teaspoon salt
¾ cup uncooked couscous

1 Coat a large nonstick skillet with cooking
  spray; place over medium-high heat until hot.
Add squash, zucchini, mushrooms, and red pepper; sauté until vegetables are crisp-tender.

2 Combine squash mixture and 3 tablespoons
  Italian dressing in a large serving bowl; toss
well. Set aside, and keep warm.

3 Combine remaining 2 tablespoons Italian
  dressing, water, and salt in a small saucepan;
bring to a boil. Remove from heat. Add
couscous; cover and let stand 5 minutes or
until liquid is absorbed and couscous is tender.

4 Add couscous to vegetable mixture, and toss
  gently. Yield: 8 (½-cup) servings.

✍ Couscous is a
grain made from
cracked wheat or
millet. It's low in
fat and sodium and
is an excellent source
of complex carbohy-
drate. Couscous
cooks in 5 minutes
and is an alternative
to rice.

CURRIED COUSCOUS WITH WALNUTS

YIELD: 4 servings

EXCHANGES PER SERVING:
2½ Starch
1 Fruit
½ Fat

PER SERVING:
Calories 272
Carbohydrate 51.6g
Protein 10.1g
Fat 2.9g
Cholesterol 0mg
Fiber 3.0g
Sodium 92mg

1 (14¼-ounce) can fat-free, reduced-sodium chicken broth
¼ cup water
½ teaspoon curry powder
1 (10-ounce) package couscous
2 tablespoons chopped walnuts
½ cup sliced green onions

1 Combine first 3 ingredients in a medium saucepan, and bring to a boil. Stir in couscous; cover, remove from heat, and let stand 5 minutes.

2 Stir in walnuts and onions; fluff couscous with a fork. Yield: 4 servings.

BROCCOLI COUSCOUS

YIELD: 4 servings

EXCHANGES PER SERVING:
2 Starch
1 Vegetable

PER SERVING:
Calories 180
Carbohydrate 36.2g
Protein 7.8g
Fat 0.6g
Cholesterol 0mg
Fiber 3.5g
Sodium 399mg

1 (14¼-ounce) can fat-free, reduced-sodium chicken broth
½ teaspoon salt
¼ teaspoon freshly ground pepper
1 cup uncooked couscous
1 (10-ounce) package frozen chopped broccoli, thawed and drained

1 Combine broth, salt, and pepper in a medium saucepan; bring to a boil. Add couscous and broccoli to broth. Cover, remove from heat, and let stand 5 minutes or until liquid is absorbed. Fluff with a fork. Yield: 4 servings.

GARLIC CHEESE GRITS

YIELD: 6 servings

Vegetable cooking spray
1½ tablespoons chopped onion
1 clove garlic, minced
1¾ cups skim milk
1½ cups water
¾ cup quick-cooking grits, uncooked
1 egg, lightly beaten
1 egg white, lightly beaten
1 cup (4 ounces) shredded reduced-fat
   sharp Cheddar cheese
¼ teaspoon salt
⅛ teaspoon hot sauce
2¼ teaspoons low-sodium Worcestershire
   sauce
Cracked black pepper (optional)

**EXCHANGES PER
SERVING:**
1 Medium-Fat Meat
1 Starch

PER SERVING:
Calories 168
Carbohydrate 19.7g
Protein 11.4g
Fat 4.8g
Cholesterol 50mg
Fiber 1.0g
Sodium 303mg

1 Coat a large saucepan with cooking spray; place over medium-high heat until hot. Add onion and garlic; sauté until tender. Stir in milk and water; bring to a boil. Stir in grits. Cover, reduce heat, and simmer 5 minutes or until thickened, stirring occasionally. Remove from heat.

2 Combine egg and next 5 ingredients; stir well. Gradually stir about one-fourth of grits mixture into egg mixture; add to remaining grits mixture, stirring until cheese melts.

3 Pour grits mixture into a 1½-quart casserole coated with cooking spray. Bake at 350° for 30 to 35 minutes or until set. Sprinkle with pepper, if desired. Yield: 6 servings.

ASPARAGUS RICE

YIELD: 11 servings

EXCHANGES PER
SERVING:
1 Starch
1 Vegetable

PER SERVING:
Calories 104
Carbohydrate 21.3g
Protein 2.7g
Fat 0.7g
Cholesterol 0mg
Fiber 0.7g
Sodium 81mg

🌿 Cook rice in a saucepan with a tight-fitting lid. Avoid removing the lid or stirring the rice as it cooks; this can make rice gummy.

Vegetable cooking spray
1 teaspoon margarine
¼ cup chopped onion
1 clove garlic, minced
2 cups canned no-salt-added chicken broth, undiluted
1⅓ cups water
1¼ cups long-grain rice, uncooked
½ pound fresh asparagus
¼ cup diced sweet red pepper
¼ cup diced sweet yellow pepper
2 tablespoons chopped fresh parsley
1 tablespoon lemon juice
¼ teaspoon salt
¼ teaspoon pepper

1 Coat a large saucepan with cooking spray; add margarine. Place over medium-high heat until margarine melts. Add onion and garlic; sauté until tender. Add chicken broth and water; bring to a boil. Stir in rice. Cover, reduce heat, and simmer 20 minutes or until liquid is absorbed and rice is tender.

2 Snap off tough ends of asparagus. Remove scales from stalks with a knife or vegetable peeler, if desired. Cut asparagus into 1-inch pieces. Arrange asparagus, red pepper, and yellow pepper in a vegetable steamer over boiling water. Cover and steam 6 to 8 minutes or until vegetables are crisp-tender.

3 Add steamed vegetables to rice mixture; toss gently. Stir in parsley and remaining ingredients. Yield: 11 (½-cup) servings.

super·quick

CURRIED RICE

YIELD: 4 servings

1 package regular boil-in-bag rice,
  uncooked
¼ teaspoon salt
½ teaspoon curry powder
2 tablespoons raisins
2 chopped green onions

**EXCHANGES PER
SERVING:**
2 Starch

PER SERVING:
Calories 149
Carbohydrate 32.9g
Protein 3.0g
Fat 0.4g
Cholesterol 0mg
Fiber 0.4g
Sodium 539mg

1 Prepare 2 cups cooked rice according to package directions, omitting salt and fat.

2 Remove rice from bag, and stir in salt, curry powder, raisins, and green onions.
Yield: 4 (½-cup) servings.

super·quick

ORANGE RICE

YIELD: 6 servings

2 packages regular boil-in-bag rice,
  uncooked
½ teaspoon grated orange rind
¼ teaspoon salt
¼ teaspoon ground ginger
  Fresh orange slices (optional)

**EXCHANGES PER
SERVING:**
1½ Starch

PER SERVING:
Calories 108
Carbohydrate 24.1g
Protein 2.0g
Fat 0.1g
Cholesterol 0mg
Fiber 0.5g
Sodium 98mg

1 Prepare 3 cups cooked rice according to package directions, omitting salt and fat.

2 Remove rice from bag; stir in orange rind, salt, and ginger. Garnish with fresh orange slices, if desired. Yield: 6 (½-cup) servings.

CREOLE RICE RING

YIELD: 12 servings

EXCHANGES PER
SERVING:
½ Medium-Fat Meat
1 Vegetable

PER SERVING:
Calories 75
Carbohydrate 7.0g
Protein 5.4g
Fat 3.3g
Cholesterol 7mg
Fiber 2.0g
Sodium 213mg

3 cups instant rice, uncooked
  Vegetable cooking spray
½ cup chopped onion
½ cup chopped celery
½ cup chopped green pepper
½ teaspoon paprika
¼ teaspoon salt
¼ teaspoon hot sauce
⅛ teaspoon dried thyme
⅛ teaspoon ground white pepper
⅛ teaspoon ground red pepper
⅛ teaspoon black pepper
1 (14½-ounce) can no-salt-added whole
  tomatoes, undrained
½ cup canned no-salt-added chicken
  broth, undiluted

1 Cook rice according to package directions, omitting salt and fat; set aside.

2 Coat a large nonstick skillet with cooking spray; place over medium-high heat until hot. Add onion, celery, and green pepper; cook 5 minutes or until tender. Add paprika and next 6 ingredients; stir well.

3 Chop tomatoes. Measure 1 cup chopped tomatoes with juice; reserve remaining chopped tomatoes for another use.

4 Add cooked rice, 1 cup chopped tomato, and chicken broth to vegetable mixture. Reduce heat, and cook, uncovered, 15 minutes or until liquid is absorbed.

5 Pack hot rice mixture into a 6-cup ring mold coated with cooking spray. Let stand 10 minutes. Invert onto a serving platter. Yield: 12 (½-cup) servings.

"Not-Fried" Rice

Slice the vegetables for this recipe while the rice cooks. Or for even quicker preparation, use leftover cooked rice.

Vegetable cooking spray
1 tablespoon vegetable oil, divided
¾ cup diagonally sliced celery
½ cup diagonally sliced carrot
1 small onion, thinly sliced
2 teaspoons to 1 tablespoon peeled, minced gingerroot
1 clove garlic, minced
½ cup sliced fresh mushrooms
1 (8-ounce) can bamboo shoots, drained
3 cups cooked brown rice (cooked without salt or fat)
1 egg, lightly beaten
3 tablespoons reduced-sodium soy sauce
3 tablespoons dry sherry
2 tablespoons sliced green onions
Green onion fans (optional)

YIELD: 10 servings

EXCHANGES PER SERVING:
1 Starch
1 Fat

PER SERVING:
Calories 115
Carbohydrate 18.6g
Protein 3.6g
Fat 2.7g
Cholesterol 22mg
Fiber 2.7g
Sodium 178mg

1 Coat a wok or large nonstick skillet with cooking spray; drizzle 2 teaspoons oil around top of wok, coating sides. Place over medium-high (375°) until hot. Add celery and next 4 ingredients; stir-fry 2 minutes. Add mushrooms and bamboo shoots; stir-fry 2 additional minutes or until vegetables are crisp-tender.

2 Stir in cooked rice, and cook until thoroughly heated. Push rice mixture to sides of wok, forming a well in center.

3 Drizzle remaining 1 teaspoon oil around top of wok. Pour beaten egg into well, and cook until set, stirring occasionally. Stir rice mixture into egg; add soy sauce and sherry, stirring constantly. Transfer to individual serving bowls, and sprinkle with sliced green onions. Garnish with green onion fans, if desired. Yield: 10 (½-cup) servings.

LEMON RISOTTO

YIELD: 6 servings

EXCHANGES PER
SERVING:
2 Starch
½ Fat

PER SERVING:
Calories 166
Carbohydrate 28.1g
Protein 3.6g
Fat 3.7g
Cholesterol 0mg
Fiber 0.7g
Sodium 90mg

Risotto is a creamy rice dish made by adding hot broth to a rice mixture and stirring constantly until the liquid is absorbed. This recipe works best when you use Arborio, a short-grained Italian rice.

4 cups canned no-salt-added chicken broth, undiluted
1 tablespoon olive oil
½ cup chopped onion
1 clove garlic, crushed
1 cup Arborio rice, uncooked
1 teaspoon grated lemon rind
3 tablespoons lemon juice
Lemon slice (optional)

1 Pour broth into a saucepan; place over medium heat. Bring to a simmer; reduce heat to low, and keep warm. (Do not boil).

2 Heat oil in a large skillet over medium-high heat. Add onion and garlic; sauté until tender. Add rice, stirring well. Add ½ cup simmering broth to rice mixture; cook, stirring constantly, until most of the liquid is absorbed. Repeat procedure, adding ½ cup broth at a time, stirring constantly, until liquid is absorbed and rice is tender (about 30 minutes). (Rice will be tender and have a creamy consistency.)

3 Stir in lemon rind and lemon juice. Transfer mixture to a serving bowl. Garnish with a lemon slice, if desired. Serve immediately. Yield: 6 (½-cup) servings.

MEXICAN BLACK BEANS 'N' RICE

YIELD: 8 servings

EXCHANGES PER SERVING:
1 Starch
1 Vegetable

PER SERVING:
Calories 106
Carbohydrate 19.8g
Protein 3.6g
Fat 1.5g
Cholesterol 0mg
Fiber 1.8g
Sodium 97mg

2 teaspoons olive oil
1 cup chopped onion
½ cup chopped green pepper
2 cups cooked long-grain rice (cooked without salt or fat)
½ teaspoon ground cumin
¼ teaspoon ground red pepper
⅛ teaspoon dried coriander
¾ cup chopped tomato
1 (15-ounce) can black beans, rinsed and drained

1 Heat oil in a large nonstick skillet over medium-high heat. Add onion and green pepper; sauté until tender.

2 Add rice and next 3 ingredients to skillet; sauté 3 minutes. Add tomato and beans; sauté 3 minutes or until thoroughly heated. Yield: 8 (½-cup) servings.

FIESTA SPANISH RICE

**EXCHANGES PER
SERVING:**
2 Starch

PER SERVING:
Calories 145
Carbohydrate 31.1g
Protein 3.5g
Fat 0.5g
Cholesterol 0mg
Fiber 1.5g
Sodium 70mg

Vegetable cooking spray
¼ cup chopped onion
2 cloves garlic, minced
1 (14½-ounce) can no-salt-added whole
tomatoes, undrained and chopped
1 (14¼-ounce) can no-salt-added beef
broth
1 (4½-ounce) can chopped green chiles,
undrained
1½ teaspoons chili powder
⅛ teaspoon salt
Dash of hot sauce
1 cup long-grain rice, uncooked

1 Coat a large saucepan with cooking spray;
place over medium-high heat until hot. Add
onion and garlic; sauté until crisp-tender. Stir in
tomato and next 5 ingredients; bring to a boil.

2 Stir in rice. Cover, reduce heat, and simmer
20 to 25 minutes or until liquid is absorbed
and rice is tender. Yield: 6 (½-cup) servings.

WILD RICE WITH MUSHROOMS AND ALMONDS

½ cup wild rice, uncooked
2 cups canned low-sodium chicken broth
  Butter-flavored vegetable cooking spray
2 teaspoons reduced-calorie margarine
¼ cup chopped celery
2 cups sliced fresh mushrooms
¼ cup chopped green onions
¼ cup chopped water chestnuts
¼ teaspoon salt
¼ teaspoon pepper
1 tablespoon slivered almonds, toasted
  Green onion (optional)

1 Combine rice and broth in a saucepan. Bring to a boil; cover, reduce heat, and simmer 50 minutes or until rice is tender, stirring occasionally. Drain; set aside.

2 Coat a large nonstick skillet with cooking spray; add margarine. Place over medium-high heat until margarine melts. Add celery; sauté 1 minute. Add mushrooms and next 4 ingredients; sauté 2 minutes or until vegetables are tender. Add vegetable mixture and almonds to rice; toss lightly. Garnish with a green onion, if desired. Yield: 6 (½-cup) servings.

YIELD: 6 servings

EXCHANGES PER SERVING:
1 Starch

PER SERVING:
Calories 85
Carbohydrate 13.7g
Protein 3.6g
Fat 2.2g
Cholesterol 0mg
Fiber 1.3g
Sodium 143mg

VEGETABLE PILAF

EXCHANGES PER SERVING:
1 Starch
½ Fat

PER SERVING:
Calories 82
Carbohydrate 13.2g
Protein 1.8g
Fat 2.7g
Cholesterol 0mg
Fiber 1.4g
Sodium 112mg

While the rice is simmering, toast the chopped pecans in a preheated oven at 350° for about 10 minutes.

1⅓ cups water
1 teaspoon chicken-flavored bouillon granules
½ cup long-grain rice, uncooked
1½ cups sliced fresh mushrooms
1¼ cups shredded carrot
½ cup water
½ cup chopped fresh parsley
⅓ cup thinly sliced green onions
¼ teaspoon pepper
¼ cup chopped pecans, toasted

1 Combine 1⅓ cups water and bouillon granules in a medium saucepan; bring to a boil, and add rice. Cover, reduce heat, and simmer 20 minutes or until liquid is absorbed and rice is tender.

2 Add mushrooms and next 5 ingredients to rice; stir well. Cover and cook over low heat 5 minutes.

3 To serve, transfer rice to a serving dish, and sprinkle with toasted pecans.
Yield: 8 (½-cup) servings.

Brown Rice Primavera

Using instant brown rice in this recipe is a time-saver. It's ready in 10 minutes.

¾ cup water
½ teaspoon chicken-flavored bouillon
    granules
2 cloves garlic, minced
¾ cup instant brown rice, uncooked
    Vegetable cooking spray
1 cup frozen French-style green beans,
    thawed and drained
1 cup sliced fresh mushrooms
½ cup diced sweet red pepper
2 tablespoons grated Parmesan cheese

YIELD: 6 servings

EXCHANGES PER
SERVING:
1 Starch

PER SERVING:
Calories 56
Carbohydrate 10.2g
Protein 2.4g
Fat 1.1g
Cholesterol 1mg
Fiber 1.4g
Sodium 110mg

1 Combine first 3 ingredients in a medium saucepan; bring to a boil. Stir in rice; cover, reduce heat, and simmer 5 minutes. Remove from heat, and let stand 5 minutes or until liquid is absorbed. Set aside, and keep warm.

2 Coat a large nonstick skillet with cooking spray; place over medium heat until hot. Add green beans; sauté 2 minutes. Add mushrooms and red pepper; sauté 3 minutes or until pepper is crisp-tender.

3 Add green bean mixture and Parmesan cheese to rice mixture; toss well.
Yield: 6 (½-cup) servings.

Microwave Instructions: Combine first 4 ingredients in a 1½-quart casserole. Cover with heavy-duty plastic wrap, and microwave at HIGH 6 minutes. Let stand, covered, for 5 minutes. Place green beans in a 1-quart casserole. Cover with heavy-duty plastic wrap, and microwave at HIGH 3 minutes. Stir in mushrooms and pepper. Cover and microwave at HIGH 3 to 4 minutes or until vegetables are crisp-tender. Add green bean mixture and Parmesan cheese to rice mixture; toss well.

GREEK PILAF

Orzo is a tiny, rice-shaped pasta.
Look for it in the pasta or rice section
of your grocery store.

Vegetable cooking spray
1 tablespoon olive oil
6 green onions, finely chopped
$\frac{3}{4}$ cup orzo, uncooked
$\frac{3}{4}$ cup instant rice, uncooked
1 (14$\frac{1}{4}$-ounce can) no-salt-added chicken
   broth, undiluted
1$\frac{1}{4}$ cups water
$\frac{1}{4}$ teaspoon salt
$\frac{1}{8}$ teaspoon pepper
1$\frac{1}{4}$ cups peeled, diced cucumber
$\frac{1}{3}$ cup crumbled feta cheese
2 tablespoons diced pimiento, drained
   Cucumber slices (optional)
   Diced pimiento (optional)

1 Coat a large nonstick skillet with cooking
spray; add oil. Place over medium-high heat
until hot. Add green onions, and sauté until tender. Add orzo; sauté 2 minutes. Add rice; sauté 2
minutes.

2 Stir in broth and next 3 ingredients. Bring
to a boil; cover, reduce heat, and simmer 20
to 25 minutes or until liquid is absorbed and
rice is tender.

3 Remove from heat, and stir in cucumber,
feta cheese, and 2 tablespoons pimiento.
Transfer to a serving dish. If desired, garnish
with cucumber slices and pimiento.
Yield: 12 ($\frac{1}{2}$-cup) servings.

ANGEL HAIR PASTA WITH VEGETABLES

YIELD: 9 servings

EXCHANGES PER
SERVING:
1 Starch
1 Vegetable
1 Fat

PER SERVING:
Calories 149
Carbohydrate 23.4g
Protein 5.2g
Fat 4.3g
Cholesterol 1mg
Fiber 1.8g
Sodium 158mg

You can use fettuccine or linguine in this recipe
if you don't have angel hair pasta.

¼ cup reduced-calorie margarine
2 cups sliced broccoli flowerets
1 cup thinly sliced carrot
½ cup sliced green onions
1 tablespoon dried basil
2 cloves garlic, minced
2 cups sliced fresh mushrooms
½ cup dry white wine
¼ teaspoon salt
¼ teaspoon pepper
8 ounces angel hair pasta, uncooked
3 tablespoons grated Parmesan cheese

1 Place margarine in a large nonstick skillet;
place over medium heat until hot. Add
broccoli and next 4 ingredients; sauté 5 minutes
or until vegetables are crisp-tender. Add mushrooms, wine, salt, and pepper; cook 2 minutes
or until mushrooms are tender. Remove from
heat; set aside, and keep warm.

2 Cook pasta according to package directions,
omitting salt and fat. Drain.

3 Add vegetable mixture and cheese to pasta;
toss lightly. Yield: 9 (¾-cup) servings.

INDONESIAN PASTA

YIELD: 4 servings

EXCHANGES PER
SERVING:
1 Starch
2 Vegetable
1 Fat

PER SERVING:
Calories 185
Carbohydrate 27.8g
Protein 7.9g
Fat 5.2g
Cholesterol 0mg
Fiber 3.0g
Sodium 251mg

½ cup canned low-sodium chicken broth
2 tablespoons creamy peanut butter
2 tablespoons low-sodium soy sauce
1½ tablespoons lemon juice
2 teaspoons seeded, minced serrano chile
¼ teaspoon granulated brown sugar
   substitute
⅛ teaspoon ground cumin
½ pound fresh asparagus spears
   Vegetable cooking spray
¾ cup sliced sweet red pepper
⅓ cup sliced green onions
2 tablespoons chopped fresh parsley
4 ounces capellini (angel hair pasta),
   uncooked

1 Combine first 7 ingredients in a small saucepan; bring to a boil, stirring constantly. Set aside, and keep warm.

2 Snap off tough ends of asparagus. Remove scales from stalks with a vegetable peeler, if desired. Cut into 1-inch pieces.

3 Coat a nonstick skillet with cooking spray; place over medium-high heat until hot. Add asparagus; sauté 3 minutes. Add red pepper; sauté 2 additional minutes or until vegetables are tender. Add green onions; sauté 30 seconds. Remove from heat; stir in parsley. Set aside, and keep warm.

4 Cook pasta according to package directions, omitting salt and fat; drain. Place pasta in a serving bowl. Add peanut sauce and vegetable mixture; toss lightly. Serve warm.
Yield: 4 (1-cup) servings.

Orecchiette With Fresh Vegetables and Herbs

Orecchiette is a small bowl-shaped pasta.

10 ounces fresh asparagus
1 (14½-ounce) can vegetable broth
1½ cups thinly sliced sweet yellow pepper
1 cup sliced carrot
2 cups sugar snap peas, trimmed
1 cup frozen green peas
¼ cup chopped fresh chives
2 tablespoons chopped fresh basil
1 tablespoon chopped fresh thyme
⅛ teaspoon salt
12 ounces orecchiette, uncooked
¾ cup grated Romano cheese
Freshly ground black pepper (optional)

YIELD: 8 servings

EXCHANGES PER SERVING:
2 Starch
2 Vegetable
½ Fat

PER SERVING:
Calories 250
Carbohydrate 40.4g
Protein 11.9g
Fat 4.2g
Cholesterol 11mg
Fiber 2.9g
Sodium 358mg

1 Snap off tough ends of asparagus. Remove scales from stalks with a vegetable peeler, if desired. Cut asparagus into 1-inch pieces, and set aside.

2 Bring vegetable broth to a boil in a large saucepan. Add asparagus, yellow pepper, and carrot. Reduce heat; simmer, uncovered, 4 minutes. Add sugar snap peas and English peas; cook 3 additional minutes or until vegetables are crisp-tender. Add chives, basil, thyme, and salt.

3 Cook pasta according to package directions, omitting salt and fat; drain well. Place pasta in a serving bowl. Add vegetable mixture; toss well. Add ½ cup cheese to pasta mixture; toss well. Sprinkle with remaining ¼ cup cheese. Sprinkle with freshly ground pepper, if desired. Yield: 8 servings.

VEGETABLE RADIATORE

YIELD: 6 servings

EXCHANGES PER
SERVING:
1 Starch

PER SERVING:
Calories 84
Carbohydrate 13.4g
Protein 4.0g
Fat 1.6g
Cholesterol 3mg
Fiber 0.8g
Sodium 102mg

🖋 Radiatore is a short, plump pasta that's rippled and ringed like a radiator. It's available either plain or tricolored. Look for radiatore at the grocery store on the shelves with the other varieties of packaged pasta.

If radiatore pasta is not available, substitute 1 cup uncooked corkscrew macaroni.

Vegetable cooking spray
½ cup chopped onion
2 cloves garlic, minced
1 cup canned low-sodium chicken broth, undiluted
2 tablespoons chopped fresh basil
⅛ teaspoon salt
⅛ teaspoon pepper
1 medium carrot, scraped and cut into very thin strips
1 cup tricolored radiatore, uncooked
¼ cup (1 ounce) shredded reduced-fat sharp Cheddar cheese
1 medium zucchini, cut into very thin strips
Fresh basil sprigs (optional)

1 Coat a large saucepan with cooking spray; place over medium heat until hot. Add onion and garlic; sauté until tender. Add broth and next 4 ingredients; bring to a boil. Stir in pasta. Cover, reduce heat, and simmer 20 minutes or until pasta is tender, stirring occasionally.

2 Remove pasta from heat; stir in cheese and zucchini. Cover and let stand 2 minutes or until cheese melts. Transfer to a serving dish. Garnish with basil sprigs, if desired.
Yield: 6 (½-cup) servings.

PIZZERIA PASTA

YIELD: 6 servings

1 (9-ounce) package fresh cheese-filled
   tortellini, uncooked
   Vegetable cooking spray
½ cup chopped green pepper
⅓ cup chopped onion
1 (8-ounce) can no-salt-added tomato
   sauce
¼ cup sliced ripe olives
1 teaspoon dried Italian seasoning
⅛ teaspoon garlic powder
   Fresh basil sprig (optional)

**EXCHANGES PER
SERVING:**
1 Starch
2 Vegetable
1 Fat

PER SERVING:
Calories 168
Carbohydrate 24.9g
Protein 7.2g
Fat 4.2g
Cholesterol 20mg
Fiber 1.3g
Sodium 246mg

1 Cook tortellini according to package directions, omitting salt and fat; drain well. Place in a serving bowl.

2 Coat a medium nonstick skillet with cooking spray. Place over medium-high heat until hot. Add green pepper and onion; sauté until tender.

3 Add tomato sauce and next 3 ingredients to skillet. Cook over medium-low heat until thoroughly heated, stirring occasionally. Add tomato mixture to tortellini; toss lightly. Garnish with basil sprig, if desired. Serve immediately. Yield: 6 (½-cup) servings.

super·quick

PASTA IN SOUR CREAM SAUCE

**EXCHANGES PER
SERVING:**
1 Starch
1 Vegetable
½ Fat

PER SERVING:
Calories 130
Carbohydrate 20.3g
Protein 4.7g
Fat 2.9g
Cholesterol 7mg
Fiber 0.9g
Sodium 40mg

3½ ounces fresh angel hair pasta,
    uncooked
¼ cup low-fat sour cream
2 tablespoons dry white wine
1 tablespoon plus 1 teaspoon grated
    Parmesan cheese
Dash of pepper
Vegetable cooking spray
⅔ cup sliced fresh mushrooms
¼ cup chopped green onions

1 Cook pasta in boiling water 1 minute; drain well, and set aside.

2 Combine sour cream and next 3 ingredients; stir well, and set aside.

3 Coat a medium nonstick skillet with cooking spray; place over medium-high heat until hot. Add mushrooms and green onions; sauté 2 minutes or until vegetables are tender. Add pasta and sour cream mixture; cook, stirring constantly, until thoroughly heated. Serve warm. Yield: 4 (½-cup) servings.

PENNE PASTA WITH TOMATO SAUCE

5 ripe plum tomatoes, seeded and cut into
    ½-inch pieces
½ cup chopped fresh basil
¼ cup halved ripe olives
1 clove garlic, minced
1½ tablespoons olive oil
1 tablespoon balsamic vinegar
⅛ teaspoon salt
⅛ teaspoon coarsely ground pepper
6 ounces penne pasta, uncooked
¼ cup crumbled feta cheese

1 Combine first 8 ingredients in a bowl; toss
  well. Cover and let stand 15 minutes.

2 Cook pasta according to package directions,
  omitting salt and fat; drain well.

3 Add pasta to tomato mixture; toss gently.
  Transfer to a serving dish, and sprinkle with
feta cheese. Yield: 10 (½-cup) servings.

YIELD: 10 servings

EXCHANGES PER
SERVING:
1 Starch
½ Fat

PER SERVING:
Calories 99
Carbohydrate 14.5g
Protein 2.9g
Fat 3.3g
Cholesterol 3mg
Fiber 0.9g
Sodium 88mg

LINGUINE FLORENTINE

YIELD: 9 servings

EXCHANGES PER
SERVING:
1 Starch
1 Fat

PER SERVING:
Calories 113
Carbohydrate 12.9g
Protein 6.6g
Fat 4.6g
Cholesterol 4mg
Fiber 3.8g
Sodium 148mg

2 pounds fresh spinach
4 ounces linguine, uncooked
2 teaspoons olive oil
½ cup grated Parmesan cheese
¼ teaspoon pepper
1 tablespoon chopped walnuts, toasted

1 Remove and discard stems from spinach; wash leaves thoroughly. Cover and cook in a large Dutch oven over medium heat about 4 minutes or until tender. (Do not add water.) Drain well; finely chop spinach.

2 Cook linguine according to package directions, omitting salt and fat. Drain. Combine linguine and olive oil in a large bowl; toss gently. Add spinach, cheese, and pepper; toss gently. Sprinkle with walnuts. Yield: 9 servings.

ORANGE-BASIL LINGUINE

YIELD: 6 servings

EXCHANGES PER
SERVING:
1½ Starch

PER SERVING:
Calories 134
Carbohydrate 24.4g
Protein 4.2g
Fat 1.9g
Cholesterol 1mg
Fiber 0.7g
Sodium 37mg

6 ounces linguine, uncooked
1 tablespoon reduced-calorie margarine, melted
½ cup canned no-salt-added chicken broth, undiluted
½ cup unsweetened orange juice
2 teaspoons cornstarch
1 tablespoon chopped fresh basil leaves
⅛ teaspoon grated orange rind
1 tablespoon grated Parmesan cheese

1 Cook linguine according to package directions, omitting salt and fat. Drain; set aside.

2 Combine margarine and next 3 ingredients in a saucepan; stir well. Bring to a boil; cook 1 minute. Remove from heat. Add basil and orange rind; stir well. Pour over linguine; toss gently. Sprinkle with cheese. Yield: 6 servings.

Spinach Fettuccine Toss

YIELD: 8 servings

2 ounces fettuccine, uncooked
2 ounces spinach fettuccine, uncooked
1¼ cups 1% low-fat cottage cheese
¼ cup skim milk
1 teaspoon Dijon mustard
½ teaspoon prepared horseradish
 Vegetable cooking spray
1¼ cups chopped sweet red pepper
½ cup sliced green onions
3 tablespoons grated Parmesan cheese
2 tablespoons chopped fresh parsley

EXCHANGES PER SERVING:
½ Lean Meat
1 Starch

PER SERVING:
Calories 94
Carbohydrate 13.5g
Protein 7.8g
Fat 1.4g
Cholesterol 3mg
Fiber 2.2g
Sodium 204mg

1 Cook fettuccine and spinach fettuccine according to package directions, omitting salt and fat. Drain well, and keep warm.

2 Combine cottage cheese and next 3 ingredients in container of an electric blender; cover and process until smooth.

3 Coat a large nonstick skillet with cooking spray; place over medium heat until hot. Add red pepper and onions; sauté until tender.

4 Add cooked fettuccine, cottage cheese mixture, Parmesan cheese, and parsley; toss gently. Serve warm. Yield: 8 (½-cup) servings.

✒ To cook pasta, use 3 quarts of rapidly boiling water for every 8 ounces of dried pasta. To prevent the boil from subsiding, add pasta gradually in small amounts, and follow package directions for cooking times.

MEDITERRANEAN ORZO

YIELD: 2 servings

EXCHANGES PER
SERVING:
1 Starch
1 Vegetable

PER SERVING:
Calories 119
Carbohydrate 23.1g
Protein 4.3g
Fat 1.4g
Cholesterol 0mg
Fiber 1.0g
Sodium 332mg

2 tablespoons dried tomato (packed
   without oil)
2 tablespoons hot water
¼ cup orzo, uncooked
   Olive oil-flavored vegetable cooking
   spray
2 tablespoons chopped sweet red pepper
1 tablespoon chopped green onions
1 tablespoon chopped fresh parsley
1 tablespoon chopped Greek olives
1 tablespoon canned low-sodium
   chicken broth
2 teaspoons red wine vinegar
⅛ teaspoon salt
⅛ teaspoon pepper

1 Combine tomato and water in a small bowl;
cover and let stand 15 minutes. Drain well.
Chop tomato, and set aside.

2 Cook orzo according to package directions,
omitting salt and fat; drain, set aside, and
keep warm.

3 Coat a small nonstick skillet with cooking
spray; place over medium-high heat until
hot. Add red pepper and green onions; sauté until crisp-tender. Add tomato, parsley, and
remaining 5 ingredients to skillet; cook until
thoroughly heated, stirring often.

4 Combine vegetable mixture and orzo in
a small bowl; toss lightly.
Yield: 2 (½-cup) servings.

CREOLE LIMA BEANS

YIELD: 8 servings

Vegetable cooking spray
½ cup chopped celery
½ cup chopped green pepper
½ cup chopped onion
1 (16-ounce) package frozen baby lima
  beans, thawed
1 cup diced tomato
1 cup spicy hot vegetable juice cocktail
¼ teaspoon dried crushed red pepper

**EXCHANGES PER
SERVING:**
1 Starch

PER SERVING:
Calories 90
Carbohydrate 17.3g
Protein 4.9g
Fat 0.4g
Cholesterol 0mg
Fiber 1.9g
Sodium 197mg

1 Coat a large nonstick skillet with cooking spray; place over medium-high heat until hot. Add celery, green pepper, and onion; sauté until tender.

2 Stir in lima beans and remaining ingredients; bring to a boil over medium heat. Cover, reduce heat, and simmer 12 to 15 minutes or until beans are tender.
Yield: 8 (1½-cup) servings.

GERMAN-STYLE LIMA BEANS

YIELD: 7 servings

EXCHANGES PER
SERVING:
1 Starch
1 Vegetable

PER SERVING:
Calories 98
Carbohydrate 19.2g
Protein 5.4g
Fat 0.3g
Cholesterol 0mg
Fiber 1.7g
Sodium 17mg

1 (16-ounce) package frozen lima beans
½ cup water
⅓ cup cider vinegar
2 tablespoons granulated sugar substitute
2 tablespoons all-purpose flour
½ teaspoon chicken-flavored bouillon
    granules
¼ teaspoon freshly ground black pepper
¾ cup chopped celery
½ cup chopped sweet red pepper
¼ cup sliced green onions

1 Cook lima beans in boiling water to cover 15 minutes or until tender; drain. Set aside, and keep warm.

2 Combine ½ cup water and next 5 ingredients in a saucepan, stirring well. Cook over medium heat, stirring constantly, 5 minutes or until mixture thickens.

3 Combine lima beans, celery, red pepper, green onions, and vinegar mixture, tossing well. Serve warm. Yield: 7 (½-cup) servings.

RANCHER'S BEANS

YIELD: 9 servings

Vegetable cooking spray
- ¼ cup chopped onion
- 1 (16-ounce) can light red kidney beans
- 1 (15.8-ounce) can Great Northern beans
- 1 (8-ounce) can no-salt-added tomato sauce
- 3 tablespoons no-salt-added tomato juice
- 1 tablespoon prepared mustard
- 2 tablespoons granulated brown sugar substitute
- ¼ teaspoon garlic powder
- ⅛ teaspoon pepper

EXCHANGES PER SERVING:
1 Very Lean Meat
1½ Starch

PER SERVING:
Calories 138
Carbohydrate 25.5g
Protein 9.1g
Fat 0.5g
Cholesterol 0mg
Fiber 4.0g
Sodium 263mg

1 Coat a medium saucepan with cooking spray; place over medium-high heat until hot. Add onion; sauté until tender.

2 Add kidney beans and remaining ingredients. Cook over medium heat, uncovered, 20 minutes or until slightly thickened.
Yield: 9 (½-cup) servings.

SUMMER SWEET CORN

YIELD: 10 servings

EXCHANGES PER
SERVING:
1 Starch

PER SERVING:
Calories 83
Carbohydrate 18.4g
Protein 3.1g
Fat 1.1g
Cholesterol 0mg
Fiber 3.1g
Sodium 75mg

If you don't have fresh corn, use
6 cups frozen whole kernel corn.

6 cups fresh corn cut from cob
   (about 12 ears)
1½ cups water
½ cup chopped green onions
¼ cup chopped green pepper
2 tablespoons chopped fresh basil
2 tablespoons white wine vinegar
½ teaspoon granulated sugar substitute
¼ teaspoon salt
¼ teaspoon ground white pepper
¼ teaspoon hot sauce
   Fresh basil sprigs (optional)

1 Combine first 4 ingredients in a medium saucepan. Bring to a boil; reduce heat, and simmer, uncovered, 20 minutes.

2 Add chopped basil and next 5 ingredients; cook 10 minutes or until corn is tender. Transfer to a serving bowl; serve with a slotted spoon. Garnish with basil sprigs, if desired. Yield: 10 (½-cup) servings.

Hearty Corn Casserole

1 (16½-ounce) can no-salt-added
  cream-style corn
½ cup egg substitute
½ cup sliced green onions
½ cup chopped green pepper
¼ cup cornmeal
2 tablespoons all-purpose flour
¼ teaspoon salt
1 (17-ounce) can no-salt-added
  whole kernel corn, drained
1 (8-ounce) carton plain nonfat yogurt
1 (2¼-ounce) can sliced jalapeño-flavored
  ripe olives, drained
1 (2-ounce) jar diced pimiento, drained
  Vegetable cooking spray
  Green pepper rings (optional)

**EXCHANGES PER
SERVING:**
1½ Starch

PER SERVING:
Calories 127
Carbohydrate 23.7g
Protein 5.6g
Fat 1.6g
Cholesterol 1mg
Fiber 1.4g
Sodium 184mg

1 Combine cream-style corn and egg substitute in container of an electric blender; cover and process until smooth, stopping once to scrape down sides. Transfer mixture to a bowl; add sliced green onions and next 8 ingredients, stirring well.

2 Pour mixture into a 2-quart baking dish coated with cooking spray. Bake, uncovered, at 350° for 45 minutes. Remove from oven, and stir well. Return to oven, and bake 25 additional minutes or until set. Garnish with pepper rings, if desired. Yield: 8 servings.

SOUTH-OF-THE-BORDER CORN

YIELD: 12 servings

EXCHANGES PER SERVING:
1 Starch

PER SERVING:
Calories 89
Carbohydrate 19.1g
Protein 2.5g
Fat 1.8g
Cholesterol 0mg
Fiber 2.8g
Sodium 123mg

1 tablespoon plus 1 teaspoon hot water
2 teaspoons reduced-calorie margarine, melted
¼ teaspoon dried cilantro
½ teaspoon ground cumin
½ teaspoon paprika
¼ teaspoon salt
¼ teaspoon garlic powder
  Dash of ground red pepper
12 half ears frozen corn

1 Combine first 8 ingredients in a small bowl; stir well.

2 Cook corn according to package directions; transfer to a serving platter, and brush margarine mixture over corn. Yield: 12 servings.

HERBED CORN ON THE COB

YIELD: 4 servings

EXCHANGES PER SERVING:
1 Starch
1 Fat

PER SERVING:
Calories 106
Carbohydrate 18.1g
Protein 2.5g
Fat 4.1g
Cholesterol 0mg
Fiber 2.2g
Sodium 5mg

1 tablespoon dried dillweed
1 tablespoon dried thyme
1 tablespoon water
1 tablespoon vegetable oil
1 clove garlic, minced
4 medium ears frozen corn

1 Combine first 5 ingredients in a small bowl; stir well. Spread over corn. Place each ear on a piece of heavy-duty aluminum foil; wrap tightly.

2 Bake at 450° for 25 minutes, turning occasionally. Yield: 4 servings.

super·quick

GREEN PEAS WITH GARLIC

Vegetable cooking spray
1 teaspoon reduced-calorie margarine
2 (1-ounce) slices lean ham, cut into very thin strips
6 cloves garlic, halved
2 (10-ounce) packages frozen English peas, thawed
1 tablespoon plus 1 teaspoon slivered almonds, toasted

1 Coat a large nonstick skillet with cooking spray; add margarine. Place over medium heat until hot. Add ham and garlic; sauté 2 minutes or until garlic is tender. Add peas, and sauté 3 minutes or until thoroughly heated. Remove and discard garlic. Transfer to a serving bowl, and sprinkle with almonds. Yield: 8 (½-cup) servings.

Microwave Instructions: Place margarine, ham, and garlic in a 2-quart casserole. Cover with wax paper and microwave at HIGH 1 minute or until garlic is tender. Add peas; cover mixture with wax paper, and microwave at HIGH 2 to 3 minutes or until peas are tender. Remove and discard garlic. Transfer to a serving bowl, and sprinkle with almonds.

YIELD: 8 servings

EXCHANGES PER SERVING:
1 Starch

PER SERVING:
Calories 83
Carbohydrate 10.8g
Protein 5.5g
Fat 1.3g
Cholesterol 3mg
Fiber 2.6g
Sodium 191mg

� Store fresh garlic in an open container (away from other foods) in a cool, dark place. Unbroken bulbs can be kept up to 8 weeks. Once broken from the bulb, individual garlic cloves can be kept for 3 to 10 days.

YIELD: 12 servings

EXCHANGES PER
SERVING:
1 Starch

PER SERVING:
Calories 79
Carbohydrate 13.8g
Protein 2.1g
Fat 2.1g
Cholesterol 6mg
Fiber 1.8g
Sodium 231mg

HASH BROWN POTATO CASSEROLE

1 (24-ounce) package frozen hash brown
   potatoes with onions and peppers,
   thawed
1 (10¾-ounce) can reduced-fat, reduced-
   sodium cream of mushroom soup,
   undiluted
1 (2-ounce) jar diced pimiento, drained
⅔ cup 1% low-fat milk
½ cup low-fat sour cream
½ teaspoon salt
2 cloves garlic, minced
   Vegetable cooking spray
½ cup soft reduced-calorie whole wheat
   breadcrumbs, toasted
   Chopped sweet red pepper (optional)
   Chopped green onions (optional)

1 Combine first 7 ingredients in a medium bowl, stirring well. Spoon potato mixture into an 8-inch square baking dish coated with cooking spray.

2 Sprinkle breadcrumbs over top of potato mixture; bake at 350° for 45 to 50 minutes or until bubbly. If desired, sprinkle top of casserole with chopped sweet red pepper and green onions after baking.
Yield: 12 (½-cup) servings.

TWICE-BAKED POTATOES

YIELD: 4 servings

2 small baking potatoes (about 6 ounces each)
¼ cup plus 2 tablespoons low-fat sour cream
¼ teaspoon garlic powder
¼ teaspoon salt
¼ teaspoon pepper
2 tablespoons chopped fresh chives
¼ cup (1 ounce) shredded reduced-fat sharp Cheddar cheese

EXCHANGES PER SERVING:
1 Starch
1 Fat

PER SERVING:
Calories 146
Carbohydrate 23.0g
Protein 4.7g
Fat 4.2g
Cholesterol 13mg
Fiber 1.6g
Sodium 214mg

1 Scrub potatoes; bake at 425° for 1 hour or until tender. Let potatoes cool to touch.

2 Cut potatoes in half lengthwise; carefully scoop out pulp, leaving ¼-inch-thick shells. Set shells aside. Place pulp in a small bowl; mash until smooth. Combine mashed potato, sour cream, and next 3 ingredients, beating until smooth. Stir in chives.

3 Spoon mixture evenly into potato shells, and sprinkle evenly with cheese. Place potato shells in a small ungreased baking dish. Bake at 425° for 5 minutes or until cheese melts. Yield: 4 servings.

YIELD: 2 servings

EXCHANGES PER
SERVING:
1½ Starch
½ Fat

PER SERVING:
Calories 133
Carbohydrate 24.7g
Protein 3.3g
Fat 2.7g
Cholesterol 0mg
Fiber 2.7g
Sodium 157mg

GARLIC-ROASTED NEW POTATOES

If you don't have fresh rosemary, substitute
¼ teaspoon dried rosemary.

6 small round red potatoes (about 1
    pound), cut in half
    Olive oil-flavored vegetable cooking
    spray
1 teaspoon olive oil
3 bay leaves
2 cloves garlic, peeled and cut in half
2 sprigs fresh rosemary
¼ teaspoon coarsely ground pepper
⅛ teaspoon salt

1 Coat potato halves with cooking spray.
  Coat a 9-inch cast-iron skillet with cooking
spray; add oil. Place skillet over medium heat
until hot; add potato, bay leaves, garlic, and
rosemary, stirring lightly. Sprinkle with ground
pepper and salt.

2 Bake at 450° for 40 minutes or until potato
  is browned, stirring twice. Remove and discard bay leaves and rosemary. Yield: 2 servings.

Scalloped Potatoes With Leeks

Vegetable cooking spray
2 cups thinly sliced leek
2 cloves garlic, minced
1½ tablespoons margarine
2½ tablespoons all-purpose flour
2 cups skim milk
½ teaspoon salt
½ teaspoon ground red pepper
¼ teaspoon ground white pepper
6 cups frozen diced potato, thawed
1 cup (4 ounces) shredded Gruyère cheese
2 tablespoons freshly grated Parmesan cheese

YIELD: 14 servings

EXCHANGES PER SERVING:
½ High-Fat Meat
1 Starch

PER SERVING:
Calories 119
Carbohydrate 14.8g
Protein 5.7g
Fat 4.3g
Cholesterol 10mg
Fiber 1.3g
Sodium 166mg

1 Coat a Dutch oven with cooking spray; place over medium heat until hot. Add leek and garlic; cook until tender. Remove from Dutch oven, and set aside.

2 Melt margarine in Dutch oven over low heat; add flour, stirring until smooth. Cook 1 minute, stirring constantly with a wire whisk. Gradually add milk, stirring constantly. Cook over medium heat, stirring constantly, until mixture is slightly thickened and bubbly. Stir in salt, red pepper, and white pepper.

3 Return leek mixture to Dutch oven. Add potato, stirring to combine. Spoon half of potato mixture into an 11- x 7- x 1½-inch baking dish coated with cooking spray. Top with half of Gruyère cheese. Repeat layers with remaining half of potato mixture and Gruyère cheese. Sprinkle with Parmesan cheese.

4 Bake at 400° for 25 to 30 minutes or until bubbly and golden. Yield: 14 (½-cup) servings.

Rosemary Potatoes

YIELD: 4 servings

EXCHANGES PER
SERVING:
1 Starch

PER SERVING:
Calories 66
Carbohydrate 14.8g
Protein 1.9g
Fat 0.2g
Cholesterol 0mg
Fiber 1.5g
Sodium 40mg

2 baking potatoes
3 tablespoons water
1 tablespoon commercial oil-free Italian
   dressing
1 teaspoon dried rosemary, crushed
¼ teaspoon paprika
⅛ teaspoon pepper

1 Cut potatoes in half lengthwise; slice each half into 4 wedges. Combine water and next 4 ingredients in a bowl; add potato wedges, and toss to coat.

2 Place in an 11- x 7- x 1½-inch baking dish lined with aluminum foil. Bake at 400° for 35 minutes or until wedges are tender. Yield: 4 servings.

Garlic Potato Sticks

YIELD: 4 servings

EXCHANGES PER
SERVING:
1 Starch
½ Fat

PER SERVING:
Calories 108
Carbohydrate 19.4g
Protein 2.6g
Fat 2.6g
Cholesterol 0mg
Fiber 1.9g
Sodium 82mg

2 medium baking potatoes (about 1
   pound)
   Vegetable cooking spray
2 teaspoons olive oil
2 cloves garlic, minced
⅛ teaspoon salt
⅛ teaspoon ground red pepper
⅛ teaspoon paprika

1 Cut potatoes into 2- x ¼-inch strips, place strips in a large bowl of ice water until slicing is complete. Drain potato strips; press between paper towels to remove excess moisture.

2 Coat a nonstick skillet with cooking spray; add to oil. Place over medium heat until hot. Add potato strips, and cook 10 minutes. Add garlic, and cook 10 to 15 additional minutes or until potato strips are lightly browned and tender, stirring frequently. Sprinkle with salt, pepper, and paprika. Yield: 4 servings.

Two-Potato Puree

YIELD: 4 servings

1½ cups peeled, cubed baking potato
1 cup peeled, cubed sweet potato
1 tablespoon reduced-calorie margarine
2 tablespoons unsweetened orange juice
1 tablespoon skim milk
⅛ teaspoon salt
⅛ teaspoon ground white pepper

EXCHANGES PER SERVING:
1½ Starch

PER SERVING:
Calories 109
Carbohydrate 21.4g
Protein 2.1g
Fat 2.0g
Cholesterol 0mg
Fiber 2.2g
Sodium 112mg

1 Arrange cubed potatoes in a steamer basket over boiling water. Cover and steam 10 minutes or until tender. Cool slightly.

2 Place potato in a medium bowl; add margarine. Beat at medium speed of an electric mixer 1 to 2 minutes or until mixture is smooth. Gradually add orange juice and milk while beating. Stir in salt and pepper.
Yield: 4 (½-cup) servings.

CITRUS SWEET POTATOES

EXCHANGES PER
SERVING:
1 Starch
½ Fruit

PER SERVING:
Calories 105
Carbohydrate 24.4g
Protein 1.5g
Fat 0.4g
Cholesterol 0mg
Fiber 2.3g
Sodium 13mg

1 pound sweet potatoes
  Vegetable cooking spray
1 tablespoon cornstarch
1 tablespoon granulated brown sugar
  substitute
¾ cup unsweetened orange juice
2 tablespoons lemon juice

1 Peel sweet potatoes; cut into ½-inch-thick slices. Place potato slices in a 1-quart baking dish coated with cooking spray.

2 Combine cornstarch and brown sugar substitute. Add orange juice and lemon juice, stirring well; pour over potato slices.

3 Cover and bake at 425° for 45 to 50 minutes or just until potato slices are tender.
Yield: 5 (½-cup) servings.

SOUFFLÉED POTATOES

YIELD: 4 servings

2 cups peeled, cubed potato
⅓ cup evaporated skimmed milk
3 tablespoons light process cream cheese
¼ teaspoon salt
⅓ cup chopped sweet red pepper
2 tablespoons chopped green onions
⅛ teaspoon ground white pepper
2 egg whites
  Vegetable cooking spray
2 teaspoons grated Parmesan cheese

EXCHANGES PER SERVING:
1 Starch
1 Vegetable

PER SERVING:
Calories 123
Carbohydrate 19.6g
Protein 6.2g
Fat 2.4g
Cholesterol 8mg
Fiber 1.4g
Sodium 276mg

1 Place potato in a saucepan; add water to cover. Bring to a boil. Cover, reduce heat, and simmer 15 minutes or until tender. Drain.

2 Combine potato and milk in a large bowl; beat at medium speed of an electric mixer 1 minute or until smooth. Add cream cheese and salt; beat at low speed until well blended. Stir in red pepper, green onions, and white pepper.

3 Beat egg whites at high speed of an electric mixer until soft peaks form. Gently fold egg whites into potato mixture. Spoon into a 1-quart casserole coated with cooking spray. Bake at 350° for 35 minutes. Sprinkle with Parmesan cheese; bake 5 additional minutes or until cheese is golden. Serve immediately. Yield: 4 (½-cup) servings.

BAKED ACORN SQUASH

YIELD: 4 servings

EXCHANGES PER
SERVING:
1 Starch
1 Vegetable
1 Fat

PER SERVING:
Calories 117
Carbohydrate 20.7g
Protein 1.7g
Fat 4.4g
Cholesterol 0mg
Fiber 2.3g
Sodium 40mg

2 medium acorn squash (about 1 pound)
3 tablespoons granulated brown sugar
   substitute
2 tablespoons unsweetened orange juice
2 teaspoons reduced-calorie margarine,
   melted
¼ teaspoon ground cinnamon
¼ teaspoon ground nutmeg
2 tablespoons finely chopped pecans,
   toasted

1 Cut squash in half crosswise; remove and discard seeds. Place squash halves, cut side down, in a 13- x 9- x 2-inch baking dish. Add water to depth of ½ inch. Bake, uncovered, at 350° for 40 minutes. Remove baking dish from oven, and invert squash halves.

2 Combine brown sugar substitute and next 4 ingredients in a small bowl, stirring well. Spoon brown sugar mixture evenly into squash halves. Bake, uncovered, 20 additional minutes, basting occasionally. Sprinkle with pecans. Yield: 4 servings.

Vegetable & Fruit Side Dishes

PER SERVING:
Calories 105
Carbohydrate 13.1g
Protein 3.7g
Fat 4.9g
Cholesterol 7mg
Fiber 1.0g
Sodium 335mg

ARTICHOKES IN MUSTARD SAUCE

Artichoke hearts are not only for appetizers. Serve this side dish with your favorite baked or broiled meat.

2 (9-ounce) packages frozen artichoke hearts, thawed and drained
¼ cup reduced-calorie mayonnaise
¼ cup low-fat sour cream
2 tablespoons Dijon mustard
1 tablespoon white wine Worcestershire sauce
1 clove garlic, minced
¼ cup fine, dry breadcrumbs
1 tablespoon chopped fresh parsley

1 Place frozen artichoke hearts in a 1-quart casserole.

2 Combine mayonnaise and next 4 ingredients in a small bowl; stir well. Spread mayonnaise mixture evenly over artichokes; sprinkle with breadcrumbs.

3 Bake at 350° for 25 minutes or until thoroughly heated. Remove from oven, and sprinkle with fresh parsley. Yield: 6 servings.

Microwave Instructions: Place frozen artichokes in a 1-quart casserole, and thaw in microwave according to package directions. Drain. Spread mayonnaise mixture evenly over artichokes. Microwave, uncovered, at HIGH 5 minutes, rotating a half-turn after 3 minutes. Sprinkle with breadcrumbs; microwave at HIGH 4 to 5 minutes or until thoroughly heated. Sprinkle with fresh parsley, and serve warm.

super·quick

LEMON-ASPARAGUS PACKETS

½ pound fresh asparagus
2 teaspoons reduced-calorie margarine
¼ teaspoon lemon-pepper seasoning

1 Snap off tough ends of asparagus. Remove scales from stalks with a knife or vegetable peeler, if desired.

2 Place asparagus on a square of heavy-duty aluminum foil. Top asparagus with 2 teaspoons reduced-calorie margarine, and sprinkle with ¼ teaspoon lemon-pepper seasoning. Fold aluminum foil tightly to seal. Place on grill rack, and grill over medium-hot coals 10 minutes. Yield: 2 servings.

YIELD: 2 servings

EXCHANGES PER
SERVING:
1 Vegetable
½ Fat

PER SERVING:
Calories 35
Carbohydrate 2.9g
Protein 1.4g
Fat 2.6g
Cholesterol 0mg
Fiber 1.3g
Sodium 38mg

super·quick

ROASTED ASPARAGUS

1 pound fresh asparagus
Olive-oil flavored vegetable cooking
spray

1 Snap off tough ends of asparagus. Remove scales from stalks with a knife or vegetable peeler, if desired.

2 Coat asparagus with olive oil-flavored cooking spray, and bake at 450° for 10 minutes or until tender. Yield: 4 servings.

YIELD: 4 servings

EXCHANGES PER
SERVING:
1 Vegetable

PER SERVING:
Calories 18
Carbohydrate 2.9g
Protein 1.5g
Fat 1.3g
Cholesterol 0mg
Fiber 1.3g
Sodium 1mg

Asparagus With Almond Sauce

YIELD: 4 servings

EXCHANGES PER
SERVING:
1 Vegetable
1 Fat

PER SERVING:
Calories 71
Carbohydrate 5.9g
Protein 3.2g
Fat 4.7g
Cholesterol 0mg
Fiber 2.4g
Sodium 116mg

Fresh asparagus tastes best in this recipe, but you can use frozen. Use 1 (10-ounce) package frozen asparagus in place of 1 pound fresh.

1 pound fresh asparagus
 Vegetable cooking spray
1 teaspoon margarine
3 tablespoons slivered almonds
⅓ cup water
1 teaspoon cornstarch
2 teaspoons lemon juice
½ teaspoon chicken-flavored bouillon
 granules
 Dash of pepper

1 Snap off tough ends of asparagus. Remove scales from stalks with a knife or vegetable peeler, if desired. Cover and cook in a small amount of boiling water 5 to 7 minutes or until crisp-tender. Drain; arrange asparagus on a serving platter, and keep warm.

2 Coat a small nonstick skillet with cooking spray; add margarine. Place over medium-high heat until margarine melts. Add almonds; sauté 3 to 5 minutes or until lightly browned. Remove skillet from heat, and set aside.

3 Combine water and cornstarch; stir until smooth. Add lemon juice, bouillon granules, and pepper to cornstarch mixture; stir well. Add cornstarch mixture to almonds. Cook over medium heat, stirring constantly, until mixture is thickened. Remove from heat; spoon sauce over asparagus. Serve immediately. Yield: 4 servings.

ASPARAGUS DIJON

YIELD: 6 servings

1½ pounds fresh asparagus spears
1 tablespoon cornstarch
1 cup nonfat buttermilk
2 teaspoons Dijon mustard
¾ teaspoon lemon juice
½ teaspoon dried tarragon
¼ teaspoon ground white pepper
  Fresh tarragon sprig (optional)
  Lemon slices (optional)

EXCHANGES PER SERVING:
1 Vegetable

PER SERVING:
Calories 42
Carbohydrate 7.4g
Protein 3.5g
Fat 0.4g
Cholesterol 1mg
Fiber 1.8g
Sodium 94mg

1 Snap off tough ends of asparagus. Remove scales from spears with a vegetable peeler, if desired. Arrange asparagus in a steamer basket over boiling water. Cover and steam 7 minutes or until crisp-tender. Set aside, and keep warm.

2 Combine cornstarch and buttermilk in a small saucepan; stir well. Cook over medium heat until thickened and bubbly, stirring constantly. Remove from heat; stir in mustard and remaining 3 ingredients.

3 Arrange asparagus on a serving platter. Spoon sauce over asparagus. If desired, garnish with tarragon sprig and lemon slices. Serve immediately. Yield: 6 servings.

SAVORY ITALIAN ASPARAGUS

YIELD: 4 servings

EXCHANGES PER
SERVING:
1 Vegetable

PER SERVING:
Calories 32
Carbohydrate 5.1g
Protein 2.9g
Fat 0.7g
Cholesterol 1mg
Fiber 1.3g
Sodium 35mg

To prepare asparagus for cooking, hold the stalk and snap off the end where it seems to break naturally. The end removed is the tough part; the remaining stalk should be tender after cooking.

1 pound fresh asparagus
1 medium tomato, seeded and chopped
2 tablespoons chopped green onions
⅛ teaspoon dried oregano
⅛ teaspoon dried thyme
⅛ teaspoon pepper
2 teaspoons freshly grated Parmesan cheese

1 Snap off tough ends of asparagus. Remove scales with a knife or vegetable peeler, if desired. Arrange asparagus in a vegetable steamer over boiling water. Cover and steam 4 minutes or until crisp-tender. Drain; arrange on a serving platter, and keep warm.

2 Combine tomato and next 4 ingredients in a small bowl; stir well. Spoon tomato mixture over asparagus; sprinkle with cheese. Yield: 4 servings.

Microwave Instructions: To microwave asparagus, snap off tough ends and remove scales with a vegetable peeler, if desired. Arrange spears in an 11- x 7- x 1½-inch baking dish with stem ends toward outside of dish; add ¼ cup water. Cover with heavy-duty plastic wrap, and vent. Microwave at HIGH 6 to 7 minutes or until crisp-tender. Let stand, covered, 1 minute; drain. Proceed with recipe as directed.

GREEN BEAN CASSEROLE

YIELD: 8 servings

Vegetable cooking spray
1/4 cup finely chopped onion
2 tablespoons all-purpose flour
1 cup skim milk
1/2 cup (2 ounces) shredded reduced-fat, reduced-sodium Swiss cheese
1/2 cup low-fat sour cream
1 teaspoon granulated sugar substitute
1/2 teaspoon salt
2 (9-ounce) packages frozen French-style green beans, thawed and drained
1 egg white, lightly beaten
1 1/2 cups herb-seasoned stuffing mix
2 teaspoons margarine, melted

EXCHANGES PER SERVING:
1 Starch
2 Vegetable
1 Fat

PER SERVING:
Calories 176
Carbohydrate 26.9g
Protein 8.1g
Fat 4.5g
Cholesterol 9mg
Fiber 0.2g
Sodium 563mg

1 Coat a medium saucepan with cooking spray; place over medium heat until hot. Add onion to pan; sauté 5 minutes or until onion is tender.

2 Add flour to saucepan, and cook, stirring constantly, 1 minute. Gradually add milk, stirring until blended. Stir in cheese and next 3 ingredients. Cook, stirring constantly, 5 minutes or until mixture is thickened and bubbly.

3 Place beans in an 8-inch square baking dish, and pour cheese sauce over beans. Combine egg white, stuffing mix, and margarine in a medium bowl. Stir well, and sprinkle over green bean mixture. Bake at 350° for 25 minutes or until thoroughly heated. Yield: 8 (1/2-cup) servings.

✿ When selecting olive oil, keep in mind how much olive flavor appeals to you. Virgin and extra virgin have the most olive flavor. Pure, refined, and extra light olive oils are milder. All olive oils contain the same amount of beneficial monounsaturated fat and the same number of calories.

PEASANT-STYLE GREEN BEANS

Two flavors of southern French cooking–olive oil and garlic–give this simple summer vegetable a foreign accent. It goes well with broiled chicken.

1 pound fresh green beans
1 tablespoon olive oil
1 cup chopped onion
2 cloves garlic, crushed
1 (14½-ounce) can no-salt-added whole
   tomatoes, drained and chopped
⅓ cup dry red wine
½ teaspoon dried oregano
½ teaspoon pepper

1 Wash beans; trim ends, and remove strings. Arrange beans in a vegetable steamer over boiling water. Cover and steam 5 minutes or until crisp-tender. Set aside, and keep warm.

2 Heat oil in a large nonstick skillet over medium-high heat until hot. Add onion and garlic; cook until tender. Add tomatoes and remaining ingredients. Cook over low heat 15 minutes, stirring occasionally. Remove from heat; add beans, tossing well to combine. Yield: 7 (½-cup) servings.

Green Beans Parmesan

YIELD: 2 servings

1 teaspoon reduced-calorie margarine
1 large shallot, sliced and separated
   into rings
½ pound fresh green beans
½ cup canned low-sodium chicken broth,
   undiluted
2 tablespoons shaved fresh Parmesan
   cheese

1 Melt margarine in a small nonstick skillet over medium-heat. Add shallot; cook 10 to 12 minutes or until golden, stirring occasionally. Remove from heat, and set aside.

2 Wash beans; trim ends, and remove strings. Place beans and broth in a medium saucepan; bring mixture to a boil. Cover, reduce heat, and simmer 12 to 14 minutes or until beans are tender. Drain beans, and stir in shallot. Transfer to a serving dish, and sprinkle with cheese. Yield: 2 (1-cup) servings.

EXCHANGES PER SERVING:
2 Vegetable
½ Fat

PER SERVING:
Calories 81
Carbohydrate 9.4g
Protein 4.8g
Fat 3.2g
Cholesterol 5mg
Fiber 2.4g
Sodium 140mg

✒ To shave Parmesan cheese into thin slivers, use a vegetable peeler and pull it across the top of a wedge of fresh Parmesan.

ROASTED GREEN BEANS

YIELD: 2 servings

EXCHANGES PER
SERVING:
1 Vegetable

PER SERVING:
Calories 52
Carbohydrate 9.0g
Protein 2.2g
Fat 1.6g
Cholesterol 0mg
Fiber 2.5g
Sodium 7mg

½ pound fresh green beans
1 clove garlic, sliced
  Olive oil-flavored vegetable cooking
  spray
1 teaspoon lemon juice
½ teaspoon olive oil
1 teaspoon salt-free lemon-pepper
  seasoning

1 Wash beans, and trim ends. Place beans in a 13- x 9- x 2-inch pan; add garlic. Coat beans and garlic with cooking spray; toss well. Drizzle lemon juice and olive oil over beans and garlic; sprinkle with lemon-pepper seasoning.

2 Bake, uncovered, at 450° for 8 minutes or until beans are crisp-tender, stirring once. Yield: 2 servings.

SEASONED GREEN BEANS

YIELD: 6 servings

EXCHANGES PER
SERVING:
2 Vegetable

PER SERVING:
Calories 56
Carbohydrate 7.6g
Protein 4.8g
Fat 0.9g
Cholesterol 8mg
Fiber 1.9g
Sodium 340mg

1 pound fresh green beans
1 cup canned no-salt-added beef broth
1 medium onion, chopped
⅓ cup chopped lean cooked ham
¼ teaspoon salt
¼ teaspoon freshly ground pepper

1 Wash beans, and trim ends. Cut beans into 1½-inch pieces.

2 Combine beans, broth, and remaining ingredients in a saucepan. Bring to a boil; cover, reduce heat, and simmer 25 minutes or until beans are tender, stirring occasionally. Yield: 6 servings.

ORANGE-GLAZED BEETS

¾ cup unsweetened orange juice
1 tablespoon cornstarch
½ teaspoon grated orange rind
¼ teaspoon ground ginger
⅛ teaspoon salt
1 (15-ounce) can whole beets, undrained
Orange zest (optional)

1 Combine first 5 ingredients in a medium saucepan; stir until blended.

2 Add beets to saucepan. Bring to a boil over medium heat; cook 1 minute or until sauce thickens, stirring constantly. Garnish with orange zest, if desired. Yield: 4 servings.

YIELD: 4 servings

EXCHANGES PER SERVING:
1 Starch

PER SERVING:
Calories 62
Carbohydrate 15.0g
Protein 1.2g
Fat 0.1g
Cholesterol 0mg
Fiber 0.8g
Sodium 116mg

SPICED BEETS

1½ pounds medium beets
½ cup low-sugar apricot spread
2 tablespoons lemon juice
½ teaspoon ground ginger
¼ teaspoon ground nutmeg

1 Leave root and 1 inch of stem on beets; scrub with a vegetable brush. Place beets in a large saucepan; add water to cover. Bring to a boil; cover, reduce heat, and simmer 35 to 40 minutes or until tender. Drain; pour cold water over beets, and drain. Trim off stems and roots, and rub off skin. Dice beets, and set aside.

2 Combine apricot spread and remaining 3 ingredients in a medium nonstick skillet; stir well. Cook over low heat until spread melts. Add beets, and cook over medium heat until thoroughly heated. Yield: 6 (½-cup) servings.

YIELD: 6 servings

EXCHANGES PER SERVING:
1 Starch

PER SERVING:
Calories 73
Carbohydrate 17.7g
Protein 1.4g
Fat 0.2g
Cholesterol 0mg
Fiber 0.6g
Sodium 482mg

YIELD: 6 servings

EXCHANGES PER
SERVING:
1 Vegetable
1 Fat

PER SERVING:
Calories 86
Carbohydrate 7.7g
Protein 5.7g
Fat 4.3g
Cholesterol 9mg
Fiber 2.5g
Sodium 169mg

BROCCOLI WITH PARMESAN SAUCE

1½ pounds fresh broccoli
 1 cup water
   Vegetable cooking spray
¼ cup chopped sweet red pepper
¼ cup chopped onion
 1 tablespoon margarine
 2 teaspoons all-purpose flour
¾ cup skim milk
 2 ounces light process cream cheese
¼ cup grated Parmesan cheese
¼ teaspoon garlic powder

1 Trim off large leaves of broccoli. Remove tough ends of lower stalks, and wash broccoli thoroughly. Cut into spears. Place spears in a Dutch oven; add water. Bring to a boil; cover, reduce heat, and simmer 10 to 15 minutes or until crisp-tender. Drain; arrange on a serving platter, and keep warm.

2 Coat a large nonstick skillet with cooking spray; place over medium heat until hot. Add red pepper and onion; sauté until tender. Remove from skillet, and set aside.

3 Melt margarine in skillet; stir in flour. Gradually add milk. Cook, stirring constantly, until slightly thickened. Add red pepper and onion, cream cheese, Parmesan cheese, and garlic powder; cook over low heat, stirring constantly, until smooth and thoroughly heated. Spoon over broccoli. Serve immediately. Yield: 6 servings.

super·quick

SZECHUAN BROCCOLI

YIELD: 4 servings

1 tablespoon low-sodium soy sauce
1 tablespoon cider vinegar
½ teaspoon granulated sugar substitute
1 tablespoon sesame seeds
2 teaspoons vegetable oil
¼ teaspoon crushed red pepper
½ teaspoon peeled, minced gingerroot
2 cloves garlic, minced
5 cups coarsely chopped broccoli

EXCHANGES PER SERVING:
2 Vegetable
½ Fat

PER SERVING:
Calories 70
Carbohydrate 8.0g
Protein 4.2g
Fat 3.6g
Cholesterol 0mg
Fiber 2.9g
Sodium 115mg

1 Combine first 3 ingredients in a small bowl; set aside.

2 Place a large nonstick skillet over medium heat until hot. Add sesame seeds; cook 1 minute or until browned. Remove seeds, and set aside.

3 Add oil to skillet; place over medium-high heat until hot. Add red pepper, gingerroot, and garlic; sauté 30 seconds. Add broccoli; sauté 1 minute. Add soy sauce mixture; stir well. Cover and cook 2 minutes or until broccoli is crisp-tender. Sprinkle with sesame seeds. Yield: 4 (1-cup) servings.

One stalk of broccoli has more calcium than ½ cup cottage cheese and more vitamin C than a navel orange. Broccoli is also a good source of iron, folic acid, and fiber.

YIELD: 8 servings

EXCHANGES PER
SERVING:
1 Vegetable

PER SERVING:
Calories 42
Carbohydrate 8.5g
Protein 2.2g
Fat 0.5g
Cholesterol 0mg
Fiber 2.7g
Sodium 37mg

BRUSSELS SPROUTS WITH CHESTNUTS

Unlike other nuts, chestnuts are low in fat. Their texture is a cross between a potato and peanut, and their flavor complements vegetable side dishes like this one.

2 (8-ounce) packages frozen brussels sprouts
1 teaspoon reduced-calorie margarine
12 shelled chestnuts, quartered
4 shallots, cut in half lengthwise and thinly sliced crosswise
½ cup unsweetened orange juice
¼ cup water
1 tablespoon brown sugar substitute
½ teaspoon chicken-flavored bouillon granules
⅛ teaspoon pepper

1 Cook brussels sprouts according to package directions, omitting salt. Drain and set aside.

2 Melt margarine in a large skillet over medium-high heat. Add chestnuts and shallot; sauté 5 minutes or until tender.

3 Combine orange juice and remaining 4 ingredients in a small bowl; stir well. Add orange juice mixture to chestnut mixture. Bring to a boil; reduce heat, and simmer 3 minutes. Stir in brussels sprouts; cook 5 minutes, stirring occasionally. Serve with a slotted spoon. Yield: 8 (½-cup) servings.

Cabbage Au Gratin

7¼ cups chopped cabbage
3 tablespoons reduced-calorie margarine
3 tablespoons all-purpose flour
1¼ cups skim milk
¼ teaspoon salt
¼ teaspoon ground white pepper
⅛ teaspoon ground nutmeg
¼ cup (1 ounce) shredded Swiss cheese
¼ cup grated Parmesan cheese
Vegetable cooking spray
2 tablespoons fine, dry breadcrumbs

1 Cover and cook cabbage in a small amount of boiling water in a large saucepan 10 minutes or until tender. Drain well, and set aside.

2 Melt margarine in a large saucepan over medium-low heat; add flour, stirring with a wire whisk until smooth. Cook 1 minute, stirring constantly. Gradually add milk; cook over medium heat, stirring constantly, until thickened and bubbly. Stir in salt, pepper, and nutmeg. Add cabbage and cheeses; stir well.

3 Spoon mixture into a 1½-quart baking dish coated with cooking spray. Sprinkle with breadcrumbs. Bake at 375° for 20 minutes or until thoroughly heated and bubbly. Yield: 8 (½-cup) servings.

YIELD: 8 servings

EXCHANGES PER
SERVING:
2 Vegetable
1 Fat

PER SERVING:
Calories 94
Carbohydrate 9.0g
Protein 4.6g
Fat 4.8g
Cholesterol 6mg
Fiber 1.7g
Sodium 216mg

✿ To avoid the blue color that sometimes occurs when cooking red cabbage, cut the cabbage with a long-blade stainless steel knife or use the slicing disc of a food processor. Adding an acid such as vinegar during cooking helps maintain the rich color of red cabbage.

SWEET-AND-SOUR RED CABBAGE

Firm apples such as Granny Smith hold up best in this vegetable side dish. Or try a less tart Jonathan, Rome, or Winesap apple.

1 medium Granny Smith apple, cored and
  sliced
2 tablespoons lemon juice
  Vegetable cooking spray
1 small onion, sliced and separated into
  rings
5 cups shredded red cabbage
¼ cup unsweetened white grape juice
2 tablespoons dry white wine
2 tablespoons balsamic vinegar
¼ teaspoon salt
⅛ teaspoon pepper

1 Combine sliced apple and lemon juice in a small bowl; toss gently, and set aside.

2 Coat a large nonstick skillet with cooking spray; place over medium-high heat until hot. Add onion; sauté until tender. Add cabbage; sauté 3 to 4 minutes or until crisp-tender.

3 Add apple mixture, grape juice, and remaining ingredients; stir gently. Cook 1 to 2 minutes or until thoroughly heated. Transfer to a serving bowl, using a slotted spoon. Yield: 10 (½-cup) servings.

super·quick

LEMON-DILL BABY CARROTS

1 (16-ounce) package fresh or frozen baby
    carrots
1 tablespoon lemon juice
1 teaspoon cornstarch
⅓ cup water
1 teaspoon dried dillweed
1 teaspoon reduced-calorie margarine
¼ teaspoon grated lemon rind
⅛ teaspoon salt
    Dash of pepper
    Fresh dill sprigs (optional)

YIELD: 5 servings

**EXCHANGES PER
SERVING:**
2 Vegetable

PER SERVING:
Calories 43
Carbohydrate 9.0g
Protein 1.0g
Fat 0.7g
Cholesterol 0mg
Fiber 1.3g
Sodium 120mg

1 Cook carrots according to package directions, omitting salt. Drain and set aside.

2 Combine lemon juice and cornstarch in a medium saucepan; stir until smooth. Gradually add water; cook over medium heat, stirring constantly, 1 minute or until thickened. Remove from heat; stir in dried dillweed and next 4 ingredients. Add carrots, and toss gently. Transfer to a serving bowl. Garnish with dill sprigs, if desired. Yield: 5 servings.

CAULIFLOWER WITH CHEESE SAUCE

YIELD: 10 servings

EXCHANGES PER SERVING:
½ Medium-Fat Meat
1 Vegetable

PER SERVING:
Calories 75
Carbohydrate 7.0g
Protein 5.4g
Fat 3.3g
Cholesterol 7mg
Fiber 2.0g
Sodium 213mg

1 large cauliflower (about 2½ pounds)
2 cups water
    Vegetable cooking spray
2 tablespoons minced green pepper
1 tablespoon minced onion
2 tablespoons margarine
2 tablespoons all-purpose flour
1 cup skim milk
6 (⅔-ounce) slices low-fat process
    American cheese, cut into strips
¼ teaspoon dry mustard
⅛ teaspoon ground white pepper
2 teaspoons chopped fresh parsley

1 Remove and discard outer leaves and stalk of cauliflower. Wash cauliflower, leaving head whole. Place cauliflower in a large saucepan; add water. Bring to a boil; cover, reduce heat, and cook 10 to 12 minutes or until tender. Drain well. Place cauliflower on a serving platter, and keep warm.

2 Coat a small nonstick skillet with cooking spray. Place over medium-high heat until hot. Add green pepper and onion; cook until tender. Set aside.

3 Melt margarine in skillet over low heat; add flour, stirring until smooth. Cook 1 minute, stirring constantly. Gradually add milk; cook over medium heat, stirring constantly, until mixture is thickened and bubbly. Add cheese, mustard, and white pepper, stirring until cheese melts. Remove from heat; stir in vegetables.

4 Spoon sauce over cauliflower; sprinkle with parsley. Serve immediately.
Yield: 10 servings.

CURRIED CAULIFLOWER

YIELD: 5 servings

Choose cauliflower that's firm and white or creamy white in color. Yellow leaves and spreading flower clusters indicate poor quality.

Vegetable cooking spray
1½ teaspoons vegetable oil
⅓ cup thinly sliced green onions
1½ teaspoons curry powder
½ teaspoon garlic powder
¼ teaspoon salt
1 large sweet red pepper, seeded and cut into ¼-inch squares
1 medium cauliflower (about 2 pounds), broken into flowerets
½ cup water

EXCHANGES PER SERVING:
2 Vegetable

PER SERVING:
Calories 55
Carbohydrate 8.7g
Protein 3.0g
Fat 1.9g
Cholesterol 0mg
Fiber 3.8g
Sodium 158mg

1 Coat a large nonstick skillet with cooking spray; add oil. Place over medium-high heat until hot. Add green onions, and sauté 1 minute. Add curry powder, garlic powder, and salt; sauté 30 seconds. Add red pepper, and sauté 1 minute.

2 Add cauliflower and water; stir well. Cover, reduce heat, and simmer 15 minutes or until cauliflower is crisp-tender, stirring occasionally. Yield: 5 (1-cup) servings.

CELERY BAKE

YIELD: 8 servings

EXCHANGES PER
SERVING:
2 Vegetable
1 Fat

PER SERVING:
Calories 99
Carbohydrate 11.9g
Protein 2.8g
Fat 5.0g
Cholesterol 0mg
Fiber 1.3g
Sodium 255mg

To ease the dinnertime rush, you can
assemble the casserole the night before,
and refrigerate it overnight.

2¾ cups diagonally sliced celery
1 (10½-ounce) can low-sodium cream
   of mushroom soup, undiluted
1 (8-ounce) can sliced water chestnuts,
   drained
1 (2-ounce) jar diced pimiento, drained
   Vegetable cooking spray
½ cup Italian-seasoned breadcrumbs
¼ cup slivered almonds, toasted
1 tablespoon reduced-calorie margarine,
   melted
   Green onion fan (optional)
   Fresh mushroom slices (optional)

1 Combine first 4 ingredients in a large bowl;
stir well. Spoon mixture into a 1-quart baking dish coated with cooking spray.

2 Combine breadcrumbs, almonds, and margarine in a small bowl; stir well. Sprinkle
over celery mixture.

3 Bake, uncovered, at 400° for 30 minutes
or until celery is tender. Let stand 5 minutes before serving. If desired, garnish with
a green onion fan and mushroom slices.
Yield: 8 (½-cup) servings.

Italiano Eggplant and Squash

Vegetable cooking spray
1 teaspoon olive oil
½ cup chopped onion
1 (8-ounce) package fresh mushrooms
2 (14½-ounce) cans no-salt-added whole
    tomatoes, undrained and chopped
1 medium eggplant, cubed
1 medium-size green pepper, seeded and
    cut into pieces
2 cloves garlic, minced
½ teaspoon dried Italian seasoning
⅛ teaspoon salt
⅛ teaspoon pepper
1 (10-ounce) package frozen sliced yellow
    squash, thawed and drained
8 ripe olives, halved
1 tablespoon red wine vinegar
2 teaspoons dried parsley flakes

1 Coat a Dutch oven with cooking spray; add olive oil. Place over medium-high heat until hot. Add onion and mushrooms; sauté 5 minutes or until vegetables are tender.

2 Add tomato and next 6 ingredients. Bring to a boil. Reduce heat, and simmer 5 minutes; add squash and simmer 15 additional minutes or until vegetables are tender. Stir in olives, vinegar, and parsley. Cook until thoroughly heated. Yield: 8 servings.

YIELD: 8 servings

EXCHANGES PER SERVING:
2 Vegetable

PER SERVING:
Calories 66
Carbohydrate 12.8g
Protein 2.7g
Fat 1.4g
Cholesterol 0mg
Fiber 2.3g
Sodium 92mg

✖ In addition to dark purple eggplant, other varieties are available. Italian eggplant resembles the common type in shape; it has a delicate skin and fine flesh. White eggplant usually has a tougher skin and is less bitter. Oriental eggplant is slender, straight, and often sweeter and smoother than larger eggplant.

YIELD: 4 servings

EXCHANGES PER
SERVING:
1 Vegetable
1 Fat

PER SERVING:
Calories 64
Carbohydrate 7.4g
Protein 1.6g
Fat 3.5g
Cholesterol 0mg
Fiber 1.9g
Sodium 5mg

super·quick

GRILLED ANTIPASTO

1 medium-size sweet red pepper
1 small eggplant (about ½ pound)
1 small zucchini
1 small yellow squash
2 tablespoons red wine vinegar
1 tablespoon olive oil
½ teaspoon dried oregano
⅛ teaspoon pepper
　Vegetable cooking spray

1 Cut red pepper lengthwise into quarters. Remove and discard membranes and seeds. Cut eggplant into ½-inch-thick slices. Cut zucchini and squash lengthwise into quarters.

2 Combine vinegar and next 3 ingredients in a small bowl; stir well with a wire whisk. Brush vegetables with oil mixture.

3 Coat grill rack with cooking spray; place on grill over medium-hot coals (350° to 400°). Place vegetables on rack, and grill, uncovered, 2 minutes or until crisp-tender, turning occasionally. Yield: 4 (¾-cup) servings.

super·quick

OKRA-TOMATO-ZUCCHINI MEDLEY

1 small zucchini
  Vegetable cooking spray
1½ cups sliced fresh okra
  2 tablespoons chopped onion
  1 cup seeded, chopped tomato
  ⅛ teaspoon dried basil
  ⅛ teaspoon dried thyme
  Dash of freshly ground pepper

YIELD: 4 servings

EXCHANGES PER SERVING:
1 Vegetable

PER SERVING:
Calories 31
Carbohydrate 6.3g
Protein 1.5g
Fat 0.4g
Cholesterol 0mg
Fiber 1.3g
Sodium 8mg

1 Cut zucchini in half lengthwise; cut into ¼-inch-thick slices.

2 Coat a nonstick skillet with cooking spray; place over medium-high heat until hot. Add zucchini, okra, and onion; sauté 4 minutes. Stir in tomato and remaining ingredients. Cover and cook over low heat 5 minutes or until thoroughly heated, stirring often. Yield: 4 (½-cup) servings.

STEWED OKRA AND TOMATOES

  Vegetable cooking spray
½ cup finely chopped onion
¼ cup finely chopped green pepper
  2 cups sliced fresh okra
  2 cups seeded, coarsely chopped tomato
  1 tablespoon lemon juice
  1 teaspoon dried oregano
¼ teaspoon salt
¼ teaspoon hot sauce

YIELD: 6 servings

EXCHANGES PER SERVING:
2 Vegetable

PER SERVING:
Calories 44
Carbohydrate 9.0g
Protein 1.9g
Fat 0.4g
Cholesterol 0mg
Fiber 1.7g
Sodium 110mg

1 Coat a medium saucepan with cooking spray; place over medium heat until hot. Add onion and green pepper; sauté 2 minutes. Add okra and remaining ingredients. Cover and cook over medium-low heat 15 minutes or until okra is tender, stirring occasionally. Yield: 6 (½-cup) servings.

CHEESY SCALLOPED ONIONS

YIELD: 6 servings

EXCHANGES PER
SERVING:
1 Starch
1 Vegetable
1 Fat

PER SERVING:
Calories 145
Carbohydrate 19.7g
Protein 7.2g
Fat 4.8g
Cholesterol 7mg
Fiber 3.1g
Sodium 247mg

4 large Vidalia or other sweet onions,
   thinly sliced
2 tablespoons reduced-calorie margarine
2 tablespoons all-purpose flour
1½ cups skim milk
½ cup (2 ounces) shredded reduced-fat
   sharp Cheddar cheese
1½ tablespoons chopped fresh parsley
½ teaspoon dry mustard
¼ teaspoon salt
¼ teaspoon freshly ground pepper
   Vegetable cooking spray
1½ tablespoons soft breadcrumbs, toasted
   Chopped fresh parsley (optional)

1 Separate onion into rings. Cook onion in boiling water to cover 5 minutes or until tender. Drain well.

2 Melt margarine in a medium saucepan over medium heat; add flour. Cook 1 minute, stirring constantly with a wire whisk. Gradually add milk, stirring constantly. Cook, stirring constantly, 10 additional minutes or until thickened and bubbly. Add onion, cheese, and next 4 ingredients; stir well.

3 Spoon mixture into a shallow 1½-quart baking dish coated with cooking spray; sprinkle with breadcrumbs. Bake, uncovered, at 375° for 20 minutes or until bubbly. Sprinkle with additional chopped parsley, if desired. Yield: 6 servings.

SAUTÉED SUGAR SNAP PEAS

Vegetable cooking spray
2 teaspoons reduced-calorie margarine
¼ cup chopped purple onion
2 cups frozen Sugar Snap peas, thawed
¼ teaspoon garlic powder
⅛ teaspoon salt
⅛ teaspoon ground white pepper

1 Coat a nonstick skillet with cooking spray; add margarine, and place over medium heat until hot. Add onion, and sauté 2 to 3 minutes or until tender.

2 Add peas and remaining ingredients; sauté 3 to 4 minutes or until peas are tender. Yield: 4 (½-cup) servings.

YIELD: 4 servings

EXCHANGES PER SERVING:
1 Vegetable

PER SERVING:
Calories 47
Carbohydrate 6.7g
Protein 2.1g
Fat 1.5g
Cholesterol 0mg
Fiber 2.1g
Sodium 95mg

---

super·quick

SUGAR SNAP PEAS WITH PAPAYA SALSA

½ cup peeled, seeded, and diced papaya
¼ cup chopped fresh cilantro
½ tablespoon minced onion
1 teaspoon lime juice
1 teaspoon rice wine vinegar
Dash of salt
Dash of ground white pepper
½ pound fresh Sugar Snap peas, trimmed

1 Combine first 7 ingredients in a small bowl; toss lightly, and set aside.

2 Arrange peas in a steamer basket over boiling water. Cover and steam 3 minutes or until peas are crisp-tender. Drain well. Transfer peas to a bowl, and top with papaya mixture. Yield: 4 (½-cup) servings.

YIELD: 4 servings

EXCHANGES PER SERVING:
1 Vegetable

PER SERVING:
Calories 34
Carbohydrate 6.8g
Protein 1.8g
Fat 0.2g
Cholesterol 0mg
Fiber 2.0g
Sodium 41mg

HERBED PEPPER MEDLEY

YIELD: 2 servings

EXCHANGES PER
SERVING:
1 Vegetable

PER SERVING:
Calories 42
Carbohydrate 8.5g
Protein 1.3g
Fat 0.8g
Cholesterol 0mg
Fiber 2.2g
Sodium 154mg

1 medium-size sweet red pepper
1 medium-size sweet yellow pepper
1 medium-size green pepper
  Olive oil-flavored vegetable cooking
  spray
½ cup onion strips
1 tablespoon canned low-sodium chicken
  broth
½ teaspoon granulated sugar substitute
⅛ tablespoon salt
⅛ teaspoon dried thyme
  Fresh thyme sprigs (optional)

1 Cut peppers in half lengthwise through stems. Remove and discard seeds and membranes. If desired, set 2 pepper halves with stems aside, and reserve third half for another use. Remove and discard stems from remaining 3 pepper halves; slice pepper halves into thin strips.

2 Coat a medium nonstick skillet with cooking spray; place over medium-high heat until hot. Add pepper strips and onion; sauté 4 minutes. Add chicken broth and remaining 3 ingredients; sauté 2 minutes. If desired, spoon pepper mixture evenly into reserved pepper halves. Garnish with thyme sprigs, if desired. Yield: 2 servings.

POTATO-ZUCCHINI PANCAKES

Leaving the peel on the potato and zucchini adds color, flavor, and fiber to this vegetable side dish.

- 4 egg whites, lightly beaten
- 3 tablespoons all-purpose flour
- 1 tablespoon fine, dry breadcrumbs
- 1/4 teaspoon baking powder
- 1/4 teaspoon salt
- 1/8 teaspoon ground white pepper
- 2 1/2 cups shredded baking potato (about 2 medium)
- 2 cups shredded zucchini (about 2 medium)
- 1/2 cup finely chopped onion
  Vegetable cooking spray
  Fresh parsley sprigs (optional)

1 Combine first 6 ingredients in a large bowl; stir well with a wire whisk. Fold in potato, zucchini, and onion.

2 Coat a large nonstick skillet with cooking spray; place over medium-high heat until hot. For each pancake, spoon 1/4 cup batter into hot skillet; flatten to 3-inch rounds. Turn pancakes after 3 minutes. Cook 3 to 4 additional minutes or until pancakes are golden. Transfer to a serving platter, and garnish with parsley sprigs, if desired. Yield: 15 pancakes.

YIELD: 15 pancakes

EXCHANGES PER PANCAKE:
1 Vegetable

PER SERVING:
Calories 42
Carbohydrate 8.1g
Protein 2.2g
Fat 0.2g
Cholesterol 0mg
Fiber 0.8g
Sodium 60mg

🍃 Shred potatoes with a hand grater or in a food processor. If you use a food processor, press the shredded potato gently between paper towels to absorb excess moisture.

DILLED SPINACH WITH FETA

YIELD: 4 servings

EXCHANGES PER
SERVING:
1 Vegetable

PER SERVING:
Calories 52
Carbohydrate 5.9g
Protein 5.2g
Fat 2.0g
Cholesterol 6mg
Fiber 5.7g
Sodium 192mg

1 tablespoon water
2 (10-ounce) packages fresh spinach
¼ cup crumbled feta cheese
2 tablespoons chopped fresh dillweed
1 tablespoon fresh lemon juice
⅛ teaspoon freshly ground pepper
 Lemon slices (optional)
 Fresh dillweed sprigs (optional)

1 Place water and spinach in a Dutch oven. Bring to a boil; cover and cook over medium heat 2 to 3 minutes or just until spinach wilts. Add cheese and next 3 ingredients; toss well. If desired, garnish with lemon slices and dillweed sprigs. Yield: 4 (1-cup) servings.

SIMPLE SESAME SPINACH

YIELD: 4 servings

EXCHANGES PER
SERVING:
1 Vegetable

PER SERVING:
Calories 40
Carbohydrate 4.6g
Protein 3.9g
Fat 1.7g
Cholesterol 0mg
Fiber 4.6g
Sodium 236mg

1 pound fresh spinach
 Vegetable cooking spray
1 tablespoon sesame seeds, toasted
1 teaspoon lemon juice
¼ teaspoon salt

1 Remove and discard stems from spinach. Wash spinach, and pat dry with paper towels.

2 Coat a Dutch oven with cooking spray; place over medium heat until hot. Add spinach; cover and cook until spinach wilts, stirring occasionally. Remove from heat, and stir in sesame seeds, lemon juice, and salt. Toss lightly. Yield: 4 (½-cup) servings.

super·quick
SPINACH CAESAR SAUTÉ

For a change of pace, try this sautéed version of a Caesar salad.

1 pound fresh spinach
1 tablespoon white wine vinegar
1 large garlic clove, crushed
½ teaspoon anchovy paste
¼ teaspoon white wine Worcestershire sauce
¼ teaspoon country-style Dijon mustard
⅛ teaspoon freshly ground pepper
   Vegetable cooking spray
2 teaspoons olive oil
⅓ cup commercial seasoned croutons
1 tablespoon freshly grated Parmesan cheese

1 Remove stems from spinach; wash leaves, and pat dry thoroughly with paper towels. Set spinach aside.

2 Combine vinegar and next 5 ingredients in a small bowl, stirring well.

3 Coat a large Dutch oven with cooking spray; add to oil. Place over medium-high heat until hot. Add spinach and vinegar mixture; cook 2 minutes or until spinach begins to wilt, stirring constantly. (Do not overcook.)

4 Transfer to a serving bowl; top with croutons and Parmesan cheese. Serve immediately. Yield: 8 (½-cup) servings.

YIELD: 8 servings

EXCHANGES PER SERVING:
1 Vegetable

PER SERVING:
Calories 39
Carbohydrate 3.5g
Protein 2.1g
Fat 2.1g
Cholesterol 1mg
Fiber 2.0g
Sodium 103mg

✎ Spinach is available at the supermarket in ½-pound or 1-pound bags or bunches. Some stores also offer it loose leaf, so you can bag your own. Look for spinach with crisp, dark green leaves. Avoid spinach with leaves that are spotty, limp, or yellow.

SPINACH SOUFFLÉ

YIELD: 6 servings

EXCHANGES PER
SERVING:
1 Medium-Fat Meat
1 Vegetable

PER SERVING:
Calories 116
Carbohydrate 8.3g
Protein 8.2g
Fat 5.9g
Cholesterol 113mg
Fiber 1.6g
Sodium 272mg

Vegetable cooking spray
2 tablespoons reduced-calorie margarine
3 tablespoons all-purpose flour
1 cup skim milk
2 teaspoons cornstarch
1 tablespoon water
¼ teaspoon salt
   Dash of ground red pepper
   Dash of ground nutmeg
3 egg yolks
1 (10-ounce) package frozen chopped
   spinach, thawed and well drained
5 egg whites
¼ teaspoon cream of tartar
2 tablespoons grated Parmesan cheese

1 Cut a piece of foil to fit around a 1-quart soufflé dish; allow a 1-inch overlap. Fold lengthwise into thirds. Coat 1 side of foil and bottom of dish with cooking spray. Wrap foil around outside of dish, coated side against dish. Allow foil to extend 3 inches above rim. Secure with string.

2 Melt margarine in a saucepan over medium heat; stir in flour. Cook 1 minute, stirring constantly. Add milk; cook, stirring constantly, until thickened and bubbly. Combine cornstarch and water, stirring well; add to milk mixture. Cook over low heat 1 minute, stirring constantly. Stir in salt, pepper, and nutmeg.

3 Beat yolks until thick. Stir about one-fourth of hot milk mixture into yolks; add to remaining hot mixture. Cook 3 minutes, stirring constantly. Transfer to a bowl; stir in spinach.

4 Beat egg whites at high speed of an electric mixer until foamy. Add cream of tartar; beat until stiff peaks form. Fold egg whites into spinach. Spoon into dish. Sprinkle with cheese. Bake at 375° for 30 minutes. Remove foil. Serve immediately. Yield: 6 servings.

Broiled Squash

YIELD: 4 servings

2 large yellow squash
2 teaspoons chopped green chiles
1 teaspoon chopped pimiento
¼ teaspoon garlic powder
¼ teaspoon ground white pepper
⅛ teaspoon dried thyme
⅛ teaspoon dried oregano
1 tablespoon plus 1 teaspoon fine, dry
   breadcrumbs
   Vegetable cooking spray
   Fresh oregano sprigs (optional)

EXCHANGES PER SERVING:
1 Vegetable

PER SERVING:
Calories 33
Carbohydrate 6.4g
Protein 1.5g
Fat 0.5g
Cholesterol 0mg
Fiber 1.6g
Sodium 27mg

1 Place squash in a saucepan; add water to cover, and bring to a boil. Cover, reduce heat, and simmer 6 minutes or until tender but still firm. Drain.

2 Cut squash in half lengthwise, leaving stems intact. Remove pulp, leaving ¼-inch-thick shells. Set shells aside.

3 Mash pulp. Add green chiles and next 5 ingredients; stir well. Spoon mixture into shells. Sprinkle with breadcrumbs. Arrange squash on a rack in a roasting pan coated with cooking spray. Broil 5½ inches from heat (with electric oven door partially opened) 8 to 10 minutes or until browned. Garnish with oregano sprigs, if desired. Yield: 4 servings.

YIELD: 4 servings

EXCHANGES PER
SERVING:
1 Vegetable

PER SERVING:
Calories 24
Carbohydrate 5.3g
Protein 1.6g
Fat 0.2g
Cholesterol 0mg
Fiber 1.4g
Sodium 151mg

super·quick

SUMMER SQUASH MEDLEY

2 yellow squash
2 zucchini
½ teaspoon grated lemon rind
1 tablespoon fresh lemon juice
1 teaspoon dried dillweed
¼ teaspoon salt

1 Cut squash and zucchini crosswise into ¼-inch-thick slices.

2 Cook in a large skillet in a small amount of boiling water 3 to 5 minutes or until crisp-tender; drain.

3 Add lemon rind and remaining ingredients, and toss. Yield: 4 (¾-cup) servings.

SUMMER SQUASH CASSEROLE

YIELD: 8 servings

1¾ pounds yellow squash, sliced
1 cup chopped onion
½ cup canned reduced-fat, reduced-
sodium cream of chicken soup,
undiluted
½ cup soft whole wheat breadcrumbs
½ cup nonfat sour cream
½ teaspoon salt
¼ teaspoon freshly ground pepper
¼ teaspoon garlic powder
¼ teaspoon dried basil
1 (4-ounce) jar diced pimiento, drained
Vegetable cooking spray
1 cup soft whole wheat breadcrumbs
⅓ cup (1.3 ounces) shredded reduced-fat
sharp Cheddar cheese
2 tablespoons reduced-calorie margarine,
melted
½ teaspoon paprika

EXCHANGES PER SERVING:
½ Starch
1 Vegetable
1 Fat

PER SERVING:
Calories 107
Carbohydrate 14.5g
Protein 5.3g
Fat 3.7g
Cholesterol 5mg
Fiber 2.3g
Sodium 342mg

1 Cook squash and onion in a small amount of boiling water in a large saucepan 12 to 15 minutes or until tender. Drain well. Mash squash mixture with a potato masher.

2 Combine squash mixture, soup, and next 7 ingredients; stir well. Spoon into a 1½-quart baking dish coated with cooking spray.

3 Combine 1 cup breadcrumbs and remaining 3 ingredients in a small bowl; stir well. Sprinkle over squash mixture. Bake, uncovered, at 350° for 25 to 30 minutes or until thoroughly heated. Yield: 8 servings.

SAUTÉED SPAGHETTI SQUASH

YIELD: 6 servings

EXCHANGES PER
SERVING:
1 Vegetable

PER SERVING:
Calories 44
Carbohydrate 7.6g
Protein 0.9g
Fat 1.5g
Cholesterol 0mg
Fiber 1.5g
Sodium 229mg

1 small spaghetti squash (about 2 pounds)
1 tablespoon reduced-calorie margarine
1 cup chopped onion
1 clove garlic, minced
1 teaspoon dried oregano
½ teaspoon salt
¼ teaspoon pepper

1 Wash squash; cut in half lengthwise. Remove and discard seeds. Place squash, cut side down, in a Dutch oven; add water to depth of 2 inches. Bring to a boil; cover, reduce heat, and simmer 20 to 25 minutes or until tender.

2 Drain squash, and let cool. Using a fork, remove spaghetti-like strands; set aside, and keep warm. Discard squash shells.

3 Melt margarine in a nonstick skillet over medium-high heat. Add onion and garlic; sauté until onion is tender. Add oregano, salt, and pepper; stir well. Add squash; toss lightly. Transfer to a serving dish.
Yield: 6 (½-cup) servings.

Microwave Instructions: Pierce squash several times with a fork; place squash on paper towels. Microwave, uncovered, at HIGH 12 minutes, turning halfway through cooking time. Cut squash in half lengthwise; remove and discard seeds. Using a fork, remove spaghetti-like strands. Proceed with recipe as directed.

SCALLOPED TOMATOES

For a complete dinner, try this dish with roasted chicken, black-eyed peas, and a salad.

5 (1-ounce) slices white bread
   Vegetable cooking spray
2 teaspoons olive oil
½ cup finely chopped celery
½ cup chopped onion
2 tablespoons all-purpose flour
2 (14½-ounce) cans no-salt-added whole
   tomatoes, undrained and chopped
1 tablespoon granulated sugar substitute
½ teaspoon salt
½ teaspoon dried Italian seasoning
   Dash of pepper
2 teaspoons grated Parmesan cheese

YIELD: 8 servings

EXCHANGES PER SERVING:
½ Starch
1 Vegetable

PER SERVING:
Calories 68
Carbohydrate 11.8g
Protein 2.1g
Fat 1.7g
Cholesterol 1mg
Fiber 0.5g
Sodium 221mg

1 Trim crusts from bread slices; reserve crusts for another use. Cut 3 bread slices into ¾-inch cubes. Cut remaining 2 bread slices into 4 triangles each. Place cubes and triangles on an ungreased baking sheet, and bake at 400° for 5 minutes or until crisp; set aside.

2 Coat a large nonstick skillet with cooking spray; add oil. Place over medium-high heat until hot. Add celery and onion; sauté 2 to 3 minutes or until vegetables are crisp-tender. Add flour, stirring well. Add bread cubes, tomato, and next 4 ingredients. Cook over medium heat, stirring constantly, 3 to 4 minutes or until slightly thickened.

3 Transfer to a 1½-quart baking dish coated with cooking spray. Bake, uncovered, at 375° for 15 to 20 minutes or until bubbly. Arrange bread triangles around edge of tomato mixture; sprinkle with cheese, and bake 5 additional minutes. Yield: 8 (½-cup) servings.

HOT 'N' SPICY VEGETABLES

YIELD: 8 servings

EXCHANGES PER SERVING:
2 Vegetable

PER SERVING:
Calories 61
Carbohydrate 10.5g
Protein 3.1g
Fat 1.7g
Cholesterol 0mg
Fiber 3.2g
Sodium 21mg

🌿 Before starting to stir-fry, line up ingredients near the cooktop. Be sure the ingredients are as dry as possible before adding them to the skillet to prevent hot oil from spattering. Always keep the food in motion when stir-frying—as if you were tossing a salad.

Since stir-fried vegetables cook quickly, they're packed with more nutrients, flavor, and color than vegetables that are cooked by slower methods.

2 teaspoons cornstarch
2 teaspoons granulated sugar substitute with aspartame (such as Equal Spoonful)
¼ to ½ teaspoon dried red pepper flakes
½ cup water
¾ pound fresh broccoli
2 teaspoons vegetable oil
1 medium onion, thinly sliced and separated into rings
3 medium carrots, scraped and diagonally sliced
1½ pounds small fresh mushrooms, halved

1 Combine first 4 ingredients in a small bowl, stirring well.

2 Trim off large leaves of broccoli. Remove tough ends of lower stalks. Cut flowerets off broccoli spears; cut spears into ¼-inch diagonal slices. Set flowerets and spears aside.

3 Coat a wok or large heavy skillet with oil; heat at medium-high (375°) until hot. Add onion; stir-fry 2 minutes. Add broccoli and carrot; stir-fry 5 minutes or until crisp-tender. Add mushrooms; stir-fry 2 minutes.

4 Stir in cornstarch mixture; cook, stirring constantly, until sauce is thickened. Serve immediately. Yield: 8 (⅔-cup) servings.

Winter Vegetables with Vinaigrette

2 medium carrots, scraped and cut into
    very thin strips
2 medium turnips, peeled and cut into
    very thin strips
¼ pound parsnips, scraped and sliced
    diagonally
2 tablespoons granulated sugar substitute
3 tablespoons vinegar
1 tablespoon water
1 tablespoon lemon juice
2 teaspoons Dijon mustard
2 tablespoons vegetable oil

YIELD: 8 servings

EXCHANGES PER
SERVING:
1 Vegetable
1 Fat

PER SERVING:
Calories 62
Carbohydrate 7.4g
Protein 0.6g
Fat 3.6g
Cholesterol 0mg
Fiber 1.4g
Sodium 71mg

1 Arrange vegetables in a steamer basket over boiling water. Cover and steam 10 to 12 minutes or until vegetables are crisp-tender. Transfer to a large serving bowl; set aside, and keep warm.

2 Combine sugar substitute and next 4 ingredients in container of an electric blender; cover and process until smooth. With blender running, gradually add oil in a slow, steady stream; process until smooth. Pour over vegetable mixture. Yield: 8 (½-cup) servings.

Microwave Instructions: Combine vegetables in a 2-quart baking dish. Cover with heavy-duty plastic wrap, and microwave at HIGH 8 to 10 minutes or until vegetables are crisp-tender, stirring after 4 minutes. Transfer to a serving platter, and keep warm. Proceed with recipe as directed.

super·quick

SKILLET ZUCCHINI

EXCHANGES PER
SERVING:
1 Vegetable

PER SERVING:
Calories 16
Carbohydrate 2.3g
Protein 1.3g
Fat 0.5g
Cholesterol 1mg
Fiber 0.3g
Sodium 318mg

Olive-oil flavored vegetable cooking spray
1 teaspoon minced garlic
2 medium zucchini, sliced and halved
½ teaspoon salt
¼ teaspoon pepper
1 tablespoon Parmesan cheese

1 Coat a large nonstick skillet with cooking spray, and place over medium heat until hot. Add garlic, and sauté 1 minute. Add zucchini; sprinkle with salt and pepper. Cook until zucchini is tender, stirring occasionally. Sprinkle with 1 tablespoon Parmesan cheese. Yield: 4 (½-cup) servings.

super·quick

ZUCCHINI STICKS

YIELD: 4 servings

EXCHANGES PER
SERVING:
1 Vegetable

PER SERVING:
Calories 19
Carbohydrate 1.6g
Protein 0.6g
Fat 1.4g
Cholesterol 0mg
Fiber 0.3g
Sodium 2mg

Vegetable cooking spray
1 teaspoon olive oil
2 medium zucchini, sliced lengthwise into strips

1 Coat a nonstick skillet with cooking spray; add olive oil, and place over medium-high heat until hot. Add zucchini, and sauté 4 minutes or until crisp tender.
Yield: 4 (½-cup) servings.

super·quick

ZUCCHINI WITH PESTO

Pesto's pungent taste gives zucchini new appeal. The stimulating flavor of this dish goes well with grilled chicken.

¾ cup tightly packed fresh basil leaves
¼ cup grated Parmesan cheese
1 tablespoon pine nuts
⅛ teaspoon pepper
2 cloves garlic, cut in half
1 tablespoon water
1 tablespoon olive oil
  Vegetable cooking spray
4 small zucchini, cut into very thin strips
  (about ¾ pound)
2 teaspoons pine nuts, toasted
  Fresh basil sprigs (optional)

1 Wash basil leaves thoroughly in lukewarm water, and drain well.

2 Position knife blade in food processor bowl; add basil, Parmesan cheese, and next 3 ingredients. Process until smooth. Combine water and oil; with processor running, pour oil mixture through food chute in a slow, steady stream until combined. Set aside.

3 Coat a nonstick skillet with cooking spray; place over medium heat until hot. Add zucchini; sauté until crisp-tender. Add basil mixture; toss well. Transfer to a serving dish. Sprinkle with pine nuts. Garnish with basil sprigs, if desired. Yield: 6 (½-cup) servings.

YIELD: 6 servings

EXCHANGES PER SERVING:
1 Vegetable
1 Fat

PER SERVING:
Calories 79
Carbohydrate 5.7g
Protein 3.2g
Fat 6.0g
Cholesterol 3mg
Fiber 1.3g
Sodium 68mg

CHUNKY APPLESAUCE

YIELD: 4 servings

EXCHANGES PER
SERVING:
1 Fruit

PER SERVING:
Calories 72
Carbohydrate 18.5g
Protein 0.2g
Fat 0.4g
Cholesterol 0mg
Fiber 2.7g
Sodium 1mg

Varieties of cooking apples include Rome, Granny Smith, Yellow Delicious, and Winesap.

4 medium-size cooking apples (about 1½ pounds)
½ cup unsweetened apple juice
¼ teaspoon ground cinnamon
⅛ teaspoon ground nutmeg

1 Peel, core, and coarsely chop apples. Combine apple and unsweetened apple juice in a small saucepan. Cook apple mixture, uncovered, over medium-low heat 15 to 20 minutes or until apple is tender, stirring occasionally.

2 Stir in cinnamon and nutmeg. Mash slightly, using a potato masher or fork. Serve applesauce warm or chilled in individual dessert dishes. Yield: 4 (½-cup) servings.

super·quick

GLAZED PEARS AND PINEAPPLE WITH ALMONDS

Feature this fruit side dish with roast beef, pork, grilled chicken, or baked ham.

2 (16-ounce) cans pear halves in juice
2 teaspoons granulated brown sugar substitute
1 teaspoon cornstarch
½ teaspoon almond extract
½ teaspoon vanilla extract
   Vegetable cooking spray
1¼ cups fresh pineapple chunks
¼ cup vanilla low-fat yogurt sweetened with aspartame
1 tablespoon sliced almonds, toasted
   Fresh mint sprigs (optional)

YIELD: 8 servings

EXCHANGES PER SERVING:
1 Fruit

PER SERVING:
Calories 51
Carbohydrate 10.8g
Protein 0.6g
Fat 0.7g
Cholesterol 0mg
Fiber 0.5g
Sodium 5mg

1 Drain pear halves, reserving ⅓ cup juice; set pear halves aside. Combine reserved juice, sugar substitute, and next 3 ingredients in a small bowl; stir well, and set aside.

2 Coat a large nonstick skillet with cooking spray. Place over medium-high heat until hot. Add pear halves; sauté 1 minute. Add pineapple chunks; sauté 1 minute. Add cornstarch mixture to pear mixture. Cook, stirring constantly, 1 minute or until thickened and bubbly.

3 Transfer to a serving dish. Drizzle yogurt over fruit mixture, and sprinkle with almonds. Garnish with mint sprigs, if desired. Yield: 8 (½-cup) servings.

YIELD: 8 servings

EXCHANGES PER
SERVING:
1 Fruit
1 Fat

PER SERVING:
Calories 91
Carbohydrate 13.8g
Protein 2.5g
Fat 3.7g
Cholesterol 5mg
Fiber 2.3g
Sodium 100mg

POACHED PEARS WITH BLUE CHEESE AND TOASTED WALNUTS

4 firm ripe Bartlett pears
1 cup water
½ cup dry red wine
¼ cup lemon juice
2 ounces crumbled blue cheese
2½ tablespoons coarsely chopped walnuts, toasted
Watercress sprigs (optional)
Freshly ground pepper (optional)

1 Peel and core pears; cut each in half length-wise. Combine water, wine, and lemon juice in a skillet; bring to a boil. Place pear halves, cut side down, in skillet. Cover, reduce heat, and simmer 20 minutes, turning and basting once with wine mixture.

2 Remove pears from wine mixture, using a slotted spoon. Discard remaining wine mixture. Place pear halves on a serving platter; sprinkle evenly with cheese and walnuts. If desired, garnish with watercress sprigs, and sprinkle with pepper. Yield: 8 servings.

super·quick

GRILLED PINEAPPLE SLICES

YIELD: 6 servings

1 small fresh pineapple, peeled and cored
2 tablespoons granulated brown sugar
  substitute
1 tablespoon reduced-calorie margarine,
  melted
1½ teaspoons rum extract
3 tablespoons shredded unsweetened
  coconut, toasted

EXCHANGES PER SERVING:
1 Fruit
½ Fat

PER SERVING:
Calories 105
Carbohydrate 19.2g
Protein 0.7g
Fat 3.4g
Cholesterol 0mg
Fiber 2.3g
Sodium 26mg

1 Cut pineapple into 6 (¾-inch-thick) slices. Combine brown sugar substitute, margarine, and rum extract in a small bowl; stir well. Brush pineapple with rum extract mixture.

2 Place grill rack over medium-hot coals (350° to 400°). Place pineapple slices on rack, and grill 5 to 7 minutes or until tender, turning once. Transfer to a serving dish, and sprinkle with coconut. Serve warm. Yield: 6 servings.

Broiling Instructions: Brush pineapple with rum extract mixture. Place pineapple on rack of broiler pan coated with cooking spray. Broil 5½ inches from heat (with electric oven door partially opened) 4 minutes on each side or until tender.

WARM FRUIT COMPOTE

YIELD: 6 servings

EXCHANGES PER
SERVING:
2 Fruit

PER SERVING:
Calories 105
Carbohydrate 26.2g
Protein 1.3g
Fat 0.7g
Cholesterol 0mg
Fiber 1.6g
Sodium 9mg

✿ Dried fruits, such
as prunes, apricots,
and dates, can be
stored, unopened, at
room temperature
for about six months.
Once the package is
opened, store the
fruit in an airtight
container in the
refrigerator or
freezer.

2 cups frozen unsweetened dark cherries,
    thawed
½ cup dried pitted prunes, halved
⅓ cup dried apricot halves, sliced into
    thin strips
6 unsweetened whole pitted dates,
    quartered
½ cup unsweetened orange juice
1 teaspoon granulated brown sugar
    substitute

1 Combine all ingredients in a medium saucepan; bring to a boil. Cover, reduce heat, and
simmer 20 minutes.

2 Transfer to individual serving dishes, and
serve warm. Yield: 6 (½-cup) servings.

Microwave Instructions: Combine first 4 ingredients in a 2-quart casserole, tossing gently. Set
aside. Combine orange juice and brown sugar
substitute in a 1-cup liquid measure; stir well.
Microwave, uncovered, at HIGH 1 minute or
until mixture boils. Pour over fruit mixture, stirring to coat fruit. Cover with wax paper, and
microwave at HIGH 2 additional minutes or
until fruit is thoroughly heated, rotating dish
after 1 minute.

Recipe Index

480   Index

478 Index

VEAL CORDON BLEU

YIELD: 4 servings

8 veal cutlets (about 1 pound)
½ teaspoon freshly ground pepper
2 (¾-ounce) slices low-fat process Swiss cheese
1 (1-ounce) slice lean cooked ham
2 tablespoons all-purpose flour
¼ cup plus 2 tablespoons egg substitute
½ cup fine, dry breadcrumbs
  Vegetable cooking spray
1 tablespoon reduced-calorie margarine
  Fresh parsley sprigs (optional)
  Lemon slices (optional)

EXCHANGES PER SERVING:
4 Very Lean Meat
1 Starch
1 Fat

PER SERVING:
Calories 250
Carbohydrate 13.7g
Protein 31.2g
Fat 7.1g
Cholesterol 98mg
Fiber 0.7g
Sodium 498mg

1 Place cutlets between 2 sheets of wax paper; flatten to ⅛-inch thickness, using a meat mallet or rolling pin. Sprinkle 4 cutlets with pepper.

2 Cut each cheese slice in half; place 1 half-slice in center of each of 4 peppered cutlets. Cut ham slice into 4 pieces; place evenly on top of cheese slices. Place remaining 4 cutlets over ham; gently pound edges to seal. Dredge sealed cutlets in flour, shaking off excess. Dip cutlets in egg substitute. Dredge in breadcrumbs.

3 Coat a large nonstick skillet with cooking spray; add margarine. Place over medium-high heat until margarine melts. Add cutlets; cook 2 minutes on each side or until lightly browned.

4 Place cutlets in an 11- x 7- x 1½-inch baking dish coated with cooking spray. Bake, uncovered, at 375° for 20 minutes. Transfer cutlets to a serving platter. If desired, garnish with parsley sprigs and lemon slices.
Yield: 4 servings.

VEAL-FONTINA POCKETS

YIELD: 4 servings

EXCHANGES PER
SERVING:
4 Lean Meat
1 Starch

PER SERVING:
Calories 274
Carbohydrate 17.5g
Protein 29.7g
Fat 11.4g
Cholesterol 158mg
Fiber 2.4g
Sodium 179mg

1 pound veal cutlets (¼ inch thick)
¼ teaspoon pepper
8 fresh sage leaves, minced
2 (½-ounce) slices fontina cheese
3 tablespoons fine, dry breadcrumbs
1 tablespoon ground blanched almonds
2 tablespoons all-purpose flour
1 egg, lightly beaten
  Vegetable cooking spray
2 teaspoons margarine
8 lemon wedges
  Plum tomatoes (optional)
  Fresh sage leaves (optional)

1 Trim fat from cutlets; cut into 4 serving-size pieces. Place cutlets between two sheets of heavy-duty plastic wrap; flatten to ⅛-inch thickness, using a meat mallet or rolling pin. Sprinkle cutlets with pepper and minced sage.

2 Cut cheese slices in half. Top each cutlet with ½ slice cheese. Fold cutlets in half; pound edges together to seal.

3 Combine breadcrumbs and almonds in a small bowl. Place flour in a shallow dish. Dredge cutlets in flour. Carefully dip in egg, and coat with breadcrumb mixture.

4 Coat a large nonstick skillet with cooking spray; add margarine. Place over medium-high heat until hot. Add cutlets; cook 2 minutes on each side or until browned. Arrange in a 11- x 7- x 1½-inch baking dish coated with cooking spray. Cover and bake at 375° for 15 minutes. Transfer to a serving platter. Top with lemon wedges. If desired, garnish with tomatoes and fresh sage leaves. Yield: 4 servings.